This is a very important and timely book, providing an in-depth assessment of the first ten years of the United Nations' Peacebuilding Architecture. It provides an historical overview of its creation and development over time, an appraisal of its performance and recommendations for improvements. I strongly recommend this book to anyone interested in peacebuilding, not in the least the Member States who are making decisions on the role of peacebuilding in the United Nations.

Oscar Fernández-Taranco, *United Nations Assistant Secretary-General for Peacebuilding Support*

The rigorous and rich research contained in this volume is invaluable for efforts to move the Peacebuilding agenda forward at the UN and, ultimately, for strengthening our collective ability to prevent and respond to conflicts.

Ambassador Olof Skoog, *Swedish Permanent Representative to the United Nations in New York and Chairperson of the UN Peacebuilding Commission (2015)*

Riveting and essential reading on how the UN translates decades of grassroots peacebuilding efforts into a global project that is "internally led and externally supported" with a brew of "good intentions, confused expectations, and faulty assumptions."

Lisa Schirch, *Research Director, Toda Institute for Global Peace and Policy Research and Research Professor, Center for Justice and Peacebuilding, Eastern Mennonite University, USA*

UN Peacebuilding Architecture

Since its establishment, the UN's Peacebuilding Architecture (PBA) has been involved in peacebuilding processes in more than 20 countries. This edited volume takes stock of the overall impact of the PBA during its first decade in existence, and generates innovative recommendations for how the architecture can be modified and utilized to create more synergy and fusion between the UN's peace and development work.

The volume is based on commissioned research and independent evaluations, as well as informed opinions of several key decision-makers closely engaged in shaping the UN's peacebuilding agenda. It seeks to find a balance between identifying the reality and constraints of the UN's multilateral framework, while being bold in exploring innovative ways in which the UN can enhance the results of its peace and development work through the PBA.

The research and writing of each chapter is guided by four objectives:

- to assess the overall impact of the PBA;
- to generate innovative ideas for how the PBA can be made more effective post-2015;
- to analyze the PBA's role at the nexus of the UN's peace and development work;
- to consider what would be required for the PBA to increase and improve its impact in the future.

It will be of interest to diplomats, UN officials, the policy community, and scholars engaged in the debate following the 2015 review and the implementation of its recommendations, and will be an essential resource for UN and peacebuilding scholars.

Cedric de Coning is a Senior Research Fellow in the Peace and Conflict Research Group at the Norwegian Institute of International Affairs (NUPI) and a Peacebuilding Advisor with ACCORD. His research focus is on AU, EU and UN peacekeeping and peacebuilding policies and practices.

Eli Stamnes is a Senior Research Fellow in the Peace and Conflict Research Group at the Norwegian Institute of International Affairs (NUPI). Her research interests revolve around critical approaches to peace and security, peacebuilding, conflict prevention, gender and the Responsibility to Protect (R2P)

Global Institutions

Edited by Thomas G. Weiss
The CUNY Graduate Center, New York, USA
and Rorden Wilkinson
University of Sussex, Brighton, UK

About the series

The "Global Institutions Series" provides cutting-edge books about many aspects of what we know as "global governance." It emerges from our shared frustrations with the state of available knowledge—electronic and print-wise, for research and teaching—in the area. The series is designed as a resource for those interested in exploring issues of international organization and global governance. And since the first volumes appeared in 2005, we have taken significant strides toward filling conceptual gaps.

The series consists of three related "streams" distinguished by their blue, red, and green covers. The blue volumes, comprising the majority of the books in the series, provide user-friendly and short (usually no more than 50,000 words) but authoritative guides to major global and regional organizations, as well as key issues in the global governance of security, the environment, human rights, poverty, and humanitarian action among others. The books with red covers are designed to present original research and serve as extended and more specialized treatments of issues pertinent for advancing understanding about global governance. And the volumes with green covers—the most recent departure in the series—are comprehensive and accessible accounts of the major theoretical approaches to global governance and international organization.

The books in each of the streams are written by experts in the field, ranging from the most senior and respected authors to first-rate scholars at the beginning of their careers. In combination, the three components of the series—blue, red, and green—serve as key resources for faculty, students, and practitioners alike. The works in the blue and green streams have value as core and complementary readings in courses on, among other things, international organization, global governance, international law, international relations, and international political economy; the red volumes allow further reflection and investigation in these and related areas.

The books in the series also provide a segue to the foundation volume that offers the most comprehensive textbook treatment available dealing with all the major issues, approaches, institutions, and actors in contemporary global governance—our edited work *International Organization and Global Governance* (2014)—a volume to which many of the authors in the series have contributed essays.

Understanding global governance—past, present, and future—is far from a finished journey. The books in this series nonetheless represent significant steps toward a better way of conceiving contemporary problems and issues as well as, hopefully, doing something to improve world order. We value the feedback from our readers and their role in helping shape the on-going development of the series.

A complete list of titles appears at the end of this book. The most recent titles in the series are:

Displacement, Development, and Climate Change (2016)
by Nina Hall

UN Security Council Reform (2016)
by Peter Nadin

International Organizations and Military Affairs (2016)
by Hylke Dijkstra

The International Committee of the Red Cross (2nd edition, 2016)
by David P. Forsythe and Barbara Ann J. Rieffer-Flanagan

The Arctic Council (2016)
by Douglas C. Nord

Human Development and Global Institutions (2016)
by Richard Ponzio and Arunabha Ghosh

NGOs and Global Trade (2016)
by Erin Hannah

UN Peacebuilding Architecture
The first 10 years

**Edited by
Cedric de Coning and Eli Stamnes**

LONDON AND NEW YORK

First published 2016
by Routledge
2 Park Square, Milton Park, Abingdon, Oxon OX14 4RN

and by Routledge
711 Third Avenue, New York, NY 10017

Routledge is an imprint of the Taylor & Francis Group, an informa business

© 2016 Cedric de Coning and Eli Stamnes

The right of Cedric de Coning and Eli Stamnes to be identified as authors of the editorial material, and of the individual authors as authors of their contributions, has been asserted by them in accordance with sections 77 and 78 of the Copyright, Designs and Patents Act 1988.

All rights reserved. No part of this book may be reprinted or reproduced or utilised in any form or by any electronic, mechanical, or other means, now known or hereafter invented, including photocopying and recording, or in any information storage or retrieval system, without permission in writing from the publishers.

Trademark notice: Product or corporate names may be trademarks or registered trademarks, and are used only for identification and explanation without intent to infringe.

British Library Cataloguing in Publication Data
A catalogue record for this book is available from the British Library

Library of Congress Cataloging in Publication Data
Names: De Coning, Cedric, editor. | Stamnes, Eli, editor.
   Title: The UN peacebuilding architecture : the first 10 years / edited by Cedric de Coning and Eli Stamnes.
   Description: Milton Park, Abingdon, Oxon ; New York, NY : Routledge, 2016. |
Includes bibliographical references and index.
   Identifiers: LCCN 2015047388| ISBN 9781138650374 (hardback) | ISBN 9781138650503 (pbk.) | ISBN 9781315625409 (ebook)
   Subjects: LCSH: United Nations–Peacekeeping forces–History.
   Classification: LCC JZ6374 .U49 2016 | DDC 341.5/84–dc23
LC record available at http://lccn.loc.gov/2015047388

ISBN: 978-1-138-65037-4 (hbk)
ISBN: 978-1-138-65050-3 (pbk)
ISBN: 978-1-31562-540-9 (ebk)

Typeset in Times New Roman
by Taylor & Francis Books

Contents

List of illustrations	xii
List of contributors	xiii
Acknowledgments	xxii
Abbreviations	xxiv
Foreword: Reflections on the birth of the UN	
Peacebuilding Architecture	xxvii
CAROLYN MCASKIE	

Introduction: Assessing the impact of the UN
Peacebuilding Architecture   1
CEDRIC DE CONING AND ELI STAMNES

PART I
Setting up the UN Peacebuilding Architecture   21

1 The vision and thinking behind the UN
   Peacebuilding Architecture   23
   ABIODUN WILLIAMS AND MARK BAILEY

2 The dynamics that shaped the establishment of the
   Peacebuilding Architecture in the early years   40
   NECLA TSCHIRGI AND RICHARD PONZIO

PART II
The Peacebuilding Architecture's instruments in practice   59

3 The Peacebuilding Fund: From uncertainty to promise   61
   JUPS KLUYSKENS

x *Contents*

4 Achievements of the UN Peacebuilding Commission and
   challenges ahead   77
   MARISKA VAN BEIJNUM

PART III
The institutional and conceptual impact of the
Peacebuilding Architecture   95

5 The gender(ed) impact of the Peacebuilding Architecture   97
   TORUNN L. TRYGGESTAD

6 Bridging the gap?: The UN civilian capacity initiative   109
   JOHN KARLSRUD AND LOTTE VERMEIJ

PART IV
Country-specific impact of the Peacebuilding Architecture   125

7 The impact of the Peacebuilding Architecture in Burundi   127
   SUSANNA CAMPBELL, JOSIAH MARINEAU, TRACY DEXTER,
   MICHAEL FINDLEY, STEPHANIE HOFMANN AND DANIEL WALKER

8 The impact of the Peacebuilding Architecture on
   consolidating the Sierra Leone peace process   145
   FERNANDO CAVALCANTE

9 The impact of the Peacebuilding Architecture on
   consolidating Liberia's peace process   159
   MARINA CAPARINI

10 The impact of the Peacebuilding Architecture in Guinea-Bissau   181
   ADRIANA ERTHAL ABDENUR AND
   DANILO MARCONDES DE SOUZA NETO

11 Searching for a niche: UN peacebuilding in the Republic
   of Guinea   196
   IAN D. QUICK

PART V
Findings and conclusion   215

12 The future of the UN Peacebuilding Architecture   217
   CEDRIC DE CONING AND ELI STAMNES

Contents xi

13 Epilogue: The UN Peacebuilding Architecture—good
intentions, confused expectations, faulty assumptions   233
JUDY CHENG-HOPKINS

Index   251
Routledge Global Institutions Series   263

List of illustrations

Figure

13.1 The UN Peacebuilding Architecture   237
13.2 Relationships and reporting lines   238

Table

8.1 Distribution of PBF monies to projects in Sierra Leone,
by thematic area   152

List of contributors

Adriana Erthal Abdenur (Brazil) (PhD Princeton, BA Harvard) is a professor at the Institute of International Relations of the Pontifical Catholic University of Rio de Janeiro (PUC-Rio) and a senior researcher at the BRICS Policy Center. She researches the role of rising powers, including the BRICS (Brazil, Russia, India, China, South Africa), in global governance, focusing on development cooperation and international security. Her recent publications include journal articles in *Global Governance, Third World Quarterly, Journal of Peacebuilding and Development, Africa Review*, and *IDS Bulletin*, as well as policy briefs for the Norwegian Peacebuilding Resource Centre (NOREF), the South African Institute of International Affairs (SAIIA), the Konrad Adenauer Stiftung, the Woodrow Wilson Center, and the Chr. Michelsen Institute. She is a former Fulbright Research grantee and fellow of the India China Institute. From 2011 to 2013, she was general coordinator of the BRICS Policy Center.

Mark Bailey (United Kingdom) is special assistant to the president at The Hague Institute for Global Justice, where he oversees projects on the future of peacebuilding, UN reform, and transatlantic relations. He also coordinates The Hague Institute's policy roundtables and Distinguished Speaker Series. He previously worked as a policy analyst in humanitarian affairs, including at the United Nations, European Union, and Save the Children UK, where he authored a flagship report on humanitarian and development issues in Afghanistan, launched on the tenth anniversary of the international intervention. Mark studied Modern History and Modern Languages at Keble College, Oxford, receiving his Bachelor's Degree with First Class Honours and was subsequently a postgraduate Fulbright Scholar at Georgetown University's School of Foreign Service, where he

xiv *List of contributors*

obtained his Master's Degree with Distinction. In addition to his career in humanitarian affairs, Mark has also worked at the European Parliament and the Council on Foreign Relations.

Mariska van Beijnum (The Netherlands) is the director of the Conflict Research Unit of the Netherlands Institute of International Relations ("Clingendael"). She has been working in the field of peacebuilding and post-conflict reconstruction since 2001 by providing analytical support—conducting evaluations and reviews—both to bilateral donors (The Netherlands Ministry of Foreign Affairs, Department for International Development—DFID, Danida, the Swedish International Development Cooperation Agency—SIDA, Norwegian Agency for Development Cooperation—NORAD, the Canadian International Development Agency—CIDA) and multilateral organizations (Development Assistance Committee of the Organisation for Economic Co-operation and Development—OECD/DAC, UN Peacebuilding Support Office—PBSO, the UN Development Programme—UNDP, the World Bank, European Union—EU). Specializing in transition financing and aid architecture issues, she has supported the international community in enhancing the effectiveness of their engagements in fragile and conflict-affected situations. Since 2015, Mariska has been a member of the Secretary-General's Advisory Group to the UN Peacebuilding Fund. She studied political science and governance at the Vrije Universiteit Amsterdam, and humanitarian assistance at the University of Groningen and the University of Uppsala.

Susanna Campbell (United States) is a post-doctoral researcher at the Centre on Conflict, Development, and Peacebuilding at the Graduate Institute for International and Development Studies, Geneva. Dr Campbell's research focuses on intergovernmental organizations, international nongovernmental organizations, organizational behavior, foreign aid, development, peacebuilding, civil wars, and state formation in Africa. She has extensive experience doing fieldwork in conflict-affected countries and has conducted peacebuilding evaluations for various UN organizations and the World Bank.

Marina Caparini (Canada) is a widely published researcher focusing on peacebuilding and security and justice reform in post-conflict and post-authoritarian settings. She is currently senior research associate with the Institute for Security Studies in South Africa, providing research and policy support on development of the police component of African peace support operations. She has held senior positions at the Norwegian Institute of International Affairs, the International Center for Transitional Justice, and the Geneva Centre for the Democratic Control of Armed Forces. She holds a PhD in War Studies from King's College London.

Fernando Cavalcante (Brazil) currently works in the Peacekeeping Best Practices Services of the UN Department of Peacekeeping Operations. In 2014, he acted as security sector reform officer and as special assistant in the UN Integrated Peacebuilding Office in Guinea-Bissau (UNIOGBIS), where he provided policy advice, and substantive and technical support to initiatives related to the mission's core peace consolidation mandate. Previously, he held positions at the Global Governance Institute and the University of Bradford's Department of Peace Studies, among others. Fernando has extensive experience conducting empirically based research and analysis on peacekeeping and peacebuilding issues, with a special focus on UN concepts, institutions, and practices. He holds a PhD (summa cum laude) from the University of Coimbra and a BA from the University of Brasilia, both in the area of International Relations.

Judy Cheng-Hopkins (Malaysia) was assistant Secretary-General of the UN PBSO from 2009 to 2014. She was previously the UN assistant high commissioner for refugees (2006–09). She holds a Master's degree in International Affairs (Economic Development) from Columbia University's School of International and Public Affairs (SIPA), where she is currently an adjunct professor of the UN and peacebuilding. Ms Cheng-Hopkins's UN career has spanned 36 years and covered several organizations/agencies besides PBSO and UNHCR, such as UNDP (20 years including 10 spent in Zambia and Kenya and two as deputy assistant administrator, Africa Bureau), eight years in the World Food Programme as director for Asia and Eastern Europe, based in Rome, and as head of the New York office. She was chair of the Conflict Prevention Council of the World Economic Forum (2012) and received Columbia University's (SIPA) Global Leadership award in 2013. She was also honored with a "Datuk" title (a sort of Malaysian knighthood) by Malaysia for her international work.

Cedric de Coning (South Africa) is a senior research fellow with the Peace and Conflict Research Group at the Norwegian Institute of International Affairs and he is also a senior advisor on peacekeeping and peacebuilding for ACCORD. He served on the Secretary-General's Advisory Group for the UN Peacebuilding Fund from 2012 to 2014. He is on the editorial boards of the journals *Global Governance* and xvi *List of contributors*

Peacebuilding. Cedric has a PhD in Applied Ethics from the Department of Philosophy at the University of Stellenbosch. Selected publications include: "The BRICS and Coexistence," co-editor (Routledge, 2015); "Enhancing the Efficiency of the African Standby Force" (*Conflict Trends*, 2014); "Understanding Peacebuilding as Essentially Local" (*Stability*, 2013); "Coherence & Coordination: The Limits of the Comprehensive Approach" (*Journal of International Peacekeeping*, 2011); and "The Unintended Consequences of Peacekeeping," co-editor (UNU Press, 2007).

Tracy Dexter (United States) is an expert in peacebuilding programming, implementation, and evaluation in post-conflict countries. Ms Dexter has extensive experience working with donors, government officials, UN agencies and beneficiaries in difficult contexts, both as a nongovernmental organization (NGO) director and as an independent consultant. She has been living and working in the Great Lakes region of Africa for several years and specializes in political analysis, transitional justice, security sector reform, and gender mainstreaming in these countries.

Michael Findley (United States) is an assistant professor in the Department of Government at the University of Texas at Austin. Dr Findley's research addresses civil wars, terrorism, international relations, and development. He uses field experiments, statistical and computational models, and some interviews. He also conducts fieldwork in Uganda, South Africa, and Malawi.

Stephanie Hofmann (Germany) is an associate professor in the Department of Political Science and International Relations at the Graduate Institute of International and Development Studies and the Deputy Director of the Graduate Institute's Centre on Conflict, Development, and Peacebuilding. Dr Hofmann's research focuses on the creation of peace and stability with emphasis on international crisis management institutions and preference formation.

John Karlsrud (Norway) is a senior research fellow of the Peace and Conflict Group at the Norwegian Institute of International Affairs working on peacekeeping, peacebuilding, and humanitarian issues. He has published peer-reviewed articles in, *inter alia*, *Conflict, Security and Development*; *Global Governance*; and *Global Responsibility to Protect*. He previously served as special assistant to the UN special representative of the Secretary-General to Chad and has done research in Chad, Haiti, and South Sudan.

List of contributors xvii

Jups Kluyskens (The Netherlands) is Director of Kluyskens Consulting, a firm specializing in evaluation, public sector reform, and governance in fragile and post-conflict situations. She was the team leader for the Review of the UN Peacebuilding Fund commissioned in 2013, which focused on evaluating the Fund's first business plan. She is a specialist in complex evaluations of development partners' country strategies and programs, aid modalities, and funds. She has extensive experience in evaluating conflict prevention, peace and stability, administrative reform, DDR, justice reform, police and security. She has worked in both Asia and Africa for multilateral and bilateral donors, including the World Bank, the UN, the EU, regional banks, OECD/DAC, DFID, SIDA, NORAD, Danida, and the Dutch Ministry of Foreign Affairs. She holds degrees in Philosophy (University of Amsterdam), African Studies (School of Oriental and African Studies, University of London), and Public Management (University of Twente, the Netherlands).

Josiah Marineau (United States) is a PhD student in the Government Department at the University of Texas at Austin. His research interests include foreign aid, civil wars, and post-war reconstruction. He has conducted field research in Burundi and Tanzania.

Carolyn McAskie (Canada) was the first UN assistant Secretary-General (ASG) for peacebuilding support, helping to launch the UN's new Peacebuilding Commission in its first two years (2006–08); previously special representative of the Secretary-General and head of the UN peacekeeping mission in Burundi (2004–06); and ASG for Humanitarian Affairs, Office for the Coordination of Humanitarian Affairs (OCHA) (1999–2004), also serving as the Secretary-General's humanitarian envoy for the crisis in Côte d'Ivoire (2003). Prior to her UN career, she was vice-president (assistant deputy minister) of CIDA, responsible for Africa and the Middle East (1993–96) and for Multilateral Affairs (1996–99), culminating a 30-year career with CIDA including service abroad in the Canadian High Commission in Kenya (1971–74), five years on assignment with the Commonwealth Secretariat in London (1975–80), and as Canada's high commissioner to Sri Lanka (1986–89). She is an Officer of the Order of Canada, holds honorary degrees from the University of British Columbia and the University of Ottawa. Since her retirement she has served as a mentor for Canada's Trudeau Foundation, as a mentor/trainer for the UN's Senior Leadership Programme (Peacekeeping), as a senior fellow at the Graduate School of Public and International Affairs of the University of Ottawa, and was vice-chair of the

xviii *List of contributors*

Pearson Peacekeeping Centre until its closure. She is currently a member of the McLeod Group in Ottawa, and lives in Wakefield, Quebec.

Richard Ponzio (United States) joined The Hague Institute in March 2014 as head of the Global Governance Program and serves as project director for the Commission on Global Security, Justice & Governance. He was formerly a senior advisor in the US State Department's Office of the Special Representative for Afghanistan and Pakistan, where he conceptualized and coordinated Secretary Hillary Clinton's and later John Kerry's New Silk Road initiative. He has served with the UN in Afghanistan, Bosnia, Kosovo, New York (PBSO and UNDP), Pakistan, Sierra Leone, and the Solomon Islands. Dr Ponzio has published widely, including *Democratic Peacebuilding: Aiding Afghanistan and other Fragile States* (Oxford University Press, 2011). He has undertaken studies in political-economy and international relations at the University of Oxford, The Fletcher School of Law & Diplomacy, The Graduate Institute for International Studies-Geneva, and Columbia University.

Ian D. Quick (United Kingdom) is a consultant in strategic design and evaluation, and director of the boutique firm Rethink Fragility. His experience runs the gamut of initiatives over the last decade to improve the coherence and accountability of work in fragile states. This includes long stints coordinating initiatives in Sri Lanka and the Democratic Republic of the Congo, and policy work with a broad cross-section of the UN system. Mr Quick is also a deployable expert for the Australian government. He holds a degree in public policy from Harvard University, and degrees in law and finance from the University of New South Wales.

Danilo Marcondes de Souza Neto (Brazil) is a PhD candidate at the Department of Politics and International Studies (POLIS) at the University of Cambridge, where he is the holder of a CAPES-Cambridge Trust Scholarship. Prior to that he was a lecturer at the Institute of International Relations at the Pontifical Catholic University of Rio de Janeiro, Brazil (PUC-Rio) (2010–12). Danilo also holds a BA and an MA from the Institute of International Relations at PUC-Rio, and between October and December 2013 he was a visiting researcher at the Institute of Economic and Social Studies in Maputo (Mozambique). His recent publications include journal articles in *Journal of Peacebuilding and Development, Africa Review, Journal of the Indian Ocean Region,* and *CIDOB Cahier d'Afers*

List of contributors xix

Internacionals, as well as policy briefs for NOREF, SAIIA, the Konrad Adenauer Stiftung, and the Chr. Michelsen Institute.

Eli Stamnes (Norway) is a senior research fellow at the Norwegian Institute of International Affairs (NUPI). She was the head of the UN Program at NUPI from 2006 to 2008, and led the institute's work on the Responsibility to Protect (R2P) from 2008 to 2011. Her research interests include critical approaches to peace and security, peacebuilding, peace support operations, gender, and R2P. She holds a PhD and a Master's degree from the University of Aberystwyth, United Kingdom. Her recent publications include *Responsibility to Protect and Women, Peace and Security: Aligning the Protection Agendas* (Brill, 2013), which she edited together with Sara E. Davies and Zim Nwokora; and "The Responsibility to Protect: Integrating Gender Perspectives into Policies and Practices," *Global Responsibility to Protect.* She wrote the paper "Values, Context and Hybridity: How Can the Insights from the Liberal Peace Critique be Brought to Bear on the Practices of the UN Peacebuilding Architecture," for the NUPI/International Committee for the Development of Peoples (CISP) 2010 project, The Future of the UN Peacebuilding Architecture, which was published in Tom Young (ed.) *Readings in the International Relations of Africa* (Indiana University Press, 2016).

Torunn L. Tryggestad (Norway) is a senior researcher and director of the PRIO Centre on Gender, Peace and Security at the Peace Research Institute, Oslo. She holds a PhD in Political Science (University of Oslo) on the topic "International Norms and Political Change: 'Women, Peace and Security' and the UN Security Agenda." Her research focuses on the UN and the gendered dimensions of conflict resolution, conflict management, and peacebuilding. She has extensive experience from teaching, training, and providing policy advice to Norwegian ministries, the Norwegian Armed Forces and the justice sector. In recent years she has also been centrally involved in conducting the High-Level Seminars on Gender and Inclusive Mediation Processes, in cooperation with the UN Department of Political Affairs and the Crisis Management Initiative. Her most recent publications include a book chapter titled "UN Security Council Resolution 1325 on Women, Peace and Security and its Relevance to the Norwegian Armed Forces" (2014), and a journal article, "State Feminism Going Global: Norway on the UN Peacebuilding Commission" (*Cooperation and Conflict,* 2014). Tryggestad was one of the principal authors of the Norwegian government's xx *List of contributors*

National Action Plan on the Implementation of UN Security Council Resolution 1325 on Women, Peace and Security (2006). She is member of the UN Secretary-General's fourth UN Peacebuilding Advisory Group (2015–17).

Necla Tschirgi (Turkey) is professor of practice in human security and peacebuilding at the Kroc School of Peace Studies, the University of San Diego, and co-executive editor of the *Journal of Peacebuilding and Development*. She received her BA and MA in political science at the American University of Beirut and her PhD in political economy at the University of Toronto. Her international career has spanned research, policy analysis, and teaching at the intersection of security and development. Prior to joining the Kroc School, she served as in-house consultant/senior policy advisor with the PBSO at the UN Secretariat in New York from 2007 to 2009. Previously, she was the vice-president of the International Peace Academy (IPA) in New York, where she also led the IPA's Security-Development Nexus research program from 2001 to 2005. Her recent publications include: "Rebuilding War-torn Societies: A Critical Review of International Assistance," in *Managing Conflict in a World Adrift*, edited by Chester A. Crocker, Fen Osler Hampson, and Pamela Aall (USIP, 2015); "Securitization and Peacebuilding," in the *Routledge Handbook of Peacebuilding* (2013); and *Security and Development: Searching for Critical Connections*, edited with Michael S. Lund and Francesco Mancini (Lynne Rienner Publications, 2010).

Lotte Vermeij (The Netherlands) is currently based in Bukavu, Democratic Republic of the Congo, as chief of the Gender and Sexual Violence Advisory Section/women protection advisor for the UN Organization Stabilization Mission in the Democratic Republic of the Congo (MONUSCO) in South Kivu. Previous to this, she was the head of the Peace Capacities Programme at the Norwegian Institute of International Affairs and regularly facilitated peace operations training for UN and NATO personnel (military, police, and civilian). As a senior research fellow at NUPI her research mainly focused on peacekeeping operations; peacebuilding; children and armed conflict; disarmament, demobilization and reintegration; conflict-related sexual violence; civilian capacities; and child protection. She holds a PhD in Disaster Studies from Wageningen University, The Netherlands, where she focused her research on child soldiers and African rebel groups. She has done extensive field work in the Democratic Republic of the Congo, Liberia, Mali, Mozambique, northern Uganda, Rwanda, and Sierra Leone.

Daniel Walker (United States) is a graduate student in Political Science at the University of Illinois Urbana-Champaign. He studies international development policy, post-colonial politics, and foreign aid. He is also a specialist in experimental methods and spatial models.

Abiodun Williams (United States) was appointed the first president of The Hague Institute for Global Justice on 1 January 2013. From 2008 to 2012 he served at the United States Institute of Peace in Washington, DC, first as vice-president of the Center for Conflict Analysis and Prevention, and later as senior vice-president of the Center for Conflict Management, leading its work in major conflict zones such as Afghanistan, Pakistan, Iraq, Libya, Tunisia and Egypt. From 2001 to 2007 Dr Williams was director of Strategic Planning for UN Secretaries-General Ban Ki-moon and Kofi Annan in New York. He gained valuable field operational experience, serving with the UN from 1994 to 2000 in peacekeeping operations in the Balkans and Haiti, in senior political and humanitarian roles. He served as associate dean of the Africa Center for Strategic Studies at the National Defense University in Washington, DC, and held faculty appointments at Georgetown, Rochester, and Tufts Universities, winning several awards. Dr Williams is the chair of the Academic Council on the UN System, and a member of the Executive Board of the Institute for Global Leadership at Tufts. He has published widely on conflict prevention and management. He holds MAs from Edinburgh University and The Fletcher School of Law and Diplomacy, and a doctorate in International Relations from the latter.

Acknowledgments

At the 2005 World Summit, the world's heads of state and government decided to establish a United Nations "Peacebuilding Architecture," consisting of the Peacebuilding Commission, the Peacebuilding Fund, and the Peacebuilding Support Office, in order to assist and focus attention and resources on countries emerging out of violent conflict. By investigating the impact that this architecture has had during its first decade in existence, this book ultimately reflects an appreciation of this momentous decision and all the people involved subsequently in implementing it.

Intellectually, we—the chapter authors and editors of the book—are indebted to a large group of people; they are simply too many to be mentioned here. We have also taken inspiration from, and relied upon information provided by, many peacebuilding practitioners as well as local stakeholders in the countries with which the UN Peacebuilding Architecture has engaged. Without these individuals, and their willingness to contribute, this book would not have seen the light of day.

In particular, we would like to acknowledge the previous assistant Secretary-General for peacebuilding, Judy Cheng-Hopkins, for her support and encouragement throughout this project, including contributing the epilogue. A special thanks also to the current assistant Secretary-General for peacebuilding, Oscar Fernández-Taranco, and the team at the UN Peacebuilding Support Office for their advice, feedback, and support throughout the project.

There are several colleagues at the Norwegian Institute of International Affairs (NUPI) who deserve our heartfelt thanks for helping us with finalizing the book manuscript: Susan Høivik lent her excellent language and proofreading skills to the chapters, while Liv Høivik and Paul Troost offered great help in preparing the manuscript for submission to the publisher. It is a privilege to be able to rely on such a good support team. We would also like to thank Kari Osland, the head of

Acknowledgments xxiii

the Peace and Conflict Research Group at NUPI, for her interest in this project as well as her support and patience during the period in which the book materialized. We have also benefitted greatly from assistance outside NUPI, and are thankful for Martin J. Burke's professional eye and efficient work in preparing the manuscript for publication.

A grant from the Norwegian Ministry of Foreign Affairs enabled NUPI to engage with and offer support to the 2015 review of the UN Peacebuilding Architecture, and contribute to generating information and opportunities to engage with the Peacebuilding Support Office, the Peacebuilding Commission, the Advisory Group of Experts, and the African Union Commission, amongst others. We are grateful for this support and for the opportunities it created to exchange ideas and to discuss our findings with the Ministry of Foreign Affairs.

Many thanks are also owed to the Global Institutions Series editors, Professor Thomas G. Weiss and Professor Rorden Wilkinson, and their team, for their efficient, professional, and friendly handling throughout the publishing process.

Finally, we, the editors, want to express our gratitude to the contributors to this book, for sharing their insight into different aspects of the UN Peacebuilding Architecture's work, for their enthusiasm and support for this project, and for their thorough work. It has been a pleasure to be book editors when collaborating with such a skilled, experienced, and dedicated group of researchers.

Abbreviations

AFL	Armed Forces of Liberia
AIAF	Afghan Interim Authority Fund
ASG	assistant Secretary-General
AU	African Union
BCPR	Bureau for Crisis Prevention and Recovery (UNDP)
BIN	Bureau of Immigration and Naturalization (Liberia)
BINUB	UN Integrated Office in Burundi
BNUB	UN Office in Burundi
BRICS	Brazil, Russia, India, China, South Africa
C34	Special Committee on Peacekeeping Operations
CAR	Central African Republic
CCC	Civilian-Contributing Country
CERF	Central Emergency Response Fund
CIVCAP	civilian capacity
CMRN	Military Committee for National Recovery (Guinea)
CNDD	National Council for Democracy and Development (Guinea)
CNDD-FDD	Conseil National Pour la Défense de la Démocratie—Forces pour la Défense de la Démocratie (Burundi)
CNIDH	National Independent Commission for Human Rights (Burundi)
CPLP	Community of Portuguese-Speaking Countries
CSC	Country-Specific Configuration
CSSO	civil service support officer
DAC	Development Assistance Committee (OECD)
DDR	disarmament, demobilization, and reintegration
DOCO	UN Development Operations Coordination Office
DPA	UN Department of Political Affairs
DPKO	UN Department of Peacekeeping Operations
ECOSOC	UN Economic and Social Council

ECOWAS	Economic Community of West African States
ECPS	Executive Committee on Peace and Security
EISAS	ECPS Information and Strategic Analysis Section
EOSG	Executive Office of the Secretary-General
ERSG	executive representative of the Secretary-General
EU	European Union
FAO	Food and Agriculture Organization
FDN	Burundian Armed Forces
FNL	Forces pour la Libération Nationale (Burundi)
GPI	Gender Promotion Initiative
GPP	government-provided personnel
ICG-GB	International Contact Group on Guinea-Bissau
ICT	information communications technology
IDPS	International Dialogue on Peacebuilding and Statebuilding
IFI	international financial institution
IGAD	Intergovernmental Authority on Development
ILO	International Labour Organization
INGO	international nongovernmental organization
IOM	International Organization for Migration
IPBS	Integrated Peacebuilding Strategy
IRF	Immediate Response Facility
JSC	Joint Steering Committee
LNP	Liberian National Police
LPP	Liberia Peacebuilding Programme
MDTF	multi-donor trust fund
M&E	monitoring and evaluation
MINUSTAH	UN Stabilization Mission in Haiti
MPTF-O	Multi-Partner Trust Fund Office
NAM	Non-Aligned Movement
NAP	National Action Plan
NATO	North Atlantic Treaty Organization
NGO	nongovernmental organization
NUPI	Norwegian Institute of International Affairs
OC	Organizational Committee (PBC)
OCHA	UN Office for the Coordination of Humanitarian Affairs
OECD	Organisation for Economic Co-operation and Development
OHCHR	Office of the High Commissioner for Human Rights
OIOS	UN Office for Internal Oversight Services
ONUB	UN Operation in Burundi

xxvi *Abbreviations*

P5	Permanent Five Members of the Security Council
PBA	UN Peacebuilding Architecture
PBC	UN Peacebuilding Commission
PBF	UN Peacebuilding Fund
PBSO	UN Peacebuilding Support Office
PCF	Peacebuilding Cooperation Framework (Sierra Leone)
PDA	Peace and Development Advisor
PNG	persona non grata
PRF	Peacebuilding and Recovery Facility
R2P	Responsibility to Protect
RC	resident coordinator
REC	Regional Economic Community
RM	Regional Mechanisms
RUNO	Recipient UN Organization
SMC	Statement of Mutual Commitments
SNR	National Intelligence Service (Burundi)
SPU	Strategic Planning Unit
SRSG	special representative of the Secretary-General
SSR	security sector reform
TFC	Technical Follow-up Committee
ToR	Terms of Reference (PBF)
TRC	Truth and Reconciliation Commission (Liberia)
UN	United Nations
UNCT	UN Country Team
UNDP	UN Development Programme
UNFPA	UN Population Fund
UNHCR	Office of the UN High Commissioner for Refugees
UNICEF	UN Children's Fund
UNIFEM	UN Development Fund for Women
UNIOGBIS	UN Integrated Peacebuilding Office in Guinea-Bissau
UNIPSIL	UN Integrated Peacebuilding Office in Sierra Leone
UNMIL	UN Mission in Liberia
UNMISS	UN Mission in South Sudan
UNOPS	UN Office for Project Services
USG	under-Secretary-General
VfM	value for money
WGLL	Working Group on Lessons Learned
WPS	Women, Peace and Security

Foreword: Reflections on the birth of the UN Peacebuilding Architecture

Carolyn McAskie

It was my privilege to serve as the first Assistant Secretary-General (ASG) for peacebuilding support—a title deliberately meant to underscore the non-operational nature of the office—from May 2006 to August 2008. While I have not been involved in the work of the Peacebuilding Architecture (PBA) since that time, I have been following it from a distance and believe there is great potential, although some of the problems of the early days are still with us. It will take political will, real commitment on the part of member states and United Nations (UN) senior management, and will require combined dedication to the purpose and to the task if we are to realize this potential.

In this foreword I have set out some "behind the scenes" perspectives on the struggles and achievements of the early days, followed by questions which I believe still need to be addressed. I conclude with some general comments on why this important experiment should continue to be supported. These are purely my personal views based on my own experiences.

Early days

The Peacebuilding Architecture had a long provenance. Peacebuilding per se goes back several decades, with its UN roots in the then Secretary-General's 1992 *Agenda for Peace*.[1] With the evolution of mediation, peacekeeping, development, human rights, and humanitarian tools, the concept of peacebuilding evolved substantially. After 2000 it became more and more evident, from academic and practical work on the link between conflict and development and with the strengthening of UN integrated peace operations, that longer-term efforts would be required to ensure the sustainability of peace in post-conflict countries. Populations in war-affected countries need to see the benefits of peace, and governments need support in rebuilding institutions, if countries are to xxviii *Foreword*

avoid the all-too-frequent relapse into conflict. Peacekeepers and humanitarians cannot stay on forever, nor can they do everything. Despite efforts on the part of development players, particularly in the evolving field of adapting development tools to conflict situations, it became evident that special efforts would be needed to bring together all the elements of peacebuilding, be they political, peacekeeping, development, humanitarian, or human rights.

It was in this context that the 2004 High-Level Panel on Threats, Challenges and Change[2] recommended a new UN structure to support transitions from conflict to post-conflict, particularly to "marshal and sustain" international support "over whatever period may be necessary." The Secretary-General's 2005 response, *In Larger Freedom*,[3] proposed the creation of a Peacebuilding Commission, along with a Peacebuilding Support Office (PBSO) and a standing fund for peacebuilding. The commission would "help to ensure predictable financing for early recovery" and would "extend the period of political attention to post-conflict recovery." Subsequently, the UN General Assembly and the Security Council each passed identical resolutions in December 2005 creating the Peacebuilding Commission (PBC), whose primary objective was "to bring together all relevant actors to marshal resources and to advise on and propose integrated strategies for post conflict peacebuilding and recovery," as well as to lay the "foundation for sustainable development."[4]

It took from January to May 2006 for member states to complete negotiations on commission membership, with the first meeting of the Organizational Committee taking place in June. The first country-specific meetings on Burundi and Sierra Leone followed in October, with the launching of the Peacebuilding Fund (PBF) that same month. One year after the founding resolution, members of the PBC were able to see what might be possible.

The PBA was launched at a time of deep mistrust among member states due to the behavior of some countries in the negotiation of the 2005 World Summit document. This spilled over into negotiations for the PBC, and the debates over seats and positions on the commission were often acrimonious. Prior to the launch of the Organizational Committee in June, there had not been a great deal of time for discussions on how the PBC would operate, with the exception of one excellent seminar for new members in May 2006 organized by the International Peace Academy (now "Institute"). There had been substantive negotiations on the PBF to establish guidelines and to set targets (which were met rapidly). There had been little guidance from member states as to how the PBSO should operate, other than that it should "support" the PBC.

No funding had been allocated in the budget for this new office, and everything was to be done, in that famous Fifth Committee phrase, "within existing resources." We all know what that means.

The October 2006 meetings represented a palpable turnaround. High-level delegations from Sierra Leone and Burundi arrived with questions on what this would mean for their countries and with high expectations that this could help to put their development back on track. The PBC responded very positively: its first substantive engagement elevated the discourse from internal New York politics to the reality and enormity of the task before them. All of a sudden the PBC had a real role—and the PBA was launched. Now it was a question of defining the route and equipping themselves for the task.

This included the business of developing operating procedures for the PBC, including the thorny question of who could be present. Representatives of civil society organizations were deliberately excluded from participating, but could observe if invited. Because many UN bodies are overwhelmed by representatives of myriad UN agencies, programs, and departments sitting at the back of the room, the PBC went too far the other way and did not allow any seats for UN players, even though the resolution had called for the a representative of the Secretary-General to be on the Organizing Committee (the ASG/PBSO sat on the podium with the chair). This initially excluded critical players such as the UN Development Programme (UNDP), the Department of Political Affairs (DPA), the Department of Peacekeeping Operations (DPKO), and the Office of the High Commissioner for Human Rights (OHCHR). Over time, we managed to invite them regularly.

The most important operating procedure was how to implement the resolution's call for "integrated strategies for post-conflict peace-building and recovery." Member states were reluctant to engage in a major exercise of designing strategies for each client country, holding that many studies had already been done, whether by the World Bank, the UN, other donors, or via their own budget and development strategies. They were, however, persuaded that in order to be true to the mandate of bringing "together all relevant actors," it would be critical to get all the strategic players to the table to share their knowledge. In this way, the PBC and the client country could agree on the key first priorities to be implemented in support of the population and to support the government on the path to peace. Burundi's was the first strategy out of the gate, due to a sincere interest on the part of the government, strong leadership by the chair of the Country-Specific Committee and the committed UN team leadership on the ground. Sierra Leone took longer, as elections were underway; later, the newly elected xxx *Foreword*

government, a dedicated committee chair and a newly appointed UN team leadership completed this strategy in the second year.

For PBSO, the task was to get support within the Secretariat for a modest internal re-allocation of resources, personnel and office space. We started off with only three or four staff; the Office of the UN High Commissioner for Refugees (UNHCR), UNDP, the UN Children's Fund (UNICEF), and the Department of Management helped; later on governments made junior professional officers (JPOs) or interns available. However, very few were long-term staff on whom the office could count. Differences of opinion arose over the role of the PBSO. For the PBC, support to the PBC and the PBF was paramount, but the PBF included a requirement that funding be made available to non-PBC countries; and the PBSO had to have a role within the UN if headquarters and field-level peacebuilding were to support the peacebuilding strategies of the PBA.

Setting up coordination on peacebuilding among UN departments and programs hit a wall. The PBSO, DPA, DPKO, UNDP, OHCHR, the UN Office for the Coordination of Humanitarian Affairs (OCHA), and the Executive Office of the Secretary-General (EOSG) began to meet at the ASG level, but it was only after about 18 months that meetings were held quasi-regularly. The main concern of operational entities was that the PBSO should not be operational. While we understood this, we also understood that if there were to be operational consequences of peacebuilding decisions, then the operational departments would need to take on board the peacebuilding strategies of the PBC and provide field capability to deliver on the strategies. In the early days, this depended much more on the field than on headquarters support.

A major issue was how to establish country eligibility for consideration by the PBC. How would a country come on the agenda, how long should it stay on the agenda, and what would be the criteria for moving off the agenda? Importantly, what should the PBC's relationship be with the country? If countries were added gradually without thought as to later removal, the PBC could end up with a long list of clients and a large number of country-specific committees. Ideally a process was needed to discuss potential client countries, but in the UN such matters are best dealt with informally. Although this was not mentioned explicitly in the resolution, the Security Council decided that they would manage requests from client countries and then pass them on, in this way confirming the subsidiary/advisory role of the PBC. The ASG network inside the Secretariat could discuss eligibility, including in regard to the PBF, but there was no formal mechanism for sharing this with member states.

Foreword xxxi

As for the relationship between client countries and the PBC, the PBC could not (and should not) direct in the same way as could the Security Council. The commission would have to build up partnership relationships in which options could be discussed, and advice and support given. Some members felt the PBC should not even have opinions, and that the country should be 100 percent in the driver's seat. Others argued that if this were the case, what was the point of having a PBC? Eventually, a respectful relationship did develop, based on a useful definition of peacebuilding as being "internally led" and "externally supported." Without internal leadership, nothing was possible; without external support, plans could falter or fail.

A great deal of time was spent discussing whether the General Assembly should have as much influence in the PBC as the Security Council, but how to manifest General Assembly "interest" was unclear—nor in fact was there much interest on the part of the Security Council. Relations with the UN Economic and Social Council (ECOSOC) had been defined in the resolution, given their role in receiving reports from the development bodies in the UN. The idea was that the PBC would work with the Security Council when countries were on the latter's agenda, and with ECOSOC once countries had moved on to a development track, but ECOSOC does not have the direct role in-country that the Security Council does in crisis management, so there was little practical outcome to these discussions.

Setting up the Country-Specific Committee memberships was a positive process, but once the PBC reached four client countries it became cumbersome, particularly as the Lessons Learned Committee also met regularly. The resolution had identified the need to invite "all relevant actors"—but some of these actors (the African Union—AU, the African Development Bank—AfDB, World Bank, etc.) were not available in New York, whereas in other cases the committee membership grew to an unwieldy number. Countries wanted donor member states as their committee chairs, hoping that would bring in money for development. This was the case for Burundi with the first chair, Norway (as vice-chair of the PBC), as Norway brought in substantial funding and high-level leadership and attention. Sierra Leone refused to have the second vice-chair of the PBC, Ecuador, to chair their committee, causing a diplomatic incident. The Lessons Learned Committee became a useful position for Ecuador as a country which itself had come out of conflict. Unfortunately, however, the donor ambassador who valiantly took over as chair for Sierra Leone did not get any financial or leadership support from his capital.

xxxii *Foreword*

One of our most disappointing discoveries was the realization that many donor governments on the PBC were not prepared to finance recovery and reconstruction in the PBC post-conflict client countries. When asked what they were going to do concerning the first two countries, Burundi and Sierra Leone, some ministers and senior officials politely explained that these countries were not on their lists of countries eligible for aid. This came as a serious shock; it undermined the whole raison d'être of the PBA if one accepted prior neglect as a central element in state failure.

The Peacebuilding Fund went through some rocky times in the beginning. After weeks, if not months, of internal negotiations it was decided that the UNDP financial network was best suited to deliver funding to the field. This did not mean that UNDP would be the sole implementer; in fact, efforts were made to ensure that implementation would be done by several UN organizations, including political and peacekeeping missions and also including the proviso that civil society organizations could be implementers in the field. A major tussle took place between the PBC and Secretariat over management of the PBF, with some member states wanting the commission to make funding and project decisions—not a normal process in international organizations. Member-state bodies can provide oversight, and the PBC was kept regularly informed, but the PBF was clearly under the authority of the UN Secretary-General. Moreover, it was not until its second year of operation that the PBSO was able to bring in dedicated staff to manage the fund, when PBF donors agreed that a modest percentage of the fund could be applied to the hiring of a staff member. The current good standing of the PBF is one of the success stories of the PBA.

Finally, we must bear in mind that much of the process of developing the ideas behind the PBC took place during the time of the previous Secretary-General and his team—from the *Brahimi Report*, which gave birth to a more integrated approach to peace operations, through the work of the High-Level Panel which proposed the PBA in 2004, to the Secretary-General's response in 2005 and the resolution that came out of the Millennium Plus 5 Summit in 2005. With a change of leadership at the top in January 2007, this history was lost in the upper echelons of the UN Secretariat, including key departments. The understanding of the long road taken to bring the PBA to light was simply not there, and the PBA found itself virtually orphaned within the Secretariat before it could establish itself. Its survival depended on a few key member states and sympathetic staff members.

Questions remaining

Since that time, it would appear that progress has definitely been made, as outlined in this volume. However, there also remain pressing questions that must be addressed if we are to realize the potential of the PBA.

In general

Does the international community agree with the eloquent statement by then Secretary-General Kofi Annan in *In Larger Freedom*, that "we will not enjoy development without security, we will not enjoy security without development and we will not enjoy either without respect for human rights"?[5] Is this concept accepted as one of the elements in preventing conflict, and especially in preventing relapse into conflict?

Have we learnt whether we can in fact build peace through concerted action in support of post-conflict countries by working and investing together strategically as partners? Do we agree that post-conflict fragility will not end if we do not provide post-conflict fragile states with the financial and technical means to invest in recovery, reconstruction, and sustainable development for peace? Have we learnt how to work with governments to strengthen institutions and to partner with them, to avoid the political and governance pitfalls that threaten peace?

Have we learnt how to support populations so that they may quickly reap the benefits of peace, with investments in health, education, and employment as investments in sustainable peace? Do UN departments and programs work together in headquarters and the field to ensure that efforts and resources are focused on priority actions aimed at sustaining peace and improving the quality of life for populations—and not just in PBA countries? Why, after six years on the PBC agenda, are some countries still at the bottom of the Human Development Index?[6]

Can we avoid the pitfall of treating peacebuilding as "just another added activity"? Peacebuilding must guide the full range of activities—through mediation, peacekeeping, development, and human rights. Is there a role for the commission in advising on peacebuilding perspectives in all these areas? It is as much the "how" as the "what." It is the lens through which we view and focus our activities to ensure the greatest impact on the long-term goal of building sustainable peace.

Therefore, does peacebuilding have a place in the discourse of senior management, other than in relation to managing the institutions of the PBA? Are peacebuilding objectives taken into consideration when planning and implementing political mediation, human rights programming, peace operations planning, and post-conflict development operations?

xxxiv *Foreword*

Have we moved beyond the language of what has long been known as the North-South dialogue? The answer to this old debate lies in the correlation between peace and security, development, and human rights embedded in the PBA. If the North prioritizes peace and security investment and the South prioritizes development investment, then peacebuilding at the nexus between security and development should surely be the key.

More specifically

Can the PBA streamline its approach to bringing countries onto their agenda and later letting them go? Is there "agenda gridlock"? That can only weaken the capacity for providing integrated strategic thinking; and the ability to mobilize resources lacks focus when the agenda is unclear.

For the Security Council and the PBC, how do we move beyond the questions of turf? There are many engaged member states on the commission that have a great deal to offer. Not including them can only weaken the effectiveness of the UN, particularly in the light of stalled negotiations to reform the Security Council. Momentum was lost in the first years, with many emerging powers on the PBC suspicious of any relationship with the Security Council, while at the same time the Security Council ignored the commission.

With one or two early notable exceptions, why is it that most chairs of the Country-Specific Configurations have not succeeded in "marshalling resources" for the client countries of the PBC? This is a major failing of the Peacebuilding Architecture. The current success of the PBF is one of the highlights of the PBA, but it cannot make up for this. Too many donors have confused "funding for peacebuilding" with their generous contributions to the Peacebuilding Fund. The PBF has been well managed and has become a valued tool of the system, providing quick-response funding for critical peacebuilding efforts, but it was never intended to substitute for long-term recovery, reconstruction, and sustainable development in post-conflict countries. If the Security Council can mandate US$8 billion for peace operations, while member states provide much less for peacebuilding, that only contributes to the belief that security trumps development—and that the old notion of the North-South dialogue is alive and well and living in New York.

Has the PBA managed to get the division of labor right? The commission is normally staffed by ambassadors and political officers who do not need to be involved in detailed discussions of technical areas of peacebuilding. These discussions can take place in the Country-Specific Configurations, while the PBC's Organizational Committee could confine

Foreword xxxv

itself to broader issues, providing guidance to client countries on political issues, ensuring a more dynamic relationship with the Security Council and the Secretary-General, and developing relationships with other organizations such as the World Bank and the regional development banks.

Can the PBSO be provided with the operating budget and the mandate it needs for three broad responsibilities: to support the PBC, manage the fund, and support integrated peacebuilding within the UN? The current operation, which still depends on borrowed staff, government interns, and JPOs is untenable. Staff do not have the capacity to cover all three areas, and must make difficult choices. The office needs high-level attention within the Secretariat, ideally reporting to the Office of the Deputy Secretary-General (DSG). The DSG should consult with member states of the commission to clarify the PBSO's mandate and to ensure that adequate resources are made available. In addition, the DSG could convene heads of UN departments and programs from time to time, to review how internal coordination can best achieve the peacebuilding objectives inherent in the creation of the PBA. This would provide clearer guidance to a strengthened ASG Peacebuilding group, whose members today are unable to deliver the full weight of their respective departments.

Reflections

It is useful to reflect on some of the thinking behind the extraordinary effort of creating a whole new architecture within the United Nations. That was the first time that a new body of this nature had been created within the structure of the UN. Over time, new funds and programs and new functional secretariats have been created, but the Peacebuilding Commission remains unique. The effort to make this happen was founded on the belief that we all have a joint responsibility for ensuring the sustainability of global peace, based on peace within individual countries and regions, in the belief that all countries have a right to peace, and in the belief that we now had the tools to help make it happen. This venture should not be abandoned or allowed to slip into mediocracy. It was, and should remain, a noble project with a clear mandate, the power to implement it and the resources to make it work.

This will depend on political will by member states of all parts of the spectrum, to come together, to share the burden of power and of resources, and then to stay the course. It will depend a great deal on the good will of new governments in countries coming out of conflict to truly "beat their swords into ploughshares."[7] It will depend on the Security Council to support the project; on member states of the commission, the council, and the General Assembly to define their enlarged xxxvi *Foreword*

vision of peacebuilding as an essential element of the security/peace/human rights/development nexus; on senior Secretariat leadership to rally the UN system; and finally on donors, new and old, to marshal the resources to which they committed in the founding resolutions.

However, also, and here I would like to expand a little, it will depend on our knowing our global history. Where do fragile states come from? Do we understand the external factors as well as internal factors that have brought them to this state?

One of the lessons we have forgotten is how the history of development assistance evolved over the past few decades. After the terrible effects of the Third World debt crisis of the 1970s—which was caused as much by irresponsible First World lending institutions as by Third World borrowers—and the excesses of structural adjustment in the ensuing decade, donors in the 1990s entered into more equal contractual relationships, providing assistance to countries that committed to agreed performance standards and targets. Donors drew up their eligibility lists not only on the basis of historical and economic partnerships but on whether their aid money would bring returns in growth and progress in partnership with recipient countries' efforts: an improvement over the aid relationships characterized by Cold War politics or structural adjustment conditionality. The basis was now a more shared understanding of development, based on decades of UN World Conferences—on social development, the environment, women's equality, population, human rights, and other areas. This was the environment that gave rise to the UN Millennium Development Goals and underpinned the discussions on mutual responsibility between donor and recipient partners in the Development Assistance Committee of the Organisation for Economic Co-operation and Development (OECD).

However, there was an unintended consequence. This process neglected to deal with the question of how to assist non-performing countries to reach effective levels of governance as a takeoff point to sustainable development. Several of these countries—whether because of corruption, poor governance, weak institutions, or civil conflict—became less attractive to donors. We are now paying the price for walking away as suffering populations descended into what Paul Collier has called "The Bottom Billion."[8] Many of us saw the PBA as the opportunity to reverse this cruel trend and put into practice our understanding of the interrelatedness of political and security concerns with economic, social, and human rights concerns. So, for donors joining the Peacebuilding Commission to state simply that neglected post-conflict client countries of the PBC "are not on our lists" was contrary to the principles that brought the

Foreword xxxvii

PBA into being. This brought the fundamental mandate of the PBC "to marshal resources" to a grinding halt, before it had even begun.

All the countries on the PBC agenda, including Sierra Leone, Guinea-Bissau, and Liberia, remain at the bottom of the UN's Human Development Index. It is those countries that are now faced with the scourge of Ebola, with little or no health administration capacity for dealing with it. We must ask ourselves: could the impact of this dreadful disease have been lessened somewhat if major investments had been made in health, education, and government administration in the previous eight to nine years?

Conclusions

The volume before us touches on many of these issues, and provides some of the answers. The 2015 evaluation will address many more. It is my deeply held view that the Peacebuilding Architecture remains a worthwhile project which must be strengthened and to which member states and UN senior management must re-commit. The 2015 evaluation provides the opportunity to make that recommitment, but it must be realistic. There are major conflicts around the world that are not within the current capacity of the PBA to deal with, whether Syria, Iraq, or the broader Middle East. However, the focus of the world on these major conflicts increases the worry that struggling post-conflict situations, mainly in African countries, will continue to be neglected. The PBA, properly managed and properly resourced, must be strengthened so that it may deal with bringing these countries and their peoples into the twenty-first century.

This will be a test of our willingness to pay up front for prevention. Whether in fragile states, post-conflict, or the environment, we must realize that this will require significant response. It is pay now—or pay more later.

On a final note, I would like to repeat a recommendation that I made many times informally in my time with the PBA. The UN member states should agree that the Trusteeship Council Chamber be turned over to the Peacebuilding Commission. The PBC could then take its true place between the General Assembly Hall and the Chambers of the Economic and Social Council and the Security Council.

Notes

1 United Nations, *An Agenda for Peace: Preventive Diplomacy, Peacemaking and Peace-keeping*, Report of the Secretary General, UN doc. A/47/277, 17 June 1992.

xxxviii *Foreword*

2 United Nations, *A More Secure World: Our Shared Responsibility*, The Report of the Secretary-General's High-Level Panel on Threats, Challenges and Change, United Nations, UN doc. A/59/565, 2004, 84.

3 United Nations, *In Larger Freedom: Towards Development, Security and Human Rights for All*, Report of the Secretary-General, United Nations, UN doc. A/59/2005, 2005.

4 UN General Assembly, A/RES/60/180, and UN Security Council, S/RES/1645, December 2005, 31–32.

5 United Nations, *In Larger Freedom*, 6.

6 United Nations Development Programme, *The Human Development Report*, 2014.

7 Isaiah 2:4, and the subject of a sculpture in the garden at UN Headquarters in New York.

8 Paul Collier, *The Bottom Billion* (Oxford: Oxford University Press, 2007).

Introduction

Assessing the impact of the UN Peacebuilding Architecture

Cedric de Coning and Eli Stamnes

- **The main challenges facing peacebuilding**
- **An overview of the book**
- **Part I: Setting up the UN Peacebuilding Architecture**
- **Part II: The Peacebuilding Architecture's instruments in practice**
- **Part III: The institutional and conceptual impact of the Peacebuilding Architecture**
- **Part IV: Country-specific impact of the Peacebuilding Architecture**
- **Part V: Findings and conclusion**
- **Conclusion**

Since its establishment in 2005, the United Nations (UN) Peacebuilding Architecture (PBA) has supported peace processes in more than 20 countries, through the Peacebuilding Commission's (PBC) Country-Specific Configurations (CSCs) and via the Peacebuilding Fund (PBF). In this book we assess the impact of the PBA over its first 10 years in existence.

The PBA consists of the Peacebuilding Commission, the Peacebuilding Fund, and the Peacebuilding Support Office (PBSO). It was formally established in December 2005. The main rationale behind the PBA was to ensure that the UN system does not take its eyes off countries emerging from conflict too soon, and to provide a sustained and concerted approach to the international community's hitherto ad hoc, fragmented, and piecemeal support for post-conflict peacebuilding.[1]

Over the course of its first decade the PBA has developed its own understanding of and approach to peacebuilding through its interaction with the six countries that were on the Peacebuilding Commission's agenda, as well as the more than 20 countries that have benefitted from the Peacebuilding Fund. The first formal review of the commission and fund was the five-year review of the PBA that was undertaken in 2010,

2 Cedric de Coning and Eli Stamnes

and co-facilitated by the permanent representatives of Ireland, Mexico, and South Africa. The five-year review found that the PBA, and more specifically the commission, had not lived up to expectations. The reviewers argued that the PBC was at a crossroads: "either there is a conscious recommitment to peacebuilding at the very heart of the work of the United Nations, or the Peacebuilding Commission settles into the limited role that has developed so far."[2]

A more comprehensive 10-year review started in 2015. The UN Secretary-General appointed an Advisory Group of Experts, led by the former foreign minister of Guatemala, Gert Rosenthal, to review the UN's approach to and experience with peacebuilding more generally, and the PBA in particular. The Advisory Group of Experts published their report at the end of June 2015, which was to serve as the basis for discussions at the UN General Assembly 2015/16 session. The subsequent decisions taken in the General Assembly and the Security Council will determine the direction of the PBA for the next decade.

There were also several related reviews that started in 2015, which will further impact on the future of peacebuilding in the UN system. Most importantly perhaps is the new Sustainable Development Goals which will shape not only the UN system-wide approach to development, but that of the whole development community. One of the ways in which the Sustainable Development Goals differ from the Millennium Development Goals they replace is that they include a goal that promotes peaceful and inclusive societies for sustainable development, provides access to justice for all, and builds effective, accountable, and inclusive institutions at all levels. This is significant because this goal and its indicators can serve as an internationally agreed basis for how sustaining peace is tracked and progress assessed, including by the PBA. Other influential reviews are the UN High-level Independent Panel on Peace Operations, which assessed the UN's special political missions and peacekeeping operations, and the review of Security Council resolution 1325, as well as important meetings on international financing for development and climate change. All of these reviews provide stimulus for decisions that will influence the future direction of peacebuilding and reflect the high degree of interconnectedness of the UN system, and especially its development and peace dimensions.

This book contributes to this debate by offering an assessment of the impact of the PBA from an informed group of practitioners and scholars who have been closely involved in, and supported the work of the PBA when it was established and as it evolved. By "impact" we simply mean the effect that the establishment and subsequent actions of the

Introduction 3

PBA have had on how we understand peacebuilding today, especially in the UN context, as well as the effect the PBA has had on peace processes in the countries where it has been active.

In the next section we will introduce and discuss the 2015 report of the Advisory Group of Experts appointed by the Secretary-General to review the PBA, and contextualize the report in a wider discussion around the main challenges facing the PBA. Then we will present the structure of the book and briefly introduce each chapter so that the reader can get an overview of how we have approached the topic, what is covered, and where to find it.

The main challenges facing peacebuilding

The Advisory Group of Experts argues that peacebuilding is at the core of the identity and purpose of the UN, and as such the whole UN system should be responsible for and contribute to peacebuilding. The advisory group uses the concept "sustaining peace" to show that all of the UN's work in prevention, peacemaking, peacekeeping, post-conflict recovery and reconstruction, human rights, and development contributes towards the same purpose. By adopting the same concept that is used in the Sustainable Development Goals, the advisory group tries to address one of the main shortcomings of the UN's approach to peacebuilding—namely, its fragmentation and compartmentalization. For some actors, peacebuilding is the responsibility of the PBA, and therefore not their concern. Others are only interested in the political, development, or human rights dimensions of peacebuilding. The advisory group argues that if the UN fails to find a way to coordinate and integrate the efforts of the UN's peace and security, development, and human rights pillars, UN peacebuilding will continue to fail.

The advisory group suggests that this fragmentation can be addressed at the intergovernmental level, if the Peacebuilding Commission becomes the bridge between the Security Council, the UN Economic and Social Council (ECOSOC), the General Assembly, and the Human Rights Council. The advisory group also recommends that these bodies place peacebuilding more directly on their respective agendas, including through annual sessions devoted to the topic.

The advisory group has also a range of recommendations for improving coherence and coordination within the Secretariat and between the Secretariat, agencies, funds, and programs of the UN system. At the field level, the advisory group is particularly concerned with the breakdowns and interruptions caused by poor institutional transfers when the UN system transitions functions and responsibilities from a

4 Cedric de Coning and Eli Stamnes

UN Country Team to a Special Political Mission to a Peacekeeping Operation, or variants of these, and back again. It also highlights the challenges that occur when responsibilities are passed on to national government institutions and offers recommendations for alleviating some of these risks.

The UN High-level Panel on Peace Operations also highlighted these transitional breakdown points as a major concern. The peace operations panel shares the concern with the lack of coherence across the UN system and it proposes a new spectrum approach to peace operations—where all the different types of engagements of the UN system in a particular conflict system over time are understood as one continuous engagement that adapts to the changing needs of the system as it evolves—with the aim of encouraging continuation and strategic coherence across the UN system. The peace operations panel also adopts the sustaining peace terminology and it recommends that the Secretary-General appoints a deputy Secretary-General dedicated to ensuring coherence across the peace operations spectrum; develops a shared strategic analysis and planning capacity; and creates a single peace operations account. The latter recommendation is one of several related to the financing of peace operations, including peacebuilding, that both the peace operations panel and the Advisory Group of Experts offer to ensure that assessed contributions are used to support the whole spectrum of UN engagements, not only peacekeeping. Both the panel and the advisory group argue that the way assessed contributions have been used to date has resulted in a distortion in the balance of effort devoted to prevention, peacemaking, peacekeeping, and peacebuilding.

In addition, when it comes to the financing of peacebuilding, the advisory group recommends that the PBF should continue to play to its comparative advantage as a rapid, impactful, procedurally light, and risk-taking investor of first resort, and they make several recommendations for further improving its effectiveness.

In a significant departure from the PBA's past engagement with mainly state institutions, the advisory group encourages both the PBC and the PBF to find ways to better engage with and support civil society. It recommends that the commission consults, perhaps annually, with civil society, and that the fund considers ways in which to involve civil society in all aspects of its program cycle, including analysis, planning, implementation, monitoring, and evaluation.

The advisory group and the peace operations panel also both stress the importance of "inclusive national ownership." In fact, the advisory group argues that national and local actors are key to successfully

Introduction 5

sustaining peace and that the role of the international community is to support inclusive national ownership. Similarly, the peace operations panel argues that peace operations should be focused on supporting the national and local actors that have the agency to make the decisions and effect the changes the peace operations mandates require.

The advisory group also stresses the importance of partnerships and urges the PBC and PBF to find ways to more meaningfully support and relate to regional and sub-regional organizations like the African Union (AU) as well as with international financial institutions, such as the World Bank and regional banks, and special mention is made of the new Asia Infrastructure Investment Bank and the New Development Bank being established by the Brazil, Russia, India, China, South Africa (BRICS) group of countries.

An overview of the book

In Part I, the book introduces the historical and political context within which the PBA was established, as well as the political compromises that needed to be negotiated to set up the PBSO, the PBC, and the PBF. This context is crucial in order to understand and assess the impact of the PBA and will continue to set the parameters for what it can hope to achieve in the coming decade.

In Part II, the book assesses the PBA's two main instruments, namely the PBC and the PBF. The PBSO exists to support both the commission and the fund, and its role will be discussed in the context of the commission and fund.

In Parts III and IV, the book turns to assessing impact. In Part III, the book addresses institutional and policy impact by looking at two specific examples, namely gender and civilian capacity. In Part IV the book assesses the impact of the PBA in five of the six countries that were on the PBC's agenda during this first decade, namely Burundi, Sierra Leone, Liberia, Guinea-Bissau, and Guinea.

In Part V, the final section of the book, we synthesize the findings and recommendations of the preceding four parts and offer an overall assessment of the impact that the UN PBA has had over its first 10 years of existence, and offer recommendations for what can be done to improve its impact in the decade to come.

In addition to the 12 main chapters, the book offers a foreword and epilogue by the two longest-serving assistant secretaries-general for peacebuilding, who were responsible for the PBA over its first decade, Carolyn McAskie and Judy Cheng-Hopkins.[3]

6 Cedric de Coning and Eli Stamnes

In her foreword, Carolyn McAskie sheds light on the struggles and achievements of the early days of the UN's PBA—days characterized by deep mistrust among UN member states, following the 2005 World Summit document negotiations. This led to a slow and, at times, acrimonious start. Moreover, there was little clarity as to how the PBSO should operate "within existing resources," or what its supporting role would entail. There were also drawn-out negotiations over which the UN entity was best suited to deliver field funding and to manage the fund. It took a year before the PBC could reach substantive engagements with Burundi and Sierra Leone, the first two countries on its agenda, and even longer to bring in dedicated staff to manage the fund. In addition, the change of leadership at the top, in January 2007, represented a serious challenge to the PBA due to their lack of understanding of the complicated genesis of the architecture, and, according to McAskie, the PBA found itself virtually orphaned within the Secretariat before it could establish itself. Its survival depended on a few key member states and sympathetic staff members.

The foreword concludes that the PBA was, and should remain, a noble project with a clear mandate, the power to implement it, and the resources to make it work. This will depend on political will and (re)commitment by member states and UN senior management, and as such represents a test of our collective willingness to pay up front for prevention.

In an equally frank epilogue, Judy Cheng-Hopkins seeks to shed light on the problems associated with the creation and management of the PBA. While there was no doubt that peacebuilding was considered by most UN member states to be an indispensable activity, the reality was that confusion reigned over structures, roles, and responsibilities. This was further exacerbated by the PBC's relationship with the Security Council, and with the Secretary-General's representatives at the field level. The Security Council questioned the added value of the advice of the PBC, and the Secretary-General's special representatives (SRSGs) in the field complained about a duplication of roles. In addition, faulty assumptions accompanied the rationale for the PBA. Secretary-General Kofi Annan claimed that there was "a gaping hole in the United Nations institutional machinery" in that no part addressed the transition from war to lasting peace.[4] Cheng-Hopkins argues, however, that this was not the case. Initiatives taken by the UN Department of Political Affairs (DPA), the Department of Peacekeeping Operations (DPKO), and the UN Development Programme (UNDP) since the early 2000s showed that there was an awareness of the need for peacebuilding and the prevention of the recurrence of conflict, and that the new

Introduction 7

structure meant a risk of duplication of activities. Nevertheless, Cheng-Hopkins concludes that sustainable peace and development for fragile and failing states is more needed than ever, but that contradictions, shortcomings, confused expectations, and faulty assumptions must be tackled and corrected if the PBA is to achieve its full potential.

Part I: Setting up the UN Peacebuilding Architecture

In Chapter 1, Abiodun Williams and Mark Bailey shed light on the vision and thinking at the time of the establishment of the PBA—a rare international moment when political will aligned with intellectual momentum to produce genuine organizational change. The PBA was a compromise of what expertise held was needed and what proved politically feasible. As such, it was a signature accomplishment, but there was a significant gap between the original reform proposals and what was ultimately achieved. The authors shed light on the reasons for this. The contentious debate on the extent to which prevention was an appropriate concern for the UN and for any new peacebuilding architecture, had a significant impact on the discussions that led to the creation of the PBA. Consultations between the Secretary-General and member states, primarily from the G-77 group of developing countries, had made it clear that the strength of feeling against a preventive mandate—seen as unduly impinging on sovereignty—would be likely to erode support for the general idea of establishing a Peacebuilding Commission.

The chapter examines the process whereby certain member states guided the adoption of the PBA through the General Assembly, as well as the negotiations on the composition of the PBC and the agreement eventually reached, namely that it would report jointly to the General Assembly and to ECOSOC. Also noteworthy during this phase was the role of civil society and the private sector—which shaped the terms of debate around the commission's mandate. Williams and Bailey conclude that the creation of the PBA reflects the UN's ability, under agile and principled leadership, to adapt in light of operational experience. Finally, they argue that the contrast between the eventual form of the PBA and the initial blueprint—especially as regards the salience of conflict prevention—indicates the direction that future reform efforts should take.

In Chapter 2, Necla Tschirgi and Richard Ponzio examine the broader context and early decisions that shaped the PBA. Although based at the UN, it was envisaged that the PBA would be a catalytic mechanism for peacebuilding by convening all relevant actors, mobilizing new resources, and serving as a repository of knowledge, policy, and practice. Yet, many of the early decisions regarding the structure and

8 Cedric de Coning and Eli Stamnes

operations of the PBA set it on a path that has seriously constrained it from meeting these ambitious expectations.

These early decisions included the configuration of the PBC into the Organizational Committee, Country-Specific Meetings, and the Working Group on Lessons Learned, and the following lack of cross-fertilization between them, as well as the development of its instrument, the so-called Integrated Peacebuilding Strategy, and the resulting lack of a lighter peacebuilding strategy instrument with concrete and time-bound benchmarks. Yet another issue was the tension inherent in the PBSO's dual mandate of serving as the secretariat for the commission and acting as a peacebuilding knowledge base for both the UN member states and operational bodies.

The chapter also examines the PBF's initial struggle to define its niche, and how revision of its Terms of Reference and management structure in 2009 made it an agile and effective catalyst for peacebuilding in high-risk situations. Based on this analysis of the PBA's various components and interaction with UN member states and other international partners during its early years, the chapter identifies three main achievements and four major missed opportunities, namely: achieving greater coherence to and a common appreciation of peacebuilding by myriad international actors; after a slow start, demonstrating the PBF's "proof of concept"; establishing the foundations for a peacebuilding knowledge base; limited progress in addressing effectively critical conflict drivers through light, host nation-driven integrated peacebuilding strategies; inadvertently attaching a stigma to serving on the PBC's agenda, while failing to demonstrate that foreign aid would dry up faster without commission engagement; wrongly separating conflict prevention from UN peacebuilding; and failing to co-lead the International Dialogue on Peacebuilding and Statebuilding.

Part II: The Peacebuilding Architecture's instruments in practice

In the second part of the book we discuss the achievements and challenges of the PBA's constitutive parts. In Chapter 3, Jups Kluyskens assesses the impact of the PBF. The fund provides support to activities, actions, programs, and organizations that seek to build a lasting peace in countries emerging from conflict. In 2015 it is supporting around 20 countries a year through its two financing modalities: the Immediate Response Facility (IRF) and the Peacebuilding and Recovery Facility (PRF). They respond to country needs by supporting the implementation of peace agreements and political dialogue; promoting coexistence and peaceful resolution of conflict; revitalizing the economy and

Introduction 9

generating peace dividends; and re-establishing essential administrative services. The PBF allocates between US$75 million and $100 million per year, and has set $100 million as an indicative target for annual allocations. It delegates extensive responsibility and authority in-country to UN agencies and national governments. At headquarters it collaborates with other entities in the PBSO as well as the PBC. The six countries on the PBC's agenda receive more than half of its resources.

The IRF is the fund's project-based financing facility, which provides rapid funding for immediate peacebuilding needs and critical transitions. According to Kluyskens, it has been underutilized, but the fund's recent decision to raise its threshold to $15 million is encouraging. The PRF is a program-based financing facility for longer-term support to post-conflict countries and is the primary vehicle for PBF funding, providing three-quarters of the total funding to date. The PRF could be further improved by speeding up proposal development, improving the Joint Steering Committees of stakeholders in-country, and targeting.

The catalytic effect of the fund is emerging, but needs to increase in terms of resource mobilization and undertaking innovative, risky, or politically sensitive interventions. Kluyskens argues that the fund will need to invest in strong partnerships with the regional banks, the European Union (EU), and the World Bank as a way of better articulating its niche and increasing its impact. Equally important are its partnerships within the UN, including working with the DPA and the DPKO. In some countries, joint funding with other partners may be appropriate. This could strengthen the fund's strategic position and make its peacebuilding contributions more visible. Demonstrating that it can work effectively and cost-efficiently, including using international nongovernmental organizations (NGOs) and governments to implement programs, will further build trust in the fund.

Although synergies between the PBF and the PBC have improved, their relationship remains challenging, and more needs to be done to harmonize and institutionalize their approaches and instruments. The question of whether the PBF is the best instrument to continue funding in PBC countries in the long term should also be examined.

In Chapter 4, Mariska van Beijnum assesses the achievements of the PBC and the way ahead. She discusses some of the key challenges to, and achievements of, the PBC and its three configurations—the Organizational Committee (OC), the CSCs and the Working Group on Lessons Learned (WGLL)—and identifies key issues that should be taken into account when discussing the PBC's future. A major obstacle facing the PBC is skepticism. This is caused by the fact that, since

10   *Cedric de Coning and Eli Stamnes*

2011, no more countries have requested to be put on the PBC agenda as well as its inability to prevent conflict escalation in countries on its own agenda, and its inability to inform the Security Council on major violent conflicts on *its* agenda.

In addition there are conflicting expectations, understandings, and agendas amongst key stakeholders from the Global North and the Global South. Working relations between the PBC and the Security Council have not improved significantly since the 2010 review, and remain a major constraint on the PBC's position within the UN system. Moreover, the decision to create a separate support structure for the PBC (the PBSO) rather than building on existing UN capacities has limited the institutional backing for the PBC.

The OC is perceived as inefficient, while the CSCs are seen as more effective, but operate rather independently of formal structures, and rely upon the efforts of individuals. The WGLL, for its part, has made no systematic efforts to draw lessons from the PBC's own experiences. Furthermore, the PBC is insufficiently connected to the UN system's lead peacebuilding departments, and has missed a major opportunity by not linking up with the International Dialogue on Peacebuilding and Statebuilding (IDPS) process and its "New Deal for Engagement in Fragile States." As a result, the PBC is increasingly becoming marginalized from much of the action in the field—even in countries on its agenda.

Nevertheless, the PBC has contributed to putting peacebuilding more firmly on the international agenda, within and outside the UN system. Its achievements are most evident in three of its five core functions: advocacy for peacebuilding and for countries' needs; promoting coordination and coherence; and supporting resource mobilization. The strength of the PBC lies in the fact that it is an intergovernmental body involving significant actors from North and South, thus offering unique potential diplomatic leverage, providing a diplomatic forum for countries that otherwise lack diplomatic presence, and bringing "non-usual suspects" to the peacebuilding table. Unlike the Security Council, the PBC supports the countries' own peacebuilding efforts, and can offer "political accompaniment" by diplomats who are not part of in-country processes and dialogues.

Van Beijnum argues that in future the PBC should focus more on the "internal track" of advice. The Security Council and the General Assembly should bring relevant issues on their respective agendas to the commission's attention. In this way, the PBC could step in when a country is getting ready to "graduate" from the Security Council agenda. Moreover, the PBC should find ways to complement and act in

Introduction 11

synergy with the New Deal and the IDPS, for example in the political dialogue elements of the New Deal, including the recent initiative to strengthen South-South dialogue. In addition, the organizational set-up of the PBC entities should be adjusted according to a clearer PBC objective, for example by also allowing for discussions of crises in non-PBC countries and supporting peacebuilding at the global level, as well as considerably reducing its meeting activity; increasing the capacity of the PBSO; clarifying how the Support Office is linked to the key UN peacebuilding entities and how it is to "serve" the PBC; and integrating the lessons learned elements into the functions of the OC.

Part III: The institutional and conceptual impact of the Peacebuilding Architecture

In Part III the book turns to the institutional and conceptual impact of the PBA. In Chapter 5, Torunn Tryggestad assesses the gender(ed) impact of the PBA. In October 2000 the UN Security Council adopted resolution 1325 on Women, Peace and Security. This marked the start of what has now become known as the Women, Peace and Security Agenda (WPS). By now, the political commitment to implement this agenda has gained considerable ground within the UN and beyond. The PBA was off to a promising start with its early, formal acknowledgment of the importance of the WPS agenda to peacebuilding. However, 10 years on from the formal establishment of the PBA, the challenges of what is now termed "gender-responsive peacebuilding" are still many. Although strong political commitment and targeted efforts at improving policy development seem to speak to the contrary, women and gender concerns are still not effectively integrated into the activities of the PBA. This applies both to how the normative framework of WPS is conceptualized and understood, and how it is operationalized.

A culture appears to prevail within the UN system of viewing the WPS as an "add-on" component, not an element central to conflict resolution and peacebuilding—and this culture seems to apply to the PBA as well. The 2014 independent thematic review of gender-responsive peacebuilding, commissioned by the PBSO, lists several concerns: the distinct gap between policy commitments and operational reality still remains; there is a need for far greater momentum and scale in gender-responsive peacebuilding; there is a continuing lack of proper gender analysis of conflict situations; and there is a pressing need for operational guidance on how to implement gender-responsive peacebuilding and how to measure results and impacts.

12 Cedric de Coning and Eli Stamnes

On this basis Tryggestad makes several recommendations. First, the senior management of the various PBA entities must address the issue of gender-sensitive conflict analysis more vigorously. Gendered dimensions must be introduced early on in elaborations on any conflict situation or peacebuilding process on the agenda of the PBC. Second, analytical capacity within the PBSO must be strengthened to also include proper gender analysts in full-time positions. Gender-responsive peacebuilding requires both targeted and mainstreaming measures. Finally, stronger linkages must be established in the implementation of the outcomes of the different review processes within the UN system, as regards how to become more effective and gender-responsive in peacebuilding efforts.

In Chapter 6, John Karlsrud and Lotte Vermeij consider the Civilian Capacity initiative as an example of a spin-off from the PBA. The Civilian Capacity (CIVCAP) reform process emerged from the understanding that civilians play a crucial role in helping conflict-affected states rebuild institutions and achieve lasting stability and progress. The reform aimed to help the UN in tackling the challenges that post-conflict countries and the international community face in the immediate aftermath of conflict. Civilian capacities are at the heart of the solutions to these challenges, whether the question is how to deploy relevant, adequate, and effective civilian capacities rapidly, or build national competence and capacities for core government functions, and achieve national ownership. To achieve these goals, the CIVCAP reform called for more flexible, locally owned solutions by the UN, multilateral organizations and member states.

The senior advisory group's report on CIVCAP was the beginning of a global effort by the UN and its member states to restructure how civilian capacity is mobilized in crisis and post-conflict settings. It sought to wrest the debate out of a deadlock on managerial issues in New York, to a focus on how to achieve lasting, locally owned, and long-term results for host populations. While the process may have had limited impact on the UN system as such, it has succeeded in putting greater focus on locally relevant solutions such as triangular cooperation and South-South cooperation initiatives where capacity is sourced from neighboring countries, and the need to ensure more use of local capacities.

The CIVCAP reform process started out with a recommendation in the 2009 "Peacebuilding in the Immediate Aftermath of Conflict" report issued by the UN Secretary-General. This is an important point: the reform process came as the explicit result of the establishment of the PBA at the UN and the increased attention given to the role of peacebuilding, and within this the civilian capacities that perform key functions in supporting peacebuilding activities in countries emerging

Introduction 13

from conflict. As such it is an example of the impact that this book seeks to explore.

However, it is uncertain whether the CIVCAP reform initiative will have a lasting impact on UN institutions and strategies. The UN has a tendency to revert to what it knows best—how to develop new guidelines and tools—getting embroiled in long-winded strategy processes that turn into a wrestling ground for inter- and intra-organizational rivalries, with reform becoming incremental.

Part IV: Country-specific impact of the Peacebuilding Architecture

In Part IV the focus shifts to an assessment of the impact of the PBA on the countries where it has been active, both as a result of being on the agenda of the PBC's CSCs, and as a recipient of support from the PBF. In Chapter 7, Susanna Campbell, Josiah Marineau, Tracy Dexter, Michael Findley, Stephanie Hofmann, and Daniel Walker assess the impact of the PBA on Burundi's peace process. Between 2007 and 2013, the PBF allocated $49 million to help in consolidating peace in Burundi, making it one of the top recipients of PBF funds. This chapter assesses the contribution of these funds to the peacebuilding process in Burundi. Campbell and colleagues find that combined with the efforts made by the chair of the PBC's Burundi Country Configuration, the PBF was a powerful tool that helped the UN to implement several innovative and influential peacebuilding activities in Burundi. Funding was disbursed quickly and went to peacebuilding projects implemented by the UN only. There was no equivalent funding source for the UN in Burundi and thus, several PBF-funded projects made crucial positive contributions to the country's peacebuilding process.

Despite clear successes, there were significant flaws in most of the projects that the PBF funded in Burundi. During the first tranche (PBF I) of $35 million, only seven out of 18 projects achieved their goals and were relevant to Burundi's peacebuilding process—while some of the unsuccessful PBF projects even had a negative impact on the peacebuilding process. During the second tranche (PBF II) of $9.2 million, many PBF-funded ventures were not designed as peacebuilding activities, but were standard development or humanitarian activities. In two out of the 13 villages covered by this study, PBF-funded activities were found to have had a negative impact on the intended beneficiaries.

While the PBF aims to support "high-risk" projects and is therefore willing to accept a certain failure rate, this chapter shows that the failures of many PBF-funded activities were caused by poor project

14   *Cedric de Coning and Eli Stamnes*

design, implementation, and monitoring—not their high-risk nature. Campbell and colleagues find that PBF-funded projects were *successful* when they: were implemented by teams that combined political, local, peacebuilding programming, and monitoring knowledge; were supported by innovative feedback mechanisms from a representative group of local stakeholders; and had national partners who were committed to both the idea and the implementation of the project.

In Chapter 8, Fernando Cavalcante assesses the impact of the PBA on Sierra Leone's peace process. Sierra Leone has achieved considerable progress in its peacebuilding process since the end of the civil war in 2002. In terms of the disarmament and demobilization of former combatants, the holding of credible presidential elections, and developments in the official diamond trade, progress is good. The same can be said for the economic domain. Despite such progress, Sierra Leone remains one of the poorest nations in the world. Moreover, some challenges still persist—like the centralization of power in Freetown and youth exclusion, which led to the outbreak of civil war in 1991 in the first place.

Sierra Leone was among the first countries to be included on the agenda of the PBC, serving as a "test case" for much of the institutional set-up of the new body, including the format and content of the PBC's instruments of engagement. Key areas of the peacebuilding process were advanced through the PBC's role in facilitating dialogue among national and international partners, as well as in gathering political support for the implementation of concrete initiatives. Sierra Leone has also obtained an above-average level of support from the PBF. More recently, progress has been made in New York for a renewed engagement of the PBC in Sierra Leone as the country prepares to "graduate" from the commission and focus on more long-term development challenges.

According to Cavalcante, the PBA has made at least three contributions to the peacebuilding process in Sierra Leone: it has been able to foster strategic coordination of international stakeholders through the adoption of an integrated peacebuilding strategy agreed with the Sierra Leone government; it has adopted a comprehensive understanding on the concept of peacebuilding in Sierra Leone, allowing the inclusion of wider areas of intervention under the umbrella of the Sierra Leone Peacebuilding Cooperation Framework, and ultimately resulting in greater peace dividends to the population; and finally, the PBF has been used to provide support in a range of key initiatives in the peacebuilding process, including the holding of elections, and during the drawdown phase and subsequent closure of the special political

Introduction 15

mission in the country. However, the PBA has been less successful in getting national actors fully involved during the development of the Peacebuilding Cooperation Framework, which focused support to the peacebuilding process around targeted priorities, and in designing more effective programs and projects for PBF support based on comprehensive analyses of the drivers of conflict and needs on the ground. Following the closure of the UN special political mission in Sierra Leone, and considering the request that the PBC should remain engaged in the country, the PBA is now expected to help to support the national government in taking a more active role in the peacebuilding process from now on.

In Chapter 9, Marina Caparini assesses the impact of the PBA on Liberia's peace process. She presents a critical appraisal of the PBA in its engagement with Liberia in three priority areas—rule of law, security sector reform, and national reconciliation—and argues that the PBA's approach in Liberia is aligned closely with the "liberal peace" approach adopted by the UN and international financial institutions. The PBA has adopted an approach that is "problem-solving" in orientation, aimed at consolidating peace through top-down institutional reforms. The main focus has been on state building, reconstituting formal institutions in the rule of law and security sectors, through the provision of technical assistance. Close cooperation has been cultivated with the government of Liberia, the political elite and international donors in this regard. This has brought advantages in terms of access and accountability, but also drawbacks in a context where political elites have been associated with corruption, lack of accountability, and impunity.

However, the PBC has also sought to secure local ownership and a bottom-up approach through consultative procedures and comprehensive public opinion surveys when mapping perceptions of, and needs for, justice and security, for program planning purposes, as well as in reconciliation efforts. The PBA's focus on building the formal justice sector may also be considered successful for cases involving groups typically disadvantaged under customary/traditional justice mechanisms (typically women, minorities, and the poor). This indicates that critics may have been too indiscriminate in condemning the liberal peacebuilding focus on institution building. On the basis of the assessment of PBA experiences in Liberia, Caparini recommends that future peacebuilding expand its focus beyond state institutions to encompass non-state, customary actors in the justice and security spheres—the primary providers of justice and security services in rural areas. In order to address the continuing marginalization and under-serving of

16 Cedric de Coning and Eli Stamnes

rural populations by public services, the PBA should also work with Liberian actors in not only "de-concentrating" formal security and justice, but also in supporting decentralization with a view to making government more responsive and accountable to local communities. Finally, it is vital to avoid any further deprioritization of, or delays to, the reconciliation process.

In Chapter 10, Adriana Erthal Abdenur and Danilo Marcondes de Souza Neto assess the impact of the PBA on Guinea-Bissau's peace process since 2007. Peacebuilding efforts have been weakened by the proliferation of differing perspectives on, and approaches to, the root causes of instability in Guinea-Bissau, as well as inadequate allocation of resources and the relatively low attention given to Guinea-Bissau by the international community—despite recurring political violence, frequent interruptions to the constitutional order, and persistent underdevelopment. The appointment of Brazil as chair of the CSC and to the PBC presidency has improved this, but a key challenge persists: the need to mobilize broader support for the effort, especially from international donors. The April 2012 *coup d'état* that led to the suspension of PBC activities in the country made clear the need to balance security-focused initiatives with development-oriented efforts, in order to address the basic causes of underdevelopment and political instability.

Guinea-Bissau has not been the typical PBA case. It has not recently emerged from conflict, nor has it been a pressing humanitarian emergency. It is rather marked by recurring political instability, complicated by severe underdevelopment and illegal transnational flows, especially drug trafficking. Second, peacebuilding efforts were suspended for a substantial period (2012–14), due to the 2012 government overthrow, with only some political coordination remaining during this period. According to the authors, these two factors underscore several limitations of the PBA, and reveal the need for the PBC to develop strategies for reacting, flexibly and effectively, to rapidly changing situations on the ground. In addition, the case of Guinea-Bissau draws attention to the need for long-term engagement with the peacebuilding process, vital in a situation of chronic political instability in which there is a need for trust building among the various stakeholders, including civil society and women. Finally, the case of Guinea-Bissau also makes clear the need for greater integration between the PBA and other UN actors dedicated to development and human rights.

In Chapter 11, Ian D. Quick assesses the impact of the PBA on Guinea's peace process from January 2010 to January 2014. Guinea is also unusual amongst the cases in this volume. It has not experienced a major war or hosted UN peacekeepers, despite a bleak political history

Introduction 17

and recent armed conflicts across every one of its borders. Instead, the context is the transition from a military to an elected civilian regime. Throughout this period Guinea was manifestly unstable, but just shy of a crisis that would keep it on the agenda of the UN Security Council or ECOWAS. It was also something of an aid orphan, as potential bilateral partners adopted a "wait-and-see" attitude to the transition. Both the PBC and the PBF approached the situation with simultaneous political, military, and economic dimensions.

On the political front, the "priority of priorities" was to establish the institutions envisaged in the country's new constitution. Thus it is striking that the period began and ended with old-fashioned crisis diplomacy, led by ECOWAS in 2010 and the UN Office for West Africa in 2013. Both interventions responded to a near-total breakdown of political dialogue over elections. Violent street politics escalated and many observers feared a crisis, but it is a credit to the Guinean people that they came back from the brink once again. According to Quick, the peacebuilding institutions did not play major roles throughout this four-year drama. In-country, the PBC was rarely physically present, and few Guinean political actors or outside observers saw it as a relevant interlocutor. At New York level, the approach was characterized as "polite peer advice"—and that for a junior member of government. Meanwhile, the UN team in-country emphasized that its proper role was to accompany the new presidential administration. It did not attempt to unblock political dialogue or work directly with electoral institutions. The major use of the PBF allocation was for "pacification" work with civil society actors. This was aimed at helping to contain the Guinean brand of street politics, and did have some positive impact.

For the security sector and female/youth employment, the record was mixed. The major goal in both cases was to lay the groundwork for engagement of other donors. In financial terms this did not happen, and there were few significant inflows. However, a secondary goal of "quick wins" did produce some important interim benefits. Most notable were interventions to build early momentum for civilian control over the volatile security sector, and support to election security. These played a role, if difficult to quantify, in averting catastrophe during the political crises in 2010 and 2013.

Overall the Guinea experience points to major questions relating to the role of the CSCs of the PBA. Are they solely to provide peer advice to the government of the day or should they engage more thoroughly in forging consensus amongst different national stakeholders? The case also sheds light on the assumption that the UN can chart a third way

18　*Cedric de Coning and Eli Stamnes*

between a full-fledged peacekeeping/political mission dispatched by the Security Council, and "development business as usual."

Part V: Findings and conclusion

In Chapter 12, Cedric de Coning and Eli Stamnes conclude by synthesizing and analyzing the findings and recommendations of the book and by considering the future of the PBA. The chapter finds that the PBA has contributed to the peacebuilding concept being adopted as an overarching framework for peace consolidation; that it has contributed to improved coordination across the UN system, especially at country level; and that it has helped the UN system to realize that too much focus on resource mobilization generates unintended consequences, including reducing peacebuilding to a programmatic and technical undertaking, thus undermining attention to its political dimension.

However, de Coning and Stamnes finds that the space for the PBA, and thus also for its further development and evolution, is constrained by internal UN structural boundaries as well as the current turbulent state of global governance. However, they argue that despite these constraints, there are still a number of things the PBA can do to enhance its effectiveness, and their recommendations include that the PBA revert back to its original intended role of addressing the root causes of conflict; that it use its broad representative base to agree on ways of addressing external factors such as corruption, transnational organized crime, and extractive industries; that it give serious attention to incorporating regional approaches into its work, including developing a much more cooperative relationship with the AU, sub-regional bodies and civil society; and that it should help to empower national and local ownership by giving a greater role to the governments and civil society of the countries on its agenda to undertake self-assessments, to brief the PBC on its vision, plans, and progress, as well as its perception of peacebuilding challenges, including those posed by its regional and international partners, and by playing a leading role in monitoring its own progress towards sustainable peace.

Conclusion

Some argue that 10 years is a very short time in the overall lifetime of an international institution like the PBA, and that it is unhelpful to compare it with the Security Council, ECOSOC, and the Human Rights Council, all of which have had a much longer history. Others are frustrated with the PBA and perceive it to lack relevance, vigor,

Introduction 19

and impact. In this volume we show how both arguments reflect different aspects of the early history of the PBA. A lot has happened during the 10 years since its establishment. Some of the pillars of the PBA, like the PBF, have shown significant progress, despite a slow start, whilst others, like the PBC, are still struggling to make their mark. We argue in this book that the PBA has had some impact, but that the way it operates and relates to the rest of the UN system has significantly constrained its effect, and will have to change before more impact can be realized. The Advisory Group of Experts has made a number of recommendations that could help to accelerate its evolution, and several further recommendations are offered in this volume.

However, as various chapters in this book illustrate, the PBA has been severely constrained, since its establishment, by the political and institutional space within which it has to operate. It thus follows that the degree to which it can be reformed, without changes in the way the larger UN system is interconnected and governed, is limited. To make the PBA more effective, one will have to improve the coherence and interconnectedness of the UN system, including at the intergovernmental level, at the levels of the Secretariat, agencies, funds and programs, and importantly, at the regional, country, and field levels where the UN operates in its various forms.

In this book we analyze the Peacebuilding Architecture's establishment and the first 10 years of its performance by looking at the process leading up to its creation, the early years of setting up the Peacebuilding Commission, Peacebuilding Fund, and Peacebuilding Support Office, as well as how it has performed in the context of five of the six countries that were on the agenda of the commission and have received a significant portion of the support provided by the fund. At the same time, we contextualize the PBA within the UN system, and within the larger international development, human rights, and peace and security governance system, with a view to show how the PBA is both enabled and constrained by the larger global institutional context of which it forms a part.

We hope that the analysis and recommendations offered by the practitioners and scholars gathered together in this volume will help those engaged in making decisions about global governance reform more generally, and about the PBA in particular, to understand how the PBA and the UN system within which it operates are interconnected. Changes are necessary not just in the PBA itself, but also in the peace and development paradigm and in the structural relationships among especially the intergovernmental bodies and global institutions that make up the UN system writ large.

20 *Cedric de Coning and Eli Stamnes*

Such changes can be glacial in pace, and some degree of strategic patience is necessary to manage expectations, but in the context of the larger shifts that are taking place in the post-unipolar global order, as well as the significant number of reviews undertaken or started in 2015, the next decade is already likely to witness significant changes and developments. We trust this volume will help the reader to understand where, in this larger context, the UN Peacebuilding Architecture comes from, what impact it has had during its first 10 years, and which directions its evolution is likely to take over the next 10 years and beyond.

Notes

1 Rob Jenkins, *Peacebuilding: From Concept to Commission* (London: Routledge, 2013), 62.
2 A/64/868–S/2010/393, Annex to the identical letters dated 19 July 2010 from the Permanent Representatives of Ireland, Mexico and South Africa to the United Nations, to the President of the General Assembly and the President of the Security Council, Review of the United Nations Peacebuilding Architecture, 21 July 2010, 3. See also Necla Tschirgi and Cedric de Coning, "Ensuring Sustainable Peace: Strengthening Global Security and Justice through the UN Peacebuilding Architecture," background paper for the Commission on Global Security, Justice, and Governance, The Hague Institute, 2015.
3 The other two were Jane Holl Lute, who served for only a few months in 2008/09 before being recalled to serve as the US deputy secretary for Homeland Security, and Oscar Fernández-Taranco, who took over the reins at the end of 2014.
4 United Nations, "In Larger Freedom: Towards Development, Security and Human Rights for All," Report of the Secretary-General, United Nations, UN doc. A/59/2005, 2005.

Part I

Setting up the UN Peacebuilding Architecture

1 The vision and thinking behind the UN Peacebuilding Architecture

Abiodun Williams and Mark Bailey

- Vision for peacebuilding: what was needed?
- Cleavages in the peacebuilding debate by 2005
- Momentum gathers for reform
- Towards a Peacebuilding Commission
- Debating the terms of the new Peacebuilding Architecture
- Role of civil society and the private sector
- The World Summit and beyond
- The Peacebuilding Support Office
- The Peacebuilding Fund
- The establishment of the Peacebuilding Architecture
- Conclusions

The United Nations (UN) Peacebuilding Architecture (PBA) was born at a rare international moment when political will aligned with intellectual momentum to produce genuine organizational change. The story of the origins of the PBA, and the contours it eventually took, is fundamentally one of the search for such an alignment. Attempts to translate scholarship and operational experience into new institutional forms entail a constant struggle to reconcile what expertise says is needed, and what is politically feasible. The Peacebuilding Commission (PBC) that emerged in 2005 was a product of such negotiation—as were the strengths and flaws that it exhibited. Along with the other two pillars of the new PBA—the Peacebuilding Fund (PBF) and the Peacebuilding Support Office (PBSO)—the commission represented a middle path between optimum policy and political reality.

By the time of the 2005 World Summit, whose Outcome Document[1] provided the mandate for the creation of these three new entities, there was widespread agreement within the UN system that building sustainable peace in countries susceptible to conflict was critical to the world

24 *Abiodun Williams and Mark Bailey*

organization's work in upholding international peace and security, promoting sustainable development, and protecting human rights.

The UN's experience in the immediate aftermath of the Cold War underlined the relevance of such a focus, as well as the need to improve its own efforts. Increasingly, the UN became the international community's "actor of choice" to manage difficult post-conflict transitions. It had been vested with unparalleled authority, and had registered some noteworthy successes, as in Namibia and Croatia.[2] All too often, however, it had labored under the weight of its new responsibilities, which could extend to plenipotentiary authority, as in Kosovo and Timor-Leste.[3]

The impetus for reform in 2005 may have proven decisive, but it was not wholly new. Previous UN reports had introduced the concept of peacebuilding, and further refined the UN's understanding. However, they had done little to foster momentum towards a coherent approach across the UN system. In contrast, the reforms of 2005 not only demonstrated that peacebuilding was an idea whose time had come, but offered normative coherence with broader efforts to reform the UN in the early twenty-first century.[4] They also provided a chance to affirm the UN's relevance, and Secretary-General Kofi Annan's own reforming credentials, at a time when the leadership of the organization and its leader had been called into question.

This chapter argues that the creation of the PBA was a signature accomplishment, but recognizes the significant gap between original reform proposals and what was ultimately achieved. Scholarly attention has focused on accounting for the ultimate form that other landmark reforms took—not least the Responsibility to Protect (R2P), where the consensus achieved in the World Summit Outcome Document differed substantially from the recommendations of the International Commission on Intervention and State Sovereignty.[5] However, there has been little analysis of what accounts for the discrepancies between the eventual form of the PBA and the initial vision for the new peacebuilding institutions, particularly as laid out by the High-Level Panel on Challenges, Threats and Change, which had recommended the creation of a Peacebuilding Commission in its 2004 report.[6]

This chapter examines the UN's thinking on peacebuilding in the period immediately before the creation of the PBA, and provides an analysis of the negotiation process that led to the creation of the architecture as it is today. We highlight key cleavages in the debate, particularly around a potential preventive mandate for the proposed commission, which put into clear relief the stakes for key member states, including the G-77 and the United States, as well as UN Secretariat and wider UN system actors. The negotiations around this sensitive issue were emblematic of the disagreements between member states, particularly between donors and countries that might themselves end up on the PBC docket, as well as implicating the interests of various other actors within the wider UN.

Vision for peacebuilding: what was needed?

That the failure to build sustainable peace was proving inimical to the wider aims of the United Nations seemed self-evident by 2005, and was also supported by scholarly work which increasingly spoke with one voice on the relevance of a peacebuilding paradigm, if not the form it should take. Particularly influential was the work of Paul Collier, who argued that between one-quarter and one-third of all negotiated peace settlements ended in failure, with reversion to civil war within five years.[7] Collier's earlier finding, that half the countries emerging from violent conflict reverted to conflict within five years, had gained considerable currency within the UN, and amongst influential member states.[8]

Senior UN officials, including the Secretary-General, agreed that more effective mechanisms were needed to prevent the recurrence of conflict after civil wars and to ensure that longer-term efforts toward development were not undermined by a renewal of conflict—a process that Collier memorably referred to as "development in reverse" in a paper that estimated the cost of an average civil war at US$54 billion.[9] Central to these efforts was the need to support institution building and promote the rule of law in post-conflict societies. There was concomitant concern that the UN and the wider international system were too poorly equipped, and too poorly coordinated, to handle such problems. Peacebuilding activities were mired in bureaucratic turf battles, lack of funding and failure to share best practices. These twin problems—external trends and an internal inability to check them—ultimately produced a consensus that innovations were necessary, and that they should take the form of a new peacebuilding architecture that could better enable the UN system to meet the challenge of helping countries successfully complete the transition from war to peace.

The new architecture was congruent with Kofi Annan's own vision of twenty-first-century sovereignty,[10] which he saw as implying responsibility and which was vested in a state's citizenry, not just in the state itself.[11] This was a silver thread that ran throughout his 2005 reform agenda. If the intellectual foundations for peacebuilding had been compellingly laid, the norm-entrepreneurship of an activist Secretary-General with an instinctive understanding of the "political traffic" in New York was also essential to peacebuilding's "coming of age."

26 *Abiodun Williams and Mark Bailey*

Cleavages in the peacebuilding debate by 2005

The overwhelming economic, political, and human cost of the failure to build lasting peace, the UN's own experience of peace operations in the 1990s, and the increased scholarly focus on the topic aligned to produce a growing body of work on peacebuilding which had a significant impact on UN reform initiatives. In this section, we highlight some of the key cleavages that influenced thinking within the UN itself, particularly during the 2005 negotiations.

"Peacebuilding" as a term has given rise to considerable definitional variance between scholars,[12] and therefore also between those in the policy sphere attempting to institutionalize a particular understanding of peacebuilding: its scope.[13] The primordial question of what peacebuilding was attempting to achieve was one such open question as the 2005 negotiations approached, with a spectrum of views developing from Galtungian "positive peace"[14] to an absence of violence with some basic standards of governance.[15] In the negotiation stage, the ambiguity surrounding peacebuilding facilitated progress by allowing actors within the UN bureaucracy and member-state delegations to project their own conceptual aspirations into the reform process,[16] even if underlying divergences could not be ignored once the PBA became operational.

The contentious nature of some issues could, however, not be avoided. One such issue was the role of prevention activities in peacebuilding. For Michael Doyle and Nicholas Sambanis, for example, peacebuilding is in effect "the frontline of preventive action."[17] This view was consistent with the call for coherence between conflict-prevention efforts and post-conflict peacebuilding implied in the seminal report on UN peacekeeping, the *Brahimi Report*, issued in 2000.[18] Although earlier UN reform documents, including Boutros-Ghali's *An Agenda for Peace*, had explicitly situated peacebuilding as a "post-conflict" activity,[19] reformists nevertheless hoped that it could be linked more coherently to activities aimed at conflict prevention.

The need for institutional coherence between prevention and peacebuilding efforts was underlined in a landmark presidential statement of the UN Security Council in 2001:

> The Security Council recognizes that peacebuilding is aimed at *preventing the outbreak*, the recurrence or the continuation of armed conflict and therefore encompasses a wide range of political, development, humanitarian and human rights programmes and mechanism. This requires short- and long-term actions tailored to address the particular needs of societies *sliding into conflict* or emerging from it ...[20]

The vision and thinking behind the UN PBA 27

This view was in line with Kofi Annan's own emphasis on the importance and interconnectedness of conflict prevention. He had "pledged to move the United Nations from a culture of reaction to a culture of prevention,"[21] and expected that the new PBA—along with R2P, the principal reform on peace and security during his tenure—would reflect this aspiration. Yet, even though the high-level panel agreed with this view, prevention was to be the principal casualty of the ensuing negotiations with and between member states.

The debate about prevention was part of a wider discussion in the academic literature about the sequencing of peacebuilding: was it to be undertaken "across the conflict cycle,"[22] or was it explicitly a "post-conflict" activity?[23] A linked question was whether there was a discernible "peacebuilding period." When, for example, could peacebuilding be declared to have been achieved? Could one measure a period of time where recurrence had been avoided, or were all post-conflict states (including, for example, Germany and Japan) forever in a peace-building stage? The view taken on this contentious subject had ramifications for the relationship of peacebuilding to other activities undertaken by the UN in conflict zones—mediation, peacekeeping, peace enforcement, and peace monitoring—and for where authority lay. Unlike these enterprises, which were generally attached to specific departments within the UN Secretariat, peacebuilding was seen as a holistic enterprise, necessarily bringing together different elements of the UN system.

Connecting the debate on peacebuilding to concurrent reform processes, not least the effort to replace the moribund Commission on Human Rights with a more effective Human Rights Council, were different views about the characteristic of the state whose capacities international actors were engaged in (re)building. Some scholars placed the emphasis on the ability of a state to provide a modicum of security, while others stressed that legitimacy rested on the ability to deliver services.[24]

Discussions about the nature of the state that was to emerge from peacebuilding efforts raised questions of democratic legitimacy. Was peacebuilding an inherently liberal process, as many argued, owing to its co-emergence at the high point of economic liberalization, the temptation of Western donors to adhere to "end of history" thinking and the intellectual attractiveness of democratic peace? Finally, a key debate in the literature that led directly into the negotiations between member states and within the UN itself was who peacebuilders actually were. This was to have implications for the institutional locus of the PBA within the UN system, as well as its reporting lines. At the time

28   Abiodun Williams and Mark Bailey

when the PBA was created, there was increasing emphasis, in the literature as well as operationally, on a "whole-of-system" approach intended to facilitate activities by a "coalition of the relevant"—including national and local authorities, the UN, regional organizations, donors, multilateral banks and the international financial institutions (IFIs), international nongovernmental organizations (INGOs), corporations, diasporas, and local civil society. The PBA attempted to reflect the understanding that an overly top-down model would be unsuccessful; nevertheless, the architecture that emerged does not itself represent a maximalist version of participation, and still does not maximize the potential of organizational learning at field level.[25]

Momentum gathers for reform

It was in the climate of such debates that viable—if unsuccessful—reform proposals began to be made, ultimately culminating in the creation of the PBA. The *Brahimi Report* proposed building upon the Executive Committee on Peace and Security (ECPS), convened by the UN Department of Political Affairs (DPA), to create an early warning mechanism: the ECPS Information and Strategic Analysis Section (EISAS). That such a facility proved stillborn foreshadowed the debates about a preventive mandate for the PBA, as well as the wariness of major powers to share their hard-earned intelligence and the reluctance of departments within the UN system to countenance losing institutional authority.[26]

Early reform proposals drew on intellectual currents, initiatives emerging from the UN itself and institutional entrepreneurship by scholars and the think-tank community. In 2001, for example, Shepard Forman, Stewart Patrick, and Dirk Salomons proposed a "Strategic Recovery Facility" "to ensure a timely and effective response to the needs of societies recovering from conflict";[27] and in 2004, James Fearon and David Laitin suggested that a revamped Trusteeship Council could provide a stakeholder-based model with a role for troop-contributing countries.[28] The contours of the eventual PBA were beginning to take shape.

Towards a Peacebuilding Commission

Within the UN, and especially the Executive Office of the Secretary-General (EOSG), there was recognition that the UN needed to adapt to these operational and scholarly currents, especially given the fragmented nature of its prevailing approach to achieving sustainable

The vision and thinking behind the UN PBA 29

peace. In light of debates about the meaning and scope of peacebuilding—tied to organizational interests and member-state imperatives—this was inevitably going to be a highly political process.

The high-level panel provided a fillip to the peacebuilding paradigm, embracing the view that UN failures to prevent conflict—and atrocities—in the post-Cold War period had essentially been failures of peacebuilding. It concluded that "neither the United Nations nor the broader international community, including the international financial institutions, are well organized to assist countries attempting to build peace,"[29] and called for "a single intergovernmental organ dedicated to peacebuilding, empowered to monitor and pay close attention to countries at risk, ensure concerted action by donors, agencies, programmes and financial institutions, and mobilize financial resources for sustainable peace."[30]

The PBC that the high-level panel recommended was "a reasonably small" one,[31] understood at the time to mean between 10 and 24 members,[32] far smaller than the number eventually settled upon (31). The panel recommended representation from the Security Council and the UN Economic and Social Council (ECOSOC), but did not mention the General Assembly. It also recommended attendance (though not membership) of relevant donors, troop-contributing countries, and representatives of the IFIs (at chief executive level). The panel's vision for the PBC was a manifestly preventive one. It defined its "core functions" as "identify[ing] countries that are under stress and risk sliding towards State collapse" and, in coordination with national authorities, organizing "proactive assistance in preventing that process from developing further."[33]

The release of *In Larger Freedom* by Kofi Annan in March 2005 was an attempt by the Secretary-General to repackage the high-level panel's recommendations in a form more acceptable to (all) member states. He agreed with the broad strokes of the panel's analysis, concurring that when it came to peacebuilding, there was "a gaping hole in the UN institutional machinery."[34] However, it had by then become clear that fears among some G-77 countries that the PBC would pave the way for a more militarily interventionist UN would make a preventive mandate for the new commission a non-starter. Given the reluctance of major powers to share intelligence, and the fears by others that such intelligence-gathering tools would be used against them, it was evident that prevention had too few allies to survive formal negotiations.[35]

Sensitive to concerns that the lack of such a mandate would weaken the PBC and deprive the UN's efforts to address violent conflict of much-needed coherence, but swayed by the strength of feeling likely to erode the wide support for the general idea of the establishment of a

30   *Abiodun Williams and Mark Bailey*

PBC, the Secretary-General announced that, in his view, the new commission should not have a conflict prevention mandate.[36] In the *Addendum* to his report, Annan noted that while "it would be valuable if Member States could *at any stage* make use of the Peacebuilding Commission's advice and could request assistance from a standing fund for peacebuilding to build their domestic institutions ... [the PBC] would not have an early warning or monitoring function."[37] Moreover, in his proposal, Annan called for countries not on the agenda of the Security Council to be considered by the PBC only at their own request. Contentious issues still remained. Following the publication of *In Larger Freedom*, member states entered a stage of bartering on the precise institutional location of the PBC, reporting lines, and membership.

Debating the terms of the new Peacebuilding Architecture

The General Assembly took up the mantle of reform, holding informal plenary debates in April 2005 on *In Larger Freedom*, followed by thematic consultations under the leadership of the 10 facilitators named by the president of the General Assembly, Jean Ping, on the four clusters in the Secretary-General's report. Deft handling of the issues by the facilitators in cluster two (Freedom from Fear) resulted in near-universal agreement that the PBC and the PBSO (within the UN Secretariat) should be established.

Conceptual debates about the scope and sequencing of peacebuilding carried over into disagreement about where the institutional locus of the PBC should be, and to which organ it would report. A large majority of delegations favored a role for the Security Council as well as for ECOSOC, but preferences tended to reflect traditional North–South divisions. While most donor countries (as well as a significant number of countries in sub-Saharan Africa) preferred a strong link to the Security Council, many G-77 countries—fearing that peacebuilding might be used as a "Trojan Horse" for the Security Council to extend its authority into development issues[38]—argued in favor of establishing the PBC under ECOSOC. The Secretary-General, in an explanatory note,[39] proposed a sequenced arrangement, whereby the PBC would report to the Security Council in the immediate aftermath of a conflict, and to ECOSOC as the military phase wound down. The overriding view from the thirty-eighth floor was that whatever the eventual set-up or reporting lines, it was imperative that the PBC should not report to more than one institution at a time.

Several delegations, including Brazil and Sweden, endorsed the Secretary-General's proposal for a sequenced relationship between the

The vision and thinking behind the UN PBA 31

Security Council and ECOSOC; a few delegations stressed the primary (though not exclusive) role of the Security Council (China, Russia, the United States); a few proposed simultaneous reporting to the Security Council and ECOSOC (Pakistan; and in a different format, the United Kingdom), whereas yet others preferred exclusive reporting to ECOSOC (Uganda). The preference from some quarters for involvement by the General Assembly itself (India, Iran, Malaysia), not anticipated in *In Larger Freedom*, laid the foundations for the dual reporting to the General Assembly and Security Council reflected in the final outcome. ECOSOC, which lacked the powerful backers of the Security Council's role or the universal representation of the General Assembly, remained at a second tier of reporting.

Although the arrival of a skeptical new US ambassador, UN-critic John Bolton, did result in the opening of dozens of new brackets in the text during the General Assembly's informal plenary consultations in June 2005, positions on the establishment of the PBC, PBSO, and PBF did not change; the broad and substantial support continued. Several delegations, including European Union (EU) member states, called for decisions to be taken at the September summit for a concrete timetable, making the PBC operational by the end of 2005. They were sensitive to the need to capitalize on the momentum generated by the process; meanwhile, the limits of political feasibility, and thus the contours of the eventual PBA, had by this stage become clearer.

Role of civil society and the private sector

Reflecting the operational and scholarly understanding that successful peacebuilding depended on engagement with all relevant actors, the General Assembly held informal interactive hearings with representatives of nongovernmental organizations (NGOs) and the private sector in June 2005. The NGOs supported the establishment of the PBC, but emphasized the importance of including civil society in the process, including decision making, and creating clear channels for regular consultation.[40]

Just as bureaucratic actors within the UN attempted to shape the conception of the peacebuilding that the PBA would advance, several rights-based advocacy groups stressed the importance of their issue agendas, such as a mainstreamed focus on gender.[41] An explicit reference to consultation with "women's organizations" was duly included in the resolutions that established the commission.[42] Some advocacy groups also called for regional offices of the PBC or PBSO, occasionally conflating the two. Engagement with civil society in the PBC's

32 Abiodun Williams and Mark Bailey

establishment and operations showed growing recognition of its importance, though some felt this did not go far enough, given the lack of nongovernmental representation on the eventual Organizational Committee of the PBC.[43] The critical role of the private sector in post-conflict reconstruction had yet to garner sufficient attention, notwithstanding the growing role of the innovative Global Compact launched by Kofi Annan in 2000.

The World Summit and beyond

Deliberations over the draft Outcome Document for the World Summit, in its various versions, were critical, given the Secretariat's view that the PBA could be established by the Outcome Document itself (if the latter took the form of a General Assembly resolution). Member states chose to establish the PBC through the Outcome Document, but, in line with the Secretariat's position, opted only to establish a broad framework, leaving the details to a subsequent General Assembly resolution.[44]

Nevertheless, heads of state and government left on the table several matters that the Secretariat felt should be addressed in the Outcome Document. Although decisions were made on the composition and mandate of the PBC, the Outcome Document did not resolve the question—which the Secretariat deemed important—of whether the PBC would advise upon request or also *proprio motu.* [45] This reflected ongoing divisions between member states about just how much authority the PBC would have, but its explicit establishment as an "intergovernmental advisory body" clearly suggested the direction.

Five outstanding issues had been left to the final negotiations on resolutions that would set up the PBA: establishment, precise membership, extent of national ownership, institutional location, and agenda setting. Informal consultations on these five issues were convened in October to examine operational aspects of peacebuilding, which would draw on UN expertise from Headquarters—the UN Development Group Office, the UN Department of Peacekeeping Operations (DPKO) and the UN Office for the Coordination of Humanitarian Affairs (OCHA)—and the field—three special representatives of the Secretary-General (SRSGs) briefed from the UN Mission in Liberia (UNMIL), the UN Operation in Burundi (ONUB), and the UN Stabilization Mission in Haiti (MINUSTAH). A World Bank representative and Ashraf Ghani also joined these consultations—the first time that speakers participated in General Assembly informal consultations via video link.

The Peacebuilding Support Office

In the meantime, the Secretariat was working on the establishment of the PBSO and PBF, to which the Outcome Document had given only brief coverage.[46] The preparatory work for establishing the PBSO was taken up by the Secretariat, led by the EOSG/Strategic Planning Unit (SPU). The Secretary-General's Policy Committee—staffed by the EOSG/SPU—discussed the establishment of the PBSO in July 2005, at which time the Secretary-General made the crucial decision that, subject to the intergovernmental processes then underway, the PBSO should be established in the EOSG as soon as possible after the summit. Recognizing the institutional rivalry between existing parts of the UN Secretariat—particularly between the DPKO and the DPA— locating the PBSO in the EOSG underlined that peacebuilding was not to be the exclusive preserve of a single department or agency.

The authority of the EOSG helped the PBSO to get off the ground and went some way to countering (without overcoming entirely) the reticence of other agencies to accept PBSO primacy on peacebuilding. The Secretary-General decided that the PBSO should be made up of staff with substantial field experience of a multidisciplinary character, drawing on the relevant departments and agencies. He also tasked the deputy Secretary-General with directing the compilation of an inventory of existing UN capacities for peacebuilding, to include recommendations on how to rationalize the system and address identified gaps.[47]

Notwithstanding the personal patronage shown by the Secretary-General, subsequent debates in the General Assembly's administrative and budget committees over "extremely small sums and minor personnel issues"[48] for the PBSO demonstrated how existing agencies, and member states that saw their interests as advanced by them, marshaled their forces in favor of a minimalist version of a support office.

The Peacebuilding Fund

Both the high-level panel and *In Larger Freedom* had identified the need for a standing fund for peacebuilding, from which disbursements could quickly be made to fill gaps between peacekeeping and longer-term development assistance. There had been a steady increase in the number of multi-donor trust funds (MDTFs) in the preceding years, driven to some extent by donors who wanted to support selected themes in a more visible manner, as distinct from providing financial support for agency programs. Several existing trust funds sought to address immediate needs in post-conflict environments, either with a country

34 *Abiodun Williams and Mark Bailey*

focus (for example, the Afghan Interim Authority Fund—AIAF) or within a thematic context (for example, the Bureau for Crisis Prevention and Recovery—BCPR/UN Development Programme Thematic Trust Fund for Crisis Prevention and Recovery).

Other funds, such as the proposed expanded Central Emergency Response Fund (CERF) run by OCHA, would also have a bearing on the design of the PBF since humanitarian interventions intersected with early-recovery activities. The challenge was to avoid possible duplication with other funding mechanisms: therefore, the PBF would need to occupy a clearly defined niche within the existing landscape of special UN funds while building on the lessons learnt from the MDTFs.

During the thematic consultations, whether driven by enthusiasm for the pooled fund principle, or by caution about duplication, member states expressed differing views about the viability or necessity of a new fund (PBF): some encouraged forward movement (France, the United Kingdom, Sweden), whereas others expressed caution (Denmark, Norway). Within the Secretariat, at the same time as it worked out the institutional design of the PBSO, the EOSG/SPU led work on the design of the PBF. The Summit Outcome Document dedicated a brief paragraph to the PBF[49] which called for a multi-year standing fund, funded through voluntary contributions while taking account of existing mechanisms. The stated objectives were to ensure the immediate release of resources needed to launch peacebuilding activities, and the availability of appropriate financing for recovery.

It was important for the PBF to have clearly defined funding priorities, while allowing for some flexibility in activities that could be supported in a specific transition context. The Secretariat believed that priority should be given to activities related to essential peacebuilding roles performed by the government or other national institutions (for example, security sector reform and rule of law); direct support for rapid build-up of national capacity; critical peacebuilding interventions for which no funding has been received (for example, the reintegration component of a disarmament, demobilization, and reintegration, or DDR, program); and high-visibility interventions to demonstrate the "peace dividend" (including support to emerging NGOs). The current priorities of the PBF show some congruence with this early thinking, with four distinct "priority areas": supporting the implementation of peace agreements; promoting coexistence and peaceful resolution of conflict; revitalizing the economy and generating peace dividends; and re-establishing essential administrative services.[50]

The Secretariat's view was that clear criteria would have to be applied to ensure that allocations met the funding priorities. Three selection

The vision and thinking behind the UN PBA 35

criteria were identified: the intervention must be of direct and critical relevance to the peacebuilding process; funding should be short term and should support interventions that create maximum impact on the sustainability of the peacebuilding process; and PBF funding should have a catalytic effect and help to attract other, more sustained support by development agencies and bilateral donors. Since then, thinking has evolved beyond a sole focus on short-term funding in the immediate aftermath of conflict. The PBF now allocates funds through two windows: an Immediate Response Facility and a Peacebuilding and Recovery Facility.[51]

The establishment of the Peacebuilding Architecture

On 20 December 2005, concurrent resolutions were adopted by the General Assembly and Security Council, establishing the Peacebuilding Commission and requesting the Secretary-General to establish a Peacebuilding Support Office and Peacebuilding Fund. The resolutions identified three functions for the new PBC:

1 To bring together all relevant actors to marshal resources and to advise on and propose integrated strategies for post-conflict peacebuilding and recovery;
2 To focus attention on the reconstruction and institution-building efforts necessary for recovery from conflict and to support the development of integrated strategies in order to lay the foundations for sustainable development; and
3 To provide recommendations and information to improve the coordination of all relevant actors within and outside the United Nations, to develop best practices, to help to ensure predictable financing for early recovery activities and to extend the period of attention given by the international community to post-conflict recovery.[52]

The resolutions also established the exact composition of the Organizational Committee of the PBC, which was to consist of seven members of the Security Council; seven members from ECOSOC; five top budgetary contributors to the UN; five top troop-contributing countries; and—reflecting concerns from G-77 countries that they were likely to be underrepresented in this arrangement—seven members of the General Assembly.

The resolutions reflect the compromises made on the other issues that the World Summit Outcome Document had not resolved,

36   *Abiodun Williams and Mark Bailey*

including national ownership and agenda setting. As the foregoing overview of the negotiations throughout 2005 indicates, the direction of these compromises tended to reflect concerns about sovereignty, which had been further heightened in the wake of the Iraq War. This was the root of the failure to translate into reality the recommendation of the high-level panel for a preventive focus, as well as the language in the final resolution on the PBC, "work[ing] in cooperation with national or transitional authorities, where possible, in the country under consideration with a view to ensuring national ownership of the peace-building process."[53] It also resulted in agreement that only with the consent of the relevant state itself would countries not on the Security Council's agenda be considered by the PBC.[54]

Such limitations have frustrated both scholars and practitioners—but the creation of the commission was itself a significant step forward, and a testament to the ability of the Secretary-General to test the boundaries of political reality as defined by member states and the UN bureaucracy itself, and respond accordingly. The optimism expressed by Kofi Annan, that the "historic" establishment of the commission went "a long way towards bridging ... a critical institutional gap,"[55] reflected this sense of accomplishment.

Conclusions

The creation of the Peacebuilding Architecture reflected the UN's ability, under agile and principled leadership and within an international environment conducive to reform, to adapt in light of operational experience and scholarly evidence concerning the need for change. However, reform is an intrinsically political process that must take due account of the core equities of member states and entities within the UN system. The many imperfections exhibited by the eventual Peacebuilding Commission, fund, and support office are a result of the middle path between optimum policy and political reality which the Secretary-General and his coalition of reformers carefully trod.

Contrasting the form that the PBA took with some of the desirable attributes lost in the course of the mammoth negotiations of 2005 can provide us with a blueprint for further improvements to peacebuilding instruments. It remains desirable for peacebuilding activities to take full account of the importance of conflict prevention, and for the UN to maximize its own potential for institutional coherence in this regard.[56] The translation of the vision of 2005 into organizational form also provides several salutary lessons to would-be reformers. In the context of the political environment facing proponents of the PBA,

The vision and thinking behind the UN PBA 37

those to whom the torch of UN reform will be passed could do worse than to heed the successes of this enterprise.

Notes

1 UN General Assembly, *World Summit Outcome Document*, UN doc. A/RES/60/1, 24 October 2005, paras. 97–105.
2 Roland Paris, *At War's End: Building Peace After Civil Conflict* (New York: Cambridge University Press, 2004), 153.
3 Carsten Stahn, "The United Nations Transitional Administrations in Kosovo and East Timor: A First Analysis," in *Max Planck Yearbook of United Nations Law Vol. 5*, ed. Jochen A. Frowein and Rüdiger Wolfrum, 2001, 105–83.
4 Richard Caplan and Richard Ponzio, "After Exit: The UN Peacebuilding Architecture," in *Exit Strategies and State Building*, ed. Richard Caplan (Oxford: Oxford University Press, 2012), 3.
5 See, for example, Cristina G. Badescu and Linnea Bergholm, "The Responsibility to Protect and the Conflict in Darfur: The Big Let-Down," *Security Dialogue* 40 (2009): 287–309; Alex Bellamy, *Responsibility to Protect: The Global Effort to End Mass Atrocities* (Cambridge: Polity Press, 2009); Gareth Evans, *The Responsibility to Protect: Ending Mass Atrocity Crimes Once and for All* (Washington, DC: Brookings Institution Press, 2008); and Thomas G. Weiss *Humanitarian Intervention* (Cambridge: Polity Press, 2007).
6 United Nations, *A More Secure World: Our Shared Responsibility*, The Report of the Secretary-General's High-Level Panel on Threats, Challenges and Change, United Nations, UN doc. A/59/565, 2004.
7 Paul Collier and Anke Hoeffler, "Conflicts," in *Global Crises, Global Solutions*, ed. Bjorn Lomborg (Cambridge: Cambridge University Press, 2004).
8 Paul Collier, V.L. Elliott, Havard Hegre, Anke Hoeffler, Marta Reynal-Querol, and Nicholas Sambanis, *Breaking the Conflict Trap: Civil War and Development Policy* (Washington, DC: World Bank and Oxford University Press, 2003).
9 Paul Collier, *Development and Conflict*, Paper for the Centre for the Study of African Economies, Department of Economics, University of Oxford, 1 October 2004.
10 Rob Jenkins, *Peacebuilding: From Concept to Commission* (London: Routledge, 2013), 3.
11 Kofi Annan, "Two Concepts of Sovereignty," *The Economist*, 16 September 1999.
12 Michale Barnett, Hunjoon Kim, Madalene O'Donnell, and Laura Sitea, "Peacebuilding: What is in a Name?," *Global Governance* 13 (2007): 35–58.
13 Barnett et al., "Peacebuilding," 54.
14 Johan Galtung, "Three Approaches to Peace: Peacekeeping, Peacemaking and Peacebuilding," in *Peace, War and Defense: Essays in Peace Research, Vol. 2* (Copenhagen: Christian Ejlers, 1975).
15 Charles T. Call and Elizabeth M. Cousens, "Ending Wars and Building Peace: International Responses to War-Torn Societies," *International Studies Perspective* 9 (2008): 7.

38 *Abiodun Williams and Mark Bailey*

16 Barnett et al., "Peacebuilding," 53.
17 Michael Doyle and Nicholas Sambanis, "International Peacebuilding: A Theoretical and Quantitative Analysis," *The American Political Science Review* 94, no. 4 (2000): 779.
18 United Nations, *Report of the Panel on United Nations Peace Operations*, UN doc. A/55/305-S/2000/809, 21 August 2000.
19 *An Agenda for Peace* was the first UN report to use the term. Paragraph 55 refers to "action to identify and support structures which will tend to strengthen and solidify peace in order to avoid relapse into conflict." United Nations, *An Agenda for Peace: Preventive Diplomacy, Peacemaking and Peace-keeping*, Report of the Secretary General, UN doc. A/47/277, 17 June 1992. The term was further refined in the *Supplement to an Agenda for Peace*, which mentioned national institutions and capacity to operate them impartially. United Nations, *Supplement to An Agenda for Peace*, Position Paper of the Secretary-General on the Occasion of the Fiftieth Anniversary of the United Nations, UN doc. A/50/60-S/1995/1, 3 January 2005.
20 United Nations, "Security Council Address Comprehensive Approach to Peacebuilding in Presidential Statement" (S/PRST/2001/5), Press Release, UN doc. SC/7014 20 February 2001. Emphasis added.
21 United Nations, "Secretary General Says Global Effort Against Armed Conflict Needs Change from Culture of Reaction to Culture of Prevention," Press Release, UN doc. SC/6759, 29 November 1999.
22 See, for example, Organisation for Economic Co-operation and Development, *Guidance on Evaluating Conflict Prevention and Peacebuilding Activities* (Paris: OECD, 2008).
23 One taxonomy is offered by William Durch, "Exit and Peace Operations: When and How to Leave Kinshasa, Kabul, Dili and Darfur," presentation, 2009 Annual Meeting of the International Studies Association, New York, 15 February 2009. Cited in Jenkins, *Peacebuilding*, 41.
24 A maximalist view on "state effectiveness" was expounded by Ashraf Ghani and Clare Lockhart, *Fixing Failed States: A Framework for Rebuilding a Fractured World* (Oxford: Oxford University Press, 2009).
25 Lise Howard for example, argues that this is essential. Lise M. Howard, *UN Peacekeeping in Civil Wars* (Cambridge: Cambridge University Press. 2007).
26 Jenkins, *Peacebuilding*, 54.
27 Jenkins, *Peacebuilding*, 56.
28 James D. Fearon and David D. Laitin, "Neotrusteeship and the Problem of Weak States," *International Security* 28, no. 4 (2004): 8.
29 United Nations, *A More Secure World: Our Shared Responsibility, Report of the High-Level Panel on Threats, Challenge and Change*, 2004, para. 225.
30 United Nations, *A More Secure World*.
31 United Nations, *A More Secure World*, recommendation 84.
32 Jenkins, *Peacebuilding*, 60–61.
33 United Nations, *A More Secure World*, recommendation 83.
34 United Nations, "In Larger Freedom: Towards Development, Security and Human Rights for All," Report of the Secretary-General, United Nations, UN doc. A/59/2005, 2005, para. 114.
35 Richard Ponzio, "The United Nations Peacebuilding Commission: Origins and Initial Practice," *Disarmament Forum* 2 (2007): 11.

The vision and thinking behind the UN PBA 39

36 United Nations, "In Larger Freedom," para. 115.
37 United Nations, "In Larger Freedom, Addendum: Peacebuilding Commission," Explanatory Note by the Secretary-General, UN doc. A/59/2005/Add.2, 2005.
38 Jenkins, *Peacebuilding*, 69.
39 United Nations, "In Larger Freedom, Addendum: Peacebuilding Commission."
40 See, for example, Renske Heemskerk, "The UN Peacebuilding Commission and Civil Society Engagement," *Disarmament Forum* 2 (2007): 17–25.
41 Jenkins, *Peacebuilding*, 68.
42 United Nations General Assembly Resolution 60/180, 2005.
43 UN Peacebuilding Commission, *UN Peacebuilding Commission: Benefits and Challenges*, Background paper prepared by the International Peace Academy for the Regional Seminars organized by the Friedrich Ebert Stiftung, New York, 6 June 2006.
44 United Nations General Assembly, *World Summit Outcome Document*, para. 97.
45 United Nations General Assembly, *World Summit Outcome Document*, para. 98.
46 "We also request the Secretary-General to establish, within the Secretariat and from within existing resources, a small peacebuilding support office staffed by qualified experts to assist and support the Peacebuilding Commission. The office should draw on the best expertise available." See United Nations General Assembly, *World Summit Outcome Document*, para. 104.
47 The Secretary-General gave a summary of the PBSO's tasks drawn up by the Secretariat in United Nations, *Implementation of Decisions from the 2005 World Summit Outcome for action by the Secretary-General*, Report of the Secretary-General, 2005.
48 Jenkins, *Peacebuilding*, 71.
49 United Nations General Assembly, *World Summit Outcome Document*, para. 103.
50 UN Peacebuilding Fund, "What We Fund," 2015, www.unpbf.org/what-we-fund.
51 UN Peacebuilding Fund, "How We Fund," 2015, www.unpbf.org/how-we-fund.
52 UN General Assembly Resolution 60/180.
53 UN General Assembly Resolution 60/180,, 22.
54 UN General Assembly Resolution 60/180, 12(b).
55 United Nations, text of Kofi Annan's remarks on the General Assembly's Endorsement of the Peacebuilding Commission, 20 December 2005, www.un.org/News/Press/docs/2005/sgsm10277.doc.htm.
56 See The Hague Institute for Global Justice, *The Hague Approach* (The Hague: The Hague Institute for Global Justice, 2013).

2 The dynamics that shaped the establishment of the Peacebuilding Architecture in the early years

Necla Tschirgi and Richard Ponzio

- **The Peacebuilding Commission: the dynamics of intergovernmental innovation**
- **The Peacebuilding Fund: searching for a niche**
- **Peacebuilding Support Office: Stepping up to the plate**
- **Looking back, looking forward**
- **Conclusion**

Peacebuilding emerged in the early 1990s at the United Nations (UN) with the end of the Cold War. Since then, it has expanded steadily in scope and importance as a critical agenda for the international community. Its institutionalization at the UN was achieved at the 2005 World Summit with the creation of the Peacebuilding Architecture (PBA), the background to which is covered in Chapter 1 in this volume. This chapter takes a different look at the PBA, focusing specifically on the dynamics that shaped the Peacebuilding Commission (PBC), the Peacebuilding Fund (PBF), and the Peacebuilding Support Office (PBSO), from the formal establishment of the PBA through what has been called its "survival" phase (2006–08).[1] Other chapters in this collection provide a fuller account of the PBA's "revival" or consolidation phase after 2008. Written by two scholars/policy analysts who were part of the PBSO during its early years, this chapter reviews the broader context and early decisions that were instrumental in the evolution of the PBA. The chapter rests on the argument that the PBA was not intended simply as another UN body with a specific function and mandate. Rather, its supporters envisaged the PBA as a much-needed innovation for better global governance in a critical issue area.

The PBA was established to bring a concerted approach to the international community's fragmented responses to countries emerging from conflict. The expectation was that the PBA would serve as an innovative experiment to break away from "business as usual" by myriad international actors involved in peacebuilding. Although based at the UN, the PBA was intended to serve as a catalytic mechanism for bringing a new approach to peacebuilding by convening all relevant actors, mobilizing new resources, and serving as a repository of knowledge, policy, and practice. Perhaps it was inevitable that once the decision was made to establish the PBA at the UN, it would be difficult to prevent it from becoming caught up in counterproductive forms of UN politics. We hold that many of the early decisions regarding the structure and operations of the PBC also set it on a path that has seriously constrained the PBA from meeting the ambitious expectations of its many supporters, or even radically changed the UN's own policies and practices in peacebuilding. As these decisions cannot be understood or explained in isolation from the larger context in which they were taken and the range of political, normative, bureaucratic, and idiosyncratic factors obtaining at the time, we situate the establishment of the PBA within that larger framework.

While focusing on the PBA's first two years, we recognize that there has been considerable learning and institutional adaptation since then. What we seek to demonstrate is the extent to which the PBA's original conception and design shaped its subsequent evolution. It is hoped that this chapter will not only shed light on the thinking and choices that guided the early years of the PBA, but will also provide insights on the longer-term ramifications of those decisions.

The PBA was very much a creation of the UN and the international system that gave birth to it. The course taken was not so much a function of any lack of a clear vision about what was needed, as the result of the inherent shortcomings of the system. As Mats Berdal noted in 2009:

> [T]he commission's evolution from the conceptual drawing-board to its current incarnation offers important clues about the political and practical obstacles that lie in the way of a more effective and coordinated international approach to peacebuilding. As is often the case, the UN here reflects deeper fault lines with the international system. These, more than any other set of factors, are likely to determine whether, and in what form, international peacebuilding will remain the kind of growth industry it has been for much of the post-Cold War era.[2]

Thus, in identifying the dynamics in the early days of the PBA, the chapter also aims to shed light on the limits of UN reform.

The chapter consists of four sections. Section one starts with a brief analysis of the broader political context in which the PBA was created,

42   Necla Tschirgi and Richard Ponzio

and examines the structure and operations of the PBC. Section two focuses on the PBF and the uneasy relations between the commission and the fund. Section three examines the institutional dynamics that shaped the PBSO. Finally, section four draws broader lessons on the thinking and choices that were made during those early years. The structure of the chapter is designed to reflect a persistent problem that characterized the PBA from the start: the fragmented nature of the new mechanism with three distinct pillars, each pillar with its own instinct for self-preservation at the expense of working towards a more integrated mechanism for greater integration and coordination with other peacebuilding actors within and outside the UN.[3]

The Peacebuilding Commission: the dynamics of intergovernmental innovation

Departing from the model proposed by the High-Level Panel on Threats, Challenges and Change, the commission was created as an advisory body reporting both to the General Assembly and the Security Council. This meant that the commission lacked any independent authority or decision-making power over other bodies, a feature that profoundly affected its status and future evolution. The concurrent assembly and council resolutions establishing the PBC specified its main purposes as follows:

1   To bring together all relevant actors to marshal resources and to advise on and propose integrated strategies for post-conflict peacebuilding and recovery;
2   To focus attention on the reconstruction and institution-building efforts necessary for recovery from conflict and to support the development of integrated strategies in order to lay the foundation for sustainable development; and
3   To provide recommendations and information to improve the coordination of all relevant actors within and outside the United Nations, to develop best practices, to help to ensure predictable financing for early recovery activities and to extend the period of attention given by the international community to post-conflict recovery.[4]

The resolutions further stated that the commission was to meet in various configurations and have a standing Organizational Committee (OC) which would develop its own rules of procedure and working methods. Within these guidelines, the commission would have to be

The establishment of the PBA   43

tailored to the difficult political context for the UN at the time. Any expectations that the new PBA would transcend the UN's traditional cleavages or narrow national interests were already laid to rest during the heated negotiations leading up to its creation.

The overarching political context

Following a decade of constructive multilateral collaboration and activism in the 1990s, by the time the World Summit met in 2005, deep cleavages had taken shape within the UN. As detailed in Chapter 1, the PBC was created in a highly charged context. As put by Rob Jenkins: "The decade and a half of peacebuilding leading up to the creation of the PBA in 2005 bequeathed an ideological legacy that combined market democracy triumphalism (post-1989) and fear of ungoverned spaces."[5] However, the immediate backdrop to its creation was:

> the still-bitter aftermath of the 2003 US-led invasion of Iraq, which occurred without Security Council authorization. In the wake of this conflict, many countries became suspicious of any new institution created to meddle in the affairs of legally sovereign states, even if doing so in the name of rebuilding the state's de facto sovereignty.[6]

The traditional North–South divide at the UN played an important role in the early days of the PBC. The G-77 and the Non-Aligned Movement (NAM) were keen to emphasize state sovereignty and non-intervention as key principles. As the first assistant Secretary-General (ASG) for Peacebuilding Support, Carolyn McAskie, has observed: "From the onset, the debate was affected by G-77/NAM that the PBC not be an instrument of the Security Council."[7] The permanent members of the Security Council (P5) had already asserted their prominence in the commission by securing non-rotating seats for themselves and playing active roles in the creation of the PBC. Curiously, the P5 refrained from active engagement in the PBC once it was established, no doubt reflecting their perception of its marginal influence and utility in dealing with countries on the council's agenda.

At the PBC, the North–South divide was also reflected in the member states' differing conceptual approaches to peacebuilding. Despite over a decade of research and practice positioning peace-building at the intersection of security and development, there was little clarity among member states on what constituted peacebuilding and how it could best be achieved. Developing countries emphasized

44 Necla Tschirgi and Richard Ponzio

socioeconomic reconstruction in the aftermath of conflict, shying away from security-oriented interventions in the early, more political phases of peacebuilding as well as pre-conflict/preventative peacebuilding. It was not coincidental that the first two countries on the PBC's agenda were Sierra Leone and Burundi, already in the later phases of their transitions from war.

Another important factor that influenced the early years of the PBC was the arrival of Ban Ki-moon as Secretary-General in January 2007. Peacebuilding had been one of the signature initiatives of Kofi Annan, and his departure just as the new architecture was taking shape meant the loss of leadership at a critical time. The new Secretary-General was preoccupied with other pressing concerns, including setting up his own team and priorities. Reporting directly to the Secretary-General, McAskie was caught in the institutional power struggles during the transition. Her early departure after only two years on the job, and her replacement by Jane Holl Lute for less than a year, before the arrival of the third ASG, Judy Cheng-Hopkins, also contributed to prolonging the PBA's formation process. In short, the early years of the PBC were marked by political discord among member states over the post-Iraq world order, the arrival of an unknown and untested Secretary-General, and high turnover in the PBSO leadership in the first three years.

Designing the commission's variable geometry

Despite the extensive planning, negotiations, and institutional revisions preceding its creation, there was no master plan to help the PBC implement its ambitious mandate. Indeed, there was considerable confusion as to how the new architecture was to conduct its work. Following a period of uncertainty, the commission organized itself into three distinct configurations: the Organizational Committee, the Country-Specific Configurations (CSCs), and the Working Group on Lessons Learned (WGLL). In view of their novelty and the need to develop appropriate operational procedures for each, the three entities developed on separate tracks, and their performance depended greatly on their membership and leadership.

As the committee of the whole, the OC was drawn from 31 member states representing the PBC's five main constituencies—the Security Council (seven members), the General Assembly (seven), the UN Economic and Social Council ECOSOC (seven), top UN donors (five), and top troop-contributing countries (five). The OC's first chair was Angola, a developing country that had experienced prolonged violent conflict and was therefore considered qualified to lead the OC. Norway

The establishment of the PBA 45

and El Salvador became vice-chairs. The OC spent considerable time on procedural issues, including the participation of other entities in the commission's work and the constitution of other PBC configurations. The question of nongovernmental organization (NGO) participation was particularly vexing, with member states expressing reservations, even though other UN entities had long accepted the growing role of the NGO sector. Finally in June 2007, the OC issued provisional guidelines for the formal and informal participation of civil society in the meetings of the PBC at UN headquarters as well as at the country level, which created dissatisfaction among NGOs. In its first year, the OC played a conservative procedural role, shying away from engaging in policy questions or positioning itself as a key player in the peacebuilding field. It was only with Japan's chairmanship during the second year that the OC took a proactive role by organizing regular meetings, developing discussion papers on broader policy questions, and undertaking greater outreach. A PBC retreat held in January 2008 and attended by the Secretary-General proved instrumental in generating a greater sense of coherence among member states.

The second and undoubtedly the most important configuration was the CSCs, which became the PBC's main instrument for peacebuilding. The CSCs were created once Sierra Leone and Burundi became the first countries on the PBC's agenda, and senior delegations from the two countries made powerful presentations at the OC, confronting member states with the challenge of devising an effective modality for country-level engagement. The Sierra Leone and Burundi CSCs were experimental laboratories, as both host countries and member states had little guidance or relevant experience to draw from. Despite the extensive thematic debates on peacebuilding and the range of policy documents preceding its creation, it was not clear how an advisory UN body based in New York would support peacebuilding on the ground. The PBSO played a critical role in these early days, working closely with the OC and the chairs of the two CSCs to steer the process.

The Sierra Leone and Burundi CSCs were chaired respectively by the Netherlands and Norway—key donors and strong supporters of the PBC—largely reflecting the expectation that the CSCs would catalyze much-needed financial support. Rumor had it that the host governments saw the PBC as an "ATM" at the UN and were reluctant to have non-donor countries (like El Salvador) chairing the CSCs. It was fortunate that Netherlands and Norway assumed their role as chairs with utmost dedication and provided substantive as well as procedural leadership from the start. According to the PBC's founding resolutions, the CSCs were open to all members of the commission as well as other

46   *Necla Tschirgi and Richard Ponzio*

key stakeholders—including the host-country government, the international financial institutions, regional organizations, neighboring countries, donor countries, and national as well as international NGOs.

Working in tandem, the Sierra Leone and Burundi CSCs developed their own working methods in response to multiple constituencies in New York, member-state capitals, UN entities, and host countries. There was continual innovation and adaptation—often prodded by pressing needs on the ground. In due course, the CSCs adopted useful innovations such as field visits, video conferencing with host-country counterparts, and ongoing consultations with key actors in New York as well as at the country level. As both Sierra Leone and Burundi already had UN missions on the ground, the relations between the PBC and the UN missions had to be negotiated delicately, since the PBSO had no field presence. Inevitably, the CSCs and the PBSO had to rely heavily on the cooperation of UN entities in New York and in the field for timely information, support, and ongoing contacts with host-government counterparts. Even more importantly, the effectiveness of the CSCs depended heavily on their being able to position themselves as influential strategic actors with respect to the two countries on the commission's agenda.

The PBC's founding resolutions had stated that one of its main purposes was "to advise on and propose integrated strategies for post-conflict peacebuilding and recovery." It was not entirely clear how this should be achieved in Sierra Leone and Burundi, where the UN had long been engaged and there were multiple strategic frameworks. Working closely with the PBSO and host-country governments, the CSCs crafted a new instrument, the Integrated Peacebuilding Strategy (IPBS). The development of the IPBS was tortuous and occasioned serious objections by host-country counterparts and UN field staff that the IPBS duplicated other strategic and planning tools and created additional burdens. Nonetheless, it became the PBC's main instrument of engagement with the countries on its agenda. The IPBS process was intended to bring diverse actors to reach a shared understanding of conflict dynamics in each context and be guided by jointly identified needs and priorities as the basis for more effective international responses. However, the IPBS process became intertwined with myriad other processes and mechanisms, adding another layer of complexity to the international engagement with national and local actors. Besides defining the terms of the PBC's engagement, perhaps the real utility of the IPBS lay in offering the commission a structured framework through which to begin understanding the realities of peacebuilding. Yet, there was a risk in adopting a template like the IPBS: that one of the key lessons of peacebuilding would get lost, that peacebuilding is context specific and cannot be reduced to a pre-determined formula. Unfortunately, as two new countries, Guinea-Bissau and the Central African Republic, were added to the PBC agenda in 2007 and 2008, respectively, the CSCs seemed to exhibit path dependency, replicating previous methods and tools of engagement. This was also partly because there was not sufficient cross-country learning or systematic efforts to draw lessons from the PBC's own experiences—despite the existence of the WGLL.

The WGLL, the PBC's third configuration, was intended as an open, inclusive, and informal platform to enhance dialogue on issues of relevance to countries on the PBC agenda. Created largely as a way to compensate El Salvador when its bid to chair the Sierra Leone CSC was thwarted, the WGLL suffered from weak leadership and lack of clarity as to its function. In principle the WGLL offered the PBC an opportunity to become a reservoir of knowledge and to distill lessons in peacebuilding by drawing upon the experiences of its members, other countries emerging from conflict, national and international actors involved in peacebuilding, as well as from scholars and practitioners. In reality, the P5 showed little interest in the WGLL and many member states regularly assigned lower-level representatives to the working group, further diminishing its effectiveness. As a result, the WGLL came to function as an informal discussion group without a strategic vision or agenda. During its first two years, the WGLL organized a series of meetings focusing on specific topics and cross-cutting issues. However, no real effort was made to relate these to the work of the PBC's two other configurations or to extract appropriate lessons for the countries on its agenda.

Indeed, one of the main shortcomings of the PBC was the lack of cross-fertilization between its three configurations. Even at the time, it was understood that the OC would need to assume a more active role in formulating policies and principles in peacebuilding, nurturing institutional relations with key actors (including the PBC's parent bodies, the Bretton Woods institutions and regional organizations) and providing strategic guidance on international peacebuilding. Meanwhile, recognizing that peacebuilding is context specific and needs to be tailored to each country, the CSC was to focus specifically on supporting the countries on its agenda, while sharing their knowledge and experience with the OC to enhance international peacebuilding policy and practice. Finally, the WGLL was to identify common challenges to peacebuilding, drawn from the commission's engagement in the countries on its agenda, and provide concrete recommendations to

48 *Necla Tschirgi and Richard Ponzio*

strengthen the PBC's advisory role and engagement in country-specific contexts. In reality, there was little synergy between the three configurations. As noted by Sarah Hearn, Alejandra Kubitschek Bujones, and Alischa Kugel, although the commission had been intended "to provide an agile platform where all actors engaged in peacebuilding in a given context could discuss and agree upon a common strategy and priorities, during the negotiations, the PBC membership became significantly more fixed and formulaic."[8]

The Peacebuilding Fund: searching for a niche

This section of the chapter provides a general overview of the first years of operation of the PBF. It was created pursuant to concurrent assembly and council resolutions requesting the Secretary-General to establish a multi-year standing fund as an essential component of the new PBA. However, the resolutions did not clarify the relationship between the three components of the PBA. As a result, there was continuing friction and contestation between the commission and the fund during the early years. Equally important, under political pressure to start disbursing quickly, the fund's design and operations did not sufficiently reflect accumulated knowledge on financing for peacebuilding in conflict contexts, creating additional tensions with donors and operational actors, and diminishing its effectiveness. The radical revision of the PBF's Terms of Reference (ToR) in 2009 reflected recognition of the shortcomings in its initial design and operations.

Defining the fund's Terms of Reference

Financing for peacebuilding had been a main area of research and advocacy throughout the 1990s since it was recognized that existing funding mechanisms did not adequately respond to the needs of conflict-affected countries. By the time the PBF was established, there was a wealth of innovative thinking and various proposals for new models for financing peacebuilding.[9] Unfortunately, this was not reflected in the design for the PBF's operations and governance system. Instead, the fund basically replicated existing funding modalities and arrangements.

The fund's ToR were developed after extensive consultations led by the PBSO, and reflected the still uncertain status of the new entity within the UN system. The ToR, defined in General Assembly resolution A/60/984 of 22 August 2006, stated that the fund "is designed to support interventions that are considered critical to the peacebuilding process. It does not seek to address all peacebuilding requirements in a

The establishment of the PBA 49

given situation; rather, it aims to have a catalytic effect that will pave the way for the sustained support and engagement of other key stakeholders." The resolution further indicated that the fund would be managed by the head of the PBSO under the authority of the secretary-general. The ToR specifically referred to the PBC's role in advising the Secretary-General on the selection of countries eligible for consideration for funding. They also indicated that both the General Assembly and the PBC would have a role in the fund's governance arrangements, and that an independent advisory group of eminent personalities with peacebuilding experience would be appointed to advise the Secretary-General on the operations of the fund. These governing arrangements were intended to ensure that the fund would be managed in a transparent manner. The ToR also specified that the use of the fund would be monitored by the PBSO.

The ToR sought to accommodate multiple constituencies, without attempting to develop an innovative model for financing peacebuilding. The external evaluation of the PBF in 2009 identified 11 different stakeholders: the PBSO as Fund Manager, the UN Development Programme (UNDP) Multi-donor Trust Fund as Administrative Agent, the PBC, the in-country steering committees and the secretariats that were created over time, the national governments, the in-country UN office, donors, recipient agencies, implementing partners, and the PBF Advisory Group.[10] Operationalizing the fund proved to be a cumbersome process, which affected its implementation and effectiveness.

The fund received strong support from the traditional and non-traditional donors alike, exceeding the US$250 million target established at its creation. From its inception until the end of February 2009, the fund received pledges of $319.3 million from 45 countries. With total deposits and available programming funds amounting to $292.4 million, the fund provided peacebuilding support to some 93 programs and projects in 11 post-conflict countries that were declared eligible to receive its support.[11] Despite broad member support, most of the funding came from eight donors, reflecting the heavy influence of the Organisation for Economic Co-operation and Development (OECD) Development Assistance Committee (DAC) and Western countries.[12]

As with the PBC, the fund was initially hampered by lack of conceptual clarity on peacebuilding and as to the stage at which its funds would be most needed. As a result, three separate windows were created: Window 1 was designated for countries on the PBC agenda; Window 2 for countries on the verge of (re)lapsing into conflict; and Window 3 for countries requiring immediate funding to respond to unforeseen and imminent threats to their peace processes. For Window 1, a

50 Necla Tschirgi and Richard Ponzio

country was declared eligible by the Secretary-General upon the recommendation of the PBC; for Window 2, the recommendation was to come from the UN Senior Policy Group; and finally for Window 3, the Secretary-General made the determination. The PBF had a two-tier decision-making structure, with the UN Secretary-General allocating certain funds for particular countries. The actual allocation of funds was made at the country level through country-specific steering committees.

Need for a change of course

A review of the projects funded by the PBF in 2009 concluded that these projects were not "much more than normal recovery/development projects, similar to others funded simultaneously through other channels that have some peacebuilding spin-offs."[13] The evaluation also noted that "questions remain about the strategic added value of funding these activities through the PBF and about the added value of the PBF as opposed to other sources of funding and ongoing development processes."[14] Perhaps more seriously, there was little evidence that the fund played a catalytic role in financing for peacebuilding. Indeed, with new pooled funds, such as the World Bank's State and Peace Building Fund, and parallel (and substantial) support coming from donor countries, it has since been argued that the "PBF's failures contributed to a diversification, not a consolidation, of financing instruments—the opposite of coordination and coherence."[15]

The inadequacy of the fund's original design and operations was recognized by member states, host countries, and UN partners, and led to internal and external evaluations. An independent evaluation was undertaken by the UN Office for Internal Oversight Services (OIOS) in 2008, focusing primarily on the fund's operations and functions. This evaluation concluded that the fund had the potential to fill an important niche but that it would have to become speedier, more efficient, and strategic in order to fulfill its vision and main objectives of identifying and funding countries' most critical needs, and catalyzing more substantial and sustainable peacebuilding funding. The PBSO responded to the OIOS evaluation in a Management Letter, and commissioned an external evaluation in early 2009. These led to a radical revision of the fund's ToR and management structures in the summer/autumn of 2009, setting it on a new course.

Like the PBC itself, the fund initially operated with little guidance and extremely limited human resources, and faced competing demands from multiple constituencies and partners. Despite its limitations as a new financing mechanism for peacebuilding, the fund has been given credit for having had a positive learning curve.[16] Interestingly, given that the lack of a common definition and understanding of peacebuilding has been a major challenge in international efforts to support war-torn societies, the 2009 external review of the PBF considered one of its main achievements to be its "contribution to a process of discussing and learning about peacebuilding issues in the broader context of post-conflict situations."[17]

Peacebuilding Support Office: Stepping up to the plate

The PBSO was the third pillar of the PBA. Led by an assistant Secretary-General, its mandate consisted of two main responsibilities: first, serving as the secretariat for the PBC; and second, acting as a peacebuilding knowledge base for UN member states as well as the operational bodies of the UN system.

The PBSO's initial design followed from its chief responsibilities, which were determined through a combination of consultations with UN Headquarters staff on the thirty-eighth floor and other key departments—especially the Department of Political Affairs (DPA) and the Department of Peacekeeping Operations (DPKO), the UNDP, and the Office for the Coordination of Humanitarian Assistance (OCHA)—as well as UN member states.[18] Leading this effort, ASG Carolyn McAskie organized the PBSO into four main sections: a small Front Office, a Policy Analysis Unit, a Strategic Planning Unit, and an External Relations Unit with responsibility for the PBF. With McAskie's arrival in June 2006, the slow process of building up the PBSO's core staff began. It is unfortunate that she left the PBSO voluntarily in just two short years—undoubtedly discouraged by the UN's Byzantine intergovernmental and bureaucratic system. However, it was during those two years that the foundations for the PBSO were laid.

Expected to operate with existing resources, the PBSO relied on staff seconded from other UN departments, programs, funds, and agencies. Coupled with the reality that other contracted staff members were either consultants or on fixed-term contracts, the incentives for building a professional esprit de corps and long-term loyalty were limited. With a PBSO numbering no more than 30 people by mid-2008 as well as overlapping functions between the PBSO's three main units, the new ASG, Jane Holl Lute, undertook a major restructuring immediately upon her arrival in August 2008. She merged the Strategic Planning Unit and part of the External Relations Unit into a new "PBC Support Branch," established a new "Financing for Peacebuilding Branch" that would

52   Necla Tschirgi and Richard Ponzio

soon include additional staff, and, reflecting the shift already underway in the portfolio of the Policy Analysis Unit, renamed it "Policy Planning and Application Branch." This reorganization was largely adopted by Holl Lute's successor, Judy Cheng-Hopkins, who arrived in July 2009.

The PBSO's first major responsibility was to serve as the secretariat for the commission. Grouped under this first responsibility were the three core PBSO functions of: convening formal and informal sessions of the CSCs; preparing country-situation progress reports; and facilitating the PBC's field visits to countries on its agenda.[19]

The CSCs on Burundi, Sierra Leone and Guinea-Bissau, chaired by Norway, the Netherlands and Brazil, respectively, placed tremendous demands on the relatively small PBSO team. However, working closely with the three chairs, PBSO staff introduced a range of peacebuilding instruments, including the Integrated Peacebuilding Strategies and their monitoring and tracking mechanisms.[20] Meanwhile, after an initial year of uncertainty, the second chair of the OC, Japan, brought new ideas and fresh energy while providing support for the PBSO's limited staff resources. Conversely, however, the WGLL was led by a relatively weak chair, seriously constraining the PBSO's efforts to strengthen this configuration.

The PBSO's second major responsibility was to serve as a peacebuilding knowledge base for member states and the operational bodies of the UN system. During the early years, this involved three main initiatives: creating the "virtual" pillar of the PBA; supporting work on peace consolidation; and contributing to system-wide efforts. Launched in March 2008, the virtual pillar consisted of a new online Peacebuilding Community of Practice initiated by the PBSO, the pre-existing Peacebuilding Portal managed jointly by the UN Department of Economic and Social Affairs and UNDP, and the peacebuildinginitative. org web portal, a project conducted in partnership with Harvard University's Program on Humanitarian Policy and Conflict Research. However, it turned out that web-based resources were a novelty for UN member states at the time, and even though these platforms provided a wealth of invaluable information, they were not put to use. The two online portals were discontinued by mid-2009, but the Community of Practice has continued to grow, with over 1,500 members today from across the UN system.

From its earliest days, the commission had to confront an essential question: When will we know when a country is ready to graduate from the PBC? PBSO staff began to investigate this in 2007. A study on Peace Consolidation, commissioned in the autumn of 2007 and conducted by Dr Richard Caplan of Oxford, was presented to the PBC

The establishment of the PBA 53

that December.[21] Based on the Caplan study, an interagency project (chaired by the PBSO and including the DPA, DPKO, UNDP, and the UN Development Operations Coordination Office—DOCO) was undertaken on "Monitoring Peace Consolidation: United Nations Practitioners' Guide to Benchmarking," aimed at assisting UN field practitioners in measuring peace consolidation by identifying principles and methodologies to establish benchmarking systems in different national and regional contexts.

Finally, two contrasting examples highlight the PBSO's new role within the peacebuilding system. The first involved its contributions to the *Report of the Secretary-General on Peacebuilding in the Immediate Aftermath of Conflict*. The drafting of the report offered an opportunity for the PBSO, between July 2008 and June 2009, to "convene the system" to identify tools and strategies for effective early peacebuilding. It also empowered the PBSO to engage more deeply in UN system efforts to strengthen international civilian capabilities while advocating for stronger local ownership of peacebuilding. During this same period—perhaps because of the distractions of work on the report and pressures from skeptical developing countries on the PBC— the PBSO declined the opportunity to serve as the co-secretariat, along with the OECD, for the International Dialogue on Peacebuilding and Statebuilding, which arguably had a significant impact on peacebuilding normative development through its *New Deal for Engagement in Fragile States*, finalized in 2011.[22]

Looking back, looking forward

The PBA was created in a particular political context which influenced its original design. In connection with the tenth anniversary, it is important to identify the PBA's early achievements as well as the continuing challenges. While there is unlikely to be sufficient interest or political will to undertake major revisions to the PBA, it is worthwhile to consider how the PBA may be empowered to play a more effective role, as envisaged by its supporters. As shown by the above review of its early years, the PBA had three main achievements, as well as several missed opportunities.

Achieving greater coherence to, and a common appreciation of, peacebuilding by myriad international actors

Prior to the establishment of the PBA, there were many actors engaged in peacebuilding. The PBA's strong advocacy for a coherent and

54   *Necla Tschirgi and Richard Ponzio*

sustained approach to peacebuilding has been a clarion call for the international community. Forging constructive deliberations between a host nation and representatives of the international community, resulting in greater certainty that longer-term commitments will be met, is a significant legacy of the UN peacebuilding reforms initiated in 2005.

After a slow start, demonstrating the Peacebuilding Fund's "proof of concept"

The PBF faced several operational and political obstacles in its early days, owing in part to limited PBSO staffing and the need to institute rules and procedures consistent with general UN norms and practice. However, by 2009/10, the benefits of investments in the PBF's staffing requirements and operational systems were beginning to pay off, as disbursement rates improved steadily alongside the capability to monitor and evaluate expended funds. Donors have taken notice, and even in the current era of fiscal austerity affecting most, if not all, UN programs, funds, and agencies, the PBF continues to receive high marks and have its relatively significant standing fund reimbursed regularly.

Establishing the foundations for a peacebuilding knowledge base

Besides backstopping the knowledge requirements of the PBC through the regular WGLL meetings and policy briefs, the PBSO demonstrated its relevance in the areas of knowledge management, networking, and applied policy research, allowing it to carve out a role for itself vis-à-vis UN system and operational actors.

However, the PBA fell short in several key areas. Some of these have already begun to be addressed while others require further reform of the PBA. They are discussed below.

Addressing effectively critical conflict drivers through light, host nation-driven integrated peacebuilding strategies

Despite a wealth of good ideas and excellent intentions, the original integrated peacebuilding strategies applied to the cases of Burundi and Sierra Leone were perceived, especially by the host countries and UN field-based officials, as unwieldy, bureaucratic, duplicative with pre-existing instruments—and, to some extent, as imposed by diplomats and UN staff in far-off New York.[23] Fortunately, this core instrument has evolved and been merged with related tools that command respect on the ground.

The establishment of the PBA 55

Inadvertently attaching a stigma to serving on the PBC agenda, while failing to demonstrate that foreign aid would dry up faster without PBC engagement

When the PBC was created, some member states felt that the new body could take up an estimated four to five countries per year, while monitoring those countries added to its agenda in previous years.[24] After nearly a decade, the PBC continues to engage only second- and third-order, albeit neglected, conflict situations in sub-Saharan Africa.

Separating conflict prevention from UN peacebuilding

In the PBA's 2005 founding resolutions, member states made a concerted effort to have it stand clear of conflict prevention, fearing that this might open the door to greater outside interference in their internal affairs. Allowing the PBA to facilitate prevention would have ensured the benefits of a holistic approach that values truly integrated and flexible peacebuilding strategies. Fortunately, beginning in 2008, PBF resources were allocated to a clear-cut instance of prevention in Guinea (Conakry), thereby setting an important precedent in a country without a significant UN presence in terms of peacekeeping or peacebuilding.

Failing to co-lead the International Dialogue on Peacebuilding and Statebuilding

The PBA missed an important opportunity when, soon after the Third International Conference on Aid Effectiveness, held in September 2008 in Accra, it declined an offer to align itself closely with the International Network on Conflict and Fragility's International Dialogue on Peacebuilding and Statebuilding, which has since become an influential platform. Fortunately, the PBSO is now working on the preparation of peacebuilding indicators for the International Dialogue's outcome document, the *New Deal Framework for Engagement in Fragile States*, and continues to expand its network among the peacebuilding community in the Global South.

Conclusion

The Peacebuilding Architecture—the commission, in particular—was established in order to bring a concerted approach to the international community's fragmented responses to countries emerging from

56 Necla Tschirgi and Richard Ponzio

conflict—not merely as yet another UN reform exercise à la the Human Rights Council. Its creators expected the PBA to serve as an innovative experiment that could break away from the "business as usual" performed by myriad international peacebuilding actors. This chapter has sought to show that many of the early decisions regarding the structure and operations of the PBC, the PBF, and the PBSO set them on a path that has not allowed the PBA to fulfill those expectations or to accomplish radical changes in well-established UN politics and practices in peacebuilding. Indeed, one senior UN official has even wondered whether "the gap" then-UN Secretary-General Kofi Annan sought to respond to in *In Larger Freedom* was widening rather than shrinking nearly a decade later.[25]

Notes

1 Rob Jenkins, *Peacebuilding: From Concept to Commission* (London: Routledge, 2013), 74.
2 Mats Berdal, *Building Peace after War* (London: Routledge, 2009), 136.
3 As Rob Jenkins has noted: "officials in the PBC, the PBSO, and the PBF have focused on 'their' individual components, engaging with the others instrumentally. This was manifested most directly in persistent contestation over control of PBF resources between the bureaucrats who manage the PBSO and the member states that constitute the PBC." Jenkins, *Peacebuilding*, 137.
4 UN General Assembly, A/RES/60/180, and UN Security Council, S/RES/1645, 20 December 2005.
5 Jenkins, *Peacebuilding*, 136
6 Jenkins, *Peacebuilding*, 136.
7 Carolyn McAskie, Unpublished Report to the Secretary General, 20 June 2008.
8 Sarah Hearn, Alejandra Kubitschek Bujones, and Alischa Kugel, *The United Nations "Peacebuilding Architecture": Past, Present and Future* (New York: Center on International Cooperation, New York University, 2014), 4.
9 See, for example, Shepard Forman, Stewart Patrick, and Dirk Salomons, *Recovering from Conflict: Strategy for an International Response* (New York: Center on International Cooperation, New York University, 2000).
10 Nicole Ball and Mariska van Beijnum, "Review of the Peacebuilding Fund," unpublished report, 2009.
11 UN Secretary-General, "Arrangements for the Revision of the Terms of Reference for the Peacebuilding Fund," 2009, www.unpbf.org/document-a rchives/terms-of-reference/#TOP.
12 Jenkins, *Peacebuilding*, 103.
13 Ball and van Beijnum, "Review of the Peacebuilding Fund," 8.
14 Ball and van Beijnum, "Review of the Peacebuilding Fund," 9.
15 Jenkins, *Peacebuilding*, 105.
16 Ball and van Beijnum, "Review of the Peacebuilding Fund," 7.

The establishment of the PBA 57

17 Ball and van Beijnum, "Review of the Peacebuilding Fund," 8.
18 Drawing on language from the founding Security Council and General Assembly resolutions of 2005, PBSO staff gave special emphasis to the PBC's role in supporting the development of integrated strategies, marshaling resources, and developing best practices.
19 Jenkins, *Peacebuilding*, 48.
20 For a comparative study of PBC and other UN strategic frameworks for peacebuilding, see Richard Ponzio, "Strategic Frameworks as Peacebuilding Tools: A Comparative Study," *Journal of Peacebuilding and Development* 5, no. 2 (2010): 6–19.
21 Richard Caplan, *Measuring Peace Consolidation and Supporting Transition* (New York: Peace Building Support Office, 2007), 1.
22 See International Dialogue on Peacebuilding and Statebuilding, "A New Deal for Engagement in Fragile States," www.pbsbdialogue.org/docum entupload/49151944.pdf.
23 See Richard Ponzio, "After Exit: The UN Peacebuilding Architecture," in *Exit Strategies and State Building*, ed. Richard Caplan (Oxford: Oxford University Press, 2012).
24 See "The UN Peacebuilding Commission: Questions and Answers," *UN Chronicle* 43, no. 1 (2009).
25 Richard Ponzio, interview with senior PBSO official, 24 June 2014.

Part II

The Peacebuilding Architecture's instruments in practice

3 The Peacebuilding Fund

From uncertainty to promise

Jups Kluyskens

- **The fund's niche in peacebuilding**
- **Financing modalities: the IRF and PRF**
- **Partnerships**
- **Peacebuilding in PBC countries**
- **Direct funding to other INGOs and government: augmenting the fund's impact**
- **Gender**
- **Value for money**
- **Achievements and challenges**
- **Recommendations**

The United Nations Peacebuilding Fund (PBF) under the United Nations (UN) Secretary-General supports activities, actions, programs, and organizations that seek to build lasting peace in countries emerging from conflict. The PBF was established in 2006, through General Assembly resolution A/60/180 and Security Council resolution S/RES/1645. The Secretary-General has delegated overall management of the PBF, including the direction of its resources and monitoring of activities, to the Peacebuilding Support Office (PBSO). Direct management of the PBF is handled by the Financing for Peacebuilding Branch, under supervision of the assistant Secretary-General (ASG) of the PBSO.

At time of writing the fund is supporting around 20 countries, delivering fast, flexible and relevant funding. Countries on the agenda of the Peacebuilding Commission (PBC) receive more than 50 percent of its funding. Other countries may also receive funding, if declared eligible by the Secretary-General.

The PBF allocates money through two funding facilities, the Immediate Response Facility (IRF) and the Peacebuilding and Recovery Facility (PRF). Both facilities fund initiatives that respond to one or more of the following four thematic areas:

62 *Jups Kluyskens*

1 Support the implementation of peace agreements and political dialogue:

- security sector reform;
- rule of law;
- disarmament, demobilization, reintegration of former combatants; and
- political dialogue for peace agreements.

2 Promote coexistence and peaceful resolution of conflict:

- national reconciliation;
- democratic governance; and
- management of natural resources (including land).

3 Revitalize the economy and generate peace dividends:

- short-term employment generation; and
- sustainable livelihoods.

4 Re-establish essential administrative services:

- public administration; and
- public service delivery (including infrastructure).

The PBF allocates between US$75 million and $100 million per year, and has set $100 million as an indicative target for annual allocations. It is dependent on voluntary contributions from member states, organizations, and individuals, and currently has 56 contributors. In 2014 the fund received $78 million from 21 member states. Top contributors in 2012–14 were the United Kingdom, Sweden, the Netherlands, Norway, Germany, Finland, Japan, Denmark, Australia, and Russia.[1] Budget allocations to countries totaled $86.7 million and $99.4 million in 2013 and 2014, respectively, a continuing and increasing trend from previous years.

The PBF is basically a mechanism for funding peacebuilding programs in post-conflict countries. It delegates extensive responsibility and authority in-country to UN agencies and national governments, especially through the Joint Steering Committee (JSC) for program development and implementation. In-country resources are handled by the relevant UN agencies. In 2014, 17 UN agencies received funding in 2014, with the largest transfers going to the UN Development Programme (UNDP), the International Organization for Migration (IOM), the UN Children's Fund (UNICEF), the UN Office for Project Services (UNOPS), and the UN Population Fund (UNFPA).[2]

The ASG and the fund are also assisted by the Multi-Partner Trust Fund Office (MPTF-O), which handles funds and project monitoring, and by the other two PBSO branches. The PBF receives support and advice from UN agencies, donors, member states, and others through the Peacebuilding Contact Group, the Senior Peacebuilding Group, and the PBF Advisory Group.

The PBF currently has a staff of 14: a core team of nine professional posts that cover leadership/business processes, portfolio management administration, overall management of design, monitoring, and evaluation; two support staff members for the fund as a whole; one secondment in the UN Department of Peacekeeping Operations (DPKO); one knowledge management officer; and one global country evaluations project manager.[3]

The fund's niche in peacebuilding

"What is peacebuilding?" can have many answers. This in part reflects the fact that the field is still fairly young, with many of its key components still under debate. It also reflects the complexity of the field, with a wide range of actors and situations.

Many of those active in peacebuilding use terms like "stabilization," "conflict management," or "early peacebuilding" to describe their work, with varying views as to how these processes relate to peacebuilding more generally. The PBF acknowledges the variety of definitions of peacebuilding, but identifies one in its current Application Guidelines—that of the May 2007 report of the Secretary-General's Policy Committee, according to which peacebuilding refers to "a range of measures targeted to reduce the risk of lapsing or relapsing into conflict by strengthening national capacities at all levels for conflict management, and to lay the foundation for sustainable peace and development."[4]

The PBF has been gathering experience in how to conduct peacebuilding guided by its principles and financing modalities. It is important to delineate the PBF's work in peacebuilding in order to clarify the line between the regular work of UN agencies (especially development work, but occasionally humanitarian work) and that of peacebuilding. The fund's joint work with the PBC also provides opportunities to examine support to long-term peacebuilding in countries on the PBC agenda. In fact, more than half of the fund's resources were spent in the six countries on the PBC agenda—all of them in Africa. In these cases the PRF has been the most used instrument to support peacebuilding.[5]

64 *Jups Kluyskens*

The PBF has made significant efforts to define its niche. These include developing guidelines for application and highlighting the key criteria of its work as well as other distinctive aspects, such as its financing modalities. The various criteria with which it operates help in defining that niche. The Global Review identified the following criteria as most central to the work of the fund: fast and flexible; relevant; catalytic; risk taking, including working with politically sensitive topics; filling donor gaps; capacity building; national ownership; inclusivity; and political commitment.

Establishing a niche is important in order to ensure that the fund provides value-added and can sustain a core financial base to assist in peacebuilding based on the above criteria. Although relatively unusual in the peacebuilding field, this is particularly important with the PBF because its programs are meant to fill gaps left by other donors and thus provide significant value-added. Depending on the country context, a combination or all of these criteria will apply. Some—such as political commitment, relevance, and national ownership—are critical to all its work. Political commitment, for example, is a requirement for the Secretary-General to declare a country eligible for the fund.

The new Business Plan underscores the importance of country demand, national ownership, and catalytic effect.[6] The fund's emphasis on risk taking, including the more political aspects of peacebuilding, is highly relevant, enabling it to focus on critical post-crisis or post-conflict transition moments. The IRF has been well suited for rapid response and has been welcomed in the field.

In the context of using the IRF more often and raising its threshold, the catalytic effect of the fund could improve as regards resource mobilization and undertaking innovative, risky or politically sensitive interventions (especially ventures that others are unwilling or unable to support). The fund defines "catalytic" as follows: "For the Peacebuilding Fund, a programme is catalytic if it enables a peace process to become unblocked and/or creates a larger or longer-term peacebuilding change to occur."[7] This definition includes financial aspects, i.e. the extent to which the PBF has leveraged other resources, but also peacebuilding process aspects, such as the extent to which activities funded by the PBF have promoted peacebuilding processes.

The Global Review noted considerable anecdotal evidence that the PBF was having a catalytic effect on resource mobilization but that few systematic data have been collected. Donors may realize that risky and sensitive peacebuilding projects need to be implemented but in many instances do not want to fund them directly, or cannot do so.

Demonstrating its catalytic and complementary potential in this area could boost the fund's own resources. This could significantly augment its impact and support long-term peacebuilding in countries that relapse into conflict or endure intermediary unstable situations. In turn, this could lead donors to recognize its value-added as a fund that can respond rapidly while also "staying the course." The fund's annual allocation target of $100 million would increase, including developing second- or third-generation programs in countries of current support, while also taking new countries on board. This would have further implications for management of the fund and its current lean staffing in New York.

The Global Review found that there was very strong donor support for seeking to catalyze additional and sustainable funding to continue its peacebuilding programming as a central feature in PBF work. The fund's emphasis on funding actions in "aid orphan" countries (countries with little international funding for peacebuilding needs), however, may make catalytic fundraising more difficult.

The view that eligibility preference should be given to aid orphans was central to the creation of the Peacebuilding Architecture (PBA). However, this stipulation has been less strictly applied in recent years, and more emphasis has been given to the PBF "filling donor gaps" where it can provide clear value-added. Precise definitions and criteria for identifying aid orphans have been lacking. The new Business Plan introduces a five-year limit for eligibility, which will help increase the strategic positioning of the fund as well as its flexibility. After five years, a review will be required to assess the impact of the fund's investments and whether it should remain active in the country.[8]

Financing modalities: the IRF and PRF

The PBF's Immediate Response Facility is a flexible and fast-funding tool for single or multiple projects, designed to jumpstart immediate peacebuilding and recovery actions. Projects submitted by the Senior UN Representative that meet the criteria receive funding within a very short time.

The PBF Peacebuilding and Recovery Facility supports a structured peacebuilding process, driven by national actors, on the basis of a joint needs analysis with the international community. The PBSO establishes a country allocation based on an approved PBF Priority Plan and delegates project approval authority to a JSC co-chaired by the national government and the UN.

These instruments are the key to the business cycle of the fund. The IRF is its project-based financing facility, created to tackle critical

66 *Jups Kluyskens*

peacebuilding needs in the immediate aftermath of conflict, or as a result of a dramatic change in the country situation. It provides rapid funding for immediate peacebuilding and addressing urgent peacebuilding needs to support critical transitions. The fund's management raised the ceiling of IRF support from $10 million to $15 million in 2014. This is a positive development, since the IRF is often utilized as the initial PBF response to a new peacebuilding situation and builds various PBF assets, such as being fast and flexible, and focusing on practical, immediate needs. In many situations, the advantages of the IRF lead to its use later in the peacebuilding phase—as when new tensions or key challenges to the peace process arise, to help bridge the "transition" of a closing UN mission, and to restart PBF programs that have been suspended following a violent change of government.

Rapid delivery of funds up front has important benefits to the UN agencies, gives credibility to peace efforts, and allows the government to deliver concrete assistance to its people. The fund's support can also deal with a wider range of actors (militaries and rebel groups) and actions (e.g. paying per diems) than some other donors can respond to, providing the PBF with an important complementary role vis-à-vis other partners. This is a noteworthy asset of the fund and contribution to UN peacebuilding efforts.

The PRF is the fund's program-based financing facility, typically intended for countries within five years following the end of the conflict. As the primary vehicle for PBF funding, it has provided three-quarters of total funding to date. PRF programs focus on medium- and long-term peacebuilding needs. By contrast, PBF programs operate longer and later in the peacebuilding phase, reflecting the fact that peacebuilding takes more time than was recognized even a few years ago.

The PRF funds longer-term peace efforts, usually between two and three years. The program development process for PRF programs is more extensive and lengthier than for the IRF. It has been the focus of considerable PBF attention in recent years, leading to a better articulated and more extensive methodology with updated guidelines and templates. It has also been envisaged that the preparation time for PRF grants would be reduced.

Further improvements are expected in improving the functioning of PRF grants, in particular the functioning of the JSCs. These committees play a key role in program development and implementation as regards decision making and oversight, ensuring adequate representation from development partners and civil society, combined with strong leadership from government. Their usefulness and performance vary, according to their composition, as well as the engagement, interest, and capacities of the host government and the UN.

In the past, the fund's PRF grants were sizeable, especially to countries on the PBC agenda with a review of achievements after completion of the projects. The Global Review recommended that the PRF is suitable for performance-based funding ensuring that prioritized peace outcomes based on the fund's niche remain on track. This is important since PRF programs that provide resources over the medium to long term can stay the course as part of the peacebuilding phase. Further, the PBF's commitment to catalytic effects for resource mobilization can be especially important for peacebuilding efforts in the later peacebuilding stages, when media, political, and aid attention has often moved on. Performance-based funding can also help in identifying whether the PBF is funding the right peace outcomes, since countries may experience spikes of new tension and even conflict within this peacebuilding phase, and may have both insecure and peaceful regions. This would also provide the fund with the opportunity to mobilize resources, demonstrating its catalytic effect, and increase its visibility as the SG's instrument for peacebuilding.

Partnerships

The fund's partnerships within and outside the UN have varied. This has often depended on which country is supported, its context, and what role the PBF can play.

The PBC is, of course, its key partner. Long-term development partners like the World Bank, regional banks, and the European Union (EU) feature more prominently in its latest Business Plan. Such partnerships have been overdue. In most cases these partners are members of the JSCs in-country, but more strategic engagement has been lacking. The PBF already collaborated with the EU in-country, for example, with election support in some African countries. Up-front collaboration with these partners, shared missions and analytical work may provide opportunities for joint financing and mutual strengthening of peacebuilding efforts. Given the EU, World Bank, and regional bank mandates it will also help identify the fund's relative strengths in the four areas in which it works. An additional advantage is that the fund can demonstrate its strategic advantage of taking risks, while the risk of failure may be lessened if other partners explicitly support its work. Such collaboration can also demonstrate that the PBF is a visible partner in in-country peacebuilding, something that has been less pronounced in recent years. The perceived relative neutrality of the UN

68   *Jups Kluyskens*

in comparison with some other donors often provides it with special opportunities to address sensitive issues that the PBF is well placed to fund. The fund's emphasis on supporting politically sensitive actions demonstrates its willingness to take risks.

A second set of partners are the UN agencies, at UN headquarters and in-country. At UN headquarters the Peacebuilding Contact Group and the Senior Peacebuilding Group are useful mechanisms for consultations. However, the Global Review noted concern about the capacity of UN agencies in-country to design and implement strong peacebuilding projects. This capacity is uneven: some agencies have more experience and pay greater attention to peacebuilding (for example, the UNDP, UNICEF, and UN Women) whereas others have significantly less institutional experience or specific commitment to peacebuilding.

As a result, some UN projects are weaker in design as well as implementation. This reality often poses a quandary for senior UN coordination officials in a country, including those dealing with PBF programs. Should they promote the participation of a wider group of UN agencies, including those with less capacity but with potentially useful approaches and skills, or should they emphasize existing in-country peacebuilding experience and capacity?

Part of this problem can be ascribed to the relative newness of the peacebuilding field and the fund, and hence the limited number of staff with peacebuilding experience, which puts a premium on PBF technical assistance to agency staff in-country. Some agencies, among them the UNDP, UNICEF, IOM, and UN Women, have created relevant peacebuilding field support components at UN Headquarters, or at least have several staff there, promoting and providing such support. Strengthening such collaboration so as to improve PBF programming and implementation in-country by the UN Country Team (UNCT) is crucial, but equally important is whether the PBF can strategically lead in the area of peacebuilding and continue to establish a niche, given the resources available.

Within the UN, the PBF also has important relationships with the Department of Political Affairs (DPA) and DPKO. The Global Review found that the fund and the DPA can mutually support each other, in particular through the fund's ability to fund peacebuilding actions and the increase in the number of joint Peace and Development Advisors (PDAs) working on peacebuilding issues in the field. While DPKO missions are usually termed "peacekeeping," some are also now receiving mandates for actions in peacebuilding. Finally, the transition period at the closure of a UN mission, whether DPKO or DPA led, is a point when PBF funding can be especially useful, as shown in the

The PBF: From uncertainty to promise   69

case of Sierra Leone. Such funding can help address unfinished peace-building needs and convey the message that the country is still receiving special UN attention.

Peacebuilding in PBC countries

The synergy between the PBF and PBC is meant to be mutually rein-forcing, with PBF benefiting from the political guidance and advice of the commission and the PBC receiving briefings by the chair of the PBF's Advisory Group on specific country priorities and projects. The PBC and PBF serve as the main instruments of the PBA but have evolved differently. In the initial years, the PBC was keen for the PBF to be a main instrument for financing peacebuilding actions in its countries, including those seen as aid orphans. The commission also assumed that it should have a strong voice in determining the level and programming focus of PBF funding in PBC countries. In this regard, PBF funding was seen as an important incentive for countries to be entered on the PBC agenda. Initially the PBC also saw the PBF as an instrument for responding to Security Council resolutions regarding countries on its agenda.

In recent years, the fund has worked at further developing its guide-lines and procedures for all the countries it supports. As a result, it has evolved into a strengthened programmatic and financial entity in its own right, with a sharper focus on peacebuilding needs in countries that meet its criteria, whether or not they are on the PBC agenda. This process has led the PBF to act more independently of the PBC, with a substantial response to non-PBC countries. While today's PBC can usefully bring attention to the funding needs of its countries, the final decision as to what to fund and how much lies with the PBF and the ASG of the PBSO. This led to controversy, as some donors hold that the PBF should continue to focus on PBC countries, whereas others say that non-PBC countries are in need and that the focus should be on them.

Synergies between the commission and the fund may have improved, but underlying structural tensions between the two still prevent the PBA from being fully effective. The Global Review identified three types of concerns:

- the roles that the PBC can play in-country;
- the levels of funding that the PBF could or should provide to PBC countries; and
- whether the PBF should continue to provide high levels of funding to PBC countries if these do not leave the PBC agenda at some point.

70 Jups Kluyskens

Both entities use various instruments to support PBC countries, and operate with a range of perspectives and strategic orientations. However, the PBC has no technical expertise on the ground.

The PBF provides funding for commonly recognized needs, but aligning and institutionalizing processes (diplomatic, programmatic, and operational) between and within the UN remain challenging. Alignments to principles like One UN, the New Deal for Engagement in Fragile States, and relevant aid effectiveness agreements have been largely ignored. In addition, an often-heard observation is that the PBC has failed to mobilize resources, leaving the PBF to be a critical contributor to countries on the PBC agenda. As this PBC task has been unrealistic from the beginning, some refer to this as "dependency on the PBF" and are concerned that funding may continue indefinitely.

As a result, discussion has emerged concerning the lack of a clear PBF policy on exit strategies for PBC countries. The Global Review found considerable support for identifying such policy that could bring further clarity in the PBF's criteria: the fund would have more resources available for other countries, whereas unending assistance to PBC countries ultimately undercuts the PBF's niche and value-added.

Direct funding to other INGOs and government: augmenting the fund's impact

Ever since the fund's establishment, concerns have been voiced that some UN agencies that do not have a peacebuilding mandate or lack peacebuilding experience might view the PBF as simply another source of funding for projects that they have identified in the course of their regular country programs, with inadequate targeting of peacebuilding needs and activities. Such concerns still exist, also among its donors, particularly in the context of the overall decline in resources available to UN agencies. The PBF has sought to mitigate this by delineating clear guidelines and providing quality assurance reviews and clear program logic requirements. Recently, as also clearly stated in the new Business Plan, the fund has been providing more up-front assistance to ensure that peacebuilding outcomes are supported by adequate conflict analysis, that they meet priorities identified within the JSCs, and that design, monitoring, and evaluation are systematically included.

That the PBF is now starting to fund international nongovernmental organizations (INGOs) and governments directly should be viewed as a positive development. In certain country contexts, INGOs or governments are better suited to implement programs. This could prove useful in the case of lack of capacity or technical expertise readily

The PBF: From uncertainty to promise 71

available in UN agencies; and also with the IRF, where preparation and implementation require rapid assessment of needs and readily available entities that can implement activities. An additional advantage is that taking high risks in terms of investment, readily available capacity in INGOs, or government may increase the impact of the program as regards speed and results. INGOs in particular often have lengthy experience in peacebuilding and have developed their own approaches and methodologies; they focus on specific groups or sectors that can supplement others; and they have a presence beyond the capital which may speed up support to specific beneficiaries. Directly funding INGOs and government may also be more cost efficient and effective, an increasingly important aspect for donors under pressure to demonstrate "value for money."

Gender

The first Gender Promotion Initiative (GPI) was a response to the UN Secretary-General's 2010 initiative on a Seven-Point Action Plan to strengthen implementation of Security Council resolution 1325 on gender. Eight countries received support during the first Business Plan, including gender targeting and mainstreaming. As part of the Seven-Point Action Plan, the PBF committed to allocating at least 15 percent of its resources to projects designed to address women's needs and to advance gender equality or empower women. In 2013, however, only 7.4 percent of PBF funding met this target. The original and revised Terms of Reference for the PBF do not specifically address gender from a peacebuilding perspective.

Both the Global Review and the 2013 Thematic Review on Gender and Peacebuilding concluded that results from the GPI have been limited, including the effective use of the gender marker.[9] The new Business Plan includes the launch of a second Gender Promotion Initiative (GPI 2) in order to stimulate further demand for projects supporting gender equality and women, particularly in their roles as actors for positive change.[10] This initiative is relevant not only in terms of achieving better results and attaining the 15 percent target, but also in providing lessons in how to program gender-responsive peacebuilding, including the potential catalytic effect such programming can have.

The PBF Application Guidelines now declare gender sensitivity as a cross-cutting priority and an essential part of the assessment of all priority plans and project proposals. If gender is indeed to be treated as a cross-cutting criterion in the four priority areas, then the fund must understand how gender can be further integrated in peacebuilding

72 *Jups Kluyskens*

programming. Specifically, electoral support, land reform, youth, and peace dividends could include gender more effectively. This will need to be monitored closely, with additional expertise at UN Headquarters. Including gender-specific indicators for improving the monitoring and evaluation (M&E) system across the fund's portfolio should help track progress. The fund's initiative to collaboration with UN Women to strengthen in-country work is a welcome development, and should help to boost the share of gender-specific and -responsive projects.

Value for money

The PBF's current focus is to ensure that projects are cost efficient, but there is little evidence that the main entities responsible for PBF programming in its countries (the UN agencies, JSC, Technical Committees, PBF secretariats) consistently apply principles designed to ensure value for money (VfM). The Global Review has proposed that the PBF should adopt as a working definition of VfM: "maximizing the impact of each dollar spent to effectively implement PBF's Business Plan in contributing to peace outcomes."[11]

This principle must be taken into consideration at the design, implementation, and evaluation stages of the fund's involvement in-country to increase effective and efficient use of resources. The PBF has been seeking to ensure that projects are cost efficient, but it is not clear how. There is little evidence that the entities responsible for PBF programming in-country consistently apply VfM principles. Discussions of cost efficiency and effectiveness may take place during project preparation, but very little is recorded. There has also been little discussion about VfM in monitoring and evaluation. This is important in view of donor concerns that their resources should be spent effectively, and their willingness to continue funding the PBF. Applying the VfM principle will also help to ensure that the most cost-efficient and effective partners are selected to implement PRF programs. In some cases this may lead donors to state that PBF resources should be provided to UN agencies based on the principle of competition. Some UNCTs have experimented with such ideas, suggesting that at an early stage concept notes should be examined and selected.

Achievements and challenges

The Global Review's overall conclusion is that the fund has matured into a unique global financing instrument for peacebuilding, enabling the UN to support critical elements of peacebuilding processes in many

The PBF: From uncertainty to promise   73

countries.[12] In recent years, the fund has been able to build a much stronger platform of policies, guidelines, and procedures to underpin its work. It has developed substantial credibility in-country and with its partners at headquarters, and has funded programs and projects that contribute to peacebuilding outcomes. Having two different financing modalities targeting different peacebuilding needs has provided the PBF with flexibility to respond to the specific needs of countries and the stage of peacebuilding efforts. The IRF has proven a rapid-response instrument that can create momentum for PBF presence. Various initiatives are now underway to strengthen PRF grants, including providing more technical assistance to UN agencies and country teams, improving the functioning of the JSCs, and further improving monitoring and evaluation.

As the fund's niche continues to evolve, various criteria are employed, including some that mark its potential: risk taking and creating catalytic effects. Articulating its niche within and beyond the UN using these criteria remains important, to provide value-added from the UN perspective and within the PBA. With its contributions to the latter and its collaboration with UN partners in-country and at headquarters, the fund is strategically positioned to collect data on peacebuilding and become a programmatic and operational Knowledge Resource Center. This has received some attention from the PBSO and PBF, but systematic efforts have not yet emerged. The fund should provide value-added by promoting learning and research on relevant peacebuilding topics, with effective sharing of this information within the UN and in the wider peacebuilding field. With active programs in some 20 countries, the PBF has extensive information databases within the field of peacebuilding. It also has important links with the PBSO Policy Branch and the PBC Lessons Learned mechanism which could further contribute to this effort. As yet, it is not possible to conclude what has or has not worked, and why.

The fund's relations with its partner, the PBC, have not been optimal. The role and responsibilities of the PBSO and its three branches—which include the management of the PBF—should be reviewed from an operational and strategic perspective. They operate in a fragmented fashion, have not been well coordinated, and lack a firm vision as regards policy and peacebuilding strategies. While the PBF anticipates that PBC countries will continue to receive the most significant share of the fund's allocations and continues to improve its working relationship with the PBC, also more systemic issues must be addressed. These include whether countries on the PBC agenda should remain eligible for PBF funding, and how the fund can develop an exit strategy for PBF funding to the current PBC country list.

74 *Jups Kluyskens*

Gender equality and gender-responsive peace programming must be improved if the PBF is to meet the target, set by the UN Secretary-General, of spending 15 percent of its total resources on gender programming. This includes closer examination of lessons learned from its first GPI, and how such actions can be improved and expanded. According to the Secretary-General's 2014 draft report on the Peacebuilding Fund, new projects totaling $7.6 million have been selected for deepening support of women's empowerment and gender equality.[13]

The PBF's business model is dependent on the progress made by its key partners in-country. UN agencies are rather uneven as regards in-country peacebuilding experience, expertise and capacities, and most lack strong capacities at their headquarters and/or regional offices to provide technical support for peacebuilding programming to their staff in-country. Moreover, after a conflict, a government's peacebuilding capacity is often limited, with a marked discrepancy between burgeoning post-conflict demands and the limited number of staff with relevant experience to address them. The fund will need to work for stronger UN agency commitments to peacebuilding and step up the fund's work building relationships with governments.

As the PBF continues to improve and consolidate its functioning, and to demonstrate value-added for its approaches and criteria, the question arises: Can it expand its overall work, including increasing the number of countries its supports? There are substantial unmet peacebuilding needs relevant to the PBF in countries where it is already working. There will probably continue to be more countries that need the PBF's type of assistance than the current 20 or so "active" countries that some have suggested might be its limit, including the capacity needed at headquarters. In any case, the PBF must tackle some of the problems mentioned above, and should also consider its current capacity at headquarters.

Recommendations

1   The PBF needs to demonstrate whether and how it has achieved results using its criteria, especially as regards catalytic effects and risk taking. Such analysis can help to strengthen the identification of its niche and promote its relevance to peacebuilding within the UN and globally. This will assist the fund in showing donors that such investments have positive peacebuilding returns, which in turn can help it to expand its resource base and increase the number of countries it can assist.

The PBF: From uncertainty to promise 75

2   The fund needs to examine the effectiveness of direct funding to INGOs and government, for both IRF and PRF. This can help the fund to target assistance better and augment its impact—not least by being cost effective and being able to demonstrate this to donors.
3   The PBF needs to take a strong lead role in the further joint inter-agency development of peacebuilding knowledge and management—also within the PBSO, the PBC's Working Group on Lessons Learned, PBF partners in-country and UN Headquarters agencies. This will help the fund to improve its strategic position, demonstrate its niche and contribute to peacebuilding policies and strategies in a range of settings.
4   The PBF should assess the results of performance-based funding and develop scenarios for upscaling, also in joint funding strategies with other partners like regional banks, the EU, and the World Bank. This can help to bolster its strategic position and relevance in-country and expand the demand for its contributions.
5   Close monitoring of the GPI 2 is necessary if the 15 percent target of PBF funding for gender programming is to be met. The PBF needs to learn how gender-sensitive peacebuilding can be designed and implemented, so that it can deploy successful approaches across its portfolio. It needs to gather further evidence showing that women are active contributors to peace and conflict resolution, and that they must be an integral part of solutions to peace and conflict programs.
6   The fund's relationship with the PBC is complex. In the short term, the PBF should develop relevant scenarios and possible benchmarks for assessing when exit from a PBC country is appropriate. It should also encourage the PBSO leadership to consider a strategy for reorganizing the PBSO to fulfill a strategic role in peacebuilding, including effective cooperation with other UN agencies at headquarters.

Notes

1   For full information concerning donors see UNDP, Multi-Partner Trust Fund Office Gateway, mptf.undp.org/factsheet/fund/PB000.
2   United Nations, *Report of the Secretary-General on Peacebuilding in the Aftermath of Conflict*, UN doc. A/69/399, 23 September 2014.
3   This reflects the need to strengthen M&E and provide more support to countries receiving PBF support.
4   United Nations, *UN Peacebuilding: An Orientation* (New York: United Nations, 2010), 49.

76 *Jups Kluyskens*

5 Burundi, Central African Republic, Guinea Bissau, Guinea Conakry, Liberia, and Sierra Leone.

6 PBSO, *PBF Business Plan 2014–2016* (New York: United Nations Peacebuilding Support Office, 2014), 4.

7 This definition was developed by the PBF in close cooperation with Peace Nexus Foundation. "Catalytic Programming and the Peacebuilding Fund," A Concept Note for the UNPBF Advisory Group, Final Draft, Peace Nexus Foundation, 2 September 2010.

8 PBSO, *PBF Business Plan 2014–2016*, 10.

9 Eleanor O'Gorman, *Independent Thematic Review on Gender and Peacebuilding* (New York: United Nations Peacebuilding Support Office, 2014).

10 O'Gorman, *Independent Thematic Review on Gender and Peacebuilding*, 11.

11 Jups Kluyskens and Lance Clark, *Review of the UN Peacebuilding Fund*, May 2014 (unpublished independent review commissioned by the PBSO), 70.

12 PBSO, *PBF Business Plan 2014–2016*, 3.

13 United Nations, *Report of the Secretary-General on the Peace Building Fund*, Draft 2014 (New York: United Nations, 2014), 3.

4 Achievements of the UN Peacebuilding Commission and challenges ahead

Mariska van Beijnum

- **Continuous challenges to the PBC**
- **Achievements of the PBC**
- **Resource mobilization**
- **Coordination and coherence**
- **Advocacy and providing strategic momentum**
- **Potential added value of the PBC**
- **Issues to be taken into account in future reforms**
- **Conclusions**

The United Nations Peacebuilding Commission (PBC) is probably the most scrutinized and criticized component of the UN Peacebuilding Architecture (PBA). From its inception, the commission has been caught in the midst of traditional intra-UN divides and turf wars, resulting in a less than clear mandate and divergent expectations as to its role and responsibilities in peacebuilding. Efforts to overcome these challenges have resulted in overly burdensome bureaucratic processes, leading to further criticism and further debate on the actual added value of the commission. The 2010 review of the PBC showed expressions of unmet expectations and disappointment that the PBC lacked an overall vision and had played a limited role, failing to give peacebuilding its proper priority within the UN system.[1] Despite efforts undertaken in response to the review's recommendations to make the PBC more relevant to the UN system and a wider range of conflict-affected countries, the PBC is today still confronted with considerable skepticism and criticism. Although several studies have indicated some notable achievements of the PBC,[2] the commission is still struggling to reform itself and find a niche in the rapidly evolving arena of peacebuilding.

Stakeholders to the PBC[3] underline a sense of urgency. While it is unlikely that the PBC will cease to exist entirely, the 10-year PBA

78 Mariska van Beijnum

review has been seen as representing a last chance to secure significant reform toward a more effective and relevant PBC and avoid it ending up as a largely ceremonial body and an added bureaucratic burden.

This chapter discusses some of the key challenges to, and achievements of, the PBC and its three configurations (the Organizational Committee—OC, the Country-Specific Configurations—CSCs, and the Working Group on Lessons Learned—WGLL) in order to identify its potential added value in the current peacebuilding arena.

Continuous challenges to the PBC

As Sarah Hearn, Alejandra Kubitschek Bujones, and Alischa Kugel note in their 2014 paper on the UN Peacebuilding Architecture (PBA), skepticism is the key obstacle facing the PBC today.[4] The PBC has not managed to reform itself in light of the criticisms expressed in the 2010 review, with major questions remaining about what the PBC is able to offer in the face of new threats and challenges to peace, security, and development.[5] Despite the recommendations made by the 2010 review to revitalize the PBC—above all noting that peacebuilding does not follow an automatic sequence of activities and that more flexible and lighter forms of engagement are required in place of the burdensome working practices that had emerged—the PBC response to the 2010 review has remained at a high level of abstraction, permitting various actors to quietly undermine or simply ignore proposals that they do not like, reflecting a sense among the PBC membership that its OC has "lacked teeth."[6]

Dan Smith's study on the impact of the PBC (December 2013) underlines that the commission's reputation is damaged by the fact that it has not managed to prevent conflict escalation in countries that are on its own agenda (i.e. Guinea-Bissau and the Central African Republic—CAR), and by the fact that it is not seen to be informing the Security Council on major violent conflicts on *their* agenda (e.g. South Sudan, Iraq).[7] This criticism has given rise to questions about the PBC's effectiveness in ensuring a coherent response to high-profile cases, and should certainly give rise to reflection in the face of arguments that the PBC should venture into conflict prevention.[8] Furthermore, the fact that since 2011 no more countries have requested to be put on the PBC agenda seems to confirm that the initial enthusiasm surrounding the PBC has waned. This in turn feeds ongoing discussions about the actual purpose of the PBC.

From the very outset, the PBC has been subject to a multitude of expectations, understandings, and agendas amongst its key stakeholders. The

Achievements of the PBC and challenges ahead 79

most obvious "stand-off" follows the traditional North–South divide that so often characterizes the UN system. The Global North—the Organisation for Economic Co-operation and Development (OECD) countries in particular—has sought to integrate the PBC into wider efforts to get the international community to work in a coherent way across diplomatic, security, and development domains when engaging in fragile and conflict-affected situations.[9] The Global South (G-77 and the Non-Aligned Movement) questions the right of the international community to interfere in the affairs of legally sovereign states, citing the key principles of state sovereignty and non-intervention. These divergent positions have translated into opposing expectations in terms of the PBC's mandate and sphere of influence: amongst the countries of the Global North there is a tendency to focus on the PBC's achievements—or lack thereof—in terms of its support to peace-building efforts on the ground (that is, an essentially operational focus); by contrast, the Global South has tended to focus on the PBC's success—or lack thereof—in influencing the Security Council and in recalibrating perceived inequalities in global governance (a main purpose attributed to the PBC in the wake of the failure of attempts to reform the Security Council's permanent membership).[10]

In addition, various stakeholders within the UN system itself have perceived the creation of the PBC as further complicating a delicate internal power balance—creating a non-conducive environment for the commission that some would argue still exists today. Central in this regard are the rather strained working relations between the Security Council and the PBC, fed by the tendency of especially the Global South countries to use the PBC as a vehicle to "right the wrongs" of the council's set-up, and the council's countering efforts to prevent the commission from intruding on its domain (for example, by negotiating core membership for seven countries from the Security Council, including non-rotating seats for the five permanent members (P5), and ensuring that the PBC was to serve as an advisory body, without independent authority or decision-making power over other bodies—including the council).

The result is that PBC stakeholders feel marginalized from the council's deliberations. Even in optimal instances, PBC representatives are allowed to present their cases to the council, but are then required to leave when the council starts its "real" deliberations which take place behind closed doors. Overall, it is clear that the working relationship between the PBC and the council has not improved significantly since the 2010 review, and remains a major constraint if the PBC is to find its position within the UN system.[11]

80 *Mariska van Beijnum*

Furthermore, many regard the decision to create a separate support structure for the PBC (the Peacebuilding Support Office—PBSO) instead of building on the capacities of existing UN entities as a major design flaw. By opting for a new structure, the UN system neglected to settle the turf battle between the Department of Political Affairs (DPA), Department of Peacekeeping Operations (DPKO), and UN Development Programme (UNDP)[12] as to which entity is best suited for closing the UN's institutional peacebuilding gap.[13] This has served to limit the potential (and much needed) institutional backing for the PBC, and the PBC is still regarded as insufficiently connected to the UN system's lead departments.[14]

Despite efforts aimed at improving the effectiveness of the PBC, its working modalities as established in 2005 remain fundamentally the same—as do the challenges linked to these modalities. The PBC membership is still significantly more fixed and formulaic than originally intended, with a core membership of 31 countries[15] and a consensus-based decision-making system, which results in long and cumbersome processes. As a result, the PBC's OC is seen as being an inefficient talk shop that focuses more on procedures than on content. The CSCs are perceived to be the most effective element of the PBC—but, as explained in Chapter 2 of this volume, there are few synergies between the CSCs and the OC. In fact, the CSCs are seen as operating rather independently of the PBC's formal structures, and questions have been raised about the sustainability of a system that seems to rely heavily on the efforts of individuals (the chairs of the CSCs and their in-country counterparts) and not on the effectiveness of the PBC as an institutional body. Reference is also made to the fact that there has not been sufficient cross-country learning and that there are no systematic efforts to draw lessons from the PBC's own experiences—this despite the existence of the WGLL.

That the PBC is insufficiently connected to the UN system's lead peacebuilding departments has become increasingly problematic as the PBC has been overtaken by developments in a highly active and dynamic field. In recent years, the UN system has invested in strengthening its integrated strategic approach to peace and security, encompassing development, the rule of law, and human rights, resulting in an increase in peace operations mandated to carry out integrated peacebuilding tasks in extremely volatile and geopolitically charged countries (such as South Sudan, Afghanistan, and Somalia). As Hearn et al. note, the original logic of the PBA would have indicated that the PBC should engage in these countries as and when needed, in order to foster coherence and advocate on behalf of peacebuilding efforts.

Achievements of the PBC and challenges ahead 81

However, they hold that this has not happened, in part because parts of the UN, including the Security Council, lack confidence in the PBC and PBSO in such high-profile contexts. That, according to Hearn et al., can be attributed to the council's reluctance to allow the PBC onto its turf; the PBC's cumbersome procedures and working practices that have not resonated with countries which have a large international presence on the ground; and the fact that the PBC has not managed to mobilize resources on a scale that could attract countries with existing large aid commitments.[16]

Importantly, the PBC has been overtaken by developments not only within the UN system, but in the wider peacebuilding field. As noted in Chapter 2, the PBC missed a major opportunity to strengthen its institutional position when it decided not to link up with the International Dialogue on Peacebuilding and Statebuilding (IDPS)[17] process and the development and subsequent implementation of the "New Deal for Engagement in Fragile States."[18] Countries from the Global South still regard the New Deal process with suspicion, viewing it as dominated by donors and tending to undermine sovereignty. Interestingly, however, there is in fact substantial overlap between the original intentions of the PBC and the IDPS/New Deal process, as both work from the basic premise that the countries on its agenda should be in the driver's seat and that mutual accountability is crucial.

The g7+ group of conflict-affected countries[19]—all part of the Global South constituency at the UN in New York—are generally perceived as playing the lead role in the IDPS and the New Deal process. Perhaps not coincidentally, all six PBC countries are part of the g7+ group and are actively involved in implementing the New Deal process at home. As Hearn et al. note, this has left the chairs of the individual CSCs to navigate between the PBC Agenda and the New Deal process, without clear guidance from the PBC as to what it regards as its complementarity and added value vis-à-vis the New Deal process.[20] Critics note the risk of an ever growing network of donor-dominated peacebuilding "New Deal Compacts" and aid allocations on the ground, all lacking buy-in from the relevant powers. Others stress that the compacts are open to all stakeholders. It is in any case clear that the PBC is increasingly being marginalized from much of the action in the field—even in countries on its agenda—which significantly undermines its potential contribution to ensuring greater international coherence in peacebuilding.[21]

A key question remains: How is a New York-based advisory body to the General Assembly and the Security Council, lacking independent authority or decision-making power over other bodies, and severely

82　*Mariska van Beijnum*

hindered by its own set-up and structures, to go about supporting peacebuilding efforts on the ground?

Achievements of the PBC

Despite the many challenges, it would be unfair to dismiss the PBC as a total failure. In fact, most stakeholders seem to agree that the establishment of the PBC has contributed to putting peacebuilding more firmly on the international agenda, within and outside the UN system.[22] As noted, several recent studies attribute some notable achievements to the PBC. Smith quite rightly argues, however, that discussions about the achievements and impact of the PBC—whether critical or supportive—have not been well anchored in the evidence. In particular there is a tendency to assess actions in isolation from both goals and capacity, resulting in rather arbitrary judgments. For instance, while it is clear that the PBC has not been able to prevent conflict escalation in the CAR and Guinea-Bissau, can this be considered a failure if judged against what the commission was established to do?[23] What is crucial—and more problematic—is the fact that the PBC's own documentation (including meeting reports and briefing notes) does not systematically assess progress or impact against the objectives of the commission. Stakeholders say they find it hard to assess at the end of a meeting (be it an OC meeting, a CSC meeting or a meeting of the WGLL) whether that meeting has contributed to the achievement of the PBC's objectives, as the set-up of meetings is not linked to the PBC's core functions, nor does the subsequent reporting link up to the overarching objectives of the PBC.

Interviewees underline that this state of affairs is directly linked to the lack of agreement (or common understanding) as to how to interpret the commission's founding resolution and its presentation of the PBC's objectives. That resolution lists five core peacebuilding functions: 1 to promote coordination and coherence; 2 to support resource mobilization; 3 to facilitate peacebuilding strategy; 4 to serve as a knowledge hub; and 5 to conduct advocacy on behalf of peacebuilding and countries' needs.[24] However, the resolution offers no clear prioritization of these functions, nor does it explicitly refer to the institutional gap the PBC was supposed to bridge—leaving open the question of *how* it was supposed to bridge this gap, and what this meant for its subsequent operating space.

However, an assessment of the achievements of the PBC concerning these individual core functions can offer insights into how they have been prioritized in practice, and which functions have proven most

Achievements of the PBC and challenges ahead 83

useful (and realistically attainable) for the commission. Recent studies seem to agree that the commission's achievements are clearest as regards three of its five core functions: advocacy for peacebuilding and for countries' needs; promoting coordination and coherence; and supporting resource mobilization.[25] It should be noted, however, that these achievements are not consistent across time and across the six countries on the PBC agenda, nor are they consistent across the three configurations that make up the PBC. Moreover, it is specifically the combination of these three objectives that has proven successful in some cases and that is perceived as holding most potential for future successes.

Resource mobilization

Assessments of the achievements of the PBC concerning its support for resource mobilization are complicated by the lack of consensus as to what "resource mobilization" entails. Thus the PBC is repeatedly criticized for not having provided much funding, although this is too narrow an understanding of its role. First, because the term "resources" refers not only to money, but also to institutional resources, technical assistance, and political support. Second, because the PBC as such has no financial resources of its own to provide to the countries on its agenda: the Peacebuilding Fund (PBF) is not owned or even managed by the commission. Countries that submit themselves to the PBC agenda are entitled to a contribution from the PBF, yet the provision of financial support from the fund is not limited to the countries on the PBC agenda. Even though there are only six countries on the PBC agenda, the PBF is currently supporting peacebuilding projects in 22.[26] Moreover, while it is true that PBC countries receive larger contributions from the PBF than do non-PBC countries, these contributions are still relatively small. The fund is specifically not intended to cover all expenses; it was established to ensure swift and flexible start-up funding for peacebuilding processes.

The confusion that has arisen around the resource mobilization role of the PBC has been compounded by the fact that, in most cases, ambassadors from donor countries have been appointed to chair the CSCs. Even though it is widely believed that the promise of financial resources was a major incentive for countries requesting to be placed on the PBC agenda, it soon became apparent that the ambassadors to the UN in New York cannot deliver on this: control of donor governments' funds for the support of peacebuilding processes remains in the respective capitals, not New York. Critics link the absence (since 2011) of more requests for being entered on the PBC agenda to the failure of

84   *Mariska van Beijnum*

the commission to generate extra funding for the countries already involved. Others, however, stress that the countries already on the PBC agenda have indicated that they wish to retain their places there, even when they "graduate" from the Security Council's agenda (as has recently been the case with Sierra Leone). Research has also shown that the six countries on the PBC agenda receive a higher per capita level of development aid than the average for other Least Developed Countries.[27] While this cannot be linked directly to the resource mobilization efforts of the PBC, the commission is nonetheless regarded as having played a useful role (alongside the World Bank and other donors) in mobilizing new rounds of peacebuilding commitments, as with Burundi and CAR.[28]

Coordination and coherence

Assessments of the achievements of the PBC in enhancing coordination and coherence differ depending on the level of analysis. Viewed at the operational level (i.e. in terms of the contribution to improving the coordination of peacebuilding efforts across the UN system), then the achievements are slight. The commission has struggled to make a meaningful impact in terms of "horizontal" peacebuilding (ensuring wider lesson learning and the development of UN-wide policies and division of labor on peacebuilding) and "vertical" peacebuilding efforts (country-specific activities). This reflects the way in which the PBC—as a new institution—was tasked with coordinating mature institutions in an area with no clearly defined boundaries, and without the requisite institutional weight, scale, or resources to demand or incentivize consent from those it was supposed to coordinate.[29]

However, examination of the founding documents of the PBC shows that it was anticipated that the coordination and coherence role would be focused on the more strategic level, where it could benefit from political clout and leverage generated by the commission's composition.[30] Assessing coordination and coherence at this level shows that the PBC has achieved some worthwhile results, specifically at the country level. Studies note how the PBC has fostered ongoing, inclusive dialogue (as in Burundi, Liberia, and Sierra Leone), and has involved important development actors like the World Bank (e.g. in CAR and Liberia) as well as important regional actors (like Turkey and Morocco in the case of CAR).[31] True, some stakeholders question these achievements, regarding the PBC as having played merely a supporting role to the (according to this reading) more critically important in-country actors. Significantly, though, interviewees from countries on

Achievements of the PBC and challenges ahead 85

the PBC agenda underline the added value arising from the presence within these processes of a driving force that is not perceived as part of the in-country playing field—as the highest UN representatives in-country inevitably are. In this way the PBC can take on the role of honest broker. That the commission is a diplomatic body rather than an operational entity is also seen as an advantage, as it is better able to facilitate government-to-government dialogue, which is important for bringing in regional actors.

Advocacy and providing strategic momentum

Assessments of the achievements of the PBC as an advocate for peacebuilding and for countries' needs emphasize that this is seen as being the core strength of the commission (and its potential added value for the future). Interestingly, this perception is shared in New York and at the country level.

As regards the PBC's advocacy role in New York, representatives of PBC agenda countries say that it is advantageous for them to have a champion for their cause at this level, one that can help them to capture the attention of the international community and to open doors to potential partner governments. This is partly a reflection of the fact that their missions in New York lack the capacity (in quantity and quality of personnel) to do this themselves. Similarly, most PBC stakeholders note the advantages for senior UN representatives in-country entailed in having an extra voice in New York that can help rally diplomatic support within the UN system. As to the PBC's advocacy role at the country level, reference is made specifically to the honest broker role that the PBC can play in supporting peacebuilding processes and preventing outbreaks of violence (as was partially achieved in the run-up to the elections in Guinea-Bissau).

Stakeholders seem to agree that the PBC can play a positive role in what Smith has referred to as "providing strategic momentum for peacebuilding processes" by bringing political weight to bear in support of an agreed strategy. He underlines the need to distinguish this role from another core function of the PBC (according to the founding resolutions): the provision of strategic advice and facilitation of a peacebuilding strategy.[32] The latter is, in fact, the most heavily criticized of the PBC's functions. In part this is because, in its early years, the commission developed its Peacebuilding Priority Plans in a less than efficient and effective manner, resulting in a very burdensome process for national governments, UN missions, and bilateral donors. Key issues in this regard are the fact that the PBC can act only on the

86 *Mariska van Beijnum*

basis of full consensus amongst its 31 members, and that the PBC relies on expertise—whether as regards peacebuilding in general or specific countries—that is generally located in member-state national capitals and not in the New York missions. An additional point of criticism concerns the perceived significant duplication of work involved in the in-country development of strategic plans, given that diplomatic mechanisms to support the development of such plans already exist at that level (as in the form of contact groups or New Deal Compacts). It is argued that countries are weighed down by strategy after strategy, with little clear idea of how it all fits together, and without the capability to implement one strategy properly, let alone all of them.[33]

Overall, stakeholders agree that the PBC adds value through its ability to bring its political weight to bear in initiating peacebuilding processes, and subsequently continuing to raise awareness about conflict-affected countries and the problems they face, thus generating the longer attention span required to sustain the peacebuilding effort—both at New York and at country levels. However, reviews also make clear that the PBC's successes here rely heavily on the goodwill and personal commitment of the CSC chairs, as well as the presence of a collaborative partner on the ground in the UN and a collaborative host government. What has not emerged is a more institutionalized way of working between the PBC, UN institutions, and the wider range of countries undergoing peacebuilding processes.[34]

Potential added value of the PBC

Critics quite rightly note that, overall, the PBC's impact has been insufficient when measured against the efforts and resources that have gone into it. However, since the commission is unlikely to cease to exist entirely, its achievements do indicate which of its core functions should receive priority in the future.

Hearn et al. found fairly broad consensus that the PBC's key added value lies in the fact that it is an intergovernmental body involving significant actors in peacebuilding from the global North and South. This is a unique configuration in the field of peacebuilding that offers potential diplomatic leverage unlike that enjoyed by any other institution. Specific reference is made to its impact as a diplomatic forum intended to advocate for greater international attention and to foster coherence across the UN system as well as a broader base of supportive regional and neighboring countries, and international financial institutions (IFIs) and regional organizations. Hearn et al. also indicate that greater clarity has begun to emerge about some viable roles of the

Achievements of the PBC and challenges ahead 87

PBC in its current form, referring in particular to two areas of diplomacy where the commission has made an impact: first, in advocacy for the countries on its agenda, providing a diplomatic forum for countries that otherwise lack diplomatic presence; second, through engaging a wide range of institutional actors, regional actors and emerging powers in supporting national development and peacebuilding strategies.[35] The political legitimacy that the PBC can derive from its founding resolutions gives it a comparative advantage, and it is regarded by its key stakeholders as having the potential to support country-led peacebuilding efforts spearheaded by senior UN in-country officials, playing a role in advocacy, resource mobilization and ensuring coherence.[36]

Stakeholders interviewed for this chapter also underscored the significance of the PBC's status as a diplomatic body, referring specifically to the added value of bringing "non-usual suspects" to the peacebuilding table (e.g. non-OECD member states, emerging powers like Brazil, Russia, India, China and South Africa (the BRICS), but also the IFIs and regional organizations). The commission has the potential to encourage and support South-South cooperation and learning on peacebuilding challenges—which might prove a more fruitful way of strengthening the position of the Global South within the UN system than continuing to focus on influencing the Security Council.

Viewed in this light, the PBC would be well advised to focus more on—and trumpet—its own strengths and comparative advantages vis-à-vis the council. Whereas being placed on the council's agenda almost invariably indicates that a country is in trouble, being on the PBC agenda can (and should) be regarded as a signal that the country is on the right track. Moreover, when countries are placed on the council's agenda they are not included in the subsequent decision-making process, in effect undermining state authority. By contrast, countries request a place on the PBC agenda in order to secure support for their efforts to implement a peacebuilding process, and to enter into comprehensive discussions with their peers and a wide range of relevant actors about the challenges that lie ahead. Stakeholders feel that the PBC should build on that positive starting point, and should focus on its strengths: providing diplomatic support to ongoing peacebuilding processes by bringing its political weight to bear when required and requested (whether by the senior UN in-country officials, or by the national government); and by serving as an honest broker, taking advantage of the fact that the PBC brings in diplomats who are not part of in-country processes and dialogues. This diplomatic support— which some refer to as "political accompaniment"—is specifically relevant to the commission's advocacy functions, the creation of

88 *Mariska van Beijnum*

strategic momentum, promoting coordination and coherence, and supporting resource mobilization.

Less positively, there seems to be fairly broad-based consensus that the PBC has made only minimal contributions through its attempts to facilitate peacebuilding strategies and serve as a knowledge hub on peacebuilding issues. This deprecation of the PBC's strategic advice role has already been explained. The negative assessments of the PBC's attempts to serve as a knowledge hub can be linked, on the one hand, to the perceived low impact of the WGLL, and, on the other, to the lack of strategic vision emanating from the PBSO. Smith points out that the broad generalizations that characterize the working group's discussions are unlikely to have an impact within a peacebuilding field that is highly active and where there is now a rich literature of evaluation, impact assessment, and lessons learned. Important in this regard is once again the fact that the PBC itself does not necessarily house considerable peacebuilding expertise.[37] Furthermore, interviewees indicate that follow-up and strategic linkages between meetings and between PBC entities (the OC, CSCs, and the WGLL) are largely missing. This is attributed to the fact that the PBC is not a normative body (it has no power and lacks the mandate to task anyone to do anything, unlike, for instance, the C34's position vis-à-vis the Security Council[38]), and also the fact that the PBSO continues to struggle to deliver on its strategic and policy functions. On the latter issue, there appears to be consensus that the PBSO lacks capacity (in quantity and quality) and mandate (vis-à-vis the PBC and other peacebuilding actors in the UN system) to play a truly effective strategic role. With regard to lesson learning and serving as a knowledge hub, specific mention is made of the perceived poor performance of the PBSO's Policy Branch: almost all interviewees say it is not clear to them what exactly this branch is doing, or what its position is vis-à-vis the PBC.

Issues to be taken into account in future reforms

As indicated, the PBC faces considerable skepticism as it struggles to free itself from the reputation of being a toothless talk shop whose own members cannot even agree on what it is that they are aiming to achieve. This confusion reflects the fact that the current objectives of the commission are too wide and not specifically geared towards what a diplomatic body in New York can actually contribute to peacebuilding writ large, and/or to peacebuilding processes in specific countries. Key strengths and weaknesses of the PBC need to be identified

Achievements of the PBC and challenges ahead 89

and assessed together with the key obstacles that it will have to overcome in order to live up to its potential.

Revisit the advisory objective of the PBC

One major obstacle seems to be the fact that the commission has been established as an advisory body to the Security Council and the General Assembly, without having any authority over these bodies, or any means to follow through on its advice. Furthermore, it is highly confusing that the PBC is to serve as an "advisor" to two bodies that are actually part of the commission itself, and indeed make up almost half its membership. Here it would make sense to focus more on the internal track of advice: that is, the extent to which the representatives of the Security Council and the General Assembly on the PBC bring relevant issues on their respective agendas to the commission's attention (in effect making them accountable for the success or failure of the PBC's advisory objective).

Unfortunately, the focus of at least part of the PBC membership has been on the external track of advice—that is, the extent to which the commission as an external actor to the council and the assembly has managed to act as a counterweight to these bodies, and has been able to influence their agendas. This has proven counterproductive as it feeds suspicions that certain countries are attempting to use the PBC to right the perceived wrongs of current governance systems of the UN, in particular the structure of the Security Council. Such suspicions in turn provoke defensive responses on the part of other members, who then take advantage of the commission's less-than-focused objectives and priorities in order to quietly undermine its potential.

While it is clear that Security Council reform remains a critical issue within the UN system, it is equally clear that this issue will not be settled via the PBC. Evidence from those cases where the PBC has had a positive impact indicates that its advisory objective needs to be revisited. The (potential) strength of the PBC lies not in its advisory role towards the council or the assembly, but in its diplomatic supportive role as regards specific countries. When this focus is taken as a starting point, the potential complementarity between the commission and the Security Council also becomes evident.

The PBC can be useful not so much in cases where conflict is still ongoing (i.e. the cases on the Security Council's agenda) but in countries that have a vested interest in consolidating a peace process. The PBC could step in when a country is getting ready to graduate from the council's agenda, for instance when a peacekeeping mission is

90 Mariska van Beijnum

preparing to withdraw, when a political peacebuilding process has been initiated and where political weight can be brought to bear to support and/or influence such a process. In this way, the UN could guarantee continued political support for a country that has embarked on peace consolidation, by providing a continued diplomatic "anchor" for the engagement of a range of UN entities in-country.

Identify PBC complementarities as regards the wider peacebuilding arena

In addition to clarifying the objectives and potential impact of the PBC in order to arrive at more realistic expectations about what the commission can and cannot achieve, stakeholders stress the need for the PBC to align itself with ongoing processes aimed at fostering international coherence in terms of peacebuilding. The most prominent of these are the New Deal and IDPS processes, which have already, in effect, taken over the peacebuilding agenda in most current PBC countries (sometimes, as in the case of Liberia, creating difficulties as regards balancing the New Deal and the PBC processes).

A possible obstacle here is the perception among many New York-based actors—a perception that crosses the usual North–South divide—that the New Deal process is donor dominated and non-inclusive, and that it undermines state sovereignty. This partly reflects how the New Deal process is driven mainly from OECD donor capitals (and the g7+), with no sense of ownership among the New York missions. One result of that may be insufficient recognition of the similarities between the New Deal and the PBC. Yet, as noted, both take country ownership as a starting point (both having self-selecting processes) and are built on the idea of mutual accountability. It is not too difficult to think of ways in which the PBC could be complementary to the New Deal and the IDPS, specifically when focusing on the political dialogue elements of the New Deal[39] and the recent initiative to strengthen South-South dialogue.[40] A future aim should be to identify areas of complementarity and potential synergies.

The PBC countries themselves also have a role to play in strengthening the commission's position in the wider peacebuilding arena, not least by clarifying what they regard as areas of complementarity between the PBC and other ongoing processes. Many stakeholders mention the absence of a collective voice from the PBC countries: these are perceived as being mostly silent during OC meetings and do not speak out about what they see as the added value derived from being on the PBC agenda—in marked contrast to how the g7+ campaigns on behalf of the New Deal and the IDPS. PBC countries should be empowered not only to strengthen the position of the commission, but also to help develop the PBC into a body that best suits their peace-building needs and is complementary to in-country processes. The PBC will need its own champions with any change process driven by the Global South in collaboration with middle and rising powers, such as those that constitute the BRICS.[41] The fact that Brazil is currently chairing the PBC is seen as a major asset in this regard.

Adjust the organizational set-up of PBC entities, with clearer PBC objectives

Finally, stakeholders see the current organizational set-up of the various PBC entities, their mutual coherence, and their relationship with the PBSO as all highly problematic and as barriers that obstruct the commission in fulfilling its potential. In particular, there is a lack of clarity on the specific roles and responsibilities of the various entities— again a reflection of the overall lack of clarity as to the commission's roles and responsibilities. Ideally, of course, the set-up of the different entities would be adjusted once the overall objectives have been clar- ified and sharpened. In the interim, however, it is clear that stake- holders believe that the only real impact achieved by the commission has been generated via the CSCs. In contrast, the value of the OC and the WGLL is questioned. That said, the CSCs are seen as relying heavily on the commitment of individuals (predominantly the chairs of the CSCs), and institutional linkages between the CSCs and the OC have remained weak.

According to interviewees, once in place, the CSCs tend to "do their own thing" with no formal obligation to report back to the OC. In fact, it could be argued that the CSCs have become a replacement for the OC: most configurations are large-scale (some with well over 50 members); and they bring together a wide range of stakeholders—from countries that use the CSCs to gather information about certain peacebuilding processes, to countries that have a vested interest in specific peacebuilding processes and are there "to do business." Most CSCs have dealt with the situation by creating a core group of stakeholders that meets regularly and identifies concrete action points, with a wider group of members meeting less frequently to exchange information.

As regards the OC, its current value is perceived to be very low: "the real business of the PBC" is conducted in the CSCs. Efforts have recently been made to render the OC more relevant. Stakeholders generally agree that the number of OC meetings should be considerably

92   *Mariska van Beijnum*

reduced (e.g. held biannually) and that they should be refocused onto developments in the PBC countries (that is, the CSCs should report back to the OC), while also allowing for discussion of crises in non-PBC countries, as well as how PBC member states might support peacebuilding processes in-country and at a more global level. This should mean that member states could no longer hide behind the PBC as an "institution," but would have to confront the fact that they themselves make up and constitute the commission, and as such are responsible for the success or failure of the PBC. The key thing is then to ensure some kind of follow-up to those meetings, and to the decisions made at them. Stakeholders have noted the contrast between the position of the PBC and the C34, with the latter able to task the UN system with following up on its findings. They also underline, however, that reform of the working practices of the OC is required. Decisions require unanimity, and the mandate/period of appointment of the OC chair is restricted to a one-year period. Stakeholders also underline the need for increased capacity of the PBSO, as well as greater clarity on how the PBSO is linked to the key UN entities in the field of peacebuilding and how it is to serve the PBC.

Finally, the WGLL seems to be regarded as a lost cause. It would be advisable to consider how lesson-learning elements can be integrated into the functions of the OC. It is certainly hard to justify the continuing existence of the WGLL and the OC as separate entities when this merely serves to add to perceptions of inefficiency and mission creep among PBC critics.

Conclusions

Reforms are vital for the future of the PBC. The commission is faced with many challenges and finds itself once again (or perhaps, still) at a crossroads: either it manages to find a way to increase its effectiveness and relevance, or it will be left with a largely ceremonial role. A focus on added value as well as on the potential complementarities between the commission and other bodies "out there" in the world of peacebuilding may provide a basis for real progress.

A key challenge will be to clarify the various expectations as to what the PBC is and what it should do—to clarify that there are differences in expectations not only between member states, but also within them (country capital versus delegations in New York), and that these differences act as barriers to the effectiveness of the commission. If common ground on objectives could be established, then it should be possible to align the commission and its entities better, renew efforts to

Achievements of the PBC and challenges ahead 93

place new countries on the PBC agenda, and re-align the role of the commission within the wider arena of peacebuilding.

Notes

1 General Assembly and Security Council, "Review of the United Nations Peacebuilding Architecture," UN doc. A/64/868-S/2010/393, 21 July 2010.
2 Such as Dan Smith, "Study on the Impact of the Peacebuilding Commission: To Play to its Strengths," 2013, unpublished paper commissioned by the Peacebuilding Support Office; and Rob Jenkins *Peacebuilding: From Concept to Commission* (London: Routledge, 2013).
3 Interviews were conducted with a range of stakeholders to the PBC in connection with work on this chapter. The author wishes to thank all those who generously gave of their time to provide input.
4 Sarah Hearn, Alejandra Kubitschek Bujones, and Alischa Kugel, *The United Nations "Peacebuilding Architecture": Past, Present and Future* (New York: Center on International Cooperation, New York University, 2014).
5 See for instance, Ivan Briscoe, *Conflict, Security and Emerging Threats* (The Hague: Clingendael Institute, 7 July 2014).
6 Hearn et al., *The United Nations "Peacebuilding Architecture."*
7 Smith, "Study on the Impact of the Peacebuilding Commission."
8 Hearn et al., *The United Nations "Peacebuilding Architecture."*
9 As underlined by the Principles for Good International Engagement in Fragile States. See OECD, *Whole of Government Approaches to Fragile States* (Paris: OECD, 2006).
10 Jenkins, *Peacebuilding.*
11 Hearn et al., *The United Nations "Peacebuilding Architecture."*
12 The DPA was nominally perceived to be the lead agency for peacebuilding, but lacked capacity; the DPKO was of course the lead agency for peacekeeping and had—through its link with the Security Council—perhaps the strongest political leverage, but lacked a mandate to cover development issues; and the UNDP (specifically its Bureau for Crisis Prevention and Recovery—BCPR) was seen as having the technical peacebuilding capacity, but lacking political leverage.
13 Vanessa Wyeth, "Peacebuilding at the UN Over the Last 10 Years," FriEnt Essay Series, Bonn, 2011.
14 Hearn et al., *The United Nations "Peacebuilding Architecture."*
15 That is, seven countries from the Security Council—including the P5; seven from the General Assembly; seven from the Economic and Social Council; five from the top 10 UN troop contributors; and five from the UN's top 10 financial donors.
16 Hearn et al., *The United Nations "Peacebuilding Architecture."*
17 See IDPS, www.pbsbdialogue.org.
18 See IDPS, "A New Deal for Engagement in Fragile States," www.pbsbdialogue.org/documentupload/49151944.pdf.
19 See g7+, www.g7plus.org.
20 Hearn et al., *The United Nations "Peacebuilding Architecture."*
21 Hearn et al., *The United Nations "Peacebuilding Architecture."*

94   Mariska van Beijnum

22 Dag Hammarskjöld Foundation, "Outcome Report," Workshop: The Peacebuilding Commission's Impact and Engagement, Greentree Estate, New York, 18–19 October 2013.

23 Smith, "Study on the Impact of the Peacebuilding Commission."

24 General Assembly, *2005 World Summit Outcome Document*, UN Doc. A/RES/60/1, 24 October 2005.

25 Such as Hearn et al., *The United Nations "Peacebuilding Architecture"*; Smith, "Study on the Impact of the Peacebuilding Commission"; and Jenkins, *Peacebuilding*.

26 See UNDP, www.unpbf.org, for more detail.

27 UN PBSO, *Resource Mobilisation for Peacebuilding Priorities: The Role of the Peacebuilding Commission (PBC)* (New York: United Nations, 2012).

28 See Hearn et al., *The United Nations "Peacebuilding Architecture"*; and Smith, "Study on the Impact of the Peacebuilding Commission."

29 Smith, "Study on the Impact of the Peacebuilding Commission."

30 General Assembly, *2005 World Summit Outcome* (New York: United Nations, 2005) (A/RES/60/1).

31 See for instance, J. Slotin, *What Next for the UN Peacebuilding Commission* (New York: International Peace Institute, 2010); Wyeth, "Peacebuilding at the UN Over the Last 10 Years"; and Smith, "Study on the Impact of the Peacebuilding Commission."

32 Smith, "Study on the Impact of the Peacebuilding Commission," 11.

33 Smith, "Study on the Impact of the Peacebuilding Commission."

34 Hearn et al., *The United Nations "Peacebuilding Architecture."*

35 Hearn et al., *The United Nations "Peacebuilding Architecture."*

36 Dag Hammarskjöld Foundation, "Outcome Report."

37 Smith, "Study on the Impact of the Peacebuilding Commission."

38 The C34 (the Special Committee on Peacekeeping Operations) was established by the General Assembly in 1965 and meets annually in month-long special session. It is mandated to undertake an annual survey on peacekeeping issues, and to task the UN system with following up on its findings and recommendations through the annual "Report of the Secretary-General on the Implementation of Recommendations of the Special Committee on Peacekeeping Operations."

39 As part of its agreed way of engaging with conflict-affected and fragile states (FOCUS), the New Deal commits to support political dialogue and leadership.

40 See www.pbsbdialogue.org.

41 Hearn et al., *The United Nations "Peacebuilding Architecture."*

Part III

The institutional and conceptual impact of the Peacebuilding Architecture

5 The gender(ed) impact of the Peacebuilding Architecture

Torunn L. Tryggestad

- **The Women, Peace and Security agenda**
- **The Peacebuilding Architecture and gender**
- **The formative years (2006–08)**
- **2010—New momentum for women in peacebuilding?**
- **Gender(ed) impact of the PBA?**
- **Concluding remarks**

The year 2015 appeared to be "the year of reviews" for many important United Nations (UN) strategies, agendas, plans, and policies. Perhaps most widely known is the review of the 2015 Millennium Development Goals. Otherwise, the reviews of UN Peace Operations, the Peacebuilding Architecture (10 years), the Women, Peace and Security agenda (15 years), and the Beijing Platform of Action (20 years) have attracted less global attention, except among those with a special interest in UN affairs or women's rights. What all these reviews seem to have had in common is a foregone dual conclusion: the international community has not managed to reach the goals set, and the UN entities established to support implementation of the strategies and policies in question have not been able to deliver in full. The reasons are many, and may involve power politics, financial constraints, and organizational turf battles. When it comes to the Peacebuilding Architecture (PBA) and its delivery on "gender-sensitive peacebuilding," an additional explanation stands out—the failure to include women effectively in peacebuilding processes and the failure to integrate gender analysis into all aspects of peacebuilding activities.[1] Without an understanding of how conflicts affect women and men differently, and the gender dynamics involved in a given conflict situation, it is also difficult to develop effective peacebuilding strategies and programs for post-conflict societies.

98   *Torunn L. Tryggestad*

In this chapter I provide an introduction to the normative framework on Women, Peace and Security (WPS), and how it relates to the PBA. I then discuss to what extent the PBA has played a major role in making UN peacebuilding efforts more gender sensitive, and conclude by offering some reflections on the status of WPS in relation to future reforms of the UN PBA.

The Women, Peace and Security agenda

Following a period of intense lobbying by an international advocacy network of women's rights activists and nongovernmental organizations (NGOs), in close collaboration with officials within the UN system and a handful of member states,[2] in October 2000 the UN Security Council adopted resolution 1325 on Women, Peace and Security.[3] This resolution calls on the international community to include women in all matters concerning international peace and security. It acknowledges women's contributions to the prevention and resolution of conflicts, and their vital roles in post-conflict reconstruction.

The adoption of resolution 1325 marked the first formal step towards what has emerged as a notable normative turn in the discourse on international peace and security. As late as the mid-1990s, it was unthinkable that the Security Council would deal with thematic issues such as women's human rights in relation to matters of international peace and security.[4] Yet, by 2010, the advancement of women's human rights, including protection from conflict-related sexual violence, had emerged as a legitimate international security concern, becoming an integral part of the discourse on international peace and security.[5] The commemoration of the tenth anniversary of resolution 1325 in October 2010 served as an important mobilizing event that reinforced the international community's commitment to this normative agenda.[6]

Since then, political commitment to the implementation of 1325 has continued to gain ground, within the context of the UN and beyond, becoming a normative framework in a process of rapid diffusion.[7] The Security Council has passed several follow-up resolutions;[8] system-wide action plans and indicators for the implementation of the WPS resolutions have been adopted within the UN Secretariat;[9] a special representative of the Secretary-General (SRSG) on sexual violence in armed conflicts has been appointed; and a steadily growing number of UN member states and regional organizations are adopting national and regional action plans for integrating and implementing this normative framework in their peace and security policies.[10] Within the UN and beyond, 1325 and its six subsequent resolutions are now

The gender(ed) impact of the UN PBA   99

formally referred to as the Women, Peace and Security agenda (WPS agenda). This is an agenda with deep roots in the international women's rights movement.[11] Over the years the WPS agenda has been lobbied and pushed forward by a dedicated group of norm entrepreneurs among NGOs, within the UN system and among member states.[12] This transnational network of norm entrepreneurs continues to play a key role in implementation of the WPS agenda at all levels—global, regional, and national.

The Peacebuilding Architecture and gender

The WPS agenda has set its mark also within peacebuilding, including the PBA. The PBA made a promising start, with early, *formal acknowledgment* of the WPS agenda and its importance to peacebuilding. However, as to actual implementation, the WPS agenda came to suffer the same fate as so many other earlier gender initiatives within the UN system. Instead of being integrated into the mainstream activities of the PBA, it soon became a sidelined activity. Gender issues were addressed separately from mainstream peacebuilding discussions; the earmarked gender advisor position within the PBSO (on secondment from what was then the UN Development Fund for Women—UNIFEM—which is now part of UN Women) was gradually tasked with additional responsibilities; and funding for "women's projects" was endorsed without such projects actually forming part of the overarching peacebuilding strategies for the countries in question.[13] The PBA had trouble translating commitments into effective action. New momentum was created in 2010 with the Secretary-General's report, *Women's Participation in Peacebuilding*. However, four years after the launching of this report, an independent thematic review of the PBA and gender concluded that a considerable gap between commitments and action still remained.[14]

The formative years (2006–08)

The UN PBA consists of the Peacebuilding Commission (PBC) and its supportive entities, the Peacebuilding Support Office (PBSO) and the Peacebuilding Fund (PBF). These three were formally established through resolutions adopted concurrently by the UN General Assembly and Security Council in December 2005.[15] The PBC became operational in June 2006. Its membership consists of 31 UN member states, on two-year membership terms.[16] The mandate of the PBC is to assist post-conflict countries in developing integrated strategies for

100 *Torunn L. Tryggestad*

post-conflict peacebuilding; to marshal resources for post-conflict recovery activities; to raise the international community's awareness of countries in the precarious post-conflict phase; and to improve strategic-level coordination among all actors involved in peacebuilding activities.[17]

The PBSO was established to support the PBC in its work and is located within the UN Secretariat under the executive office of the Secretary-General. The functions of the PBSO include the drafting of reports, conducting research and analysis, and serving the Secretary-General in coordinating UN agencies involved in peacebuilding activities. A further important role of the PBSO is to administer the PBF, which was launched in 2006. The PBF is intended to fill the gap in funding for countries in the immediate post-conflict phase but not yet on the path towards sustainable development.

The PBC was born in an atmosphere of tension stemming from distrust and power struggles between the dominant states in the Security Council and the G-77 majority in the General Assembly. This power struggle frequently paralyzed the ongoing processes of UN reform and heavily influenced the negotiations on the setup, membership, and mandate of the PBC.[18] In such an atmosphere, one might assume that it would be difficult to get women's issues onto the PBC agenda; in fact, the PBC is the first UN body to have gender concerns explicitly built into its founding resolutions.[19] Although no direct reference is made, the founding resolutions contain several paragraphs on women and women's concerns, closely reflecting the spirit of resolution 1325. For instance, the contributions that women's organizations make to peacebuilding efforts are recognized,[20] as is the important role of women in peacebuilding.[21] Most important is probably paragraph 20, which calls upon the commission to integrate a gender perspective in all its work.

Similarly, language on women was integrated within the peacebuilding strategies developed for the first two countries on the PBC's agenda—Burundi and Sierra Leone. In the case of Burundi, in particular, the strategy makes direct reference to 1325 and deals with WPS concerns in important areas like capacity-building measures for the political, social, and economic participation of women; the inclusion of women's civil society organizations in peacebuilding efforts; and the integration of women's legal and human rights in security sector reform.

The head of the PBSO during the formative years, Carolyn McAskie, was also a firm advocate of women's issues. She treated the WPS agenda as a cross-cutting issue to be mainstreamed into a broad range of peacebuilding activities. To assist in this work, a full-time gender advisor was seconded to the PBSO from UNIFEM. PBF funds were

The gender(ed) impact of the UN PBA   101

also disbursed to projects and programs of direct or indirect benefit to women. This included projects focused on raising awareness regarding 1325, preparatory work on democratic dialogue, and rehabilitation of women's roles in community reconciliation and reconstruction processes. Furthermore, gender issues were taken up in several meetings of the PBC Working Group on Lessons Learned (WGLL). One of their synthesis reports from this early period states that integration of a gender perspective is a key principle and element of peacebuilding, and that 1325 constitutes a normative framework that enjoys widespread acceptance among PBC members.[22]

What was achieved on gender during the formative years of the PBA came about due to dedicated lobbying and close collaboration among various civil society organizations (spearheaded by the NGO Working Group on WPS, located in New York), individuals within UN entities (such as UNIFEM) and a group of UN member states. In the latter category, Norway played a key role in promoting the WPS agenda in its capacity as co-chair of the PBC, chair of the Burundi Country-Specific Configuration and a major donor to the PBF.[23] The gender footprint on the PBA in this early phase represented something new in terms of integrated efforts to include women and women's concerns in peacebuilding, bringing high hopes for more gender-sensitive UN peacebuilding efforts. Then, with the change in PBC membership (due to rotation) and PBSO management in 2008, some of the momentum on gender was lost—at least for a while. Also the NGO community seemed to have lost some of its interest in the PBA. It was not long, however, until the PBSO entered a period of self-assertion and more aggressive pursuit of what was seen as its mandate[24]—and gender was one of the topics to be pursued.

2010—New momentum for women in peacebuilding?

In October 2009, following the Security Council open debate on WPS, it adopted resolution 1889.[25] It reiterates the council's commitment to the WPS agenda and expresses concern about its slow implementation. It stresses the importance of women's participation in peacebuilding and requests that the Secretary-General provide a progress report on this dimension of the WPS agenda. The PBSO was then tasked by the Secretary-General with drafting the report, and funding was provided by UNIFEM for two external consultants (one senior and one junior) to lead the process.[26]

The *Women's Participation in Peacebuilding* [27] report was developed in parallel with the Secretary-General's progress report, *Peacebuilding*

102 *Torunn L. Tryggestad*

in the Immediate Aftermath of Conflict. [28] Apart from a short paragraph referring to the ongoing work on the separate report on women and peacebuilding, the latter report hardly mentions women's issues: a clear illustration of the sidelining of gender issues within the PBA. Instead of integrating women and gender as a cross-cutting issue in the generic report—as requested in the formative documents of the PBA—the PBSO spent resources on two parallel processes, producing two separate reports that dealt with many of the same technical and operational issues, but with no integration between the two. When the *Women in Peacebuilding* report was finalized there was hefty disagreement among member states—as well as among senior UN officials—as to when and how it should be presented to the Security Council. Many diplomats and UN officials were of the opinion that it should not be considered as part of the Security Council open debate on peacebuilding, but as part of the open debate on WPS: in other words, a women's issue to be dealt with separately from the broader discussion on peacebuilding. In the end, the proponents of an integrated approach managed to convince skeptics that the *Women in Peacebuilding* report should be considered as part of the general debate on peacebuilding. However, in practice the report was not really debated, but simply taken note of.

That said, the PBSO management did pick up on the report, which points out that in many respects women's post-conflict needs resemble the five recurring priorities outlined by the Secretary-General in his 2009 report, *Peacebuilding in the Immediate Aftermath of Conflict.*[29] These are: safety and security; confidence in the political process through inclusive dialogue and post-conflict elections; access to basic services such as water and education; a functioning public administration; and economic revitalization (notably employment creation). Still, these priorities and how they should be met are not discussed from a gendered perspective. The PBC WGLL statement from 2008—that the integration of a gender perspective is a key principle in peacebuilding— was not taken into account by those who drafted the Secretary-General's 2009 report on peacebuilding.

The parallel *Women in Peacebuilding* report stated that policymakers and others involved in programming and budgeting had failed to translate political commitments and guidance materials into concrete gender-sensitive projects. Only a very low percentage of budget allocations went to addressing women's needs or the advancement of women. In the report, the Secretary-General admits that efforts to engage women and address women's issues in the context of peace processes must be accelerated, and commitments be made more concrete. This message was reiterated in the UN PBA review report, released in July 2010, advising that the PBC should be at the forefront in moving women's role in peacebuilding from a niche concern to the mainstream.[30]

In an effort to remedy the situation, the Secretary-General in his *Women in Peacebuilding* report launched a Seven-Point Action Plan on how to include women in peace talks and make gender equality a central part of post-conflict planning. The action plan was intended to be merged into the larger reform agenda of the *Immediate Aftermath* report.[31] The most progressive—and controversial—action point of the plan was a financial target of 15 percent of all UN-managed funds in support of peacebuilding to be set aside for addressing women-specific needs, advancing gender equality, or empowering women. This latter action point was immediately followed up by the PBSO, and by October 2012 PBF funds had reached two thirds of the target 15 percent.[32] Still, an indicative baseline study of UN-managed peacebuilding funds, conducted in November 2013 by UN Women, PBSO and the UN Development Programme (UNDP), found that only 6 percent had been allocated for women's empowerment and gender equality.[33]

Gender(ed) impact of the PBA?

Some 10 years after the formal establishment of the PBA, the challenges of what is now termed "gender-responsive peacebuilding" are still many. Although firm political commitments and efforts targeted at improving policy development might seem to indicate the contrary, women and gender concerns are still not being effectively integrated into the activities of the PBA. This applies both to how the normative framework of WPS is conceptualized and understood, and how it is operationalized. In her thematic review for the PBSO, Eleanor O'Gorman lists a range of concerns.[34] First, the distinct gap between policy commitments and operational reality still remains. Second, much greater momentum and scale are needed in gender-responsive peacebuilding. Third, there is a continuing lack of proper gender analysis of conflict situations. Fourth, there is a pressing need for operational guidance on *how* to implement gender-responsive peacebuilding and *how* to measure results and impact.

Within the UN system there seems to be a prevailing culture of seeing the WPS as an "add-on" component and not one central to conflict resolution and peacebuilding.[35] This also seems to apply to the PBA. The idea that initiatives aimed at including women in peacebuilding and addressing their specific concerns is something to be kept separate from generic peacebuilding activities is still prominent. The

104   *Torunn L. Tryggestad*

recent thematic gender review conducted under the auspices of the PBSO and PBF serves as a clear illustration. When the external consultants arrived in New York in September 2013 to start the gender review, they discovered that a wider management review of the PBF was already underway. The latter had no explicit reference to gender in its Terms of Reference.[36] It was the research teams themselves that established contact with one another to create synergies, including going on field visits together. Although little could be done with the decisions to have two different reviews undertaken simultaneously on issues that were clearly overlapping, O'Gorman has encouraged the PBSO to consider the review reports together in order to optimize recommendations on gender-sensitive peacebuilding.[37]

Concluding remarks

The achievements of the PBA and its prospects for future success have attracted the attention of a growing number of scholars and analysts interested in issues of global governance in general and the workings of the UN in particular.[38] There is a body of literature addressing the gender aspects of the PBA more specifically.[39] Most of these are the work of individual experts, NGOs, and think-tanks closely associated with the transnational advocacy network on women, peace, and security. Many of the publications on the PBA and gender were issued during the PBA's first four to five years of existence; they reflect a period of intense lobbying and advocacy work to have gender language integrated into the formal documents, to ensure gender competence within the PBSO, and to secure funding for women-specific peacebuilding projects and activities in PBF beneficiary countries.

This literature provides analyses, arguments, and evidence for the benefits of including women in peacebuilding. Women's inclusion is portrayed both as a rights issue (women have the right to be heard and to be part of decision making) and an issue of more effectively achieving sustainable peace. Women are crucial to economic recovery, social cohesion, and the political legitimacy of any new government, it is argued.[40] The women's rights activists and academics in question have undoubtedly played an influential role in changing mindsets and strengthening gender awareness among politicians and senior diplomats at the strategic level. They have perhaps been less successful in influencing those who translate policy into practice and make decisions on budget allocations under the auspices of the PBA.

Although the WPS agenda enjoys steadily increasing normative and political support also within the PBA, it still has some way to go before

The gender(ed) impact of the UN PBA 105

it is properly acknowledged in academic circles and among analysts in think-tanks where peacebuilding concepts are discussed, criticized, and refined. Male academics and analysts dominate the discourse on peacebuilding and inform theory development and policymaking, at the UN and in member states. Few of these scholars have paid much attention to women's issues or to the highly gendered aspects of post-conflict peacebuilding in their publications. The challenges of peacebuilding appear to be viewed as something "gender neutral" in the mainstream literature on peacebuilding. In effect, women remain marginalized—politically, socially, and economically.

The 10-year review of the PBA could pave the way for change in prevailing policies and practices. First, the senior management of the various PBA entities will need to address the issue of gender-sensitive conflict analysis more vigorously. Gender dimensions must be introduced early on in deliberations on any conflict situation or peacebuilding process on the PBC agenda. Second, the analytical capacity within the PBSO must be strengthened to include proper gender analysts. Full-time positions must be secured, not dependent on goodwill and secondments from UN entities such as UN Women. Third, achieving gender-responsive peacebuilding will be difficult unless both *targeted* and *mainstreaming* measures are pursued. These are lessons that have been drawn from similar processes in other parts of the UN system since the 1970s. Finally, in terms of synergies and lessons, much is likely to be gained from establishing stronger linkages in the implementation of the outcomes of the different review processes within the UN system, as regards how to become more effective and gender responsive in peacebuilding efforts.

Notes

1 Rob Jenkins, *Peacebuilding: From Concept to Commission* (London: Routledge, 2013); Eleanor O'Gorman, *Independent Thematic Review on Gender for the UN Peacebuilding Support Office (PBSO)—Final Report*, an independent analysis commissioned by the UN Peacebuilding Support Office, University of Cambridge, March 2014, www.un.org/en/peacebuilding/pbso.
2 Torunn L. Tryggestad, "Trick or Treat? The UN and Implementation of Security Council Resolution 1325 on Women, Peace and Security," *Global Governance* 15, no. 4 (2009).
3 UN Security Council, UN doc. S/RES/1325/2000, 31 October 2000.
4 David M. Malone, "Introduction," in *The UN Security Council*, ed. David M. Malone (Boulder, Colo.: Lynne Rienner, 2004).
5 The WPS agenda emerged in parallel with the UN nurtured debates on "human security" and "Responsibility to Protect" (R2P). However, the WPS agenda seems to have fared better than human security and R2P in

106 *Torunn L. Tryggestad*

terms of global acknowledgment and commitment to its implementation. See Natalie F. Hudson, *Gender, Human Security and the United Nations: Security Language as a Political Framework for Women* (London: Routledge, 2010); and Funmi Olonisakin, Keren Barnes and Eka Ikpe, eds, *Women, Peace and Security: Translating Policy into Practice* (London: Routledge, 2011).

6 A record number of more than 90 statements were given by member states, UN officials, civil society representatives, the International Committee of the Red Cross, and regional intergovernmental organizations such as the European Union (EU), the North Atlantic Treaty Organization (NATO), and the African Union (AU). Also, statements were delivered by a record number of high-level government representatives—including the US secretary of state.

7 Torunn L. Tryggestad, "International Norms and Political Change: 'Women, Peace and Security' and the UN Security Agenda," PhD dissertation, Faculty of Social Sciences, University of Oslo, 2014.

8 The subsequent Security Council resolutions to 1325 are 1860 (2008), 1888 (2009), 1889 (2009), 1960 (2010), 2106 (2013), and 2122 (2013). Beyond the "mother resolution," resolutions 1889 and 2122 are those that most explicitly address commitments in relation to peacebuilding.

9 See for example, "UN Strategic Results Framework on Women, Peace and Security: 2011–2020," July 2011, www.un.org/womenwatch/ianwge/taskfor ces/wps/Strategic_Framework_2011-2020.pdf.

10 As of January 2015, 48 member states had adopted National Action Plans (NAPs) for implementation of 1325 (including the United States), and several NAPs are underway (including Japan). Regional organizations such as the AU, the EU, and NATO have also adopted resolutions, action plans, and policies for the implementation of 1325. Furthermore, the AU and NATO have appointed a special envoy for WPS and an SRSG on WPS, respectively. These appointments are quite progressive organizational steps, as the high-level appointees are mandated to work on the full WPS agenda. The UN-appointed SRSG has a mandate limited to the issue of preventing and combatting Sexual Violence in Armed Conflict.

11 Cynthia Cockburn, *From Where We Stand: War, Women's Activism and Feminist Analysis* (London: Zed Books, 2007).

12 Tryggestad, "International Norms and Political Change."

13 Torunn L. Tryggestad, "The UN Peacebuilding Commission and Gender: A Case of Norm Reinforcement," in "Women, Peace and Conflict: A Decade after Resolution 1325," ed. Susan Willet, *International Peacekeeping* (special issue) 17, no. 2 (2010).

14 O'Gorman, *Independent Thematic Review on Gender for the UN Peacebuilding Support Office (PBSO)—Final Report.*

15 Security Council, UN doc. S/RES/1645, 20 December 2005; and General Assembly, UN doc. A/RES/60/180, 30 December 2005.

16 The PBC consists of an Organizational Committee, several Country-Specific Configurations and the WGLL. It has 31 members, representing key UN bodies and important groups of member states (seven members selected by the Security Council, seven elected by the Economic and Social Council, five of the top providers of financial contributions to the UN, five top providers of military personnel and civilian police to UN missions, and seven members elected by the General Assembly).

The gender(ed) impact of the UN PBA   107

17 See PBS, Mandate of the Peacebuilding Commission, www.un.org/en/pea cebuilding/mandate.shtml.
18 The PBC was first proposed by the High-Level Panel on Threats, Challenges and Change in 2004 and subsequently endorsed by UN Secretary-General Kofi Annan in his March 2005 report, *In Larger Freedom*. It was one of the few proposals the UN World Summit could agree upon. See UN General Assembly, *World Summit Outcome Document*, UN doc. A/RES/60/1, 24 October 2005. See also, New York University Center on International Cooperation and the International Peace Institute, "Taking Stock, Looking Forward: A Strategic Review of the Peacebuilding Commission," an independent analysis by the commissioned by the Permanent Mission of Denmark to the UN, April 2008. www.ipinst.org/media/pdf/publications/p bcsrev08.pdf.
19 Tryggestad, "The UN Peacebuilding Commission and Gender."
20 Security Council, UN doc. S/RES/1325/2000, 31 October 2000, para. 14.
21 Security Council, UN doc. S/RES/1325/2000, para. 15.
22 UN PBC Working Group on Lessons Learned, *Synthesis Report: Key Insights, Principles, Good Practices and Emerging Lessons in Peacebuilding*, Special Session, 2008. www.un.org/en/peacebuilding.
23 Torunn L. Tryggestad, "State Feminism Going Global: Norway on the UN Peacebuilding Commission," *Cooperation and Conflict* 49, no. 4 (2014).
24 Rob Jenkins, "The UN Peacebuilding Commission and the Dissemination of International Norms," Crisis States Working Paper Series No. 2 (Crisis States Research Centre/London School of Economics and Political Science, 2008).
25 Security Council, UN doc. S/RES/1889, 5 October 2009.
26 Jenkins, *Peacebuilding*.
27 Available at www.un.org/ga/search/view_doc.asp?symbol=A/65/354.
28 Available at www.un.org/en/ga/search/view_doc.asp?symbol=S/2010/386.
29 Available at www.un.org/en/ga/search/view_doc.asp?symbol=S/2009/304.
30 Available at www.un.org/ga/search/view_doc.asp?symbol=A/64/868.
31 Jenkins, *Peacebuilding*.
32 O'Gorman, *Independent Thematic Review on Gender for the UN Peacebuilding Support Office (PBSO)—Final Report*.
33 Security Council Report, "Women, Peace and Security," Cross-Cutting Report, April 2014. www.securitycouncilreport.org.
34 O'Gorman, *Independent Thematic Review on Gender for the UN Peacebuilding Support Office (PBSO)—Final Report*, 25.
35 Security Council Report, "Peacebuilding: Expected Council Action," March 2014 Monthly Forecast. www.securitycouncilreport.org/monthly-for ecast/2014-03/peacebuilding_2.php.
36 O'Gorman, *Independent Thematic Review on Gender for the UN Peacebuilding Support Office (PBSO)—Final Report*.
37 O'Gorman, *Independent Thematic Review on Gender for the UN Peacebuilding Support Office (PBSO)—Final Report*, 17.
38 See Mats Berdal, *Building Peace After War* (London: Routledge, 2009); International Peace Academy, "The UN Peacebuilding Commission: Benefits and Challenges," background paper prepared for the regional seminars organized by the Friedrich Ebert Stiftung, New York Office, 6 June 2006; Sarah Hearn, Alejandra Kubitschek Bujones, and Alischa Kugel, *The*

108 *Torunn L. Tryggestad*

United Nations "Peacebuilding Architecture": Past, Present and Future (New York: Center on International Cooperation, New York University, 2014); Jenkins, "The UN Peacebuilding Commission and the Dissemination of International Norms"; Jenkins, *Peacebuilding*; and Rob Jenkins, "Post-Conflict Peacebuilding," in *International Organization and Global Governance*, ed. Thomas G. Weiss and Rorden Wilkinson (London: Routledge, 2014).

39 See Action Aid, the Catholic Agency for Overseas Development (CAFOD) and CARE International, "Consolidating the Peace? Views from Sierra Leone and Burundi on the United Nations Peacebuilding Commission," NGO Report, June 2007; Sanam Naraghi Anderlini, *Women Building Peace: What They Do, Why It Matters* (Boulder, Colo.: Lynne Rienner, 2007); Catherine Guicherd, "Picking up the Pieces: What to Expect from the Peacebuilding Commission," Dialogue on Globalization, FES Briefing Paper, New York, December 2005; Hudson, *Gender, Human Security and the United Nations*; International Alert, "Integrating Women's Priorities into Peacebuilding Processes: Experiences from Burundi and Sierra Leone," report of a civil society workshop, London, 25–29 February 2008; J. Klot, "Women and Peacebuilding," Independent Expert Paper, commissioned by the UN Development Fund for Women and PBSO, 2007, www.un.org/en/peacebuilding/pdf/doc_wgll/wgll_backgroundpaper_29_01_08.pdf; NGO Working Group on Women, Peace and Security, UNIFEM, and United Nations Methodist Office, "UN Peacebuilding Commission: A Blueprint for Amplifying Women's Voices and Participation," Issue Brief, November 2005, womenpeacesecurity.org; and NGO Working Group on Women, Peace and Security, "SCR 1325 and the Peacebuilding Commission: Security Council Resolution 1325 on Women, Peace and Security— Six Years On Report," October 2006, womenpeacesecurity.org; Elisabeth Porter, *Peacebuilding: Women in International Perspective* (London: Routledge, 2007); Tryggestad, "The UN Peacebuilding Commission and Gender"; Tryggestad, "International Norms and Political Change"; and Tryggestad, "State Feminism Going Global."

40 Similar arguments and reasoning can be found in the 2009 *Women and Peacebuilding* report.

6 Bridging the gap?

The UN civilian capacity initiative

John Karlsrud and Lotte Vermeij

- **A historical background of CIVCAP**
- **Operationalizing the recommendations in South Sudan**
- **CAPMATCH**
- **The CIVCAP initiative: results, lessons learned, and the way forward**
- **Implications for the Peacebuilding Architecture**
- **Conclusions and recommendations**

The civilian capacity reform initiative was first suggested by UN Secretary-General Ban Ki-moon in his 2009 report, "Peacebuilding in the Immediate Aftermath of Conflict": "a review needs to be undertaken that would analyse how the UN and the international community can help to broaden and deepen the pool of civilian experts to support the immediate capacity development needs of countries emerging from conflict."[1]

This chapter traces the civilian capacity (CIVCAP) initiative from its inception in 2009 until the end of the UN CIVCAP team in June 2014, assessing the institutional and conceptual impact of the Peacebuilding Architecture (PBA), and offering some recommendations for the 2015 review of the PBA.

A historical background of CIVCAP

Following a request by the Security Council in May 2008, the civilian capacity reform process emerged from the understanding that civilians play a crucial role in helping conflict-affected states rebuild institutions and achieve lasting stability and progress. The reform aimed to help the UN in tackling the challenges that post-conflict countries and the international community face in the immediate aftermath of conflict. Civilian capacities are at the heart of the solutions to these challenges,

110 *John Karlsrud and Lotte Vermeij*

whether the question is how to deploy relevant, adequate, and effective civilian capacities rapidly, or build national competence and capacities for core government functions and achieve national ownership. To achieve these goals, the CIVCAP reform called for more flexible, locally owned solutions by the UN, multilateral organizations, and member states.

The Senior Advisory Group's report on CIVCAP was the beginning of a global effort by the UN and its member states to restructure how civilian capacity is mobilized in crisis and post-conflict settings. It sought to wrest the debate out of a deadlock on managerial issues in New York, to a focus on how to achieve lasting, locally owned, and long-term results for host populations. While the process may have had limited impact on the UN system as such, it has succeeded in putting greater focus on locally relevant solutions such as triangular cooperation and South-South cooperation initiatives where capacity is sourced from neighboring countries, and the need to ensure more use of local capacities.

The CIVCAP reform process started out with a recommendation in the 2009 "Peacebuilding in the Immediate Aftermath of Conflict" report issued by the UN Secretary-General. This is an important point: the reform process came about as the explicit result of the establishment of the PBA at the UN and the increased attention given to the role of peacebuilding, and within this the civilian capacities that perform key functions in supporting peacebuilding activities in countries emerging from conflict.

However, it is uncertain whether the CIVCAP reform initiative will have a lasting impact on UN institutions and strategies. The UN has a tendency to revert to what it knows best—how to develop new guidelines and tools—getting embroiled in long-winded strategy processes that turn into a wrestling ground for inter- and intra-organizational rivalries, with reform becoming incremental. Nevertheless, the UN has managed to take some positive steps. The UN Development Programme (UNDP) has merged its Bureau for Conflict Prevention and Recovery (BCPR) and the Bureau for Development Policy, removing artificial divides between its policy support for developing and fragile countries; and cooperation among various UN entities in the area of rule of law has progressed in recent years. To enable lasting reform and impact, the UN system should:

- increase the use of government-provided personnel (GPPs) from a representative cross-section of member states to UN peace operations and consider these as Civilian-Contributing Countries

(CCCs); engineering teams, ICT experts, Sexual Exploitation and Abuse teams, human rights monitors, judicial experts, organized crime and terrorism experts should be included;

- focus on and support triangular and South-South cooperation initiatives, implementing these where possible through GPP and CCC arrangements;
- support efforts to remove artificial barriers between peacekeeping and special political missions, recognizing that the challenges on the ground are complex and interconnected;
- increase cooperation between UNDP BCPR and the UN Department of Peacekeeping Operations (DPKO)/UN Department of Political Affairs (DPA) at UN Headquarters; and
- continue to pursue increased cooperation within the UN and with the World Bank and other international organizations at the field level.

In June 2009, UN Secretary-General Ban Ki-moon issued "Peacebuilding in the Immediate Aftermath of Conflict." In the report, he provided advice on how the UN could improve support to national efforts to effectively and rapidly secure sustainable peace. The report focused on the challenges facing post-conflict countries and the international community in the immediate aftermath of conflict. It reflected on past peacebuilding experience, the importance of national ownership, the unique challenges arising from the specific context of early post-conflict situations, recurring priorities for international assistance, UN efforts undertaken to enhance the efficiency and effectiveness of post-conflict response, as well as systemic challenges faced in missions. In addition, the report proposed a review that would explore how the UN together with the international community could help to expand the pool of civilian experts to support the immediate needs for capacity development in countries emerging from conflict.[2]

The Secretary-General subsequently appointed a Senior Advisory Group, led by Jean-Marie Guéhenno, to undertake an independent review of how civilian capacity is provided in the aftermath of conflict. Based on broad consultations with UN representatives, member states, civil society, and regional organizations, the Advisory Group published its independent report in March 2011. The report noted five crucial areas where civilian capacities to support countries emerging from conflict were lacking: basic safety and security; inclusive political processes; justice; economic revitalization; and core government functionality. Aiming to provide recommendations as to how to strengthen the capacity of countries emerging from conflict to enable a successful transition to sustainable peace, the report was built around four key

112 *John Karlsrud and Lotte Vermeij*

themes: ownership, partnerships, expertise and nimbleness (the "OPEN" framework). Stressing the need to strengthen civilian capacities and establish resilient institutions as necessary foundations for sustainable peace, the report made the following recommendations:

- Strengthen national *ownership* of peace processes by supporting core government functions, nurturing national capacities and improving the economic impact of international interventions.
- Encourage the UN to work in global *partnerships*, looking beyond its own staff and harnessing the full range of global capacities to be found within member states and civil society organizations.
- Urge the UN to draw on outside *expertise* and to establish clarity on the core capacities of the UN and stronger accountability to member states.
- Use available resources more effectively and efficiently, increasing the UN's *nimbleness* in the face of often very turbulent transitions.[3]

The Senior Advisory Group's report on CIVCAP marked the beginning of a global effort by the UN and its member states to restructure how civilian capacity is mobilized in crisis and post-conflict settings. Building on the vision of the Senior Advisory Group, Secretary-General Ban Ki-moon identified concrete priority actions in the report "Civilian Capacities in the Aftermath of Conflict," focusing on how the UN should collaborate with its partners to meet the challenges and strengthen the quality and effectiveness of support to post-conflict institution building.[4] The Secretary-General then appointed a steering committee of high-level representatives from entities across the UN system, to ensure that the outcomes of the initiative would be integrated across the organization.[5] Chaired by Susana Malcorra, the committee was established to "oversee the CIVCAP initiative and ensure coherence and coordination of CIVCAP-related issues across the system."[6] To support the steering committee, a working group as well as a CIVCAP support team was appointed, headed by Sarah Cliffe as special advisor and assistant Secretary-General (ASG) of civilian capacities.

Under this structure, the CIVCAP initiative aimed to engage a broader set of partners to work together on the supply of civilian assistance. The CIVCAP approach placed particular emphasis on collaboration with partners from the Global South, resting on three assumptions:

1 The Global South are important providers that are willing and able to offer civilian expertise due to their own experiences in development and transitions.

The UN civilian capacity initiative   113

2   Resources will be available to enable this exchange of civilian capacities.
3   The multilateral system for post-conflict support will be able to reorganize itself to improve the absorption of international assistance.[7]

The focus on the Global South by the CIVCAP initiative emerged:

> ... against the backdrop of a much broader and longer-term dynamic wherein major actors of the Global South have continued to grow significantly as providers of bilateral assistance. Long-standing South–South cooperation programmes have expanded in line with the growing economic interests and foreign policy aspirations of these countries. National policy frameworks, systems and institutions are evolving to manage the growth in scale and complexity of these technical cooperation programmes, a trajectory which seems likely to continue in the coming years.[8]

Operationalizing the recommendations in South Sudan

The CIVCAP initiative coincided with the birth of the youngest nation in the world—South Sudan. This country, with deep and manifold capacity needs, was given particular attention by the CIVCAP team and the rest of the UN, with special reference to the role that civilian capacities were envisaged to play in the mandate given by the UN Security Council to the UN Mission in South Sudan (UNMISS). The mandate explicitly "*Encourages* the Secretary-General to explore ideas in the independent report of the Senior Advisory Group on Civilian Capacity in the Aftermath of Conflict that could be implemented in the Republic of South Sudan."[9] Concurrently, the g7+ was established, gathering a group of 19 (now 20) countries that had experienced conflict, including South Sudan. These countries called for a new model of partnership between fragile and conflict-affected countries and their development partners, with the emphasis on national ownership, using national systems and following a common plan. The call for stronger national ownership and focusing on developing core governmental capacities was also reflected in a World Bank report, *Conflict, Security and Development;*[10] the civilian capacity reform process in the UN; the development of post-2015 development goals; and the "Peacebuilding and Statebuilding Goals" of the g7+.[11]

Various initiatives were pursued, including new modalities to recruit GPP into the UN system; establishing memoranda of understanding

114   *John Karlsrud and Lotte Vermeij*

for receiving assistance from seconded technical teams; attempting to increase procurement from national service providers; and an ambitious triangular cooperation program, facilitated by the Intergovernmental Authority on Development (IGAD).

The IGAD initiative provided 199 civil service support officers (CSSOs) to South Sudan in the first phase (2012–14).[12] These were twinned with counterparts across many ministries and sectors, to enable rapid development of core government capacity in a coaching and mentoring scheme. These CSSOs came from the civil services of Ethiopia, Kenya, and Uganda and were seconded for two-year terms. This initiative resonated well with the UN civilian capacity reform process and with the calls for greater use of regional capacity and more flexible and bottom-up approaches in supporting countries emerging from conflict.[13]

Diana Felix da Costa, Søren Vester Haldrup, John Karlsrud, Frederik Rosén, and Kristoffer Nilaus Tarp argue that the IGAD initiative was promising as a new and potentially innovative model of triangular cooperation for capacity development for four reasons. First, it provides a model of large-scale support to rapid capacity development in core government functions. Second, the use of regional capacity to a certain degree mitigates the potential for resentment when external experts are brought into capacity-poor environments. Third, the program already shows some evidence of impact on core practices. Finally, there seems to be strong ownership of the program at central levels of the South Sudanese government and among many of the twins.[14]

However, with a sudden upsurge in violence at the end of 2013, much of the progress made since 2011 seemed lost, and the future remains uncertain.

CAPMATCH

In order to work towards better partnerships and an increase of civilian capacity deployments, the UN civilian capacities team officially launched "CAPMATCH" on 21 September 2012 as a self-service online platform aimed at matching civilian capacity needs and offers from various countries and organizations. Focusing on the five areas identified as crucial capacity gaps for countries emerging from conflict or crisis—safety and security, justice, inclusive political processes, core government functionality, and economic revitalization—CAPMATCH was established "to better match the demand and supply of specialised civilian capacities for countries emerging from conflict."[15]

Owned and monitored by the CIVCAP team, the CAPMATCH pilot aimed to address the critical shortage of capacities needed to

The UN civilian capacity initiative 115

enable the transformation of institutions and secure sustainable peace. It would go about this by providing a platform for governments and organizations, where they could register to request/provide capacities. Such capacities might include experience in supporting other countries abroad, as well as domestic experiences of reform. Based on the principle of equal partnership, CAPMATCH would then offer one or more possible matches to facilitate the exchange of expertise and experience between countries, governments, and civil society. However, once potential matches were identified, it would remain the responsibility of the governments/organizations themselves to establish contact with the other entity. These countries and organizations would use their own selection and deployment processes and determine the terms of their cooperation themselves. As such, CAPMATCH was meant as an information tool, not a recruitment or selection mechanism.

Outreach efforts by the CIVCAP team through the CAPMATCH platform resulted in the engagement of 50 entities from member states, 69 percent of which were from the Global South. Some 85 percent of the requests came from UN missions and lead departments at UN Headquarters. The CAPMATCH pilot resulted in deployments of civilian experts from Iraq, Liberia, Rwanda, Senegal, Sierra Leone, and Sweden to missions in South Sudan, Liberia, Côte d'Ivoire, and Yemen, as well as nominations for GPPs by Croatia, Egypt, and Turkey for highly specialized institution-building expertise in justice and corrections.[16]

Unfortunately, CAPMATCH also encountered various challenges during its implementation phase. Countries and organizations were not aware of the platform and had to be encouraged to register. Although it was meant to serve as a self-service online platform, the outreach process proved rather labor intensive for the CIVCAP team. Not only was follow-up by the team necessary to establish contact between providers and requesters of civilian capacities, but it had to manage differences in how civilian capacities were requested and provided. The CIVCAP team thus had to work closely with member states in identifying suitable expertise and responding to questions regarding needs. Additionally, member states also identified a range of challenges related to their internal processes, particularly those states that had no tradition of providing civilian capacities through the UN. Still, "the work of the independent civilian capacities network, which brought together Brazil, China, Egypt, India, Indonesia, Norway, South Africa, Russia and Turkey for a series of meetings in Bali, Indonesia, Brasilia, Moscow and Oslo, has helped to clarify those challenges, as seen by Member States."[17]

116 *John Karlsrud and Lotte Vermeij*

Efforts to overcome these challenges and engagement that could guarantee a long-term, sustainable relationship to enable deployments were well received by member states. Drawing on the lessons learned from the CAPMATCH pilot, the idea of automated matching was discarded. It was decided that outreach efforts at headquarters to broaden and deepen the pool of civilian capacities should be strengthened instead.

The CIVCAP initiative: results, lessons learned, and the way forward

In January 2014 the Secretary-General's final stand-alone report on civilian capacity in the aftermath of conflict was issued. This report highlighted results achieved since the inception of the CIVCAP initiative; it also underlined lessons learned, and identified remaining challenges and a way forward. Moreover, the report addressed issues that had been raised by member states. While stating that the CIVCAP team would be disbanded by June 2014, the report emphasized that cross-cutting efforts aimed at improving UN support to capacity building in countries emerging from conflict would continue. The work of the CIVCAP initiative would be incorporated and mainstreamed within existing structures and business processes without requiring extra resources, allowing the promotion of effective civilian capacity in the aftermath of conflict to remain a priority across the UN system.

Results

The evaluation of the CIVCAP initiative found that progress had been made through policy frameworks and tools that allowed the UN to provide increasingly effective support to institution building, as well as improved institutional arrangements for internal coherence. These effects were also evident in the field. Furthermore, the UN had provided support and achieved significant improvements in the performance of national institutions in Côte d'Ivoire, Liberia, Sierra Leone, Somalia, and Timor-Leste over the previous two years. Within these countries, the UN had mainly engaged with sectors such as electoral and parliamentary institutions, justice and corrections, local and central government, and police as well as civil society. Particularly good progress had been made in the areas of police, justice, and corrections, with ongoing efforts in the areas of core government functionality and inclusive political processes. However, economic revitalization proved a particularly challenging area, and fewer goals had been achieved in that field, the 2014 report noted.[18]

The UN civilian capacity initiative 117

As stated in earlier reports on civilian capacities, nimble processes are a requirement for the success of effective outreach and deployment of expertise. To this end, guidelines have been developed to enhance access to specialized expertise from member states and thus the utilization of GPP. Concerning partnerships, progress has been made in collaboration with the African Union, the League of Arab States, the Organisation for Economic Co-operation and Development, and the World Bank. Still, although progress has been achieved in certain areas and potential has been demonstrated, much remains to be done, and further consolidation of the efforts made through the CIVCAP initiative is needed. Looking back at the two-year working period of the CIVCAP initiative, various lessons learned can be identified.

On the whole, the initiative bears evidence of the impact of the establishment of the UN PBA. The CIVCAP reform process was initiated by the Secretary-General's report on peacebuilding in 2009, highlighting the important role that civilians play in peacebuilding activities. The subsequent reform process has shown the increasing importance of the Secretary-General's reports on peacebuilding, and their ability to highlight gaps and muster resources and attention of the member states to deal with them.

Lessons learned

The first lesson learned from the CIVCAP initiative experience is that support to institution building in post-conflict settings must be improved further, and grounded in national ownership. This means that efforts to enhance national ownership should be based on a clear understanding of the continuous need to align with national decision-making cycles and priorities. These processes require national commitment and are often lengthy, to which the UN will have to pace itself and sequence its support accordingly. That said, rapid confidence building is essential, and in order to maintain political momentum, international support must enable national institutions to show early and visible results. During transitions, this support may take the form of timely advice, modest but prompt financial assistance, and the adaptation of program delivery in the field to demonstrate the evolving role of national institutions. Furthermore, institution building requires access to expertise as well as early and sustained financial support. During the lengthy process, the UN Secretariat departments and agencies, as well as its funds and programs, should combine their complementary strengths in order to improve UN support to the political and technical process in these contexts. This in turn calls for better-integrated efforts.

118 *John Karlsrud and Lotte Vermeij*

Second, the pool of civilian expertise available for peacebuilding should be broadened and deepened further. To achieve this, the UN will have to reach out to member states, including those of the Global South. However, as shown by the CAPMATCH pilot, the UN needs a certain amount of resources and effort to engage in close partnerships with member states. In particular, this may require additional investments when establishing partnerships with countries from the Global South, as their expertise, although valuable, may not be readily available, due to lack of sufficiently developed domestic systems that can make their experiences easily accessible to others. Other challenges in this area were faced during the CAPMATCH pilot, as noted above. As a result, the idea of automated matching has now been discarded: outreach efforts at UN Headquarters to broaden and deepen the pool of civilian capacities are to be strengthened instead. These efforts will focus on gender-related challenges, requiring an enhancement of the pool of civilian capacities that can assist national institution-building initiatives to address gender challenges in post-conflict situations.

In addition, efforts will be made to increase the availability of female protection advisors in peacekeeping missions and gender expertise, and to incorporate them in mission management as well as integrated assessment and planning. However, these initiatives are constrained by the circumstance that UN units which perform outreach are already significantly overstretched. The intention is therefore for the Department of Field Support to link future outreach activities to a strengthened workforce planning approach, in order to identify critical gaps and match them with suitable candidates. To broaden and deepen the pool of civilian capacities further, member states are encouraged to provide additional technical and financial support aimed at facilitating increased outreach to the Global South.

The third lesson learned from the CIVCAP initiative is that regional, South-South and triangular cooperation should be enhanced further, as well as partnerships with international financial institutions. As a key element of post-conflict institution building, triangular cooperation implies that the UN delivers only a proportion of the support needed for national institutions in affected areas. Successful examples of South-South or triangular cooperation can already be seen. Among the important lessons learned from such experiences are the following:

- Fragile countries and countries emerging from conflict have a clear willingness to engage and strengthen capacity to take active part in the development of capacity development strategies, as evidenced by the g7+ initiative.

The UN civilian capacity initiative   119

- South-South and triangular cooperation can enable more relevant support and strengthen ownership in the host country, not least on the individual level where capacity is being built on a day-to-day basis.
- These approaches can also be significantly less expensive and more sustainable than fly-in/fly-out Northern expert approaches.
- Cooperation should focus on core government and upstream institutions on a program or strategic level, including the national ministries of finance, planning, justice, infrastructure and health, and the central bank. Here it is important to bear in mind the political sensitivities of seconding experts from neighboring states to twin with and mentor officials in key positions.

Implications for the Peacebuilding Architecture

The approaches taken by Northern and Southern providers during such initiatives are evolving into complementary approaches and can prove increasingly productive, if coordinated well.[19] Responding to requests from member states and challenges indicated earlier, the UN will aim to provide increasingly structured support to member states to improve triangular and South-South cooperation. This support may take the form of country-level support, outreach to member states on post-conflict needs and ways of dealing with these, documentation of experiences and exchange of these, and the development of standard operational instruments. UNDP will play a vital role in supporting these developments, as well as the Peacebuilding Support Office through the Peacebuilding Fund.

Additionally, it is essential to develop partnerships with international financial institutions such as the World Bank, to further utilize the complementarity and comparative advantages of the UN and such institutions. Plans are also being developed to deepen partnerships with organizations such as the African Development Bank and the European Union.

Third, there is significant interest in deepening partnerships with regional organizations such as the League of Arab States and the African Union. Lastly, opportunities for sub-regional partnerships should be explored further, in order to utilize their ability to build cross-border institutional trust and to link regional assistance between countries. The regional organizations can lead such initiatives, with the support and active involvement of intergovernmental bodies, bilateral donors, and the UN through the Peacebuilding Commission.[20]

120   *John Karlsrud and Lotte Vermeij*

Future directions

Today the UN is involved in nationally owned institution-building efforts in highly complex transition situations, like those in Afghanistan, the Democratic Republic of the Congo, Haiti, Iraq, Libya, Mali, Somalia, South Sudan, and Yemen. As to future directions, the continued need to strengthen the support to institution building in these areas has been stressed. When investing in concerted efforts to tackle the challenges faced, it is of utmost importance to take into account lessons learned. In order to work towards more successful and sustainable institution-building results in the field, the UN will need to work through a more coherent and systematic response closely linked in with national priorities as well as international partners. This will require clear accountability within the UN system: the task must be incorporated into existing structures and business processes, to maintain the momentum established by the CIVCAP initiative between 2012 and 2014. These efforts will focus on three areas in particular:

1 Improved support to institution building grounded in national ownership.
2 Broadening and deepening the pool of civilian expertise for peacebuilding.
3 Enhancing regional, South-South, and triangular cooperation.

The need to consolidate and strengthen support, as well as the potential to deliver results, has been demonstrated in these three areas, making them key priorities. The application of lessons learned from the CIVCAP initiative, the continuation of dialogues established with partners, as well as sustained support by member states: these will be essential building blocks in the work towards closer collaboration in institution building in the aftermath of conflict.

Indeed, the end of the CIVCAP initiative could mark the "beginning of a concerted effort across the United Nations system, to apply key lessons on institution-building and deepen our partnerships with member states and other key actors."[21] That said, in addition to its efforts to improve the impact of institution building, the UN will also continue to provide basic security and support for political settlements through peacekeeping missions as well as special political missions. These aspects are seen as complementary: a stable political situation is needed in order to build national institutions, and vice versa.

The UN civilian capacity initiative 121

Conclusions and recommendations

The CIVCAP reform process can be seen as part of a larger change process that has been ongoing in the UN system since Secretary-General Boutros Boutros-Ghali issued "An Agenda for Peace" in 1992.[22] With the report, the UN focused on the longer-term institutional and peacebuilding challenges that were necessary to deal with in order to secure lasting peace, and as a consequence, civilian expertise would be in increasing demand over the next two decades. The establishment of the peacebuilding architecture in 2005 was in recognition of the lack of attention to countries that emerged from conflict and still required significant support to build their institutions to secure lasting peace, but which received diminishing attention as they were no longer on the UN Security Council agenda after the departure of a UN peacekeeping mission.

Civilian capacities are central to the support of which countries in transition are in dire need, and the CIVCAP reform sought to further the change processes that had been ongoing in the UN system for two decades. However, while the initial results and take-up of issues were disappointing, remnants of the CIVCAP reform agenda are being included in other, more recent, and larger reform efforts. In 2015, a high-level independent panel on peace operations, nominated by Secretary-General Ban Ki-moon, delivered its report, underscoring the need for a more field-oriented system that could enable the UN to rapidly deploy the expertise demanded.[23]

In conclusion, then, for lasting reform and impact the UN system should:

- increase the use of GPP from a representative cross-section of member states to UN peace operations and consider these as CCCs, including engineering teams, ICT experts, sexual exploitation and abuse teams, human rights monitors, judicial experts, and organized crime and terrorism experts;
- focus on and support triangular and South-South cooperation initiatives, and implement these where possible through GPP and CCC arrangements;
- support efforts to remove artificial barriers between peacekeeping and special political missions, recognizing that the challenges on the ground are complex and interconnected;
- increase cooperation between the UNDP, BCPR and DPKO/DPA at UN Headquarters; and
- continue with increased cooperation within the UN and with the World Bank and other international organizations at the field level.

122 *John Karlsrud and Lotte Vermeij*

Notes

1 United Nations, "Progress Report of the Secretary-General on Peace-building in the Immediate Aftermath of Conflict," UN doc. A/64/866-S/2010/386, 16 July 2010, 20.
2 UN, "Peacebuilding in the Immediate Aftermath of Conflict," Report of the Secretary-General, UN doc. A/63/881-S/2009/304, 11 June 2009.
3 Senior Advisory Group led by Jean-Marie Guéhenno, "Civilian Capacity in the Aftermath of Conflict: Independent Report of the Senior Advisory Group," UN doc. A/65/747-S/2011/85, 22 February 2011.
4 UN, "Civilian Capacities in the Aftermath of Conflict: Report of the Secretary-General," UN doc. A/66/311–S/2011/527, 19 August 2011.
5 The CIVCAP Steering Committee consisted of Susana Malcorra, chef de cabinet and chairperson; Jeffrey Feltman, under-Secretary-General (USG) of the Department of Political Affairs; Herve Ladsous, USG of the Department of Peacekeeping Operations; Bob Orr, ASG of the Executive Office of the Secretary-General; Yukio Takasu, USG of the Department of Management; Valerie Amos, USG of the Office for the Coordination of Humanitarian Affairs; Helen Clark, chairperson of the UN Development Group; Judy Cheng-Hopkins, ASG of the Peacebuilding Support Office; and Won-Soo Kim, ASG of Change Management.
6 UN, "Civilian Capacities: Building National Institutions in the Aftermath of Conflict," www.civcapreview.org.
7 UN, "Civilian Capacities: Building National Institutions in the Aftermath of Conflict."
8 UN, "Civilian Capacities: Building National Institutions in the Aftermath of Conflict."
9 Security Council, UN doc. S/RES/1996, 8 July 2011, para. 21.
10 World Bank, *Conflict, Security and Development* (Washington, DC: World Bank, 2010).
11 For more information, see g7+, www.g7plus.org.
12 The IGAD program was supported by UNDP and financed by Norway.
13 Cedric de Coning, John Karlsrud, and Ingrid Marie Breidlid, "Turning to the South: Civilian Capacity in the Aftermath of Conflict," *Global Governance* 19, no. 4 (2013): 135–52.
14 Diana Felix da Costa, Søren Vester Haldrup, John Karlsrud, Frederik Rosén, and Kristoffer Nilaus Tarp, *Triangular Co-operation for Government Capacity Development in South Sudan* (Oslo: Norwegian Peacebuilding Resource Centre (NOREF), 2013).
15 CAPMATCH, "Global Marketplace for Civilian Capacities," capmatch. dfs.un.org/CapMatch/Home/Index; and Civilian Capacities, "Building National Institutions in the Aftermath of Conflict," www.civcapreview.org.
16 UN, "Civilian Capacity in the Aftermath of Conflict: Report of the Secretary-General," UN doc. A/68/696-S/2014/5, 6 January 2014.
17 UN, "Civilian Capacity in the Aftermath of Conflict," 15.
18 UN, "Civilian Capacity in the Aftermath of Conflict."
19 UN, *Institution-building in Post-Conflict and Post-Crisis Situations: Scaling up South–South and Triangular Cooperation* (New York: United Nations Civilian Capacity Initiative, 2013).
20 UN, "Civilian Capacity in the Aftermath of Conflict."

The UN civilian capacity initiative 123

21 UN, "Civilian Capacity in the Aftermath of Conflict," 21.
22 Boutros Boutros-Ghali, "An Agenda for Peace: Preventive Diplomacy, Peacemaking, and Peace-keeping: Report of the Secretary-General Pursuant to the Statement Adopted by the Summit Meeting of the Security Council on 31 January 1992," UN doc. A/47/277-S/24111, United Nations, 17 June 1992.
23 UN, "Report of the High-level Independent Panel on Peace Operations on Uniting our Strengths for Peace: Politics, Partnership and People," UN doc. A/70/95-S/2015/446, 17 June 2015.

Part IV

Country-specific impact of the Peacebuilding Architecture

7 The impact of the Peacebuilding Architecture in Burundi

Susanna Campbell, Josiah Marineau, Tracy Dexter, Michael Findley, Stephanie Hofmann and Daniel Walker

- Context of the PBF in Burundi
- Period I: deadlock in parliament
- Period II: deadlock in negotiations with the FNL
- Period III: 2010 election period
- Period IV: the consolidation of political power in the post-2010 phase
- Analysis of PBF oversight, guidance, support, and implementation mechanisms and instruments
- The UN Peacebuilding Commission
- The UN Peacebuilding Support Office
- Country-based mechanisms
- Conclusions and recommendations

Along with Sierra Leone, Burundi was one of the first two countries placed on the agenda of the Peacebuilding Commission (PBC). It was also one of the largest recipients of support from the United Nations (UN) Peacebuilding Fund (PBF), which provided a total of US$49 million between 2006 and 2013 in two tranches.[1] The civil war in Burundi had begun in 1993; the transition out of war officially began with the signing of the Arusha Peace and Reconciliation Agreement in August 2000. The main political parties had agreed to peace, but the rebel groups were not included in the peace agreement; they continued to engage in open combat with the Burundian Army.

The involvement of the UN Peacebuilding Architecture (PBA) in Burundi came just as the country seemed finally to be emerging from war. Even though one rebel group remained outside the country's political institutions, the peaceful election of Burundi's main rebel leader as the new president in 2005 made Burundians feel as if the war might actually end.[2] The selection of Burundi as one of the first PBC countries signaled the UN's strong commitment to preventing it from

128 *Susanna Campbell et al.*

backsliding into war, serving as a true success story for international peacebuilding. Indeed, the seven-year relationship between Burundi and the PBA did help to advance Burundi's post-war transition, although not without significant difficulty. Part of the difficulty derived from the lack of guidance and support inherent in pilot initiatives, leading UN staff in Burundi and key Burundian officials to play a key role in determining what the PBA looked like at the country level, and teaching the UN Peacebuilding Support Office (PBSO) many core lessons as they went along.

Between 2007 and 2010, the PBF allocated its first tranche of funding to Burundi, giving the UN system $35 million to support core peacebuilding priorities selected by the UN and the Burundian government. These funds made it possible for the UN Integrated Office in Burundi (BINUB)—which integrated the entire UN Country Team (UNCT) under the political leadership of the executive representative of the Secretary-General (ERSG)—to carry out innovative peacebuilding projects that fulfilled aspects of its Security Council mandate, which BINUB may not otherwise have been able to achieve.[3] However, most of the activities that the PBF supported during this first tranche were ineffective, and in some cases even did harm.

The second tranche of PBF funding to Burundi, $9.2 million allocated in 2011, supported a more standard UN structure: the Security Council-mandated mission focused on high-level political processes and analyses, interfacing with the PBC, while the UNCT managed and supervised operational activities, implementing the PBF-funded projects. This standard UN structure had a negative effect on the peacebuilding activities supported by the second tranche of PBF funding. Unlike several of the projects supported by the first tranche, projects under the second were not designed to deal with the specific causes of conflict and peace in Burundi. Instead, they focused on apolitical development, and humanitarian and early recovery activities that the UN carried out in non-conflict-affected countries.

We argue that the poor quality of many of the projects funded by the PBF in Burundi was due, in part, to the lack of knowledge among UN staff of how to design or implement high-quality peacebuilding activities. Neither the headquarters of the UN organizations receiving PBF funds (Recipient UN Organizations, or RUNOs) nor the PBSO, which manages the PBF, could ensure that peacebuilding capacity existed within the teams receiving PBF funding. Many UN organizations viewed support from the PBF as simply another funding source for largely apolitical humanitarian, early recovery, or development activities.

The impact of the PBA in Burundi 129

This chapter is based on an impact evaluation of PBF and PBC support to Burundi's post-war transition between 2007 and 2013.[4] Building on the 2010 evaluation of PBF support to Burundi, conducted by the same lead evaluator, the 13-member research team employed an innovative quasi-experimental research design grounded in a household-level survey of over 250 households from randomly sampled *collines*, with and without PBF involvement, over 165 semi-structured interviews, 90 of which are drawn from the randomly sampled *collines*, as well as a detailed document review.[5]

Context of the PBF in Burundi

The broader institutional environment within which the PBF projects operated had an important, if sometimes indirect, influence on the PBF portfolio. In particular, relations between the Burundian government and the UN were strained throughout the period of PBA involvement. Between 2006 and 2013, the Burundian government requested that three actual and interim heads of the UN missions to Burundi quit their positions and leave the country. It required the UN to reduce the size and scale of its mission from a large peacekeeping mission, the UN Operation in Burundi (ONUB, 2004–06), to a smaller integrated mission without peacekeepers, BINUB (2007–10), then to a still smaller mission, the UN Office in Burundi (BNUB) (2011–14), and then to the final withdrawal of the mission at the end of 2014. These negotiations between the UN and the Burundian government about the future of the various UN missions in the country formed the subtext of the PBF's decision-making process in Burundi.

Period I: deadlock in parliament

One of the first projects funded by the PBF, the Cadre de Dialogue, was a strategic entry point for the PBF and created space for dialogue among key political actors. The Conseil National Pour la Défense de la Démocratie—Forces pour la Défense de la Démocratie (CNDD-FDD) had been the governing party in Burundi since winning both the presidency and a majority in the National Assembly in the 2005 elections. However, internal divisions within the CNDD-FDD led to a split in 2007, resulting in the party losing its majority in parliament.

That in turn led to a deadlock for much of 2007, preventing the government from passing and enacting crucial legislation. The Cadre de Dialogue contributed to unblocking the deadlock in parliament. Building on the numerous negotiation and mediation efforts led by

130   *Susanna Campbell et al.*

various states, the UN, individuals, and nongovernmental organizations (NGOs) since the outbreak of the war in 1996, the Cadre de Dialogue encouraged a culture of dialogue between political actors and civil society.

Several of the security-sector projects were also highly relevant to the overall political and security context. The PBF support to the Burundian Armed Forces (FDN) was based on a clear strategy developed by the latter which included three PBF projects: the Military Barracks Project, the Morale-Building Project, and the Displaced Families Project. All three targeted critical areas of reform for the military. In particular, they helped to reduce incidents of violence and increase intergroup social cohesion in the Burundian military, which had recently integrated former rebels into its ranks. Our survey revealed that the population felt much more secure than it did prior to the PBF interventions.[6] Among the households surveyed, 62 percent noted that the decrease in the number of active combatants in the communities helped to create a greater sense of security.

Interventions aimed at supporting the reform of the National Intelligence Service (SNR) and the Burundian police were less successful. The project that focused on training of the SNR, a body infamous for torture and other human rights abuses, succeeded in creating temporary openness and accountability, but did not initiate any sustainable reform. The police project sought to increase the capacity, positive visibility, and professionalism of the police, but then distributed poor-quality uniforms to the police, which led to a great deal of negative publicity and public accusations of corruption. The project eventually procured new high-quality uniforms, a point considered important for ongoing efforts to professionalize the police, but much of the equipment provided by the project, such as cars and radios, has since fallen into disrepair. Despite the efforts at professionalization, significant problems have remained. Our survey showed that Burundians view the police as a potential threat to their personal security, rather than a clear guarantor of it.

Period II: deadlock in negotiations with the FNL

The PBF also contributed to the completion of the peace process with the Forces pour la Libération Nationale (FNL) in 2009. This had been the last rebel group to enter negotiations with the government and, until 2009, had failed to implement a 2006 ceasefire agreement. The PBF helped to unblock a 2009 impasse in the negotiations with the FNL by supporting facilitation efforts and funding the demobilization of 11,000 "adults associated with the movement" who were not

The impact of the PBA in Burundi 131

included in the official demobilization program. The demobilization of the "associated adults" allowed the FNL to transform into a political party and participate in the 2010 elections.

The PBF also supported several projects in the area of justice and rule of law during this period. In the Transitional Justice project, the PBF funded a countrywide consultation process on Burundi's transitional justice mechanisms, seeking to maintain attention on them in a context where the government was unwilling to create them. The other justice projects focused on the construction of local tribunals as well as clearing backlogged cases in courts. Both these projects were part of ongoing judicial reform processes, but did not provide ideal entry points for the PBF as they failed to address many legal and political barriers to the independence and effectiveness of the judiciary.

Period III: 2010 election period

The PBF constructively contributed to the period surrounding the 2010 election by providing crucial funding for organizing the elections and promoting national dialogue. PBF election funding made it possible to distribute high-quality ballots to areas that had not received them and to provide ID cards to women, enabling greater participation. It also promoted national dialogue by establishing the Permanent Forum for Political Parties, an offshoot of the Cadre de Dialogue, which sought to facilitate the resolution of conflicts among the political parties. Despite the demobilization of the FNL, political violence between FNL and CNDD-FDD supporters continued.[7] In particular, youth wings of the parties, like that of the CNDD-FDD, Imbonerakure, contributed to the growing political violence.[8] Important dialogue efforts were supported by the PBF and others, but our interviews and surveys showed that Burundians considered the behavior of the political class, and its manipulation of susceptible youth, to be one of the greatest threats to their security, and the main potential cause of future violence.

Other governance initiatives that the PBF supported were less well targeted and less timely, and some were poorly implemented. The anti-corruption project failed to deal with the legal barriers to the proper functioning of anti-corruption and judicial institutions because the government was not ready to address these legal issues. The project could not therefore make progress towards its aims, which depended on a legal framework that the government was not willing to put in place. Our survey showed that people saw corruption as a major problem at the *colline* level, and one that may be increasing, especially in those *collines* that received PBF funding.

132 Susanna Campbell et al.

The youth project, women's project, and the small business project were plagued by implementation problems and failed to make any obvious contribution to the socioeconomic situation among target groups, often bringing "peace disappointments" rather than peace dividends. Staff and partners implementing the youth and women's projects argued that the allotted timeframe was far too short for them to spend the large budgets allocated to these projects, and the quality of the programs suffered. Furthermore, the method employed to identify the youth and women who would benefit was not transparent, leading to claims of corruption and favoritism.

Period IV: the consolidation of political power in the post-2010 phase

Rather than deepening liberal democracy, the CNDD-FDD victory in the 2010 elections led to three developments that undermined the consolidation of democracy. First, most of the opposition was absent from government, and several opposition leaders fled the country in order to avoid arrest.[9] Second, political violence continued, including an egregious act with possible political origins—the September 2011 attack on a bar in Gatumba, with over 30 people killed. Finally, a new draft constitution bill submitted by the CNDD-FDD in late 2013 threatened to revise the power-sharing provisions of the constitution that had helped to secure peace.[10]

During this period, the last project funded by PBF I—the first tranche of PBF support to Burundi—was finally implemented. The PBF supported the creation of the National Independent Commission for Human Rights (CNIDH), but rather than simply providing the physical infrastructure and cars that the CNIDH needed, it withheld funding from the government until it passed a law that would allow the commission to function in a truly independent fashion. It was set up in 2011 and carries out human rights investigations (including of extrajudicial executions) throughout the country, and has been seen as an important protector of human rights in a context where these rights are repeatedly violated.

The CNDD-FDD's consolidation of power and the increase in political violence coincided with the disbursement of the second tranche of PBF funding to Burundi in 2011. Unlike the first, which focused primarily on political, security, legal, and human rights institutions based in Bujumbura, the second tranche sought to integrate former combatants, refugees and internally displaced persons at the community level in Cibitoke, Bubanza, and Bujumbura Rurale, supporting the Burundian government's national reintegration plan.

The reintegration efforts have had mixed results. On the one hand, in combination with projects supported by other donors, they seem to have contributed to building positive intergroup social cohesion in communities that had been torn apart by the war. Our survey shows that 96 percent of all respondents perceive improvements in social cohesion, especially due to local associations, which the project supported, and the involvement of local authorities. The project also gave individuals who were able to form productive local associations new economic opportunities and useful training that helped some to advance in their professions (such as welding, tailoring, farming, cooking).

In other places, however, and despite the increased involvement of local administrators, PBF II activities—those involving the second tranche of PBF support to Burundi—did not alter how social services were delivered, nor did they make a clearly sustainable improvement in the financial situation of many beneficiaries. Many of those whom we interviewed complained that the project was too short to achieve its intended aims. They argued that sustainable social cohesion, much less real trust, could not be built in only three to six months. They also reported that even though they were now members of associations and had new job skills, there was no funding to ensure that these associations would continue to be profitable or that they could sustain the social cohesion created within their associations.

A major problem with PBF II was that funding went to fairly standard early recovery or humanitarian activities on the part of the six implementing UN agencies. They lacked sensitivity to the unique nature of peacebuilding projects, which requires implementing agencies to be highly attuned to the power dynamics of the contexts in which they operate, questioning their influence on those contexts, and adjusting their approach and overall "theory of change" as the context and its dynamics change.[11] Also lacking was a clear plan for sustaining the effect of their projects, threatening again to turn peace dividends into disappointments. In two out of the 13 *collines* where we conducted interviews, activities that the PBF II supported even had clearly negative effects on the intended beneficiaries because of local-level corruption and poor oversight and implementation by the UN.

Analysis of PBF oversight, guidance, support, and implementation mechanisms and instruments

There have been important innovations and professionalization of the mechanisms that oversee, guide, and support the implementation of the PBF portfolio in Burundi. Innovations that made a particular

134 *Susanna Campbell et al.*

contribution to peace consolidation were: 1 the creation of joint project units in BINUB that integrated political, peacebuilding programmatic, and local knowledge; 2 the involvement of high-level officials in BINUB and BNUB in several innovative dialogue- and security-focused projects, effectively linking the political and the operational; 3 the creation of Technical Follow-up Committees (TFCs) for PBF I projects that included a broad range of stakeholders (for example, government, civil society, and donors); and 4 the establishment of innovative accountability mechanisms in several projects that enabled participants and observers to assess regularly whether the project was progressing as planned and to propose alterations to project aims and implementation.

Once PBF II was underway, these innovations were largely forgotten or dismantled. A new TFC and Coordination Cell was established, which helped to monitor activities and created linkages among the six UN organizations that were implementing the various PBF II activities. These mechanisms lacked peacebuilding or monitoring techniques and did not seem to encourage RUNOs to reflect regularly on whether their activities were achieving the desired outcomes at the community level. Yet field-level implementation, accountability, and monitoring mechanisms are crucial components of peacebuilding projects and help to determine whether the peacebuilding activity remains relevant to the evolving context that it is intended to influence.

One problem is that the PBF is based on the assumption that the RUNOs have the capacity for high-quality peacebuilding projects and monitoring, and that the Joint Steering Committee (JSC, which monitors implementation of the peacebuilding priority plan for the country) has the time and resources to oversee their projects, ensure that they are in line with the peacebuilding priority plan, and provide additional assurance that implementation is on track. Our assessment indicates significant ruptures in this accountability and capacity chain, with negative impacts on PBF-funded activities. The innovative mechanisms mentioned above helped to fill some of these gaps, but a more systemic and sustainable solution is needed. We now examine each of the oversight and guidance mechanisms, assessing their strengths and weaknesses in the Burundian context.

The UN Peacebuilding Commission

The UN PBA was established to "help countries build sustainable peace and prevent relapse into violent conflict."[12] Our research in Burundi showed that the PBC played an important role in sustaining

The impact of the PBA in Burundi   135

the attention of the international donor community on Burundi and serving as a key interlocutor between interested Western states and the Burundian government. The influence of the PBC in Burundi seemed to rely primarily on the work of the chair of its Country-Specific Configuration (CSC), and the support that he received from the PBSO, his government, and key partnerships with other members of the CSC— which is the body in the PBC that is charged with closely following the situation in Burundi.[13]

In several cases, the CSC chair worked very closely with the UN mission in the country and implemented a complementary strategy that influenced how and what peacebuilding priorities were selected. The chair also helped to dismantle key roadblocks in Burundi's peacebuilding process, raised key political concerns of the international community directly with the government, discussed major concerns of the government directly with the international community, held regular exchanges with civil society, and helped to encourage donors to continue to contribute funds to Burundi. Within the design of the PBA, one of the major advantages of a CSC chair is that this person is a representative of a member state and is therefore able to speak with other governments, donors, and other actors with different authority from an international bureaucrat. In addition, if the CSC chair is declared persona non grata (PNG) by the host government and banned from serving as chair, he or she does not lose their "day job." This makes it possible for the chair to take more political risks in relations with the host government, perhaps applying more direct political pressure than the special representative of the Secretary-General (SRSG) or other UN staff member whose career would probably suffer if the chair were declared PNG by the host government.

In Burundi, in part because of the frequency with which top UN staff have been declared PNG, the role of the CSC chair seems to have been particularly important. The chair seems to operate largely as an individual, backed by the support team in the UN and the government. The frequency of PBC CSC meetings for Burundi gradually declined, and sources report that over time meetings rarely took place at the ambassadorial level.[14] Countries on the PBC's agenda are often not politically important for many PBC members; as a result, it seems that the original idea of the PBC being an intergovernmental body that can prevent post-conflict countries from falling back into war has been whittled down to one important and potentially powerful position. This position is held by one international diplomat and relies on this individual's skills and commitment, and the guidance and support received from the PBSO and from his or her government. The broader

136 *Susanna Campbell et al.*

PBC served as a venue for various actors to voice their concerns, but the major leverage of the PBC in Burundi came in the form of the CSC chair and that person's willingness and ability to play a key diplomatic and fundraising role. CSC chairs also often mobilized funding from their own governments (for example, Japan, Norway, and Sweden) even if these had not been traditional aid partners of Burundi.

The UN Peacebuilding Support Office

One of the primary functions of the PBSO is to "administer the Peacebuilding Fund and help to raise funds for it."[15] It works in close collaboration with the UN Development Programme's (UNDP) Multi-Partner Trust Fund Office (MPTF-O), which "serves as the Administrative Agent of the PBF and is responsible for the receipt of donor contributions, transfer of funds to Recipient UN Organizations, consolidation of narrative and financial reports and their submission to PBSO and PBF donors."[16]

The PBSO and the MPTF-O are the primary accountability agents for the PBF at UN Headquarters. The PBSO has a small team responsible for administering the PBF and supporting RUNOs and JSCs for all 23 countries that receive PBF funding. Having such a relatively small team, the PBSO relies on the staff skills, accountability procedures, and procurement mechanisms of the RUNOs to design, implement, and monitor high-quality peacebuilding projects, and on the capacity of the JSC to monitor the contribution of these projects to the Peacebuilding Priority Plan. That has proven a major flaw in the design of the PBF.

The PBSO is aware of the implications of its structure and accountability mechanisms, and the link to the overall performance of the fund. For a better success rate of global PBF projects at the local level, the PBSO recognizes that its institutional arrangement requires "a solid capacity at the level of the Joint Steering Committee, Fund users and implementers."[17] The problem is that it is the recipients of funding, and some external parties in-country, that are largely responsible for determining whether they have the capacity to implement their proposed projects and to monitor compliance with the stated objectives.

Unlike many other donors, after the initial approval process of a Peacebuilding Priority Plan and the corresponding projects, the PBSO appears to have relatively little influence on the quality of the projects that they support.[18] Instead, the JSC and the RUNOs are responsible for monitoring the quality and impact of the PBF projects. Prior to the allocation of PBF funds, there is no assessment of the capacity of the JSC or RUNO to oversee or implement peacebuilding projects. During

The impact of the PBA in Burundi   137

the entire period under study in Burundi, there were very few staff members on the JSC or within a RUNO who had training or expertise in peacebuilding project design, implementation, or monitoring. Those projects that did have staff with this skillset were of significantly higher quality than those that did not.

There is also a problem with the information that the PBSO receives about the implementation of the PBF projects and how this information is dealt with. Many difficulties experienced by RUNOs during implementation of PBF activities in Burundi were not mentioned in the reports submitted to the PBSO. Such issues were too politically sensitive in relation to the government, or staff were wary of reporting them. In addition, the successes or contributions presented in reports to the JSC and PBSO were often not supported by clear evidence. Staff monitored the project inputs and outputs and the overall amount of money spent, but not the contribution to consolidating the peace.

Furthermore, the PBSO did not systematically provide operational guidance to the PBF Secretariat in Burundi, the JSC, or the RUNOs based on the contents of the reports it received. We did not find any examples where the PBSO had requested alterations in ongoing PBF-funded projects in Burundi in response to information in the reports. The situation for the MPTF-O was not significantly different. It received reports showing how money was spent in relation to six general categories. This information was sent directly to the MPTF-O and was not included in the reports sent to the JSC, although it is available on the MPTF-O website. Moreover, RUNOs did not submit financial reports that link actual expenditures to planned activities, making it very difficult for the MPTF-O, the JSC, or the PBSO to assess whether the PBF money was spent as intended or whether the project achieved the intended value for the funding provided.

The PBSO's support to the RUNOs and JSC in Burundi has focused on conflict analysis, the development of the priority plan, helping to ensure the initial buy-in of the Burundian government and some reflection on project design. However, it has largely stayed out of the implementation process. While this is an understandable stance from the perspective of a New York-based office with very few staff, it means that the PBSO has no real assurance that the projects it funds will be relevant, efficient, or effective. The PBSO argues that it is up to the RUNOs to ensure that they have the capacity to implement PBF-funded projects, and that the existence of specific capacity or monitoring mechanisms is not a required condition for receiving PBF funds.

In sum, the complexities of the post-conflict context demand greater political awareness, more feedback and accountability mechanisms,

138 *Susanna Campbell et al.*

more accompaniment (requiring more staff and often more skilled staff), a greater focus on capacity building and the transfer of capacity to national actors, and generally more focus on the program and project implementation process. The PBF should help to ensure that its reporting and support structures, the RUNOs, and the other country-based mechanisms are designed and implemented to deal directly with this context. Because this type of project is more complex and requires more staff attention, there will most likely be a higher staff cost for higher-quality peacebuilding projects, and both the PBF and its donors should be prepared to support this.

Country-based mechanisms

The PBSO works with several key organizations in fund-receiving countries: the JSC and support structures, the RUNOs, and the host government. The JSC is "co-chaired by the Senior UN Representative and a senior government representative ... The JSC monitors the implementation of the Priority Plan, while also approving projects (including project amendments) and assessing programme-wide achievements before the end of each calendar year."[19] The RUNOs implement PBF-funded projects, sometimes in collaboration with international or national NGOs. For both PBF tranches provided to Burundi, the UN established TFCs and a PBF Secretariat to support the JSC.[20]

The mechanisms accompanying the PBF in Burundi served an important consultation and feedback function. With both tranches of PBF support, the JSC served as an important venue for discussing and resolving issues between the UN and the government. However, it was not able to monitor the quality of the projects, instead largely addressing higher-level issues of strategy, priorities, and resource sharing between the government and the UN.

During PBF I, the JSC included the active participation of many members of civil society and donors. It met more frequently and was charged with monitoring the implementation of the PBF projects. JSC membership stayed the same for the PBF II, but attendance and the active inclusion of non-UN and non-government perspectives was much weaker.[21] The community focus of PBF II projects did not seem to be of equal interest to people as the PBF I projects, which had focused on multiple sectors and on higher-level political issues and processes. As a result, during PBF II fewer people in Burundi were aware of its activities, and the JSC members generally seemed much less engaged in the PBF process.

The impact of the PBA in Burundi 139

The most powerful mechanisms that the PBF created were the TFCs and innovative monitoring structures within several projects. When they worked well, the TFCs and several of the monitoring mechanisms served the crucial role of creating regular external accountability for the intermediary outcomes of the PBF interventions and providing information about project progress, with opportunities for reflection on the purpose and effectiveness of the PBF project or activity. This type of information, based on assessments from multiple stakeholders about the contribution to the stated aims, and the space for reflection and critical analysis, are crucial for organizational learning and mid-course correction.[22]

There was an important difference between the TFCs that supported PBF I projects and the TFC that supported those under PBF II. The former were organized around various sectors (like security, human rights, and rule of law) and some included the active participation of civil society members, national NGOs, international donors, and key government officials. These individuals spent their own time and energy in critically assessing the quality of PBF projects and proposing adjustments and alterations to their design and implementation. In several cases, these persons had knowledge and understanding of peacebuilding projects and monitoring which they applied to help improve the design of the PBF projects, setting up innovative monitoring mechanisms within several security and dialogue projects, and helping important mid-course corrections to be made.

While the TFC for PBF II projects had some very active members, it was much smaller and applied less direct pressure on the RUNOs to alter their approach or make mid-course corrections. Furthermore, most of its members did not have significant experience with peacebuilding projects or monitoring and evaluation, and those that did seemed unable to encourage RUNOs to integrate this more effectively into their work. This meant that the TFC and the Coordination and Programme Design Cell monitored activity-level outputs rather than peacebuilding outcomes or contribution.

In sum, during PBF II, the TFC, the RUNOs, and the Coordination and Programme Design Cell helped to gather some important data about the implementation of activities. However, this did not lead to the necessary mid-course corrections when PBF II activities were not achieving the intended goals. These monitoring efforts did not infuse a political or peacebuilding approach into PBF II activities, nor did they address some of the lingering concerns felt by some recipients about the sustainability and catalytic effect of the support provided to local associations.

140 *Susanna Campbell et al.*

Conclusions and recommendations

The PBF was a powerful tool that helped the UN implement innovative peacebuilding projects and, on the whole, made a positive contribution to Burundi's peacebuilding process. Despite the successes, however, our research has shown that systemic problems contributed to low-quality projects which made poor use of PBF funds and sometimes even had negative effects on potential drivers of peace in Burundi. The quality and contribution of PBF-funded projects depended on whether they were implemented by staff with capabilities in peacebuilding project design and monitoring; whether they were supported by innovative feedback mechanisms from a representative group of stakeholders; and whether they had national partners involved in both the concept and the implementation of the activity.

The mechanisms and procedures that the PBSO has established to support PBF projects have focused on the identification of peacebuilding priorities and the selection of projects to achieve these priorities. However, the success of peacebuilding projects is determined by how they interact and engage with the specific context that they are intended to influence. How PBF projects are implemented, and how the original project designs are adapted to fit the context, are at least as important as the selection of the project. Unfortunately, the current mechanisms and capacities available to the UN are not sufficient to support consistently high-quality peacebuilding projects.

To improve the overall quality of PBF projects and programs, we recommend that the core actors involved in the PBF address three systemic problems: the insufficient capacity within RUNOs to design, implement, and monitor high-quality peacebuilding projects; the insufficient support capacity of the PBSO and RUNOs; and that lessons about processes, practices, and mechanisms that support high-quality peacebuilding projects are not transferred from one recipient country to the other, or between country teams in one country. These factors should determine when the PBF decides to stop funding projects in a country (its exit strategy).

Below are recommendations for the PBF's new application guidelines, the next round of PBF support to Burundi, and other countries that receive PBF funding:

1 *Ensure that RUNOs have the capacity to design, implement and monitor high-quality peacebuilding projects.* The PBSO should assess whether the RUNOs have project teams with the proper skillsets, including technical knowledge related to the peacebuilding activity,

The impact of the PBA in Burundi 141

knowledge of the broader political context, local knowledge related to the focus of the project, and expertise in designing, implementing, and monitoring reflective peacebuilding. In turn, RUNOs should ensure they have the capacity to engage high-quality peacebuilding projects before requesting funds. The PBSO should also ensure that procedures and procurement practices enable the organization to hire the necessary staff or consultants, and to procure any necessary goods, without delaying the project. Reporting practices should identify the intermediary outcomes of activities, not simply the outputs and the amount of money spent. Crucially, the country-level leadership of the RUNO should be involved in direct oversight of PBF activities, including by visiting the projects and supporting constructive problem solving when difficulties are encountered.

2   *Ensure that both headquarters and country-based mechanisms accompany the implementation of PBF activities and support critical reflection.* To enable reflective peacebuilding, PBSO should help to create spaces for reflection during the design and implementation process for each PBF project, its contributions and its challenges. The PBSO can do this by accompanying the project's implementation process through regular field missions—attending key JSC meetings, meeting with project staff, visiting project sites, and talking with partners and observers. The PBSO should also inform the senior UN leadership in the country, senior leadership of the RUNOs in the country, the JSC, and the government of their key role in supporting high-quality peacebuilding projects. This will require the PBSO to spend time with each key actor to explain the specific requirements of a peacebuilding project and their role in ensuring its quality.

3   *Collect and transfer lessons learned about the practices, mechanisms, and processes that support high-quality projects.* The PBSO should collect the lessons learned from RUNO staff, partners, the JSC, and governments about the practices, mechanisms, and processes that seemed to contribute to high-quality projects. It should provide descriptions and explanations of the various options to the RUNOs, JSC, and governments involved in PBF activities. The PBSO should also investigate the lessons learned by the broader humanitarian community about short-term socioeconomic support at the community level. PBF projects can easily turn from peace dividends to "peace disappointments" if they are not well implemented and there is no follow-up.

4   *Link the exit strategy to the country context and to the capacity of the UN and the host government to deliver high-quality projects.*

142 *Susanna Campbell et al.*

The PBSO should determine the PBF's exit strategy based on the following considerations: whether there is a clear need in the country for high-quality peacebuilding in the short term; whether the senior UN leadership has a clear vision for peacebuilding in the country and the will to implement it; whether the host government leadership has the vision and will to implement peacebuilding; and whether the RUNOs have the capacity, will, and vision to conduct high-quality peacebuilding projects. If these standards are not met in a given country, then the PBF should stop providing it with funding.

Notes

1 In early 2007, the PBF allocated US$35 million to fund Burundi's first Peacebuilding Priority Plan (PBF I), which ran from 2007 to early 2010 and covered four key areas: governance; rule of law and the security sector; protection of human rights; and land issues, with a focus on the reintegration of returning refugees and resolution of land disputes. Six RUNOs—the Office of the High Commissioner for Human Rights (OHCHR), the UN Development Programme (UNDP), the UN Department of Peacekeeping Operations (DPKO), the UN Population Fund (UNFPA), the UN High Commissioner for Refugees (UNHCR), and the UN Development Fund for Women (UNIFEM, later part of UN Women)—implemented the 18 projects funded by the first tranche. See United Nations Peacebuilding Fund, "Burundi Overview," www.unpbf.org/countries/burundi. In 2011, the PBF allocated a second tranche of funds totaling $9.2 million (PBF II) toward community-based socioeconomic reintegration of ex-combatants and displaced persons in the three Burundian provinces most affected by conflict: Bujumbura Rural, Cibitoke, and Bubanza. The second tranche was implemented by four of the same UN entities that had implemented the PBF I projects—UNDP, UNHCR, UNFPA, and UN Women—as well as two new ones: the Food and Agriculture Organization (FAO) and the International Labour Organization (ILO).
2 Peter Uvin, *Life After Violence: A People's Story of Burundi* (London: Zed Books, 2009).
3 Headed by the resident coordinator, the UNCTs exist in 136 countries; their members include representatives of the UN organizations working in-country. The UN Integrated Office in Burundi ran from 2006 to 2011, ending because its mandate was not extended.
4 For the full impact evaluation, see Susanna Campbell, Tracy Dexter, Michael Findley, Stephanie Hofmann, Josiah Marineau, and Daniel Walker, *Independent External Evaluation UN Peacebuilding Fund Project Portfolio in Burundi 2007–2013* (Geneva: Centre on Conflict, Development and Peacebuilding, The Graduate Institute, 1 February 2014).
5 Susanna P. Campbell with Leonard Kayobera and Justine Nkurunziza, "Independent External Evaluation: Peacebuilding Fund Projects in Burundi," BINUB, March 2010, www.unpbf.org/wp-content/uploads/Indep

The impact of the PBA in Burundi   143

endent-Evaluation-Burundi.pdf. *Colline* (hill) refers to the units of rural settlement in Burundi and Rwanda. A group of *collines* form a commune. In Burundi, there are 117 communes and 2,639 *collines*.

6 This increased sense of security cannot of course be attributed solely to reforms in the Burundian Armed Forces.

7 Human Rights Watch, "Pursuit of Power: Political Violence and Repression in Burundi," doc. no. 1-56432-479-6, New York, May 2009, www.hrw.org/sites/default/files/reports/burundi0509web.pdf.

8 International Crisis Group, "Burundi: Ensuring Credible Elections," Africa Report No. 155, Nairobi/Brussels, 2010, 17–18; Human Rights Watch, "'We'll Tie You Up and Shoot You': Lack of Accountability for Political Violence in Burundi," doc. no. 1-56432-634-9, New York, May 2010, www.hrw.org/sites/default/files/reports/burundi0510webwcover_2.pdf; United Nations Security Council, "Seventh Report of the Secretary-General on the United Nations Integrated Office in Burundi," UN doc. S/2010/608, 2010, 1–2.

9 International Crisis Group, "Burundi: From Electoral Boycott to Political Impasse," Africa Report No. 169, Nairobi/Brussels, 2011, 3.

10 Esdras Ndikumana, "Burundi Constitution Change Risks Opening Ethnic Wounds," *Agence France-Presse*, 1 December 2013.

11 "Theory of change" refers to the project's theory about how it will influence the likely drivers of conflict and peace that it has identified. See Susanna P. Campbell, "When Process Matters: The Potential Implications of Organizational Learning for Peacebuilding Success," *Journal of Peacebuilding & Development* 4, no. 2 (2008): 20–32; and Susanna P. Campbell, "Organizational Barriers to Peace: Agency and Structure in International Peacebuilding," PhD Dissertation, Tufts University, 2012.

12 United Nations Peacebuilding Fund, "United Nations Peacebuilding Fund: Who We Are," www.unpbf.org/who-we-are.

13 The PBSO synthesizes the key features of the PBC as follows: The PBC "helps identify clear peacebuilding priorities for the countries on its agenda—Burundi, Central African Republic, Guinea-Bissau, Liberia, and Sierra Leone; encourages national ownership, partnerships, and mutual accountability; networks closely with the UN system at headquarters and in the field, with the Secretary-General's senior representatives and UN country teams; and raises funds for peacebuilding through donor conferences and public advocacy—particularly for countries that attract less donor interest." United Nations Peacebuilding Support Office, "The United Nations Peacebuilding Architecture," 2010, 2, www.un.org/en/peacebuilding/pbso/pdf/pbso_architecture_flyer.pdf.

14 According to an analysis of meetings of the PBC configuration for Burundi, the group met formally 19 times and informally 34 times between 2006 and 2011. For the informal meetings, the ambassador was listed as chairing only 17 meetings, while records do not indicate the chair at all six times. The frequency of meetings declined from 10 in 2007 to one for 2011 for formal meetings, and from nine to two informal meetings over the same period. UN Peacebuilding Commission, "Country-Specific Configurations: Burundi," www.un.org/en/peacebuilding/doc_burundi.shtml.

15 United Nations Peacebuilding Support Office, *The United Nations Peacebuilding Architecture* (New York: United Nations, 2010), 4.

144 *Susanna Campbell et al.*

16 "As the Administrative Agent of the PBF, the MPTF-Office transfers funds to RUNOs on the basis of previously signed MoUs [memoranda of understanding] between each RUNO and the MPTF Office." United Nations Peacebuilding Fund, "The Peacebuilding Fund: What is the PBF?" www.unpbf.org/application-guidelines/the-peacebuilding-fund-pbf.

17 United Nations Peacebuilding Fund, "Monitoring and Evaluation: Reflective Peacebuilding," www.unpbf.org/application-guidelines/7-monitoring-and-evaluation-me-reflective-peacebuilding.

18 The PBC requires the countries on its agenda to prepare a Peacebuilding Priority Plan. Over the entire period studied (2007–13), the three Peacebuilding Priority Plans (or equivalent documents) were developed, largely by key UN staff and Burundian government officials, based on consultations with a broader group of Burundian and international stakeholders in the country.

19 PBC, "The Peacebuilding Fund: What is the PBF?"

20 In addition, for the second PBF tranche, the UN established a Coordination and Programme Direction Cell that reported directly to the UN resident coordinator or deputy representative of the Secretary-General. The Coordination and Programme Direction Cell also worked with the RUNOs implementing PBF activities to help create linkages among them, and monitor their activities, and, together with the PBF Secretariat, consolidate their activity reports for submission to the JSC and PBSO. The cells worked with the TFCs to provide monitoring, but tended to focus on activity-level outputs rather than the contribution to peacekeeping.

21 The JSC met every six months during PBF II and focused on monitoring the project's overall contribution to the Priority Plan and reviewing the reports that were synthesized by the Coordination and Programme Direction Cell.

22 Susanna P. Campbell, "When Process Matters: The Potential Implications of Organizational Learning for Peacebuilding Success," *Journal of Peacebuilding and Development* 4, no. 2 (2008) 20–32; Campbell, "Independent External Evaluation: Peacebuilding Fund Projects in Burundi"; and Susanna P. Campbell, "Routine Learning? How Peacebuilding Organizations Prevent Liberal Peace," in *A Liberal Peace? The Problems and Practices of Peacebuilding*, ed. Susanna P. Campbell, David Chandler, and Meera Sabaratnam (London: Zed Books, 2011), 89–105.

8 The impact of the Peacebuilding Architecture on consolidating the Sierra Leone peace process[1]

Fernando Cavalcante

- **PBC engagement in Sierra Leone: a brief assessment**
- **PBF support to the Sierra Leonean peacebuilding process**
- **Future PBA involvement in Sierra Leone**
- **Conclusions and recommendations**

Since the official end of the civil war in 2002, Sierra Leone has achieved considerable progress in its peacebuilding process. More than 70,000 former combatants have been disarmed and demobilized, credible presidential elections were successfully held in 2002, 2007, and 2012, and the official diamond trade has made progress.[2] In the economic domain, annual growth rates for Sierra Leone over the past decade were higher than the average for sub-Saharan Africa, and the short-term economic outlook remains positive, thanks especially to mining production.[3] Despite such progress, Sierra Leone remains one of the poorest nations in the world, ranking 183 of 187 in the 2014 Human Development Index and displaying poor indicators of human and social development.[4] Moreover, some challenges remain—like the centralization of power in Freetown and youth exclusion, which led to the outbreak of civil war in 1991 in the first place.[5]

Virtually since its inception in 2005/06, the UN Peacebuilding Architecture (PBA) has been engaged in peacebuilding efforts in Sierra Leone. The country was one of the first to be included on the agenda of the Peacebuilding Commission (PBC), serving as a test case for much of the institutional set-up of the new body, including the format and content of the PBC's instruments of engagement.[6] At the country level, key areas of the peacebuilding process were advanced through the PBC's role in facilitating dialogue among national and international partners, as well as in gathering political support for the implementation of concrete initiatives.[7] Sierra Leone has also obtained an above-average level of support from the Peacebuilding Fund (PBF),

146   *Fernando Cavalcante*

having received more than US$50.1 million since 2007 for quickly starting and implementing initiatives in a range of priority areas.[8] More recently, progress has been made in New York for a renewed engagement of the PBC in Sierra Leone as the country prepares to "graduate" from the commission and focus more on long-term development challenges than on core peacebuilding priorities. Considering this level of involvement from the PBA, it seems reasonable to regard Sierra Leone as a yardstick for analyzing the effectiveness of this institutional arrangement vis-à-vis countries emerging from armed conflict situations.

This chapter takes stock of the PBA's engagement in Sierra Leone, through the PBC and the PBF, and reviews some of its key achievements in consolidating peace in the country. Despite major accomplishments—in fostering greater strategic coordination from the international community, pushing forward a comprehensive understanding of peacebuilding and ensuring quick funds for critical peacebuilding areas—the PBA now faces the challenge of effectively supporting Sierra Leone in managing its peacebuilding process more actively after the closure of the UN Integrated Peacebuilding Office in Sierra Leone (UNIPSIL).

PBC engagement in Sierra Leone: a brief assessment

The PBC included Sierra Leone on its agenda in July 2006, following a request from the UN Security Council for advice on the situation of the country. The national authorities had expressed interest in the new organ earlier that year, when the government noted that "remarkable progress" had been achieved since the end of the civil war but "formidable challenges" remained to be addressed.[9] In October 2006, the PBC Country-Specific Configuration (CSC) for Sierra Leone held its first meeting, and declared the country eligible to receive support from the PBF.[10]

Immediately after its first meeting, the CSC-Sierra Leone started working to identify peacebuilding priorities and gaps on which to focus PBC engagement in the country. Five such priorities were outlined in the Sierra Leone Peacebuilding Cooperation Framework (PCF), an integrated peacebuilding framework designed to reflect "a shared vision of the UN's strategic objectives" for the country and a "set of agreed results, timelines and responsibilities for the delivery of tasks critical to consolidating peace."[11] The first priority outlined in the document was youth employment and empowerment, understood not only in terms of creating economic opportunities and jobs for youth, but also of creating long-term economic growth and an enabling

The impact of the PBA in Sierra Leone 147

environment for the private sector. The second priority referred to justice and security sector reform, which included concerns with access to justice as well as programs for constitutional reviews and reforms. The consolidation of democracy and good governance, particularly via the strengthening of national institutions (e.g. parliament, the National Commission for Democracy, and the Human Rights Commission) and the enhancement of civil society participation, were identified as the third priority. Fourth came capacity building, "in its broadest sense and at all levels," which included reforms in the civil service and a broad review of existing institutions. Finally, the fifth priority concerned the development of the energy sector, as the enormous electricity needs in Sierra Leone were identified as a cross-cutting challenge to all other priority areas. [12]

A key shortcoming of the PBC engagement in Sierra Leone at that stage concerned the length of time required to produce the PCF and the limited involvement of national authorities in its development. It took the CSC-Sierra Leone a full 18 months to identify the peacebuilding priorities for the country and to develop a specific instrument of engagement for addressing them. [13]

Moreover, because much of the process of developing the document took place in New York, the national authorities did not feel ownership of the process. [14] Attempts by New York-based stakeholders to engage in contact and communication with actors in Sierra Leone were not always successful. For instance, a visit of a PBC delegation to Sierra Leone during the process was deemed by the Secretariat as "useful in providing crucial information from the ground" [15]—however, according to one interviewee, most meetings of the delegation were scheduled with representatives from the national government and the UN system in the country, with relatively little time for direct contact with civil society representatives, especially outside Freetown. [16] Despite the best intentions, the attempt to develop a peacebuilding strategy in close cooperation with stakeholders at the country level eventually resulted in only "a distorted picture of needs and a lack of involvement from rural areas." [17] Similarly, the voices of such groups in PBC meetings in New York were underrepresented during most of the process of drafting the strategic frameworks for Sierra Leone, especially as the actual guidelines for the participation of civil society entities were not adopted until June 2007.

That said, the adoption of the PCF represents one of the main contributions of the PBC to the peace process in Sierra Leone at the level of strategic coordination. By the time the CSC-Sierra Leone became operational, several instruments and strategies focusing on various

148 *Fernando Cavalcante*

areas and adopted by a range of actors were in place, including the Poverty Reduction Strategy Paper, Vision 2025, the Peace Consolidation Strategy, and the UN Development Assistance Framework.[18] With the adoption of the PCF, the PBC consolidated a whole range of strategies into a single document that would guide the engagement of international stakeholders in Sierra Leone until the adoption of the government's Agenda for Change in June 2009.

The content of the framework was not necessarily new, as it drew heavily on existing documents. However, it offered a platform through which commitments could be agreed upon and monitored, and pressure could be put on donors and implementing partners, national and international. This is a positive aspect, in that donors are usually dissatisfied with the existence of such a range of plans which frequently (albeit unintentionally) overlap in peacebuilding contexts. Moreover, as the government adopted An Agenda for Change as a strategic framework for growth, economic development and peace consolidation, the PCF served as the basis upon which the PBC realigned its engagement in the country by focusing on the peace consolidation aspects of the government document.[19] Hence, according to one diplomat, the PCF agreed between the government and the PBC was instrumental in helping to channel international funds and support to the five targeted peacebuilding priorities outlined above.[20]

The second main contribution of the PBC to the peace process in Sierra Leone is conceptual and not restricted to that case, but speaks directly to wider peacebuilding debates on the interrelationship between security and development: the commission embraced a comprehensive concept of peacebuilding, which favored the consideration of a wide spectrum of activities as part of the peacebuilding process and resulted in more peace dividends to the population. By the time the PBA was established, the concept of peacebuilding had been significantly expanded in terms of scope, phases, timing, and envisaged activities, compared with the concept initially advanced by Boutros Boutros-Ghali in the early 1990s.[21] Notably, by then it was recognized that creating the conditions for sustainable peace required involvement not only after the end of armed conflict, but also during the full spectrum of armed conflict. Moreover, activities usually seen as pertaining to the realms of conflict prevention, peacekeeping, or development during the 1990s were progressively associated with, or recognized as having a positive impact on, peacebuilding.[22] However, differing views of exactly what was to be considered as "peacebuilding" or "development" still caused confusion, particularly as the preference for specific activities or end goals tended to reflect the interests of different actors.[23]

The impact of the PBA in Sierra Leone 149

The inclusion of Sierra Leone as one of the first countries on the PBC agenda and the identification of energy sector development as a peacebuilding priority in the PCF illustrate the PBC's comprehensive understanding of peacebuilding. The inclusion of Sierra Leone on the commission's agenda was initially a contentious issue among PBC member states and the UN Secretariat. The Peacebuilding Support Office (PBSO), for one, advocated the inclusion of the country (as well as of Burundi), whereas some member states favored including countries that were not too far beyond their armed conflicts.[24] Some donors even considered Sierra Leone as a case of "early development" rather than "post-conflict," as more than five years had elapsed since the end of the civil war in 2002.[25] At the country level, some individuals were also skeptical about the actual impact of PBC involvement so long after the end of the conflict.[26] Finally, other member states voiced concerns about ensuring some geographical balance among the countries on the PBC agenda.[27] All the same, the inclusion of Sierra Leone on the agenda at this early stage signaled that the newly established organ understood peacebuilding as a process that went far beyond concerns with the short-term or immediate post-conflict phase.

As for the inclusion of the development of the energy sector as a peacebuilding priority in the PCF, it should be borne in mind that infrastructure in Sierra Leone, including transport as well as electricity and water supply, was in poor condition after the decade-long civil war. Infrastructure, as such, had been highlighted as a matter of concern by the previous government and by other international actors.[28] Upon taking office in the second half of 2007, the newly elected government started to advocate the need to include the advancement of the energy sector as a peacebuilding priority.

Initially, however, several actors disagreed that improving the energy sector should be recognized as a peacebuilding need or gap for the PBC, claiming that it was part of development tasks to be carried out at a later stage.[29] It was only after continued negotiations at the political and technical levels that the CSC-Sierra Leone came to the understanding that the crisis in the energy sector jeopardized all other priority areas, and represented "a critical challenge for the country's recovery and economic development."[30]

In recognizing the development of the energy sector, especially electricity, as a peacebuilding priority, the PBC seemed to confirm that successful peacebuilding required attention not only to core activities like the holding of elections or disarmament, but also initiatives that could generate immediate peace dividends and mitigate the risks of instability caused by lack of progress in areas like economic

150 *Fernando Cavalcante*

development or reduction of poverty—both of which were severely affected by the poor condition of the electricity sector in Sierra Leone. According to one inside observer, recognition of the development of the energy sector as a PBC priority provided UN entities and national stakeholders with powerful political clout when looking for external funding for projects aimed at developing the electricity sector in Sierra Leone.[31] Recent reports also indicate that the provision of electricity to the population has improved, with additional capacity added to the transmission and distribution networks, and greater access to electricity in rural areas.[32]

PBF support to the Sierra Leonean peacebuilding process

The PBF has been an important source of rapid and flexible funding for peacebuilding initiatives in Sierra Leone. Since 2007, and in close coordination with the PBC, it has approved $50.1 million in financial support to the implementation of 36 peacebuilding projects in the country.[33] The use of PBF funds was a key instrument for avoiding potential relapse into armed conflict following the escalation of tensions prior to the 2007 elections, and played a vital role in ensuring funds for several activities carried out during the drawdown of UNIPSIL. Moreover, the fund is now being used to fill the gap in initiatives carried out in the immediate post-UNIPSIL phase.

Most PBF-supported initiatives fell into the thematic area of peaceful resolution of conflicts, which typically focused on the promotion of democratic governance and human rights, as well as on strengthening institutions that promote social cohesion. In Sierra Leone, projects in this area have been critical for ensuring the holding of free and fair elections in 2007 and 2012, in guaranteeing funds to the reparations program to the victims of the civil war, and, more recently, in building the capacity of political and non-state actors to contribute to the Constitutional Review Process.[34] The PBF-supported reparation program, for instance, enabled victims of the civil war to meet some of their most immediate needs (e.g. medical care) through micro-grants. The amount required to sustain the program, however, later proved inadequate, as the actual number of victims was found to be significantly higher than initially estimated.[35] The required amount was not subsequently matched by international partners, although that could have been achieved by stronger advocacy from the PBC.

The PBF also supported 11 projects focusing on the advancement of political dialogue, security sector reform and the promotion of the rule of law. Projects in the latter area were instrumental in providing

The impact of the PBA in Sierra Leone   151

adequate equipment and material for the Sierra Leonean police and armed forces, guaranteeing the material conditions for their functioning. Other PBF-funded projects focused on the restoration and/or strengthening of public administration and the provision of basic public services, with heavy emphasis on the purchase of required components to restore the provision of energy in Freetown, in line with the priorities outlined in the PCF. Finally, one project received PBF funds in the area of economic revitalization, which supported the Youth Secretariat in carrying out its activities and reflected the PBC concern with the issue of youth unemployment.[36] Table 8.1 shows the distribution of PBF monies to projects in Sierra Leone, by PBF thematic areas.

The relatively uneven distribution of PBF support in Sierra Leone may be understood as a result of two factors. The first concerns the approval of the first PBF envelope of $35 million to the country in 2007 before the adoption of the PCF: this diverted much of the political discussion away from concrete peacebuilding challenges and the definition of a common agenda for the international partners into a matter of how to divide "this sudden new injection of donor money."[37] In New York and Freetown there was keen interest in having the money disbursed quickly. Whereas member states and the Secretariat wanted to achieve quick wins in the early stages of the functioning of the PBC and PBF, the Sierra Leonean government and civil society urgently needed the money, which represented about one-tenth of annual official development assistance to the country at the time. The result was a stronger focus on security-centered projects (e.g. security sector reform) rather than on initiatives that could have helped to speed up the reconstruction of the social fabric across the country or a political agreement between the government and the opposition around sensitive reforms—such as the recommendations of the Truth and Reconciliation Commission.[38]

The second factor accounting for the relatively uneven distribution of PBF support concerns the lack of conflict analyses to inform programming decisions on the amount of investment expected to generate greater peace dividends to the population and/or more catalytic impact in the peacebuilding process. In the absence of such analyses, PBF-supported projects were initially approved without much consideration being given to the drivers of the armed conflict, and some projects contributed only marginally to the peacebuilding process.

Similarly, areas that could have benefited from more financial resources from the PBF, such as the management of national resources, received little or no attention in PBF programming at first.[39] Despite

152 *Fernando Cavalcante*

Table 8.1 Distribution of PBF monies to projects in Sierra Leone, by thematic area

Thematic areas	Projects		Approved budget	
	Quant.	*%*	*US$ million*	*%*
1 Support the implementation of peace agreements and political dialogue	11	30	18.3	37
1.1 Security sector reform	7	18	11.1	23
1.2 Rule of law	3	9	7.1	14
1.3 Disarmament, demobilization, and reintegration	–	–	–	–
1.4 Enhancing political dialogue	1	3	0.1	–
2 Promote coexistence and peaceful resolution of conflicts	20	55	18.2	36
2.1 National reconciliation	13	36	15.4	30
2.2 Democratic governance	7	19	2.8	6
2.3 Management of natural resources (including land)	–	–	–	–
3 Revitalize the economy and generate immediate peace dividends	1	3	4.1	8
3.1 Creating short-term job opportunities	1	3	4.1	8
3.2 Creating sustainable livelihoods	–	–	–	–
4 (Re)establish essential administrative services and related human and technical capacities	4	12	9.5	19
4.1 Restoring administrative structure (public administration)	2	6	0.4	1
4.2 Provision of basic public services (including infrastructure)	2	6	9.1	18
Total	1	100	50.1	100

Source: Compiled based on information available at MPTF Office, "Multi-Partner Trust Fund Office Gateway: The Peacebuilding Fund."

the growing importance the PBSO has attached to the requirement of conflict analyses to inform PBF programming, no conflict analysis has yet been conducted for Sierra Leone, and projects have continued to be designed and implemented according to alternative analyses, like evaluations from technical missions or external studies.[40]

Notwithstanding the relatively uneven distribution of PBF funding and the mixed results of some projects, an earlier assessment concluded that PBF support to Sierra Leone had been largely effective in contributing

The impact of the PBA in Sierra Leone 153

to the peacebuilding process in the country.[41] In addition, the PBF has begun to play an important role in providing rapid and flexible support for activities in the immediate period before and after the closure of UNIPSIL. As of this writing, the PBF had approved four projects in connection with the mission's drawdown, focused on capacity building of non-state actors to participate actively in the ongoing constitutional review process; the enhancement of the democratic governance of the security sector, including strengthening civilian oversight over the armed forces; support to national authorities in the area of human rights; and conflict prevention and dialogue.[42] Furthermore, the PBSO has already identified some priorities that may be addressed in the short term, especially regarding initiatives for enhancing the engagement of international financial institutions in Sierra Leone and the socioeconomic development of the diamond-rich district of Kono.[43] The use of PBF support during this critical period in the Sierra Leone peacebuilding process thus reinforces the flexibility of the PBF, as well as highlights how it might be used in other equally challenging periods, such as the start-up of peacekeeping operations or in transitions of the UN presence from peacekeeping to special political missions.

Future PBA involvement in Sierra Leone

In light of the progress achieved in the peacebuilding process since 2002, especially after the holding of credible elections in 2012, the CSC-Sierra Leone started to discuss future PBC engagement in the country.[44] Discussions were intensified particularly after the Security Council decided to draw down UNIPSIL fully by 31 March 2014.[45] The decision would in practice transform the UN presence in the country from a peace mission to a UN Country Team led by a residential coordinator tasked with long-term development goals. In the context of this transformation, international partners and the national authorities agreed that there was a need for continued PBC engagement in Sierra Leone. The chair of the CSC-Sierra Leone claimed in 2013 that "it [was] not the time for the international community to turn away from Sierra Leone," given that the country still needs appropriate levels of political and financial support from international partners.[46]

Also according to the chair, such renewed PBC involvement should reflect a "lighter approach," more responsive to concrete requests by international and national partners in Sierra Leone. The focus of the PBC's renewed engagement will continue to be based on the priorities already identified in the government's own Agenda for Prosperity, which replaced the Agenda for Change and should continue to provide

154 *Fernando Cavalcante*

overall guidance for the peacebuilding process. Furthermore, the PBC's main forum for political discussions and engagement is expected to be modified to reflect a leaner membership on the basis of need. Rather than rigid structures, future meetings will have a more open membership, with participation limited to member states that have a more direct role or more relevant experience on specific aspects of the peacebuilding process. The expectation is that this lighter form of engagement can require fewer meetings in New York and lead to a more reactive engagement based on concrete requests made by partners in the field.[47] In this connection, and in the absence of a political mission following the closure of UNIPSIL, which was an important link between the PBC and the field, it will be important to reinforce the PBC links with the UN family in Sierra Leone, to ensure that peacebuilding strategies are undertaken in a coherent and coordinated fashion at field level.

The decision to review the PBC engagement in Sierra Leone represents an important indicator of the necessarily limited duration of PBC support and engagement to countries on its agenda. On the one hand, the commission plays an advisory role, seeking to pave the way towards sustainable peace and development—which means that countries are eventually expected not to require PBC support as their societies progress towards those envisaged goals. On the other hand, some developing countries still seem to feel, as put by one senior diplomat from a country on the PBC agenda, that "being on the agenda of the PBC itself gives a different picture of that country to the world," as if it could be considered "fragile" or "failed," thus sending a negative message to potential investors from abroad. According to this view, "when [a country] is there [on the PBC agenda], it does not want to be there forever."[48] At the same time, the decision highlights that PBC engagement should be determined by conditions on the ground and by the interests and demands of the country concerned. Thus, the nature and format of PBC support and engagement should reflect the real needs and challenges faced by countries at all times, including as they start focusing on long-term development issues rather than immediate peacebuilding priorities. It is thus critical that the PBC be able to keep pace and creatively accompany countries' needs as they arise.

Conclusions and recommendations

The UN-led peacebuilding process in Sierra Leone has been successful to the extent that it has managed to prevent a relapse into violence, but several of the "formidable challenges" noted by the government when

The impact of the PBA in Sierra Leone   155

expressing interest in the PBC remain. Sierra Leone still needs to overcome some of the socioeconomic problems that led to violent conflict in the first place, such as the centralization of power in Freetown and youth exclusion. The country's relatively high economic growth rate in recent years reflects an undiversified economy driven mainly by the extractive industry and commodities, notably minerals and agriculture. However, the apparent economic gains have not necessarily been translated into social welfare for the population, as Sierra Leone remains one of the poorest countries in Africa and indeed the world. This situation raises serious concerns over the sustainability of long-term development in the country.

The PBA has played an important role in this process. This chapter has briefly reviewed three such achievements: the PBC's role in fostering strategic coordination through the adoption of an integrated peacebuilding strategy agreed with the Sierra Leonean government; the PBC's embrace of a comprehensive understanding on the concept of peacebuilding, allowing for the inclusion of wider areas of intervention under the umbrella of the PCF and ultimately resulting in greater peace dividends to the population; and finally, the quick and flexible use of PBF support in a range of key initiatives, also during the drawdown phase and subsequent closure of UNIPSIL. However, the PBA has had less success in getting national actors fully involved during the development of the PCF, which focused support to the peacebuilding process around targeted priorities, and in designing more effective programming for PBF support based on comprehensive analyses of the drivers of conflict and actual needs on the ground.

A major challenge ahead will be for the PBA to continue offering adequate support to Sierra Leone in managing its peacebuilding process more actively after the closure of UNIPSIL. The UN will remain engaged, and programs and agencies will continue to operate in Sierra Leone, but with the focus gradually more on long-term development aspects (e.g. further advancing the energy sector) than on core peacebuilding tasks like security sector reform.

Based on a brief analysis of the involvement and impact of the PBA in Sierra Leone's peacebuilding process, we may indicate these possible options for the future of the PBA:

1   *Engagement with national authorities should start as early as possible.* The PBC and PBSO should involve national authorities in political dialogue as early as possible, to identify and agree on key areas of intervention. This should include close collaboration in the development of the PBC's integrated peacebuilding strategies

156 *Fernando Cavalcante*

with a view to upholding the principle of national ownership and to ensure greater results in the peacebuilding process.

2 *Conflict analyses should be a first step in the development of PBA strategies and programming for specific country contexts.* Conflict analyses could provide member states and the UN Secretariat with a better picture of the overall context, with a view to identifying potential priority areas to be agreed between the government and the PBC, as well as in identifying targeted areas that could result in greater advances in peacebuilding processes, thus enhancing the PBF's catalytic role. However, the requirement of conflict analyses should not become a bureaucratic imperative that hinders, delays, or prevents PBA engagement.

3 *The use of PBF funding during transitional periods, such as the start-up of multidimensional peacekeeping operations and special political missions, or during transitions from the former to the latter, should be intensified.* The positive results achieved by projects supported by the PBF in Sierra Leone during the drawdown of UNIPSIL, as well as the Fund's flexible nature and ability to take calculated risks, place it in an especially privileged position for providing rapid and targeted support to initiatives during uncertain periods of change and uncertainty.

Notes

1 This chapter is partially based on the author's PhD research, which was funded by a doctoral scholarship from the Portuguese Foundation for Science and Technology and by a European Commission Marie Curie Fellowship. The views herein expressed are solely those of the author and do not necessarily represent the official positions of any institution to which he has been affiliated.

2 Jeremy Ginifer, "The Challenge of the Security Sector and Security Reform Processes in Democratic Transitions: The Case of Sierra Leone," *Democratization* 13, no. 5 (2006): 791–810; Theo Neethling, "Pursuing Sustainable Peace through Postconflict Peacebuilding: The Case of Sierra Leone," *African Security Review* 16, no. 3 (2007): 81–95.

3 African Development Bank, "Sierra Leone: Country Strategy Paper, 2013–2017," 2013.

4 UNDP, *Human Development Report 2014: Sustaining Human Progress— Reducing Vulnerabilities and Building Resilience* (New York: United Nations Development Programme, 2014).

5 Jeremy Allouche, "Is it the Right Time for the International Community to Exit Sierra Leone?" IDS Evidence Report 38, Institute for Development Studies, Brighton, 2013.

The impact of the PBA in Sierra Leone   157

6 Amy Scott, "The United Nations Peacebuilding Commission: An Early Assessment," *Journal of Peacebuilding and Development* 4, no. 2 (2008): 7–19.

7 Andrea Iro, "The UN Peacebuilding Commission—Lessons from Sierra Leone," WeltTrends *Thesis* 6, University of Potsdam, Potsdam, 2009; and ActionAid, CAFOD, and CARE International, "Consolidating the Peace? Views from Sierra Leone and Burundi on the United Nations Peacebuilding Commission," 2007, www.actionaid.org.

8 MPTF Office, "Multi-Partner Trust Fund Office Gateway: The Peacebuilding Fund," 2014, mptf.undp.org/factsheet/fund/PB000.

9 Permanent Mission of Sierra Leone to the United Nations, "Invitation to the Peace Building Commission to Operate in Sierra Leone," letter dated 27 February 2006, to the president of the General Assembly, 1.

10 PBC, "Summary Record of the 1st Meeting of the Peacebuilding Commission Sierra Leone Configuration," UN doc. PBC/1/SLE/SR.1, 2007; and PBC, "Summary Record of the 2nd Meeting of the Peacebuilding Commission Sierra Leone Configuration," UN doc. PBC/1/SLE/SR.2, 2007.

11 Richard Ponzio, "Strategic Policy Frameworks as Peacebuilding Tools: A Comparative Study," *Journal of Peacebuilding and Development* 5 (2010): 6.

12 PBC, "Sierra Leone Peacebuilding Cooperation Framework," UN doc. PBC/2/SLE/1, 2007, 4–8.

13 PBC, "Summary Record of the 1st Meeting of the Peacebuilding Commission Sierra Leone Configuration," 4–8.

14 Interview with senior diplomat from country on the PBC agenda, New York, 17 October 2012.

15 PBC, "Report of the Peacebuilding Commission on its 1st Session," UN doc. A/62/137-S/2007/458, 2007, para. 35.

16 Interview with senior diplomat from country on the PBC agenda, New York, 17 October 2012.

17 Scott, "The United Nations Peacebuilding Commission," 10.

18 PBC, "Conference Room Paper for the Country Specific Meeting on Sierra Leone," UN doc. PBC/2/SIL/CRP.1, 2008.

19 PBC, "Outcome of the Peacebuilding Commission High-level Special Session on Sierra Leone," UN doc. PBC/3/SLE/6, 2009.

20 Interview with senior diplomat from country on the PBC agenda, New York, 17 October 2012.

21 Secretary-General Boutros Boutros-Ghali, "An Agenda for Peace: Preventive Diplomacy, Peacemaking and Peace-Keeping," Report of the Secretary-General Pursuant to the Statement Adopted by the Summit Meeting of the Security Council on 31 January 1992, UN doc. A/47/277-S/24111, 1992.

22 Fernando Cavalcante, *Coming into Life: The Concept of Peacebuilding in the United Nations, from an Agenda for Peace to the Peacebuilding Commission*, PhD Dissertation, University of Coimbra, Coimbra, Portugal, 2013.

23 Charles T. Call, "Institutionalizing Peace: A Review of Post-Conflict Peacebuilding Concepts and issues for DPA," internal document, UN Department of Political Affairs, New York, 2005.

24 Carolyn McAskie, "United Nations Peacebuilding Architecture: Two Years on—A History with Recommendations for the Way Forward," internal document, UN Peacebuilding Support Office, New York, 2008, 11.

158 *Fernando Cavalcante*

25 ActionAid, CAFOD, and CARE International, "Consolidating the Peace?" 12.
26 Interview with senior diplomat from country on the PBC agenda, New York, 17 October 2012.
27 Gilda M.S. Neves, *Comissão das Nações Unidas para Consolidação da Paz: Perspectiva Brasileira* (Brasília: FUNAG, 2009).
28 See e.g., PBC, "Summary Record of the 1st Meeting of the Peacebuilding Commission Sierra Leone Configuration," UN doc. PBC/2/SLE/SR.1, 2008.
29 Interview with PBSO officer, New York, 19 July 2011.
30 PBSO, "Informal Thematic Discussion on Sierra Leone Energy Sector Development, Summary Note of the Chair of the Country-Specific Configuration for Sierra Leone," internal document, Peacebuilding Support Office, New York, 2007, 1.
31 Interview with PBSO officer, New York, 19 July 2011.
32 UNDP, "National Energy Profile of Sierra Leone," June 2012, www.sl.undp. org/content/dam/sierraleone/docs/focusareadocs/undp_sle_energyprofile.pdf.
33 Unless otherwise stated, all data in this section were drawn from MPTF Office website, 22 June 2014.
34 Juan Larrabure, Hindowa Momoh, and Alphaeus Koroma, "Report of the Final Evaluation: Peacebuilding Fund Programming in Sierra Leone, 11 January–28 February 2011," 2011, www.unpbf.org/wp-content/uploads/docs/Final%20Evaluation%20-%20Sierra%20Leone.pdf.
35 Larrabure et al., "Report of the Final Evaluation."
36 MPTF Office, "Multi-Partner Trust Fund Office Gateway"; and telephone interview with PBSO official, 23 July 2014.
37 Anne M. Street, Howard Mollett, and Jennifer Smith, "Experiences of the United Nations Peacebuilding Commission in Sierra Leone and Burundi," *Journal of Peacebuilding and Development* 4, no. 2 (2008): 39.
38 Street et al., "Experiences of the United Nations Peacebuilding Commission in Sierra Leone and Burundi."
39 Larrabure et al., "Report of the Final Evaluation."
40 Telephone interview with PBSO official, 23 July 2014.
41 Larrabure et al., "Report of the Final Evaluation."
42 Telephone interview with PBSO official, 23 July 2014.
43 Telephone interview with PBSO official, 23 July 2014.
44 PBC, "Second Review of the Outcome of the High-level Special Session of the Peacebuilding Commission on Sierra Leone," UN doc. PBC/6/SLE/2, 2012, para. 15.
45 Security Council resolution 2097, UN doc. S/RES/2097, 2013, paras. 2 and 20.
46 Security Council, "Provisional Verbatim Record of the 6933rd Meeting of the Security Council," UN doc. S/PV.6933, 2013, 5.
47 UN, "Summary of the Visit of H.E. Mr. Guillermo E. Rishchynski, Chair of the Peacebuilding Commission Sierra Leone Configuration, to Sierra Leone, 25 to 28 February 2014," www.un.org/en/peacebuilding/cscs/sl/pbc_visits/PBC%20Chair's%20Visit%20to%20Sierra%20Leone%20-%20Draft%20Report%20-%20Feb%202014%20(For%20Consultation).pdf.
48 Interview with senior diplomat from country on the PBC agenda, New York, 17 October 2012.

9 The impact of the Peacebuilding Architecture on consolidating Liberia's peace process

Marina Caparini

- **Context and engagement of the PBA in Liberia**
- **The regional justice and security hubs**
- **National reconciliation**
- **Assessment of the PBA impact on Liberian peacebuilding**
- **Assessment of Liberian experience for the peacebuilding debate**
- **Recommendations**

Efforts to build peace following intrastate conflict have become a core focus of practitioners, policymakers, and academics concerned with regional and global security. This concern is seen in the burgeoning institutional infrastructure and professionalization of peacebuilding, not least the establishment of the United Nations "Peacebuilding Architecture" (PBA), as the UN has increasingly focused on the transition from peacekeeping to the consolidation of peace.

Yet, at the same time that peacebuilding has been widely taken up as a key instrument for engaging with post-conflict countries, the concept and practice of peacebuilding have also become contested and subjected to sustained criticism. According to its critics, the dominant peacebuilding paradigm widely upheld by policymakers and practitioners focuses on short-term technocratic fixes to conflict that are largely designed and implemented by actors in the Global North. Prioritizing state institution building and top-down processes, this dominant approach imports institutions that are often inappropriate to the local context; more fundamentally, it fails to address underlying questions of power relations. In this critique of the "liberal peace," peacebuilding amounts to "a form of neo-colonialism in which western methodologies of governance are patterned over local methodologies."[1]

This chapter offers a critical appraisal of the PBA's engagement with Liberia, examining the institutionalized peacebuilding process and program, while taking into account some of the concerns expressed

160 *Marina Caparini*

above. Liberia emerged from a prolonged, devastating period of civil war, and was formally included as one of five countries on the agenda of the Peacebuilding Commission (PBC) in 2010. While a generally stable post-conflict state, Liberia is also fragile: many core governance institutions are weak and societal divisions remain as potential drivers of conflict. Following an overview of the context and trajectory of engagement, the chapter examines the PBA's approach in three priority areas: rule of law, security sector reform (SSR), and national reconciliation. Rule of law and SSR are considered primarily through the initiative of the regional justice and security hubs. The chapter then examines reconciliation efforts supported by the PBC, before discussing the PBA's overall contribution to and impact on the consolidation of peace in Liberia to date. This is followed by implications of the findings of the Liberian peacebuilding experience for contemporary debates on peacebuilding. The chapter concludes with several recommendations for practitioners and scholars of peacebuilding based on the assessment of the Liberian experience.

Context and engagement of the PBA in Liberia

From 1989 to 2003, Liberia was in the throes of civil war. The conflict resulted in an estimated 250,000 deaths, mass violations of human rights, including the indiscriminate killing of civilians, widespread rape and sexual violence, forced recruitment of child soldiers, and mass displacement of 1 million people—one-third of the population—as well as the wholesale destruction of government, economy, and infrastructure. The conflict traumatized society and exacerbated pre-existing divisions and interethnic and land-based conflict.[2] With the Comprehensive Peace Agreement of 2003, and the deployment of 15,000 peacekeepers in the largest UN peacekeeping mission at the time, intensive efforts began, aimed at stabilizing and then assisting in reconstructing the shattered state and deeply divided society. These efforts were supplemented, and then transformed, following the engagement of the PBA in Liberia. Initially on a project basis in 2007, this engagement became a full-fledged program from 2010 which has intensified its efforts with the drawdown of the UN Mission in Liberia (UNMIL).

The UN Peacebuilding Architecture, consisting of the Peacebuilding Commission, Peacebuilding Support Office (PBSO), and Peacebuilding Fund (PBF), was launched with the creation of the PBC as an intergovernmental advisory body following the UN World Summit in 2005. The purpose of the PBC was to bring together all relevant peacebuilding actors in a common forum that could assist in ensuring

The impact of the PBA in Liberia 161

sustained attention, funding, identification of best practices, and development of integrated strategies for peacebuilding and recovery in countries emerging from violent conflict, countries that risk being forgotten by the international community.[3]

In October 2007, the UN Secretary-General determined that Liberia was eligible to receive funding from the PBF, marking the beginning of PBA engagement with Liberia. From then until 2010, this engagement was project driven. Liberia received US$15 million in funding from the PBF for 25 peacebuilding projects which were determined on the basis of a joint analysis of immediate peacebuilding priorities between the government of Liberia and the PBF.[4] An independent evaluation of the 25 projects in the PBF Liberia portfolio was conducted in early 2010. It found that most projects were efficiently established, with high degrees of local participation in design and implementation, although with weak monitoring. In view of eventual UNMIL drawdown, the evaluation recommended a more sustained engagement by the PBF and the development of "a longer term strategy and vision for the sustainability and ownership of a peacebuilding concept through implementation of key projects."[5]

In May 2010 the government of Liberia submitted a formal request for the PBC to enter Liberia on its agenda as the fifth country for which it would develop a country-specific engagement, or Country-Specific Configuration (CSC), noting in particular the need for further efforts in the rule of law, security sector reform, and national reconciliation in the light of eventual UNMIL withdrawal.[6] A PBC mission to Liberia was undertaken in August 2010, involving extensive consultations with over 500 stakeholders and resulting in a detailed report on the main challenges, gaps, and risks to peacebuilding in the three core areas.[7] This report came to inform the development of the Statement of Mutual Commitments, after the government's request was formally accepted in September 2010.

A CSC was created for Liberia, under the chairmanship of Prince Zeid al Hussein, permanent representative of Jordan to the UN. The Statement of Mutual Commitments (SMC) was agreed shortly thereafter.[8] According to the SMC, subsequent PBF intervention would be based on the PBC Priority Plan, to be developed by the government of Liberia with the support of the Joint Steering Committee (JSC) and the PBSO, and based on consultations with national stakeholders. The SMC identified three core priorities: strengthening the rule of law, security sector reform, and national reconciliation.

Under rule of law, while the SMC acknowledged Liberia's dual system of customary and statutory law, it focused on the lack of capacity of

162 Marina Caparini

the formal justice system, which impeded provision of impartial service to all Liberians, and on the need to bolster public confidence in the formal justice system. It set out five main areas of focus. First, legislative review would aim at clarifying the jurisdictions of customary and statutory legal systems, primarily through the creation of a Law Reform Commission. Second, access to justice would be improved, especially in the neglected countryside, by emplacing more justice personnel and building more infrastructure. Third, efforts would be made to enhance the capacity of the judiciary at all levels of legal staff in the judicial system, as well as to establish a case management system. Fourth, oversight mechanisms for all actors in the judicial system, including police, judiciary, prosecuting counsels, and public defenders, would be strengthened. Fifth, public outreach and information about citizens' legal rights and obligations would be undertaken, to address the sense of alienation many Liberians felt concerning the state justice system.[9]

The second area of focus identified in the SMC was supporting SSR. By 2010 Liberia had already undergone seven years of reform and transformation in its security sector, and, according to the original SMC, had reached a critical point. Demobilization had been conducted and the Armed Forces of Liberia (AFL), Liberian National Police (LNP), and the Bureau of Immigration and Naturalization (BIN) had been re-established, personnel vetted, and some training and restructuring implemented. However, the public continued to lack trust in these institutions. There were also critical capacity gaps to be addressed: in view of the eventual drawdown of UNMIL peacekeepers, Liberian security forces would need to be prepared to take over responsibility for maintaining law and order.

Given this context, the SMC identified six priorities in security sector reform. First, the adoption and implementation of the omnibus national security and intelligence bill and the formulation of follow-on legislation for each security institution was required, as a framework for further reforms. Second, the effectiveness of the LNP was to be improved. Third, the SMC would prioritize the LNP deployment outside Monrovia to five regional hubs located throughout the country. Fourth, it would support further institutional reform of the BIN. Fourth, sustainability, accountability, and civilian oversight of the AFL would be prioritized, as would inter-institutional relationships through the empowerment of the National Security Council, County Security Councils, and relevant legislative oversight bodies. The final priority was regional collaboration: Liberia's participation in subregional initiatives, and harmonization between national and regional instruments.[10]

The impact of the PBA in Liberia 163

As its third area of focus, the SMC outlined the promotion of national reconciliation. Several priorities were identified, among them: supporting the resolution of land tenure issues and strengthening the Land Commission; strengthening national identity including among youth; empowering women in peacebuilding and recovery; enhancing public understanding of the Truth and Reconciliation Commission (TRC) report and supporting a traditional conflict resolution and reconciliation program involving "Palava huts", or "peace huts"; supporting the Independent National Commission on Human Rights in fulfilling its mandate; and strengthening state capacity to promote national dialogue and reconciliation.[11]

In each of these three focus areas, the government of Liberia then committed to a series of concrete actions for moving towards them— generating political will to implement certain reforms, increasing relevant budgetary allowances, establishing adequate mechanisms, etc.[12] In turn, the PBC pledged to engage in "political advocacy and support, resource mobilization, and fostering coordinated action among all relevant stakeholders," in support of the peacebuilding effort.[13] The PBC and the government also agreed to undertake a review of the SMC every nine months, whereby the essential priorities and corresponding commitments could be revised, refined, and updated in the context of ongoing implementation.

In May 2011 the Liberia Peacebuilding Programme (LPP) was agreed between the government, the UN, and international partners, to implement the peacebuilding tasks in the three core areas outlined in the SMC. The LPP was based on the PBC Priority Plan, as well as the security, justice, and reconciliation elements contained in the Poverty Reduction Strategy of 2008–11.[14] The LPP elaborated a program that intentionally went beyond what the PBF itself could finance, and sought to identify all the key peacebuilding gaps in the three priority areas identified for PBC engagement—SSR, rule of law, and national reconciliation—in the hopes that the UN member states associated with the PBC Liberia configuration could assist in raising funding.[15] This was reflected in the subsequently revised SMC, which placed greater emphasis on the role of the PBC in supporting the coherence of UN and donor efforts.[16]

The LPP grouped together justice (rule of law) and security (SSR) for joint programming: this was considered the "key component" due to the major challenges related to public order and internal security faced by Liberia and the impending UNMIL transition. The PBC similarly viewed rule of law and SSR as one integrated challenge.[17] National reconciliation was deemed secondary and would be addressed separately.

164 *Marina Caparini*

The regional justice and security hubs

PBC-supported SSR activities, and several relating to rule of law, rapidly came under the auspices of the initiative to establish five regional "justice and security hubs." Each hub would be responsible for three contiguous regions, and would help to ensure the presence of more effective and sustainable state security and justice capacities to benefit local populations outside Monrovia in outlying areas. This joint Liberian government/UN initiative, financed largely by the PBF, was considered a "catalytic" intervention, intended to foster a long-term, comprehensive approach to peacebuilding through the extension of Liberian security and justice services throughout the country.[18]

State policing and the formal justice system, two of the most fundamental and defining functions of the modern state, have been particularly weak in Liberia's outlying regions. In these traditionally marginalized and under-served regions, rural Liberians have continued to rely almost exclusively on traditional and customary justice, although justice mechanisms led by chiefs have been weakened by the war, lack of resources, and unclear mandates.[19] UN military and police contingents have been the main actors providing stability and security since the end of the civil war. As UNMIL began the progressive drawdown of its forces in Liberia with a view to later withdrawal, it was understood that the Liberian state would need to assume full responsibility for internal security.

According to the original concept, the hubs were intended as a mechanism to decentralize justice and security services and to strengthen these services holistically, emphasizing the development of interlinkages between them. State justice and security actors would be physically co-located at each of these hubs: police, courts, state prosecution, public defenders, border management, and even corrections personnel. The co-location of rule-of-law actors—robust police support units and border management, officers, with elements of the justice system including county attorneys, public defenders, magistrates and judges— was intended to enhance interagency cooperation and interoperability, and ease communications, with expected benefits in service delivery to people throughout the region.[20]

Each hub was originally projected to cost about $3 million, with an additional $1 million for the enhancement of services, deployment, and outreach. The government of Liberia was expected to take full responsibility for recurring costs necessary to sustain and administer the hubs, such as office supplies, gasoline, repairs, and maintenance and cleaning services.[21] The PBF fully financed the first hub in

Gbarnga, which experienced significant cost overruns, but co-financing was sought with donors for the subsequent hubs.[22] By 2013 some $13.3 million in funding from PBSO had been allocated to support the development of the five regional justice and security hubs, constituting "the most ambitious project undertaken by the Fund thus far," according to UN Assistant Secretary-General for Peacebuilding Support Judy Cheng-Hopkins.[23]

During the first three years of PBF support, the hub initiative focused primarily on establishing the first regional hub in Gbarnga, Bong County, with responsibility for Bong, Lofa, and Nimba counties. The development of the Gbarnga hub encountered repeated delays and difficulties, with problems relating to the lack of proper planning as well as problems of design, coordination, and the construction process. Despite these difficulties, and the largely untested assumptions about co-locating security and justice providers within a Liberian setting, the initiative has brought several specific benefits to a context where public services had been severely under-resourced or absent.

The Gbarnga hub has resulted in the introduction of a range of new programs and services to the region—including probation services, fast-track court services, and a Sexual and Gender-Based Violence Crime Unit. The hub project has made possible forward-basing of desperately needed security personnel in the Police Support Units and Border Patrol Units within the region, closer to their assigned areas of responsibility, thus enabling a faster, albeit still limited, response to public disorder and border management contingencies. This has raised the profile of the Liberian state police in the region.[24] There have also been benefits in the sharing of very scarce resources among actors based at the hub, not least as regards the few vehicles at the disposal of the police support units and border patrol units. The hub has also resulted in enhancement of corrections capacities, through the hiring of more corrections officers and the building of a health clinic at the Gbarnga regional prison. Furthermore, with the completion and opening of the new Ninth Circuit Court facility at the Gbarnga hub in early 2014, urgently needed justice-related personnel and services finally began operating from the hub.[25]

Despite these contributions to building Liberian state capacities in justice and security, development of the Gbarnga hub was also problematic. Progress in implementing the hub became bogged down due to problems linked to the building of a large infrastructure project—including lack of funding, difficulties with contractors, and the construction and logistical challenges posed by the long rainy season in Liberia. The hub was further criticized for creating logistical and

166 *Marina Caparini*

financial challenges for the consumers of those services in terms of the distance of those centralized services from the nearest major urban center, Gbarnga city. For some actors based at the hub, their location is likely to have little apparent relevance or impact on their working relations with other hub inhabitants—for example, the public outreach officer who deals with citizens and Monrovia-based complaint mechanisms. For others, such as border patrol units, being located far from the border area negated the benefits in being located in a centralized hub where resources could be shared.[26]

While promoted as a means of decentralizing security and justice, the first hub in Gbarnga was found more correctly to "deconcentrate" state security and justice personnel by relocating them from Monrovia to hubs based in the periphery. Real decentralization as regards the devolution of decision-making authority and budget allocation responsibilities to the level of local (regional) authorities had yet to emerge, as Monrovia continued to make most key decisions, which were then implemented by the regionally based actors.[27]

Some questions have been raised about the sustainability of the justice and security hubs. An analysis of the implications for security of the findings of a joint World Bank/UNMIL public expenditure review published in early 2013 forecast that a sizeable financing gap would emerge between Liberian national revenues, expected foreign assistance, and SSR (including the establishment of regional justice and security hubs).[28] "It is clear that the government will not be able to absorb the full anticipated cost of security operations expected to be transferred from UNMIL."[29] Absorption of recurrent costs—including for the PBF-funded justice and security hubs—in the national budget over a multi-year period was deemed the most challenging to the Liberian government as regards sustaining SSR, and the review recommended incorporating these costs into the medium-term budget.[30] The expenditure review further noted that "a decision must be made with regard to the phasing of construction and operation of regional hubs over time given the limited available resources and the recurrent cost to operate and maintain the hubs."[31]

Liberia decreased the amount it allocated to policing in the 2013/14 budget by 18 percent compared with the preceding year, spurring the special representative of the UN Secretary-General to warn publicly that inadequate resourcing would compromise the ability of Liberian security forces to take over from UN forces during the drawdown. The intervention secured a government promise to provide sufficient resources, including coverage of recurrent costs for hubs two and three.[32]

The impact of the PBA in Liberia 167

Concerning the development of the remaining hubs, one early lesson learned from the experience of the Gbarnga hub was that a shift in emphasis was required, at least initially—from prioritizing co-location and the large investment in infrastructure that implies, to giving priority to service delivery.[33] Consequently, the planning and development of regional hubs two and three in Harper and Zwedru have concentrated in the first phase on improvements to service delivery, giving priority to ensuring prosecution of cases at circuit court level, the provision of free legal representation at magisterial and circuit court levels, and psychosocial, medical, and legal support to victims of sexual and gender-based violence.[34]

More generally, the implementation of more rigorous monitoring and evaluation mechanisms by the PBA in Liberia has made possible close tracking of expenditures and indicators, in turn providing improved capacities to demonstrate progress in reaching identified outcomes and objectives.[35] Comprehensive public opinion surveys have also enabled a better understanding of regional justice and security needs and perceptions, now being integrated into the design and implementation of hubs two and three.[36]

National reconciliation

National reconciliation is closely linked to peacebuilding. While peacebuilding is often used to refer broadly to the process of re-establishing order, the rule of law, and stability in the aftermath of conflict, reconciliation addresses the "residues of conflict"—deep societal wounds and traumas. These may produce lingering fears, anger, and resentments that can generate "antagonistic forms of identity and community that fuel rather than solve conflict."[37] Reconciliation is embedded within the broader field of transitional justice, which generally holds that conflicts may re-erupt if the legacies of violence or past abuses are not dealt with and if no deliberate efforts are made to repair the moral and social fabric of the society in question. Post-conflict reconciliation, then, refers to ways of addressing the past in order to move a country towards sustainable peace. It typically involves elements of truth-telling, enabling victims to speak about their experiences, acknowledgment of wrong-doing, reconciling victim and perpetrator on the basis of forgiveness rather than retribution, and the articulation of a vision of a peaceful, collective future.[38] However, the issue of addressing impunity or retributive justice—that is, bringing perpetrators of past crimes and human rights abuses to justice—is highly contested. In Liberia, tension between the impetus for forgiveness and

168 *Marina Caparini*

resolving impunity through criminal justice has influenced efforts towards national reconciliation, including those facilitated by the PBA.

Reconciliation often includes the establishment of a truth commission, a process established in a post-conflict context to help establish the truth about the past and its impact on the population, abuses of human rights in particular. Based on Article XIII of the 2003 Comprehensive Peace Agreement, the Liberian TRC was established in legislation in 2005 with the mandate "to promote national peace, security, unity and reconciliation" through investigation of gross human rights abuses and violations of international humanitarian law as well as other abuses that occurred during the period of civil war from 1979 to 2003.[39] The commission began operating in 2006, and submitted its final report in December 2009.

Through dialogue and testimony, the TRC sought to establish the truth about the causes and nature of the civil war period, and was able to establish a public discourse and record to that effect. However, the TRC also experienced significant problems in terms of its poor organization, inadequate resourcing and staffing, and questionable and contested methods, as well as interpersonal tensions and rivalry among its commissioners. Moreover, internal divisions among the commissioners eroded its credibility in the eyes of the domestic public and international audiences alike.[40] The final report of the commission contained several controversial recommendations relating to retributive justice, including the recommendation to establish an extraordinary tribunal and a domestic criminal court to prosecute individuals responsible for gross violations of human rights and violations of international humanitarian law, and egregious crimes under domestic law, respectively. Among the most contentious recommendations was that which proposed that 49 individuals, including the sitting president, Ellen Johnson Sirleaf, and other important figures in government, be banned from holding public office for a 30-year period.[41] The TRC consequently became blocked; despite heavy investment in the process by international donors, implementation of its recommendations was "quietly shelved."[42]

As discussed above, in 2010 the PBC and the government of Liberia agreed on the Statement of Mutual Commitments, which included national reconciliation as its third component. However, whereas attention focused on rule of law and SSR, national reconciliation efforts by comparison saw "very limited concrete activity" in the context of the controversy aroused by the TRC. That eventually spurred the PBC to request presidential authorization to develop a national strategy on reconciliation.[43]

The impact of the PBA in Liberia 169

The PBC appeared to appreciate the importance of reconciliation, as reflected in the LPP, which defined national reconciliation in terms of three specific outputs. First, national reconciliation was seen in terms of increased social cohesion, to be developed by means of "platforms" for dialogue, including Palava huts. This is a traditional conflict resolution and reconciliation mechanism widely practiced in rural areas of Liberia. It is convened by members of the community recognized for their integrity, usually a group of male elders, and is commonly used to resolve interpersonal or intercommunal tensions over land disputes, debt, divorces, and extramarital affairs.[44] The Palava hut mechanism was adopted by the TRC "to redress outstanding transitional grievances and create both the basis and opportunity to repair and restore broken relationships at the community and national levels."[45] Social cohesion was to be served through enhanced political participation and improved conflict management, using both traditional and conventional methods, including alternative dispute resolution tools.[46]

Second, reconciliation would be pursued through land-dispute resolution at local and county levels: such disputes were a root cause of conflict, and unequal access to land and land ownership is often an underlying cause of poverty and political and economic inequalities. The creation of a Land Commission to establish an alternative approach to resolution of land disputes was seen as critical for dealing with these disputes.[47]

Training and employment for youth constituted the third component of national reconciliation in the LPP. As a group, youth are in the majority in Liberia and were highly affected by the extended civil war. Youth continue to face lack of employment opportunities and are at high risk of sexual and gender-based violence, involvement in mob justice, crime, land-based conflicts and the escalation of conflicts to violence. PBF support here has focused on developing livelihood skills, apprenticeship opportunities, and fostering a sense of service and national duty through the creation of a national youth service program.[48]

National reconciliation continued to stall, however. This was attributed to the absence of a coherent strategy and framework, as well as the diversity of actors and programs that resulted in duplication of efforts, waste, and competition. There was a need for a mechanism to coordinate the various government and civil society initiatives in this area. Consequently, the government undertook, with support from the JSC, a new initiative that resulted in the Strategic Roadmap for National Healing, Peacebuilding and Reconciliation. This was developed as an implementation plan for the reconciliation elements

170   *Marina Caparini*

contained in the pre-existing LPP, described above. The roadmap is a planning document covering 18 years, "designed to foster coherence of institutions, structures, systems, mechanisms, and human resources mobilized to foster national healing and reconciliation and build sustainable peace."[49] It constitutes a coherent strategic framework for reconciliation that would explicitly identify priorities, roles, and responsibilities, as well as implementation strategies and a coordinating mechanism for the Liberian people and other stakeholders.[50] The roadmap was aligned with other major policy frameworks, including the "Agenda for Transformation," Vision 2030, and the New Deal of the International Dialogue on Peacebuilding and Statebuilding.[51]

While drawing on the LPP, the roadmap reconceptualizes reconciliation into three categories encompassing 12 thematic areas. Under "accounting for the past" are memorialization, reparations, and psychosocial recovery. Under "managing the present" are issues concerning youth, women, and political polarization, and support for people with disabilities. This category also includes issues of identity and citizenship, and national history. Under the category "planning for the future" are constitutional and legal reform. Under this plan, UN actors— UNMIL, the UN Children's Fund (UNICEF), UN Women, the UN Development Programme (UNDP), and UN Habitat—work with relevant Liberian government institutions to implement and co-manage specific projects.[52]

The roadmap marked a new impetus to move forward on reconciliation. The implementation of the roadmap was formally kicked off in June 2013 with a three-day Reconciliation Festival, followed by a large public outreach event in Gbarnga to develop an operational implementation strategy through a participatory approach and to raise public and media awareness of the process. Also in 2013 the PBF Priority Plan 2014–16 was developed by the JSC, supported by the PBSO. The plan involved a consultative process and was closely aligned to all national frameworks. It sought to address several root causes of conflict and enhance social cohesion. The plan was allocated $15 million up to 2016, part of which would be dedicated to national reconciliation. The approved Priority Plan 2014–16 lists nine projects, most of which clearly fall under the reconciliation framework: a national youth service plan, land disputes resolution system, women's economic empowerment, community-based conflict management, the Palava hut program, strengthening local/traditional mechanisms for peace, support to the law reform commission, support to the constitutional review process, and support for the PBSO in coordinating and capacity building in conflict management.[53]

The impact of the PBA in Liberia 171

Despite these auspicious signals of new commitment to reconciliation, the PBC recognized that implementation remained slow.[54] One factor delaying implementation was lack of capacity of the Independent National Human Rights Commission, responsible under the roadmap for leading community reconciliation processes through the Palava hut mechanism at local level. Another reason given for delays in stakeholder consultations was that reconciliation was a "highly sensitive topic."[55]

The Ebola crisis of 2014 further contributed to delays in implementing the reconciliation component of the peacebuilding efforts in Liberia, as funds allocated to reconciliation were diverted to the Ebola response. By August the UN Resident Coordinator warned that $3 million funding allocated by the government of Liberia to national reconciliation would probably be diverted to addressing the Ebola crisis, and that there would be delays in the timetable for the implementation of the roadmap on reconciliation.[56] Liberia subsequently confirmed, in December, that the crisis had delayed implementation of the 2014 targets under the SMC as well as PBF projects.[57]

Furthermore, the roadmap sets out a course for reconciliation aimed at fostering a national dialogue and ultimately social cohesion, but it omits the element of bringing to account those responsible for war crimes. The approach to reconciliation embodied by the roadmap is one anchored in restorative justice, although the roadmap asserts that its pursuit is not intended to preclude the pursuit of retributive or restitutive justice.[58] As explained by the head of the Liberian PBC Configuration, the PBC's focus on national reconciliation is not about punishing perpetrators or retributive justice; it involves seeking reconciliation through activities like rewriting Liberian history with due consideration for the role played by all ethnic groups, an emphasis on developing national symbols, and encouraging the establishment of Palava huts to provide a space for Liberians to discuss the conflict.[59]

While the roadmap differs from the TRC in its emphasis on restorative justice, the former faces an array of challenges similar to those that confronted the TRC. These include lack of a national consensus or shared vision for Liberian reconciliation, and lack of political will. Those responsible for implementing the roadmap can learn from the experiences of the TRC, specifically as regards ensuring adequate public support and political buy-in for its implementation.[60] However, several other factors are likely to continue to influence public attitudes: the Liberian political and economic elite contains former leaders of the conflict; command structures dating from wartime continue to exist in certain communities; and there is continuing impunity of wartime

172 *Marina Caparini*

perpetrators. National courts remain too weak to deal with war criminals; and in the absence of a war crimes tribunal, impunity continues, leaving many wartime leaders and perpetrators of war crimes in positions of political and economic power while civil society remains divided, fragile, and weak.[61] Furthermore, national processes—including the reconciliation process—are widely perceived as being driven by external actors.[62]

The de facto lower priority of reconciliation in Liberian peacebuilding until recently, the slow and delayed implementation of the roadmap, continuing challenges in coordinating efforts among Liberia's diverse peacebuilding and reconciliation actors and mechanisms, and continuing sensitivity of certain aspects of reconciliation all indicate that progress on this element has been lagging. Given the continuing divisions within Liberian society, delays in acknowledging and working with psychosocial fears and trauma from the war period may become politicized and affect relations among communities. Establishing security and order, and rebuilding state institutions and extending state authority into the historically under-served hinterland have been important elements of post-conflict stabilization and peacebuilding. However, if we accept that reconciliation is essential to long-term peacebuilding, care must be taken not to reconstruct the state with the same grievances and societal divisions that led to the conflict in the first place.

Assessment of the PBA impact on Liberian peacebuilding

Fundamental tasks of the PBC are to focus and sustain political and donor attention on a country or subregion that is recovering from conflict, to serve as a forum for coordinating and integrating donor aid and reconstruction efforts by UN and non-UN actors, and to act as guardian of the peacebuilding process. To do so, it needs to consult with the full range of actors involved in peacebuilding, from national authorities to international donors and international financial institutions to civil society, and function as an advisory body in recommending integrated strategies for post-conflict peacebuilding.[63]

This chapter finds that the PBA's engagement in Liberia has been extensive, covering a broad range of institutional reforms in the state justice and security sectors. These reforms and initiatives, particularly in rule of law and SSR, have been largely advanced in an integrated manner, as reflected in the regional justice and security hub projects, where the links between justice sector actors and law enforcement agencies have been taken into consideration in planning and

The impact of the PBA in Liberia 173

implementation. The grouping together of rule of law and SSR priorities reflects good practice by acknowledging the essential relationship between the two domains, as identified in other peacebuilding and SSR studies.[64] Development of the PBC's program priorities was also harmonized both with the poverty reduction strategy and the national security strategy.

The development of the PBA's engagement with Liberia shows a systemic process of consultation with Liberian stakeholders and joint identification of priorities. Consultative and inclusive processes were involved in the development of key PBC-supported projects—initially conducted mainly among key stakeholders in government and the international community, but also through efforts to engage local communities and civil society in nascent national reconciliation work. Public opinion surveys aimed at monitoring local perceptions of justice and security provision in the regions where hubs are being developed have been introduced, to establish baselines and inform programming on local needs.

In addition, monitoring and evaluation mechanisms have been introduced progressively and are providing an evidence base for claimed outcomes, as apparent in program reporting.[65] The PBA operates with a level of transparency that appears to be far higher than that of any other UN agency or division engaged in peacebuilding-related tasks. Documentation of programs and projects is publicly available on the Internet, and requests for interviews and information are met by key actors.

A 2013 study of the PBF's engagement with various post-conflict countries, including Liberia, indicates that over the period 2007–11 SSR generally received the largest percentage of funding among PBF-funded activities.[66] Within the domain of SSR, the PBF primarily favored projects for providing infrastructure, vehicles, and equipment, over building staff capacities through training or strengthening governance and oversight systems.[67] The study criticizes this preference for "hardware" over "software" as being at the expense of funding of local civil society and local administration, creating "capacity deficits in the areas of outreach, management and oversight and knowledge" and thus undermining longer-term sustainable peacebuilding.[68] As the UN Secretary-General has acknowledged, building up hardware is easier to measure than the more intangible rebuilding of societal trust, institutional legitimacy, or strengthening governance and oversight of the security sector.[69] More effort is needed to target the causes of conflict and instability and to improve the benchmarks, monitoring, and evaluation of SSR.

174 *Marina Caparini*

The discussion of the development of regional justice and security hubs following the pilot hub experience in Gbarnga, and the subsequent shift in emphasis to improving service delivery before infrastructure development, would indicate that the PBA has demonstrated responsiveness and flexibility, learning from mistakes and adapting programs accordingly, at least in the short to medium term. Furthermore, the hub initiative has proven an effective vehicle for mobilizing political attention, and international and domestic funding—although it may have diverted attention from other initiatives in the security and justice delivery domain.

The PBC was intended to promote integrated peacebuilding strategies. Indeed, it has played an important role in leveraging and providing expertise from within the UN system to support reconciliation, and more broadly, transitional justice efforts in post-conflict countries. Implementing such measures is costly, and early observers of the PBC hoped it could help mobilize funding for activities.[70] However, the third focus area of the PBA in Liberia, national reconciliation, appears to have been less well integrated into the other two main peacebuilding priority areas, and continues to lag behind. The reconciliation initiatives advanced tend to be more civil society focused than institution-building focused, given their emphasis on restorative justice and mitigating actual and potential sources of societal conflict. In 2014, the Ebola epidemic interrupted peacebuilding efforts: funds were diverted from the roadmap to Ebola response, entailing further delays for the new impetus towards reconciliation.

In concentrating its efforts on formal security and justice institutions, the PBA has not yet dealt effectively with the essential "hybridity" of Liberian society: the coexistence of formal state structures with informal, traditional, or customary structures (for example, "big men," village and town chiefs, secret societies). Rule of law and SSR initiatives have largely been state-centric, focusing on formal state institution building and centralized processes, extending the authority of the state throughout the country. Customary/traditional justice providers have generally not been involved, with the exception of some efforts to harmonize customary law with the formal state justice system. Recent activities concerning local and traditional conflict resolution mechanisms indicate a growing awareness of the importance of non-state peacebuilding aspects. In a society where the vast majority of the population continues to resort to customary and informal justice mechanisms over formal state ones, whether out of preference or need, a state-centric focus on institutional capacity building can only be a partial approach towards the consolidation of peace.

The impact of the PBA in Liberia 175

Assessment of Liberian experience for the peacebuilding debate

The discussion above has shown that the PBA's approach in Liberia is aligned closely with the "liberal peace" approach taken by the UN and international financial institutions; indeed, the PBA explicitly tailored its engagement in Liberia to address capacity gaps that would be left as the UNMIL drawdown progresses. Rather than questioning the assumptions and foundations on which mainstream peacebuilding is undertaken, the PBA has chosen an approach that is "problem solving" in orientation, focused on consolidating peace through top-down, institutional reforms. The main focus has been on state building, reconstituting formal institutions in the rule of law, and security sectors through the provision of technical assistance. The PBA has cultivated close cooperation with the government of Liberia, the political elite, and international donors in this regard. The concept of "justice and security hubs" has not yet been picked up and replicated elsewhere; too little time has passed since the first hub became operational for a clear assessment of whether the expected benefits are being realized.

The Liberian case illustrates some of the dilemmas that critics have associated with liberal peacebuilding. For example, Liberian national budget shortfalls for the security and justice sectors over the past two years have given rise to the question of whether the promulgated institutional reforms in the rule of law and the security sector are sustainable.[71]

The development of a close working relationship with the government brings advantages in terms of access and accountability, but it also comes with drawbacks in a context where political elites have been associated with corruption, lack of accountability, and impunity. Several observers have indicated that widespread public mistrust of the Liberian government accounted in part for the scale of the Ebola crisis.[72]

However, the PBA's approach can also show some successes that correspond to the practices and norms advanced by the critical school of peacebuilding. Local ownership is served by the PBA's use of consultative procedures and comprehensive public opinion surveys to establish local communities' needs and perceptions of justice and security needs and perceptions, which are then fed into program planning. The PBA has also raised the possibility of bringing Southern experiences into the reconciliation strand of its activities in Liberia.[73] Although delayed and deprioritized until recently, the PBA's focus on reconciliation has the potential to facilitate bottom-up processes.

The PBA's focus on building the formal justice sector may also be considered successful for cases involving groups that have often been disadvantaged under customary/traditional justice mechanisms. While

176 *Marina Caparini*

customary justice mechanisms are easily accessed and enjoy broad legitimacy in the eyes of rural populations, they tend to be patriarchal and biased against certain social groups. A recent study has shown that plaintiffs in Liberia prefer to use the formal justice system in contexts where they are disadvantaged under the customary system (typically women, minorities, and the poor), and are more satisfied with the results of the formal justice system. Thus, women in Liberia prefer to use the formal justice system when bringing cases against men, which brings them gains in areas such as greater household and child food security.[74] This indicates that critics may have been too undiscriminating in their condemnation of liberal peacebuilding's focus on institution building.

Recommendations

Future peacebuilding should expand its focus beyond state institutions to encompass non-state, customary actors in the justice and security spheres, since they remain the primary providers of justice and security services in rural areas. In order to deal with the continuing marginalization and under-serving of rural populations by public services, the PBA should work with Liberian actors not only to "deconcentrate" formal security and justice, but to support decentralization with a view to making government more responsive and accountable to local communities. Finally, it is important to avoid any further deprioritization of, or delays to, the reconciliation process in Liberia.

Notes

1 Roger Mac Ginty, "Introduction," in *Routledge Handbook of Peacebuilding*, ed. Roger Mac Ginty (London: Routledge, 2013), 5.
2 United Nations Security Council, "Report of the Secretary-General to the Security Council on Liberia," UN doc. S/2003/875, 2003, esp. paras. 26 and 30.
3 Carolyn McAskie, "2020 Vision: Visioning the Future of the United Nations Peacebuilding Architecture," NUPI, and CIPS Working Paper, The Future of the Peacebuilding Architecture Project, 2010, 13–14.
4 Republic of Liberia and United Nations Liberia, "Priority Plan for Peacebuilding Fund (PBF)—Revised: Liberia, 2009," 2009.
5 Peacebuilding Fund Liberia, "Mid-Term Review," March 2010, 13, para. 27.
6 Marjon Kamara, Mission of the Republic of Liberia to the United Nations, "Request for the Peacebuilding Commission's Engagement with Liberia," 27 May 2010, www.un.org/en/peacebuilding/cscs/lib/key_docs/country_request_liberia.pdf.

The impact of the PBA in Liberia 177

7 PBC, "Report of the PBC Delegation Mission to Liberia, 16–27 August 2010," www.un.org/en/peacebuilding/cscs/lib/pbc_visits/stmt_pbc_mission_report_16_Aug_2010.pdf.
8 Peacebuilding Commission, "Statement of Mutual Commitments on Peacebuilding in Liberia," UN doc. PBC/4/LBR/2, 2010.
9 PBC, "Statement of Mutual Commitments on Peacebuilding in Liberia," paras.7–14.
10 PBC, "Statement of Mutual Commitments on Peacebuilding in Liberia," paras. 15–21.
11 PBC, "Statement of Mutual Commitments on Peacebuilding in Liberia," paras. 23–28.
12 PBC, "Statement of Mutual Commitments on Peacebuilding in Liberia," para. 30.
13 PBC, "Statement of Mutual Commitments on Peacebuilding in Liberia," paras. 31–32.
14 International Monetary Fund, "Liberia: Poverty Reduction Strategy Paper," IMF Country Report No.08/219, Washington, DC, 2008.
15 Government of Liberia and United Nations, "Draft Liberia Peacebuilding Programme," Revised 3rd Draft, 2011.
16 Peacebuilding Commission, "Review of Progress in the Implementation of the Statement of Mutual Commitments on Peacebuilding in Liberia—First Progress Report," UN doc. PBC/6/LBR/1, 2012, para. 15(b).
17 Interview with Staffan Tillander, head of Liberia PBC Configuration, Oslo, 12 February 2014.
18 Rory Keane, "Reviewing the Justice and Security Hub Modality as Piloted in Liberia," *Stability: International Journal of Security & Development* 1, no. 1 (2012): 87.
19 Pewee Flomoku and Lemuel Reeves, "Formal and Informal Justice in Liberia," Special Issue on Consolidating Peace: Liberia and Sierra Leone, *ACCORD* 23 (2012): 44.
20 Keane, "Reviewing the Justice and Security Hub Modality as Piloted in Liberia," 87–91.
21 World Bank, "Liberia Public Expenditure Review Note," Report No. 71009-LR, 2013, para. 54.
22 World Bank, "Liberia Public Expenditure Review Note," para. 14.
23 See UNMIL, "Government of Liberia and UNMIL Welcome Launch of Justice and Security Hub," 2013, unmil.unmissions.org.
24 Marina Caparini, "Extending State Authority in Liberia: The Gbarnga Justice and Security Hub," NUPI Report No. 5, Norwegian Institute of International Affairs, Oslo, 2014.
25 PBSO, "Liberia. Project Half Yearly Progress Update: Period Covered, January–June 2014," Programme on Enhancing Access to Security and Justice at the Decentralized Level—Gbarnga Justice and Security Regional Hub, 2014, 1.
26 Caparini, "Extending State Authority in Liberia," 33.
27 Caparini, "Extending State Authority in Liberia," 48–9.
28 World Bank, "Liberia Public Expenditure Review Note," para. 43.
29 World Bank, "Liberia Public Expenditure Review Note," vii.
30 World Bank, "Liberia Public Expenditure Review Note," paras. 39, 54.
31 World Bank, "Liberia Public Expenditure Review Note," para. 69.

178 Marina Caparini

32 Caparini, "Extending State Authority in Liberia," 32.
33 PBC, "Summary of the Visit of H.E. Mr. Staffan Tillander, Chair of the Liberia Configuration, Peacebuilding Commission, to Liberia, 2–7 February 2014," para. 20.
34 PBC, "Third Progress Report," 2014, para. 52.
35 For example, see Peacebuilding Fund, "Annual Report of the Joint Steering Committee in Liberia," 2013.
36 Liberia Peacebuilding Office, "Report on Baseline Public Perception Survey," 2012; Peacebuilding Office and Ministry of Internal Affairs, Liberia, "Public Perception Survey on Justice and Security in South-East Liberia," 2013; also PBC, "Third Progress Report," para. 50.
37 Emma Hutchison and Roland Bleiker, "Reconciliation," in *Routledge Handbook of Peacebuilding*, ed. Roger Mac Ginty (London: Routledge, 2013), 82.
38 Priyal Singh and Lesley Connolly, "The Road to Reconciliation: A Case Study of Liberia's Reconciliation Roadmap," ACCORD Policy & Practice Brief No. 30, 2014, 3.
39 National Transitional Legislative Assembly, Liberia, "Truth and Reconciliation Commission Mandate," 2005, Article IV, Section 4, trcofliberia. org/about/trc-mandate.
40 Paul James-Allen, Aaron Weah and Lizzie Goodfriend, *Beyond the Truth and Reconciliation Commission: Transitional Justice Options in Liberia* (New York: International Center for Transitional Justice, 2010).
41 The Liberian Supreme Court subsequently intervened and ruled that the recommendation to ban the 49 individuals was unconstitutional, on the grounds of lack of due process and because the TRC lacked the constitutional authority to enforce this recommendation.
42 Hannah Neumann and Joel G. Winckler, "When Critique is Framed as Resistance," *International Peacekeeping* 20, no. 5 (2013): 627.
43 Peacebuilding Commission, "Review of Progress in Implementation of the Statement of Mutual Commitments on Peacebuilding in Liberia—First Progress Report," UN doc. PBC/6/LBR/1, 2012, para. 8.
44 Ezekiel Pajibo, *Traditional Justice Mechanisms: The Liberian Case* (Stockholm: International IDEA, 2008), 18–24.
45 Truth and Reconciliation Commission, Vol. Three, Title XII, "The Palava Hut or Peace Forums," 2009, 2.
46 Government of Liberia and United Nations, "Draft Liberia Peacebuilding Programme," Revised 3rd Draft, 9–10.
47 Government of Liberia and United Nations, "Draft Liberia Peacebuilding Programme," 10–11.
48 Government of Liberia and United Nations, "Draft Liberia Peacebuilding Programme," 11–12.
49 Government of Liberia, "Towards a Reconciled, Peaceful and Prosperous Liberia: A Strategic Roadmap for National Healing, Peacebuilding and Reconciliation, June 2012–July 2030," Draft 3, 2012.
50 Government of Liberia, "Towards a Reconciled, Peaceful and Prosperous Liberia," 7.
51 Government of Liberia, "Towards a Reconciled, Peaceful and Prosperous Liberia."

The impact of the PBA in Liberia   179

52 UN Mission in Liberia, "Liberia: Joint Press Conference by the Peace Building Office and the Governance Commission," 29 July 2013.
53 Peacebuilding Fund, "Annual Programme Narrative Progress Report: Reporting Period 1 January–31 December 2013," 2013, 5–6.
54 Peacebuilding Commission, "Informal Meeting of the Liberian Country Specific Configuration: Chair's Summary of the Discussion," 24 February 2014, para. 8.
55 Joint Steering Committee, "Annual Report of Joint Steering Committee in Liberia," 28 November 2013, 7.
56 Peacebuilding Commission, "Summary of the First Joint Informal Meeting of the PBC Configuration of Guinea, Liberia and Sierra Leone on the Ebola Crisis," 18 August 2014, 3.
57 Peacebuilding Commission, "Summary of the PBC Joint Session of the Guinea, Liberia and Sierra Leone Configurations on the Ebola Crisis and Peacebuilding Efforts," New York, 3 November 2014, para. 5.
58 Government of Liberia, "Towards a Reconciled, Peaceful and Prosperous Liberia," (Roadmap), 16.
59 Interview with Ambassador Staffan Tillander, Oslo, 12 February 2014.
60 Singh and Connolly, "The Road to Reconciliation," 6–7.
61 International Crisis Group, "Time for Much Delayed Reconciliation and Reform," 2012.
62 Enrique Sanchez and Sylvia Rognvik, "Building Just Societies: Reconciliation in Transitional Settings," United Nations Workshop Report, Accra, Ghana, 5–6 June 2012, 21; and Government of Liberia, "Towards a Reconciled, Peaceful and Prosperous Liberia," (Roadmap), 14.
63 Gerhard Thallinger, "The UN Peacebuilding Commission and Transitional Justice," *German Law Journal* 8, no. 7 (2007): 689–90.
64 Ann Fitz-Gerald, *SSR and Peacebuilding: Thematic Review of Security Sector Reform (SSR) to Peacebuilding and the Role of the Peacebuilding Fund* (New York: United Nations Peacebuilding Support Office, 2012), 10, www.un.org/en/peacebuilding/pbso/pdf/SSR2_web.pdf.
65 See Peacebuilding Fund documents for Liberia on the Multi-Partner Trust Fund Office database, mptf.undp.org/document/search?fund=PB000&country=LBR&go=true.
66 Sari Graben and Ann Fitz-Gerald, "Mind the Gap: The Importance of Local Institutional Development in Peace-building-funded Security Interventions," *Conflict, Security & Development* 13, no. 3 (2013): 290.
67 Graben and Fitz-Gerald, "Mind the Gap," 287.
68 Graben and Fitz-Gerald, "Mind the Gap," 311.
69 United Nations, "Peacebuilding in the Aftermath of Conflict," Report of the Secretary-General, UN doc. A/69/399-S/2014/694, 2014, para. 26.
70 Thallinger, "The UN Peacebuilding Commission and Transitional Justice," 698–700.
71 Barnard Harborne, "The Costs of Security Sector Reform: Questions of Affordability and Purpose," Sustainable Security blog, 9 April 2014, sustainablesecurity.org/2014/04/09/costs-of-the-security-sector.
72 Helen Epstein, "Ebola in Liberia: An Epidemic of Rumors," *The New York Review of Books*, 18 December 2014, www.nybooks.com/articles/archives/2014/dec/18/ebola-liberia-epidemic-rumors; Sara Jerving, "Why Liberians Thought Ebola was a Government Scam to Attract Western

180 *Marina Caparini*

Aid," *The Nation*, 16 September 2014, www.thenation.com/article/181618/why-liberians-thought-ebola-was-government-scam-attract-western-aid#.

73 See the PBC-commissioned paper, "South–South Cooperation: Support to National Reconciliation in Liberia," 30 January 2014.

74 Justin Sandefur and Bilal Siddiqi, "Delivering Justice to the Poor: Theory and Experimental Evidence from Liberia," 15 November 2013, bilalsiddiqi.com/blog/wp-content/uploads/2013/11/Delivering_Justice_to_the_Poor_2013-11-15.pdf.

10 The impact of the Peacebuilding Architecture in Guinea-Bissau

Adriana Erthal Abdenur and Danilo Marcondes de Souza Neto

- An "awkward fit"
- Impact: How the PBC has affected Guinea-Bissau
- Guinea-Bissau and debates on UN peacebuilding
- Moving ahead

In 2005, as part of broader reform efforts at the United Nations UN) initiated by Secretary-General Kofi Annan, a new architecture devoted to peacebuilding was created. This was meant to bridge the organizational gap between the UN Security Council and Economic and Social Council (ECOSOC) in order to prevent countries marked by conflict from slipping back into violence. In the context of the 10-year review, it is necessary to consider how these mechanisms have contributed to peacebuilding in concrete cases, as well as how those experiences have fed back into the UN to reshape broader discussions on the causes of, and approaches to, recurring conflict.

This chapter focuses on the case of Guinea-Bissau, analyzing the role of the UN Peacebuilding Architecture (PBA)—the Peacebuilding Commission (PBC), Peacebuilding Fund (PBF), and Peacebuilding Support Office (PBSO)—in stabilizing the country and promoting development. We also examine how these experiences have shaped key concepts and approaches at the core of UN peacebuilding.

Analyzing the case of Guinea-Bissau is important not only because it is one of the six countries on the PBC agenda, but also because its somewhat awkward fit with the PBC's 2005 mandate sheds light on both the capacities and shortcomings of the UN mechanisms. Drawing on interviews carried out with diplomats, UN officials, and the Guinea-Bissauan government and civil society representatives, we find that efforts to stabilize the country have been constrained by the proliferation of different perspectives on, and thus approaches to, the root causes of its instability. This mismatch is exacerbated by the relatively

182   A. Erthal Abdenur and D. Marcondes de Souza Neto

scant attention that Guinea-Bissau has received within the international community. The April 2012 *coup d'état* that led to the suspension of PBC activities in the country renewed debates about the need to balance security-focused initiatives with development-oriented efforts. However, the limitations of the UN mechanisms in preventing recurrent interruptions to constitutional rule in Guinea-Bissau underscore the need to strengthen the preventive as well as remedial dimensions of peacebuilding as envisioned by the UN mechanisms.

We begin with an overview of how Guinea-Bissau entered the PBC's agenda, in light of the country's chronic political instability and persistent poverty. We then analyze the UN peacebuilding mechanisms' impact in Guinea Bissau, and finally we look at how those experiences have in turn shaped discussions about peacebuilding at the UN.

An "awkward fit"

The UN peacebuilding mechanisms were established through General Assembly resolution 60/180 and Security Council resolution 1645, drawing on nearly a decade of discussions on peacebuilding. Secretary-General Boutros Boutros-Ghali's "Agenda for Peace" provided an initial definition of the concept, and the High-Level Panel on Threats, Challenges and Change, convened by Secretary-General Kofi Annan in 2004, fed into the 2005 report *In Larger Freedom: Towards Development, Security, and Human Rights for All*. Although the initiative generated high expectations about the UN's ability to help countries marked by conflict and instability to avoid lapsing back into conflict, deliberations over the procedures of the new PBC were protracted, and its mandate as established in 2007 was narrower than many of the participating states had hoped. For instance, the function of conflict prevention in peacebuilding was minimized, mainly because of concerns with national sovereignty.

These points were underscored by the 2010 review of the UN peacebuilding mechanisms, which recognized that this architecture needed significant overhaul in order to be effective, particularly given changing views about the UN's peacekeeping model. The review noted that, against initial expectations, requests for inclusion within the PBC agenda have been few, and that the engagement of these mechanisms with situations of instability has not been very clear.[1] Stating bluntly that "this threshold of success has not been achieved,"[2] the review cites, among the reasons for lack of sufficient effectiveness, lagging commitment by some member states and the limited implementation of preventive measures, even within the narrow scope provided for in

The impact of the PBA in Guinea-Bissau 183

the PBC's mandate. Despite noting the devotion by Country-Specific Configuration (CSC) chairs and their support structures, which had managed to call greater attention on the part of the international community to the cases, the review indicated that the commission's role in advocating for the allocation of adequate resources for key issues must also be boosted,[3] including through adequate financing to peacebuilding operations.[4]

With respect to Guinea-Bissau specifically, what contextual features have limited the UN PBA in contributing to the prevention of recurring violence, before and after the 2010 review? Guinea-Bissau is among the world's poorest countries, ranked 177th on the UN's 2014 Human Development Index.[5] It has also experienced chronic political instability since achieving independence from Portugal in 1974.[6] As in many other African countries, the late 1980s were marked by economic liberalization, the abandonment of Marxist-oriented policies from the time of independence, and the establishment of a "structural adjustment program" guided by the International Monetary Fund (IMF) and World Bank. Despite changes to the national constitution made in the early 1990s, including the abolition of the death penalty and of the single-party government, economic liberalization and political reform were not translated into democratic stability.[7] After an initial democratic period, 1994–98, a civil war was fought in 1998 and 1999, during which the country's already scarce basic infrastructure was nearly completely destroyed.

As a state frequently referred to as "fragile" or "failed," Guinea-Bissau has had great difficulty in consolidating its democratic process and institutions, with its political order frequently interrupted by *coups d'état* and political assassinations. The economy is precarious, heavily dependent on the production of cashew nuts for export. Those problems are intertwined in complex ways: for instance, given the lack of income-generating activities and social safety nets, military leaders who fought in the struggle for independence have little incentive to retire, and the armed forces remain severely under-professionalized.[8] In addition, although there has been no large-scale ethnic violence in Guinea-Bissau, the prominent role of the Balanta ethnic group within the military has generated further social tensions. As a result, security sector reform in Guinea-Bissau is crucial for guaranteeing stability and democracy, particularly in order to put an end to decades of mobilization of the armed forces.[9]

Within this context of high uncertainty, peacebuilding—particularly in terms of creating an environment conducive to democratic institutions and peaceful alternation of power—is a highly complex effort.

184   *A. Erthal Abdenur and D. Marcondes de Souza Neto*

According to Birgit Embaló, the political order in Guinea-Bissau is a "heterarchical" configuration, not characterized by the idea of the state disciplining other groups, but rather by "the coexistence of different logics of order (state/non-state, civil/military, local/national etc.)."[10] There are ever-changing constellations of actors involved which tend to separate and reunite, with few stable alliances and coalitions.

In 1999, a UN mission in Guinea-Bissau was established, the UN Integrated Peacebuilding Office in Guinea-Bissau (UNIOGBIS). Its repeatedly extended mandate had goals of supporting the consolidation of constitutional rule, promoting political dialogue and reconciliation, encouraging security sector reform, and promoting respect for human rights and the rule of law. The office has assisted in several national elections, including those convened in July 2009 after the assassination of President João Bernardo "Nino" Vieira.[11] UNIOGBIS has also sought to enhance cooperation among the major international players working towards stability in Guinea-Bissau, including the UN, the African Union (AU), the European Union (EU), the Economic Community of West African States (ECOWAS), and the Community of Portuguese-Speaking Countries (CPLP).

However, with the recurrence of violence and the continuing fragility of state institutions, international drug trade groups began operating in the country. In the meantime, Guinea-Bissau had been attracting little attention from the international community, including from the most influential members of the Security Council, who have concentrated on other cases on the PBC agenda (the United States on Liberia, the United Kingdom on Sierra Leone, and France on Côte d'Ivoire).[12] Guinea-Bissau has also sometimes been sidelined by situations of more urgent humanitarian need, like the crisis in the Democratic Republic of the Congo.[13] Some donors, frustrated by the recurring instability, have either pulled out or scaled back their assistance.

According to Rob Jenkins,[14] the Guinea-Bissau authorities consented to have the country included on the PBC agenda largely because of pressure from international donors. Similarly, Rodrigo Tavares and Luís Bernardino[15] list the inclusion of Guinea-Bissau in the PBC as one of the accomplishments of the International Contact Group on Guinea-Bissau (ICG-GB).[16] In the July 2007 country request letter, the government noted its difficulty in filling the funding gap and mentioned the "risk of continuing in a downward spiral, with all the related social and political consequences that one can imagine in terms of threats to human security and peace, as well as in the whole sub-region."[17] A referral letter from the Secretary-General to the president of the Security Council on 28 November that year acknowledged the efforts by the government of Guinea-Bissau to re-engage with the international community. The letter also thanked Nigeria and ECOWAS for supporting security sector reform, necessary to help demobilized military personnel to reintegrate constructively into civilian life and thus interrupt the cycle of coups. However, the text also acknowledged "new challenges," including the threat of drug and human trafficking that would have to be addressed "in order to prevent the unravelling of the important gains made so far." In December, Guinea-Bissau was placed on the PBC agenda, as the third country after Sierra Leone and Burundi (both June 2006).

In some respects, as UN officials have noted, Guinea-Bissau had "an awkward fit" with the PBC agenda. According to PBC staff, the commission had originally been envisaged with a role starting when UN peacekeeping forces pull out of a country.[18] Guinea-Bissau's civil war, however, had ended as far back as 1999. This time gap meant that, despite recurring instability, the country was not perceived by the international community as having the same emergency dimension seen elsewhere, as in the Central African Republic (CAR)—particularly given the absence of large-scale violence in Guinea-Bissau (assassinations have targeted military and political elites). In addition, there has been no UN peacekeeping mission in Guinea-Bissau, which meant that it did not fit cleanly with the "sequencing" thinking prevalent at the UN, in which peacebuilding is viewed as the transition from peacekeeping to long-term stability and development. For Jenkins, in 2007/08 Guinea-Bissau was more a case of a fragile state than a post-conflict state, but the recurring instability justified its inclusion on the PBC agenda, since the strategies recommended for Guinea-Bissau could "be perceived as relevant throughout the wider conflict-prevention sector."[19]

Guinea-Bissau's inclusion on the PBC agenda led to the adoption of a Strategic Framework for Peacebuilding. The move also increased the attention given by the international community to the situation in the country. However, this attention focused heavily on the increasing entrenchment of the international drug and human trade, framed by Northern countries as potential threats to international security. In March 2008, UN Secretary-General Ban Ki-moon declared that Guinea-Bissau was eligible to receive assistance from the PBF. Two tranches were set up: an initial allocation of US$6 million, approved in April against a first Priority Plan, and an additional $16.8 million, approved in June 2011, for a plan focusing on employment, national dialogue, and security sector reform.

The 2010 PBA review considered Guinea-Bissau as being "further back on the road to peace when compared to Sierra Leone and Burundi."[20] The report also acknowledged that until that point, the

186 *A. Erthal Abdenur and D. Marcondes de Souza Neto*

country had experienced limited benefits from PBC engagement.[21] In 2012, President Malam Bacai Sanhá died of natural causes in Paris, and the government began organizing anticipated presidential elections. Although the CSC provided financial support for the elections, on 12 April that year the military seized power in yet another *coup d'état*. The international community denounced the overthrow, as did the CSC in briefings to the Security Council. Following the coup, the PBF steering committee for Guinea-Bissau was dismantled, and the PBF suspended its initiatives in the country pending a return to constitutional order, in line with the position of the international community, multilateral organizations, and bilateral partners alike.[22] To facilitate a return to constitutional order, the CSC began working to facilitate dialogue and coordination among the key international partners of Guinea-Bissau, focusing on ECOWAS and the CPLP. The coup, however, delayed presidential elections by more than two years,[23] and led to the suspension of practically all development cooperation in the country.

Impact: How the PBC has affected Guinea-Bissau

In light of the April 2012 coup, Guinea-Bissau's political instability underscores the need for more preventive action by the UN PBA. This is not to say that existing mechanisms have had no impact in Guinea-Bissau. First, the inclusion of Guinea-Bissau on the PBC agenda has created new institutional channels linking the international community to local politics. Communication between UNIOGBIS and the UN has been strengthened, and new channels have been created with regional players such as Senegal, Nigeria, Angola, ECOWAS, and the AU, as well as with external actors like the EU, Portugal, and Brazil. Within Guinea-Bissau, this interaction has raised awareness among domestic stakeholders of the existence and function of UN peacebuilding mechanisms, although the recurrent political upheavals constrain the institutional learning process on both sides.

In addition, the inclusion of Guinea-Bissau on the PBC agenda has gradually raised the attention paid by the international community to the country's political instability, including the possibility of cross-border spillover. Such attention is particularly important because a major challenge in promoting peacebuilding in Guinea-Bissau has been the oscillating commitment on the part of the international community. Teresa Cravo argues that the EU's engagement in the country has been motivated not by considerations of the political developments in Guinea-Bissau, but primarily by perceptions that the country had

The impact of the PBA in Guinea-Bissau 187

become an external source of insecurity for the EU.[24] Although the "attention deficit" around Guinea-Bissau is still significant, especially with other conflicts breaking out in Africa, some of the aforementioned actors have been following the situation in Guinea-Bissau more systematically, including through the monitoring function of the PBC. This attention has targeted not only the general situation in Guinea-Bissau, but more specifically, the need for urgent security sector reform and for balancing security initiatives with development-oriented efforts.

As a platform for political coordination, the PBC has managed to foster inclusive dialogue to some extent, promoting calm during turbulent periods. However, unlike in Burundi, no permanent forum for dialogue has been established. With respect to resources, the UN has helped to devise mobilization strategies in support of peacebuilding efforts in Guinea-Bissau. Most recently, the UN peacebuilding mechanisms have provided support for elections, including those held in 2014. The PBF has financed specific initiatives, although these were suspended after the coup.

Despite these improvements, the April 2012 coup shows that the UN peacebuilding mechanisms have not sufficed to break the cycle of violence in Guinea-Bissau. Some issues of effectiveness have already been identified. The planning process was drawn-out and ended up replicating some existing development initiatives, generating frustration in Guinea-Bissau and undermining confidence in the UN mechanisms. As the 2010 review put it, "given limited national capacity, the administrative burden of drawing up, implementing and monitoring the strategic framework has been particularly marked."[25] Concerning political coordination, the rapidly changing cast of characters in Guinea-Bissauan politics leads to uneven involvement of national stakeholders in the process of establishing peacebuilding priorities. As a result, civil society entities—including those focused on women's issues—have not been adequately incorporated into the process.

In addition, despite the PBC's support of elections, there is clearly a need for broader and more sustainable resource mobilization. Initially, the PBF underestimated Guinea-Bissau's needs as regards resource allocation. In April 2008, the fund approved a mere $6 million for Guinea-Bissau—as compared to $35 million for Sierra Leone in March 2007, $15 million for Liberia in December 2007 (Liberia would be entered on the PBC agenda in 2010), and $35 million for Burundi, also in 2007. UN officials have since tried to address the resource gap, as reflected in the June 2011 approval to allocate $16.8 million for Guinea-Bissau's second priority plan.[26] Nonetheless, as regards security sector reform, for instance, Guinea-Bissau has been provided with fewer resources from the PBF: by 2012, it had received less than $4

188   *A. Erthal Abdenur and D. Marcondes de Souza Neto*

million, whereas Sierra Leone had been allocated $10 million and Burundi over $12 million.[27]

For making the democratic process more sustainable, support for elections is necessary—but the case of Guinea-Bissau underscores the vital importance of going beyond procedural democracy. As seen by the Guinea-Bissauan authorities, the international community had initially focused on ensuring the conditions needed for electoral processes to take place; it was only after the appointment of José Ramos Horta as head of UNIOGBIS that greater attention was given to the post-electoral period.[28] Security sector reform is important to help demobilize older military leaders and provide them with stability in retirement, opening up space for newly trained professionals in the military and security forces. Projects such as the Special Pension Fund for the armed forces and security forces had been taken up by the CSC prior to the 12 April coup, and some individual countries, including Brazil, had provided assistance for establishing new training centers for the military and security forces. That said, however, efforts to address the needs of the women and youth of Guinea-Bissau should be included among peacebuilding priority areas.[29]

Broader institution building is necessary to consolidate the democratic process and expand state capacity between elections. In addition, given the country's precarious economic situation and heavy reliance on cashew cultivation, more development projects are needed to boost productivity and diversify the economy. The provision of public services such as education and healthcare must also be addressed. These demands are particularly challenging because the international community has tended to approach the instability in Guinea-Bissau from a military/police perspective, as reflected in the common portrayal of Guinea-Bissau as a "narco-state."[30] Such characterization can lead to an approach based narrowly on rooting out those who are believed to participate in the illicit drug trade. Although addressing illicit flows is important for ensuring stability and avoiding spillover, political instability in Guinea-Bissau dates much further back than the entrance of organized crime. Underdevelopment is a root cause, so excessive focus on addressing illicit flows and the related problem of impunity is unlikely to break the cycle of violence and poverty in Guinea-Bissau.

Guinea-Bissau and debates on UN peacebuilding

The interaction between UN peacebuilding mechanisms and actors in Guinea-Bissau can be seen as a two-way process. First, the case of Guinea-Bissau has highlighted the need to maximize the catalytic

The impact of the PBA in Guinea-Bissau   189

potential of the UN PBA by improving coordination between PBC initiatives and other UN mechanisms—especially since there are so many UN divisions, agencies, and programs dealing hands-on with aspects of peacebuilding. Although the CSC has sought convergence of perspectives with other UN bodies, including the PBSO, the Department of Political Affairs, and UNIOGBIS, it is important to enlist the participation of other agencies as well, in order to implement a comprehensive strategy for Guinea-Bissau. For instance, there could be better coordination with the India, Brazil and South Africa Fund, which has implemented small but effective development projects in the country.

Beyond the UN, there is also recognition of the need to improve coordination among stakeholders, especially in light of the interest on the part of African powers like Nigeria, Angola, and South Africa[31] in playing an important role in Guinea-Bissau. At a May 2012 working lunch meeting convened by the UN, the key partners stressed the need for improved coordination, including the elaboration of a common strategy, for instance by revitalizing the ICG-GB. In terms of positive advances, there has been greater awareness on the part of the PBC regarding the implications of transnational flows of illicit drugs, contraband arms, and human trafficking. This is particularly important because there have been occasional links between turbulence in Guinea-Bissau and instability across the border with Senegal, in the province of Casamance.[32] These cross-border issues underscore the need to integrate the countries of the region, as well as regional organizations, into the PBA's policy response.

Second, the case of Guinea-Bissau illustrates the importance of a long-term engagement with the peacebuilding process. Rebuilding relationships in the context of frequent coups and assassinations takes time as well as constant engagement. As noted by the 2010 review, peacebuilding does not lend itself to compartmentalization, and it is important to resist the urge to focus on measurable elements of peacebuilding when so many aspects are political or otherwise intangible. In Guinea-Bissau, there is particular concern about the effect that suspended cooperation has had on the resumption of peacebuilding efforts.[33] In 2012, the PBC called on international partners to "immediately reengage with Guinea-Bissau" once an acceptable political arrangement could be widely agreed upon, but there has been little guidance as to how to resume efforts that were interrupted for more than two years. It was also unclear how the suspension of funding and initiatives will affect the resumption of these efforts after the 2014 elections. In a May 2014 statement, the PBC chair, Brazilian Ambassador Antonio de Aguiar Patriota, supported the proposal of the

190   A. Erthal Abdenur and D. Marcondes de Souza Neto

special representative of the UN Secretary-General for a donor conference for Guinea-Bissau, intended to transform the pledged support into concrete reality.[34]

The case of Guinea-Bissau has also prompted questions about the PBC's responsiveness to sudden shifts in circumstances. The commission has been criticized for how it has reacted (or failed to react) to changing conditions on the ground in Guinea-Bissau. According to Necla Tschirgi, after violence erupted in 2009, the PBC issued a condemnation but failed to assess promptly how the events would affect its involvement in the country.[35] (Other UN divisions also bear responsibility for inadequate responsiveness: it took over a year for the requests of Guinea-Bissau and CAR for inclusion in the PBC to be transmitted from the Secretariat and the Security Council to the PBC.[36])

Although the PBC is not an operational body, delays in project implementation have also affected peacebuilding efforts. According to Ball and van Beijnum, the rehabilitation of the military barracks project has been postponed due not only to the political instability, but also because of practical issues like difficulties in staff recruitment and in the preparation of contracts for national and international bidders.[37] Such delays end up creating additional hurdles not only at the project level, but also as regards coordination efforts.

Third, the case of Guinea-Bissau has enriched discussions within the UN about the PBA's institutional learning process. Although the commission did reach beyond its comfort zone by incorporating both Guinea-Bissau and CAR into its agenda, its engagement in those countries has sometimes revealed an uncritical continuation of previous practices. For example, the negotiated framework for Guinea-Bissau "contained no indicators or benchmarks for any of the commitments mentioned, nor was a monitoring and tracking document circulated. Guinea-Bissau's first review took place without a progress report, or indeed a framework."[38] More broadly, the case of Guinea-Bissau has been recognized within the PBC as a clear illustration of why the idea of sequencing—that peacekeeping operations are to be followed by peacebuilding—is inadequate. UN officials recognize that in addition to the need to conduct peacebuilding activities concurrently in cases where there is a peacekeeping mission, there is also a need to reimagine the role of peacebuilding in contexts where, as in Guinea-Bissau, there has not been a UN peacekeeping mission. In other words, the case of Guinea-Bissau has shown that UN peacebuilding cannot be predicated on the prior existence of a UN peacekeeping mission.

The recurring violence in Guinea-Bissau also shows that there is inadequate knowledge within the UN about the local political situation

The impact of the PBA in Guinea-Bissau 191

and the socioeconomic issues that underpin the instability. Without such knowledge, it is difficult to keep pace with the fast-changing political scene and to facilitate the design of effective initiatives, and carry out coordination of stakeholders, nationally and regionally.

Perhaps most importantly, the case of Guinea-Bissau indicates the need to rethink and boost the preventive function of UN peacebuilding mechanisms. After the April 2012 coup, a Security Council report argued that UNIOGBIS, the PBC's Guinea-Bissau CSC, and the UN Office for West Africa had not adequately anticipated political developments in the country.[39] During the negotiations leading up to the creation of the PBA, the discussion of an early warning system generated alarm among UN member states, including African countries, whose representatives expressed concern that such a system would infringe on national sovereignty and might be used to legitimize intervention by external actors. However, the case of Guinea-Bissau shows that the PBC will have to strengthen its preventive function, even if this is limited to circumstances where local stakeholders have requested assistance. This idea was acknowledged in the 2010 review, which noted the need for "a more forthright acceptance of the preventive dimension of the Commission's role."[40] In part this could be achieved by boosting coordination with UN agencies and other efforts geared at monitoring the ongoing political situation and assessing progress and reversals in the country's socioeconomic development.

Finally, the case of Guinea-Bissau has shown that, although having another developing country lead the CSC is not a panacea for peacebuilding, there can be advantages, facilitating dialogue among local actors. As with the Moroccan leadership of the CSC for CAR, the Brazilian chairmanship of the Guinea-Bissau CSC has shown that a fellow developing country can, under certain circumstances, mobilize a wide variety of actors within the international community. In addition, developing countries may be tapped into as sources of innovation and normative entrepreneurship. In the case of Guinea-Bissau, Brazil has long advocated a more balanced approach to the security and development dimensions of peacebuilding, arguing that failure to help Guinea-Bissau to meet basic development functions tends to undermine efforts to reform the security sector and consolidate the democratic process.[41] In addition, Brazil's presence in the Security Council has served to upgrade the level of council involvement with Guinea-Bissau. On the occasions when Brazil has occupied a non-permanent seat on the council, it has advocated on behalf of Guinea-Bissau.[42] Brazilian development cooperation initiatives in the country have emphasized security sector reform as well as the strengthening of state

192 A. Erthal Abdenur and D. Marcondes de Souza Neto

institutions and capacity building, stressing the interconnectedness of security and development.[43]

The case of Guinea-Bissau also highlights the importance of the regional dimensions of peacebuilding, including the need to facilitate a protagonist role for regional actors such as ECOWAS and to diffuse rivalries that may emerge among actors. Nonetheless, a wide array of factors external to UN efforts, including geopolitical rivalries, pose challenges to peacebuilding in Guinea-Bissau. During the country's civil war, Portugal and France competed for influence in the region, via the CPLP and Francophone members of ECOWAS;[44] this rivalry weakened coordination between the two institutions.[45] Joshua Forrest argues that the CPLP was more successful than ECOWAS in mediating in the war, because it was viewed as "politically neutral."[46] According to Security Council Report, the chair of ECOWAS, President Alassane Ouattara of Côte d'Ivoire, has influenced ECOWAS's position by fuelling criticism of the Angolan Military Mission in Guinea-Bissau because Angola had supported former President Laurent Gbagbo during the Ivorian crisis.[47] Similarly, interest in Guinea-Bissau within the Security Council has depended heavily on the specific countries sitting on the council. Attention to Guinea-Bissau has decreased when Brazil has not been on the council, and greater attention has instead been paid to the possible implications of drug trafficking on peacebuilding efforts.[48]

Moving ahead

Guinea-Bissau's interaction with the UN peacebuilding mechanisms has been unusual in two key ways when compared with the other countries on the PBA's agenda. First, it is not a classic case of an immediate or near-immediate post-conflict context, but a situation of recurring political instability complicated by severe underdevelopment and illegal transnational flows. Second, out of the seven years that Guinea-Bissau has been on the agenda of the PBC, more than two have been marked by the suspension of most UN peacebuilding activities due to the 2012 *coup d'état*, with only some political coordination remaining during this period. These two factors highlight some of the limitations of the UN peacebuilding mechanisms so far, particularly given its narrow mandates and lack of effectiveness on the ground, as regards preventive as well as remedial efforts.

Despite these challenges, there are now positive expectations regarding peacebuilding in Guinea-Bissau. One important step was taken in early June 2014, after the CPLP Conference of Constitutional

The impact of the PBA in Guinea-Bissau   193

Jurisdictions, during its meeting in Benguela, Angola, decided to end the suspension of Guinea-Bissau pending the inauguration of the members of the National People's Assembly and the new president.[49] In addition, in late 2013, Brazil assumed the presidency of the PBC, generating new hopes that the commission may be strengthened, perhaps even reformed. For this, however, Brazil would have had to overcome not only inattentiveness from key players and the limitations of the position, as regards its low executive power and its short term (which expired in early 2015), but also resistance from countries that have a status quo-oriented, highly legalist approach, such as Russia. The ability to enact change at the PBA, and in Guinea-Bissau more specifically, will depend on whether support for change can be mustered across a wider range of stakeholders. If effectiveness of the PBA can be enhanced for a broader spectrum of contexts, that will help not only in stabilizing and developing Guinea-Bissau, but also in assisting other "non-traditional" cases of recurring political violence.

Notes

1 United Nations, "2010 Review of the United Nations Peacebuilding Architecture," UN doc. A/64/868-S/2010/393, 21 July 2010, www.un.org/ga/search/view_doc.asp?symbol=A/64/868.
2 UN, "2010 Review of the United Nations Peacebuilding Architecture," 8.
3 UN, "2010 Review of the United Nations Peacebuilding Architecture," 11.
4 UN, "2010 Review of the United Nations Peacebuilding Architecture," 28.
5 UNDP, "Human Development Index 2014," 2014.
6 According to Birgit Embaló, Portuguese colonialism left no strong administrative structures in the country. See Birgit Embaló, "Civil–Military Relations and Political Order in Guinea-Bissau," *Journal of Modern African Studies* 50 (2012): 255. In contrast to other Portuguese colonies such as Angola and Mozambique, Portugal had little interest in promoting settlement in Guinea-Bissau.
7 Ibid., 253–81.
8 Ibid.
9 Teresa Cravo, "Security Sector Reform and the Rule of Law: A Critique of International Intervention in the Context of Instability," paper presented at the International Studies Association Annual Conference, 26–9 March 2014, Toronto.
10 Embaló, "Civil–Military Relations and Political Order in Guinea-Bissau," 255.
11 Vieira was prime minister of Guinea-Bissau between 1978 and 1980, and president 1980–99, and again from 2005 until his assassination in 2009.
12 Security Council Report, "October 2007 Monthly Forecast: Africa—Guinea-Bissau," 2007.
13 Security Council Report, "March 2007 Monthly Forecast: Africa—Guinea-Bissau," 2007; and International Crisis Group, "Beyond Turf Wars:

194 *A. Erthal Abdenur and D. Marcondes de Souza Neto*

Managing the Post-Coup Transition in Guinea-Bissau," Africa Report, no. 190, 17 August 2012.

14 Rob Jenkins, *Peacebuilding: From Concept to Commission* (London: Routledge, 2013).

15 Rodrigo Tavares and Luís B. Bernardino, "Speaking the Language of Security: The Commonwealth, the Francophonie and the CPLP in Conflict Management in Africa," *Conflict, Security and Development* 11, no. 5 (2011): 607–36.

16 The ICG-GB was created in 2006 and includes Angola, Brazil, Cape Verde, France, the Gambia, Ghana, Guinea, Portugal, Senegal, Spain, the UN, the EU, the Community of Portuguese-Speaking Countries, the Economic Community of West African States, the West African Economic and Monetary Union, the IMF, and the World Bank. UNIOGBIS, "Sept. 24, 2007— Final Communiqué of the III Working Session of the ICG on Guinea-Bissau," uniogbis.unmissions.org/Default.aspx?ctl=Details&tabid=9921&m id=12885&ItemID=11836.

17 Letter from Prime Minister Martinho Dafa Cabi to UN Secretary-General Ban Ki-moon, Bissau, 11 July 2007.

18 Interview with PBC staff member, New York, April 2013.

19 Jenkins, *Peacebuilding*, 111.

20 UN, "2010 Review of the United Nations Peacebuilding Architecture."

21 UN, "2010 Review of the United Nations Peacebuilding Architecture," 12.

22 UN Peacebuilding Fund, "Guinea-Bissau Overview," www.unpbf.org/coun tries/guinea-bissau.

23 Presidential elections in Guinea-Bissau took place on 13 April and 18 May 2014. They had been initially scheduled for 24 November 2013 and then 16 March 2014. See "Guinea-Bissau Postpones Post-Coup Election until March," *Reuters*, 15 November 2013, www.reuters.com/article/2013/11/15/ us-bissau-election-idUSBRE9AE0Q420131115.

24 Cravo, "Security Sector Reform and the Rule of Law."

25 UN, "2010 Review of the United Nations Peacebuilding Architecture."

26 UN Peacebuilding Fund, "Guinea-Bissau Overview."

27 Ann M. Fitz-Gerald, *Thematic Review of Security Sector Reform to Peacebuilding and the Role of the Peacebuilding Fund* (New York: United Nations Peacebuilding Support Office, 2012).

28 Interview with Guinea-Bissau government official, March 2014, New York.

29 Interview with Guinea-Bissau government official, March 2014, New York .

30 Raggie Johansen, "Guinea-Bissau: A New Hub for Cocaine Trafficking," *Perspectives*, United Nations Office on Drugs and Crime (UNODC), 5 May 2008.

31 During the visit to Pretoria of Guinea-Bissau's Prime Minister Martinho Dafa Cabi, in August 2007, South Africa signed a defense cooperation agreement with Guinea-Bissau and announced that it would open an embassy in its capital, Bissau. Other areas of cooperation mentioned during the visit include infrastructure, health training, and the fight against drug trafficking. See Republic of South Africa, Department of International Relations and Cooperation, "Press Comments made by South African Deputy President Phumzile Mlambo-Ngcuka and Prime Minister Martinho Dafa Cabi of Guinea Bissau," Presidential Guesthouse, Pretoria, Monday 6 August 2007, www.dirco.gov.za/docs/speeches/2007/mngcuka0807.htm.

The impact of the PBA in Guinea-Bissau 195

32 Vincent Foucher, "Wade's Senegal and its Relations with Guinea-Bissau: Brother, Patron or Regional Hegemon?" South African Institute of International Affairs, Occasional Paper 132, January 2013.

33 According to the International Crisis Group, aid was suspended on the part of key players such as Brazil, the United States, the EU, the World Bank, and the African Development Bank. See International Crisis Group, "Beyond Turf Wars."

34 Security Council, "Statement by the Chair of the Guinea-Bissau Configuration of the Peacebuilding Commission H.E. Ambassador Antonio de Aguiar Patriota, Permanent Representative of Brazil to the United Nations 19 May 2014," www.un.org/en/peacebuilding/pdf/GB%20-%20disc%20GB %20Chair19mai%20-%20FINAL.pdf.

35 Necla Tschirgi, "Escaping Path Dependency: A Proposed Multi-Tiered Approach for the UN's Peacebuilding Commission," Working Paper, CIPS/ NUPI, 2010.

36 The request from the government of Guinea-Bissau was made in a letter to the Security Council dated July 2007. Guinea-Bissau was entered on the agenda of the PBC in December that year and was deemed eligible for PBF funding in March 2008. See UN Peacebuilding Fund, "Guinea-Bissau Overview."

37 Nicole Ball and Mariska van Beijnum, "Review of the Peacebuilding Fund," 4 June 2009, www.clingendael.nl/sites/default/files/20090604%20PBF_ Review.pdf.

38 Jenkins, Peacebuilding, 111.

39 Security Council Report, "Update Report on Guinea-Bissau," May 2012.

40 UN, "2010 Review of the United Nations Peacebuilding Architecture."

41 Gilda M. Santos Neves, Comissão das Nações Unidas para Consolidação da Paz—Perspectiva Brasileira (Brasília: FUNAG, 2010), 1.

42 The importance that Brazil has given to Guinea-Bissau has been noted by both the International Crisis Group and Security Council Report. See International Crisis Group, "Guinea-Bissau: In Need of a State," Africa Report no. 142, 2 July 2008; and Security Council Report, "March 2006 Monthly Forecast: Africa-Guinea-Bissau," 2006.

43 Adriana Abdenur and Danilo M. De Souza Neto, "Rising Powers and the Security-Development Nexus: Brazil's Engagement with Guinea-Bissau," Journal of Peacebuilding and Development 9, no. 2 (2014): 1–16.

44 See International Crisis Group, "Guinea-Bissau: In Need of a State."

45 The International Crisis Group refers to divergences between CPLP and ECOWAS in terms of the transition after the April 2012 coup. See International Crisis Group, "Beyond Turf Wars."

46 Joshua B. Forrest, "Anatomy of State Fragility in Guinea-Bissau," in Security and Development: Searching for Critical Connections, ed. Necla Tschirgi, Michael S. Lund, and Francesco Mancini (Boulder, Colo.: Lynne Rienner, 2010), 191.

47 Security Council Report, "Update Report on Guinea-Bissau," May 2012.

48 See: Security Council Report, "December 2006 Monthly Forecast: Africa— Guinea-Bissau," 2006; and Security Council Report, "November 2008 Monthly Forecast: Africa—Guinea-Bissau," 2008.

49 Saponoticías, "Conferência das Jurisdições Constitucionais da CPLP levanta suspensão da Guiné-Bissau," 5 June 2014, noticias.sapo.tl/portu gues/lusa/artigo/17818273.html.

11 Searching for a niche

UN peacebuilding in the Republic of Guinea

Ian D. Quick

- **"A rupture between population and state"**
- **Facing the triple transition**
- **Searching for a niche**
- **Questions from Conakry**

The Republic of Guinea is unusual amongst the cases in this volume. It has not experienced a war, nor hosted a United Nations (UN) peacekeeping or political mission. This is remarkable given a bleak political history and a turbulent neighborhood—it is as if the country were designed to confound statistical models for fragility.

Perhaps counter-intuitively, these same features make it a useful case study for the contributions and limitations of the UN Peacebuilding Architecture (PBA). This is because it is easier to tell the causal story. The new institutions operated in a clear field, with few other actors competing for influence, and their influence on the behavior of local and international actors can be more readily isolated. In this sense it is a test case for what might happen after the drawdown of a political or peacekeeping mission, a step just taken in Sierra Leone and envisaged in the near future in Burundi.

This chapter examines the period from January 2010 to January 2014. The interval opens with the signature of the Ouagadougou agreement for transition from the National Council for Democracy and Development (CNDD) military government to a civilian administration, and closes with the seating of the Legislative Assembly as the last major step in that process.

I divide the story into four parts. The first briefly explains the country context. The second lays out the specific challenges of the transition, while the third looks at how these evolved and tries to mark out the influence of the UN Peacebuilding Commission (PBC) and Peacebuilding Fund (PBF).

UN peacebuilding in the Republic of Guinea 197

Finally I identify some broader questions that are raised by the experience in Guinea.

"A rupture between population and state"

In 1958, Guinea was the only French colony to decline membership of the new Communauté française and opt instead for immediate independence. The country's first president, Sékou Touré, famously rebuffed Charles de Gaulle to his face, declaring "we prefer poverty in freedom to riches in slavery." The imagination thrills at the moment—Touré made himself an enemy for life and became a hero of pan-Africanists. However, as a recent intergovernmental assessment put it, "hope quickly died thereafter ... as Guinea entered a long period of political, diplomatic and economic isolation."[1] The government that ensued was single-party and aspired to totalitarianism. It steered the economy into the ground despite an abundance of natural resources, often described as a "geological scandal," and was overturned by a military coup shortly after Touré's death in 1984.

The new government dubbed itself the Military Committee for National Recovery (CMRN). It promised economic and political liberalization, and a new constitution in 1990 notionally civilianized politics and permitted competing parties. However, the elections that followed were widely derided as unserious and often boycotted. Tensions peaked with massive popular protests in 2006–07, prompting both clumsy repression and repeated government reshuffles.

Before long the instability prompted another military coup, in December 2008. The new government, the CNDD under Moussa Dadis Camara, made yet more promises on managed liberalization and enjoyed some initial popularity, but it was feckless and riven by factional rivalries. Dialogue with political parties, trade unions, and civil society quickly broke down. Then the country hit bottom in September 2009. Security forces massacred some 156 people in and around Conakry's main stadium, along with grotesque sexual assaults of a similar magnitude and widespread looting.[2]

At this point the Economic Community of West African States (ECOWAS) became more actively involved. It had already suspended Guinea's membership following the CNDD coup; it now designated President Blaise Compaoré of Burkina Faso as mediator. He was backed by a strong International Contact Group comprising Guinea's major bilateral partners. Dramatic factional shifts within the CNDD then permitted agreement on a timetable for transition to democratic rule. This was formalized in the Ouagadougou agreement of January

198 *Ian D. Quick*

2010, providing for a caretaker government under interim President Sékouba Konaté (notionally the number two of the CNDD government), with elections for a new president to be held within six months. A new constitution was adopted in April 2010, specifying that Guinea should "proceed to" legislative elections at the end of the same six-month period.[3]

The timetable was simple but the actual course of events was to prove rather complicated. Throughout, the UN peacebuilding architecture was involved on two tracks. The UN Secretary-General had designated Guinea as eligible for support from the PBF in June 2008, as a country "at risk of lapsing into conflict."[4] It was a rather risky move to provide funding support under the CNDD military junta but the decision was overtaken by events, and 90 percent of funds were actually committed during the 2010–14 transition period. As at date of writing, the PBF's total allocations had reached US$45 million—not a tremendous sum, but its third-biggest country portfolio worldwide.[5] Meanwhile the PBC added Guinea to its agenda in February 2011, with the distinction of being the only country added at its own request rather than that of the Security Council. The Country-Specific Configuration was established shortly afterwards and chaired by Luxembourg.

Facing the triple transition

The legacy of misrule laid heavily upon Guinea in 2010. Most indices of state fragility ranked the country just inside or outside the top 10 "of concern" in the world—in company with Iraq, the Central African Republic, and neighboring Côte d'Ivoire.[6] The risk-assessment methodologies that underpin these indices were picking up on a "triple transition" with simultaneous political, economic, and military dimensions.[7]

Along the political axis, the highest priority was to establish the civilian institutions anticipated in the 2010 constitution. Of these the most important and contentious were obviously the presidency and National Assembly. Both were to be directly elected, in a context with almost no experience of free and fair elections and a recent history of violent street politics. Alongside this dossier was a grab-bag of issues usually grouped under the heading "national reconciliation." Guinea had little history of communal violence, with a few notable exceptions, but violence perpetrated by state against society would need some sort of accounting. This included specific incidents—most notoriously the massacres in 2007 and 2009—but also a legacy of impunity and nonperformance of state functions that stretched back to the early days of independence.

UN peacebuilding in the Republic of Guinea 199

The PBC took almost all of this on board, with special emphasis on establishing core political institutions as the "priority of priorities."[8] Interestingly the PBF's planning document skipped this and instead emphasized softer elements: *citoyenneté* (habits and culture of good citizenship), and the responsible conduct of media and political parties. It also emphasized local mechanisms for conflict resolution to complement the new and unproven political architecture.

As for the military dimension, it was clear that the coups of 1984 and 2008 were merely acute episodes of a chronic disease. The International Commission of Inquiry mounted after the 2009 massacre aptly summarized the overall situation as characterized by "organized impunity," and the armed forces made up of "clans and factions that barely conceal their rivalries."[9] The former problem had fuelled a steady stream of disappearances since the days of Sékou Touré, along with the bloody repression of public dissent on multiple occasions. The latter problem had led to serious mutiny incidents in 1985 and 2006 alongside the two successful *coups d'état*.

An ECOWAS-led assessment mission in early 2010 elaborated on these themes. The team emphasized that basic institutions of civilian control were an immediate priority, including a coherent defense policy and budgetary control. It was also clear that military institutions were oversized. Personnel had at least doubled from 2001 to 2009, in part driven by involvement in wars in neighboring Sierra Leone (1997–98), Guinea-Bissau (1998–99), and Liberia (2000–01). The result was described by one interlocutor as a "dustbin for delinquents" with training and discipline very poor.[10] The grade pyramid had also been almost inverted by rampant over-promotion, the CMRN government's go-to solution for discontent in the ranks.

Against this background the PBC and PBF found there was considerable scope for bilateral aid, but likely difficulties in tapping it in the short term due to donors' "wait-and-see" attitude (*attentisme*) to the political transition. (Most notably the European Union—EU— which had formally conditioned resumption of most bilateral assistance on credible parliamentary elections.) This led to a focus on creating the conditions for broader donor engagement, and from the PBF's side project support to "quick wins" to build confidence among all stakeholders.

Finally, there is the economic domain. Guinea is classed as "least developed" and in 2010 was ranked 156th on the UN Development Programme's (UNDP) Human Development Index.[11] In more concrete terms, national statistics put 70 percent of the population under the extreme poverty line of $1.25 per day, with that proportion having

200   *Ian D. Quick*

increased significantly over the decade 2001–10.[12] Foreign direct investment had also nosedived back down to trivial levels after some tentative forays in 2006–07. This handicapped the mining sector, often described, as mentioned, as a "geological scandal" because the world's largest bauxite reserves sat grossly underexploited and had been subjected to a series of shady deals since independence.[13]

The political transition was not expected to have much immediate impact on these problems. It was clear that the mining sector would be the engine of overall growth, accounting for more than 90 percent of export earnings, but in Guinea's geological circumstances it was capital intensive and would generate few jobs. This contrasted with an estimated 200,000 new entrants to the labor market each year.[14] Moreover, the last two governments had survived in part by populist spending. As the World Bank noted, "the painful reforms needed to stabilize the economy such as price increases of subsidized items, including fuel, are juxtaposed with high expectations of a population that is eager to reap the benefits of democracy."[15]

With this background, the PBC and PBF decided to focus on "youth and women's employment policy." The UN team in-country had argued some years prior that the situation of Guinean youth "constituted a veritable time bomb for the country," and this belief had only been reinforced by the demographics of the massive street protests from 2006–08.[16] In contrast with the acknowledged need, however, no unified approach had materialized. Policy was split across a half-dozen ministries and the subject was almost invisible in the Poverty Reduction Strategy that had been hastily extended for 2011–12.

Searching for a niche

How did the three dimensions of the transition evolve? What role did the UN PBA play? The aspect that proved most contentious, and most dangerous, was the establishment of basic political institutions. The first acts of this drama were the two rounds of the presidential election (designed much like the French system). The first stage went ahead as scheduled in June 2010, but was followed by bitter protests by the third-place finisher, Sidya Touré. He complained of large-scale vote rigging, perhaps understandably since the Supreme Court annulled more than 25 percent of all votes cast. There followed four months of wrangling over vote totals, logistical arrangements, and the composition of the electoral commission. There was some violence, with perhaps 20 deaths, which took on ethnic overtones in a few areas.[17] Support for the two runoff candidates became polarized along ethnic

UN peacebuilding in the Republic of Guinea 201

lines, with Cellou Dalein Diallo caricatured as the "Peuhl candidate."[18] When the second poll was completed in December, it was Diallo's turn to play the part of victim. He proclaimed himself the real victor for a tense few days before finally conceding.

International actors played significant roles in managing these tensions. At each stage there was intensive mediation by the Contact Group of bilateral actors and the UN Office for West Africa, along with electoral observer teams from the EU and the Carter Center (aided immeasurably by the constructive engagement of transitional President Sékouba Konaté). All this dropped off precipitously with the inauguration of President Condé in December 2010. In response to his strong urging, ECOWAS walked away; Konaté's mandate ended; and the Contact Group dissolved, albeit continuing to meet as an informal "Group of Friends."

On paper it was thus a clean handover to the PBC. At the request of the Condé administration, Luxembourg, the chair of the new configuration, undertook a first exploratory mission in April 2011. A Statement of Mutual Commitments was then agreed in September, including a commitment from the PBC side to "facilitate the strengthening of dialogue between the Government and all actors ... with a view to reaching a consensus on issues relating to the parliamentary and local elections."[19]

The long third act of the drama was now the constitution of the National Assembly. This was a period of steadily building pressure. The new constitution specified that Guinea should "proceed to the legislative elections" at the end of a transition period of six months— therefore November 2010. The elections were then to be followed by the establishment of an array of other institutions, including the National Council for Communications and the Constitutional Court.

However, President Condé delayed in setting a date. The reasons for this remain disputed. It was argued from some quarters that it was a tactical move to advantage his own political party, but in any event there were fierce disputes on electoral processes that had to be resolved before proceeding. These included whether and how to update the electoral register; what to do with the Independent National Electoral Commission; arrangements for diaspora voting; and the choice of vendor for electoral equipment. Consensus on these *points de désaccord* was not forthcoming. The National Transition Council that was supposed to be a consultative placeholder for the National Assembly proved a dead letter. A formal Dialogue Committee comprising government and opposition notables was launched but rapidly failed, with the facilitator reporting back that the country was in a "full political crisis."[20]

202 *Ian D. Quick*

With Guinea's peculiar history this impasse was dangerous. It rapidly bred accusations of "winner-take-all" politics—a unilateral approach to governance that was inappropriate with core political institutions not yet in place. Civil society interlocutors referred openly to "RPG-ization" of the government (Condé's party); and hinted at "Malinké-zation" (Condé's ethnicity).[21] For their part, opposition figures opted for a talk-fight strategy. To give the flavor, Sidya Touré declared in one interview that "we will alternate manifestations, meetings and *ville morte* operations since we haven't obtained satisfaction on our demands."[22] Large-scale street protests became commonplace through 2012. They became considerably more violent in 2013, with incidents in February–March and May, each leading to 100-plus wounded and a handful of deaths.[23]

Generally speaking, the PBC did not play a significant role during this period. At New York level it remained resolutely intergovernmental—Guinea was represented by its ambassador to the UN or its minister for financial and economic control as "focal point." The commission's plenary meetings were polite affairs. The first review of the Statement[of Mutual Commitments "encourage[d] the stakeholders to proceed insofar as possible with the dialogue concerning as yet unresolved issues"; a subsequent press statement at the peak of the crisis exhorted "all political actors to engage constructively in dialogue launched by the President."[24] There were a total of four other press releases, all echoing this rather anodyne language.

In-country, where the disputes were raging, the commission was not really present on the stage. Luxembourg as chair of the configuration did not have permanent representation in Guinea. Its ambassador to the UN accordingly traveled there for several short trips, meeting sequentially with political and civil society interlocutors in a sort of abbreviated shuttle diplomacy. (A bigger delegation of the Guinea configuration visited in March 2012, with much the same agenda but many more logistical headaches.) This approach was not sufficient to get traction. The commission was not publicly mentioned by Guinean political actors in 2012–13, nor was its role discussed in policy papers produced by the EU, the United States, or interested think tanks.[25]

A key factor here was the lack of a country-level counterpart. For the UN team in-country, comprising a dozen or so development agencies, had squarely defined its role as "accompaniment" of the new Condé administration. It started work shortly after the inauguration on a Development Assistance Framework, a planning tool to define "the collective response of the UN system to national development priorities" all the way through to 2017.[26] Senior officials stressed that a

UN peacebuilding in the Republic of Guinea 203

Steering Committee established to manage the PBF allocation "did not have a political role" and was focused on program management.[27] At one point, the PBF's own newsletter proudly featured the UN's senior official accepting a military decoration from President Condé.[28]

As a consequence of this policy orientation, there was no specialist in conflict or political analysis on the ground until late 2012, while engagement of the UN's Department of Political Affairs (DPA) and Department of Peacekeeping Operations was limited to short technical missions in May 2011 and March 2012. The Peacebuilding Support Office's small local team was unable to take up the slack. It developed no overall metrics or situation analysis, and indeed managed to collect just 25 percent of the metrics defined in project contracts.[29] There were also no outside evaluations of project effectiveness against the strategic-level outcomes defined in the work plans of the PBF and PBC.

By mid-2013, the same actors that had crisis-managed the presidential elections had to be re-engaged. This time it was Said Djinnit who acted as mediator, as the head of the UN's Office for West Africa and a former senior official of the African Union. Key bilateral partners and ECOWAS provided strong support behind him. The approach was old-fashioned crisis diplomacy over the course of about two months, which addressed in turn the *points de désaccord*, an emergency rescheduling of the vote, and then opposition withdrawal from counting amidst cries of a *"casus belli."*[30] After some tense periods the National Assembly finally took its seats in October 2013 and elected its office holders in January 2014. (Of course, by this point the next presidential election was just one year away, with most actors beginning to turn their attention there.)

What of the security domain? With the political drama being largely played out on the streets of Conakry and regional centers, the most urgent question had become public order. The repression of mobilizations in 2007 and 2009 had been shockingly violent. A similar catastrophe was largely avoided during the transition period, a fact that should by no means be taken for granted. The most serious incidents led to a half-dozen deaths and 100 or so casualties, and it is notable that the security forces were usually well represented in the latter group rather than resorting to lethal force at the first sign of trouble.

At a practical level there were three key reasons for this. The first was the part-demilitarization of the capital, for which credit goes to the transitional government under Sékouba Konaté and then the Condé administration. A second factor was a special force for elections security (FOSSEPEL, later FOSSEL), created as a bridging measure. A third was considerable domestic mobilization against the brand of

204 *Ian D. Quick*

violent street politics that had dominated the scene from 2006 to 2010. This encompassed faith leaders, some civil society groups and political parties, women's groups, media organizations, and often local government. For the latter two factors an array of international agencies played a supporting role with funding and project support. The PBF was one of them, disbursing a few million dollars through the UN agencies to help scale up FOSSEPEL and "calming" activities.

All the while the larger issue of security sector governance hovered in the background. Here the record is rather mixed. As of May 2014 a national security policy and supporting sectoral policies had just been finalized. Bilateral partners, including the members of the PBC, were yet to commit significant funding or training contingents.[31] (Indicatively, the biggest expected donor had just advertised a multi-year contract to provide further advice on the development of national policy.[32])

This is not yet wildly slow for a major national policy process: some four years had elapsed since the Ouagadougou agreement ended the CNDD military government. However, it does require a critical look back given the stated ambitions of the PBA to "catalyze" wider involvement. On the positive side were two early interventions supported by the PBF. The first was a biometric census of military personnel, administered by a South African firm and completed in late 2011. This was an entry point for almost any credible reform plan. The second was a project to facilitate the retirement of just under 4,000 soldiers, amounting to nearly 20 percent of total strength. Taken together these did much to establish the credibility of reform efforts, and posed good first tests for civilian control.[33] It was also clear that other potential donors could not have supported such action given the sensitivity of the sector and the still-transitional nature of the government.

On the negative side, support to the national policy process took some missteps. There was strong ownership by the Condé administration, due perhaps to enlightened self-interest, with a high-level steering committee established shortly after the presidential inauguration, but a great deal of activity in 2011–12 led to few concrete results. A draft reform plan was drawn up and budgeted in minute detail, with the support of several short-term technical consultants supplied by UNDP, but it had to be reworked, if not discarded. Civil society actors and the political opposition complained that they had been excluded from the process.[34] (Anecdotally, the process may have actually done harm by fuelling the complaints about "winner-take-all" politics noted above.) Bilateral partners who were being asked for funding echoed these complaints, to the effect that "they could not support something already cooked up by the time they saw it."[35]

UN peacebuilding in the Republic of Guinea   205

A new approach was tried from 2012–13 with the secondment of a small advisory team to the Office of the President—the president also occupying the position of minister of defense. This project was again underwritten by the PBF and led to some initial improvements, with the policy process opening to a broader circle of actors, but the team soon ran into serious disagreements with the UN resident agencies on how the process should be led. Key members ended their tenure before schedule, and the positions were in the process of being re-staffed at date of writing.

Finally, there is the economic dimension. In overall terms this clearly moved the fastest. The Condé administration pursued a broadly credible package of measures for economic stabilization and governance from 2011 to 2013, capped off by $2.1 billion in debt relief under the Highly Indebted Poor Countries Initiative.[36] Much of this progress was aggressively marketed at a Donors and Investors Conference hosted by the United Arab Emirates in November 2013.

Alongside this the Condé administration continued to emphasize the "youth and women" dossier in its discussions with the PBC and PBF—actively seeking to minimize the disruptive effects of economic stabilization, but with respect to results, there was not a great deal to report. Policy remained fragmented between several ministries and the dossier was not well reflected in the governing policy frameworks, the Plan Quinquennal for macroeconomic policy, and the new Poverty Reduction Strategy for 2013–15. Nor was a concrete proposal on youth and women included in the prospectus documents presented at the 2013 donor/investor conference.[37]

For their part international partners (including the members of the PBC configuration) maintained a wait-and-see attitude. Indicatively, a manual "mapping" of donor involvement in mid-2012 found only the PBF and the World Bank active in the sector.[38] The former supported a few micro-projects executed by UN organizations, aiming to employ some 4,000 youth in waste recycling. These interventions adopted an overt supply-side logic to the problem of violent street politics, focusing on high-risk areas and coupling cash stipends with citizenship and "peace education."[39] (While this is not trivial one must wonder about targeting, given an estimate of 200,000 new entrants to the country's labor market each year.)

The World Bank project was of significantly larger scope, targeting 24,000 individuals for temporary employment and 10,000 with cash transfers for nutrition and education. This was justified along fairly orthodox lines, i.e. "assisting the Government to lessen the potential impact of ongoing reforms on poor and vulnerable households."[40] It

206 *Ian D. Quick*

does not appear that the PBC or PBF were a significant influence in the origination and design of this program. In fact, causation ran the other way, with the PBF contributing some top-up funding once the World Bank project development machine was already running.[41]

Questions from Conakry

In theory, Guinea's transition was precisely the type of situation where the UN PBA is supposed to add value. The country was manifestly unstable, but just shy of a crisis that would keep it on the agenda of the Security Council.[42] It was also rather neglected in financial terms. These factors made it a poster child for the ambition to "extend the period of political attention to post-conflict recovery" that was expressed back in 2005.[43]

In practice, however, the above assessment is not positive. Large-scale conflict was avoided, but the involvement of the PBC was book-ended by that of "traditional" mechanisms of crisis management. There is also little evidence of substantial additional funding flows, a fact due mostly to difficulties in formulating coherent national policies in the security and economic sectors. What broader challenges do these results suggest for the UN's ability to engage with this sort of "middle-range" crisis?

A first concerns member states. In short—what was expected of the countries sitting in the Guinea configuration of the PBC? To provide peer advice to the government of the day? Or did a mandate to "bring together all relevant actors" mean helping to forge consensus amongst different national stakeholders?[44]

In practice the peer-advice model prevailed. This matched the intent of the incoming Condé administration, which had just requested the dissolution of the Contact Group of bilateral partners and was in no hurry to replace it. In the face of this reluctance there was little appetite amongst the dozen or so countries on the Guinea configuration to push for a more assertive role in meetings in New York or in the press. Moreover, briefings to the Security Council as the situation worsened were handled by the UN DPA in closed session.[45] This all added up to a rather minimalist approach. Dialogue with the executive branch, just one party to the core disputes at national level, encouraged responsible behavior at the margins but did little directly to build consensus.

These results are not surprising. As the Secretary-General's 2009 report, "Peacebuilding in the Aftermath of Armed Conflict," put it, in transitional settings "the capacity and will to exercise full national ownership may be constrained because ... a stable political order is yet

UN peacebuilding in the Republic of Guinea   207

to be established."[46] This has driven a significant normative shift over the 10 years since the PBC was first established, perhaps epitomized in the International Dialogue on Peacebuilding and Statebuilding. This is a heavy process launched in 2008 with some 45 governments and a panoply of multilateral institutions. Its main outcomes document, the New Deal, put the focus squarely on "new ways of engaging" with the twin imperatives of being "country-led" yet also driven by "credible and inclusive processes of political dialogue."[47] The same ideas have become increasingly present in the UN system. The Secretary-General's 2012 update on "Peacebuilding in the Aftermath of Conflict" went considerably further than the 2009 edition and summarized its three priority themes as "inclusivity, institution-building and sustained international support." At the level of the Security Council, a March 2014 debate on peacebuilding saw the word "inclusive" used some 57 times in 2.5 hours, with the administrator of UNDP declaring that "a more inclusive approach to peacebuilding than we often see today is a key priority."[48]

In the face of these trends the PBC's own approach remains ambivalent. The 2010 review of the PBA argued that it should "facilitate and advance the kind of broad-based dialogue that will enable a society to heal and rebuild."[49] The chair of the commission, Brazil, has also weighed in to this effect:[50] "No majority Government can alone face the myriad challenges facing a society emerging from conflict [and] elected governments that fail to keep the various societal and political forces engaged can drive their countries towards untold tragedies."

However, there is not yet consensus on "what the tools are" in this regard—or as one diplomat put it, what member states represented on the commission are really expected to do.[51] In this regard it is ironic that the same Security Council debate on peacebuilding cited Guinea as an example of "inclusive" approaches, given that it referenced the exact moment at which the commission's peer-advice approach went on hiatus and the UN Office for West Africa stepped in to directly facilitate dialogue in-country.

This leads to a second challenge: Are the agencies, funds and programs of the UN viable operational partners for peacebuilding objectives? Can they chart a third way between a full-fledged peacekeeping/political mission dispatched by the Security Council, and development "business as usual"?

Here the Guinea case is not encouraging. Throughout 2010, the UN Office for West Africa had cooperated with ECOWAS and the International Contact Group to painstakingly mediate between factions in the presidential elections. However, from the day of the inauguration of President Condé it was as if a switch had been flipped—the UN

208   *Ian D. Quick*

Country Team was all-in with the new administration. This ruled out a role facilitating "broad-based dialogue" in the sense that had been advocated by the 2010 review. The consequences were most serious for the PBC's "priority of priorities," the establishment of constitutional institutions. Here it was necessary to re-engage the UN Office in West Africa for crisis mediation. The effects were also noticeable in the security sector, where international partners and Guinean civil society repeatedly complained about lack of information and involvement.

All this marks a crucial difference from cases like Sierra Leone and Burundi, where the PBC complemented UN missions that were specifically tasked with support to national political dialogue,[52] but perhaps the key point to emphasize is that the approach in Guinea was not the result of idiosyncratic choices. It rather reflected deeply embedded policy orientations for the UN development system. The senior official in-country was a first-time resident coordinator with a technical background. Point number one (literally) of the standard job description for this post is to "ensure effective support at the request of Government in its coordination of all types of external development assistance."[53] This definition of the role comes directly from the General Assembly, being reiterated *ad nauseam* in the 2012 Quadrennial Comprehensive Policy Review.[54]

Or we can descend to a more granular level. We noted above that there was a lack of politically capable staff on the ground, but the 2009 review of "Peacebuilding in the Aftermath of Armed Conflict" had stressed precisely this point, noting that "support for the Resident Coordinator is particularly weak."[55] Evaluations for the PBF have also repeatedly found a lack of human resources that are fit for purpose, with little adaptation to fit the specific needs of post-conflict situations.[56] We also noted that there were few metrics for overall peacebuilding effectiveness, nor any project-level evaluations to this effect, but at global level, UNDP recently found that it has no established practice for conflict analysis nor metrics to measure progress in this regard.[57]

It would be naïve to suppose that engagement of the new PBA could change such systemic factors at the stroke of a pen, and here the experience in Guinea can stand in for that of the UN more generally. The PBC was intended to encourage "a coherent, coordinated and integrated approach" in post-conflict settings.[58] It was launched concurrently with policy directives to "integrate" efforts of all the UN's operational entities towards common peacebuilding objectives. Both initiatives asked essentially that "optimal use is made of existing capacities,"[59] but they quickly ran into a hard reality. The next high-level

UN peacebuilding in the Republic of Guinea 209

review of UN peacebuilding, in 2009, took stock of "different mandates, guiding principles, and governing structures" amongst operational entities on the ground, and stressed that priorities had to be determined by local needs rather than "what international actors can or want to supply."[60] The most high-profile follow-up initiative, the 2011 Review of Civilian Capacities, asserted rather more bluntly that "many of the civilian capacities most needed by conflict-affected communities are not to be found within the United Nations."[61]

In sum, the ambition to "extend the period of political attention" for unstable countries was not value-neutral. It posited a new middle ground between the two extremes of the UN Charter: the default position of non-intervention in internal affairs, and the exceptional case of Security Council action to meet a threat to international peace and security.[62] Successful operation in this middle ground was always going to pose substantial adaptive challenges for both the member states sitting in the Peacebuilding Commission, and the UN bureaucracy operating on the ground.

Notes

1 ECOWAS, African Union and United Nations, "Rapport d'Évaluation du Secteur de la Sécurité en République de Guinée," 2010 May, 27 (author's translation).
2 United Nations, "Report of the International Commission of Inquiry Mandated to Establish the Facts and Circumstances of the Events of 28 September 2009 in Guinea," UN doc. S/2009/693, 18 December 2009, 2–3.
3 Republic of Guinea, "Constitution adoptée par le Conseil National de Transition le 19 avril 2010," doc. no. D/068/PRG/CNDD/SGPRG/2010, 2010, art. 159.
4 See United Nations, "Terms of Reference for the Peacebuilding Fund," UN doc. A/63/818, 13 April 2009, Annex para. 2.1.
5 Measured by approved budget as of April 2014. Data from Multi-Donor Trust Fund Unit Office, mdtf.undp.org.
6 Fund for Peace, "Failed States Index," 2010, global.fundforpeace.org; Norman Patterson School of International Affairs, "Assessing State Fragility," a Country Indicators for Foreign Policy Report, 2011; World Bank, "World Development Indicators," 2010, data.worldbank.org.
7 The term was originally coined for post-Soviet states: see Claus Offe, "Capitalism by Democratic Design? Democratic Theory Facing the Democratic Transition in Eastern Europe," *Social Research* 58, no. 4 (1991): 865–81.
8 See Peacebuilding Commission, "Initial Mission by the Chairperson of the Guinea Configuration of the Peacebuilding Commission to the Republic of Guinea, 3–10 April 2011," 2011, www.un.org/en/peacebuilding.
9 United Nations, "Report of the International Commission of Inquiry," 2009, para. 259.

210 *Ian D. Quick*

10 International Crisis Group, "Guinée: Reformer l'armée," Rapport Afrique No. 164, 2010, www.icg.org.
11 "Least developed" is a UN classification based on per capita income, human assets, and economic vulnerability. The criteria are approved by the Committee for Development Policy, a subordinate organ of the Economic and Social Council.
12 Republic of Guinea, "Progress Report and Extension of the Poverty Reduction Strategy Paper," 2011, www.imf.org.
13 Net inflows of foreign direct investment dropped from 9 percent of gross domestic product in 2007–08 to 2 percent in 2010, with the latter below average for even least developed countries. See World Bank, "World Development Indicators," 2011. On mineral resources see Muriel Devey, "Remédier au 'scandale géologique' guinéen," *Jeune Afrique*, 11 July 2011, quoting President Condé.
14 Summarized in United Nations, "UN Technical Mission to Guinea on Peacebuilding: 02–10 May 2011," internal document dated 13 June 2011.
15 World Bank, "Project Appraisal Document on a Proposed Grant to the Republic of Guinea," Report No. 66196-GN, 23 May 2012, www.worldba nk.org.
16 UNDP Guinea, "Mid-Term Evaluation for UN Development Assistance Framework 2007–12," 2012, 33. Internal document on file with author.
17 Human Rights Watch, "Guinea: Witnesses Describe Security Force Excesses," 2010, www.hrw.org; Carter Center, "Observing the 2010 Presidential Elections in Guinea: Final Report," 2011, www.cartercenter.org; Open Society Initiative for West Africa, "Rapport d'enquête sur les violences et violations des droits humains durant le processus électoral guinéen de 2010," 2011, www.osiwa.org.
18 International Crisis Group, "Guinea: Putting the Transition Back on Track," Africa Report No. 178, 2011, 5–6.
19 Peacebuilding Commission, "Statement of Mutual Commitments on Peacebuilding in Guinea between the Government of Guinea and the Peacebuilding Commission," UN doc. PBC/5/GUI/2, 23 September 2011, 9.
20 Author's conversations with senior government officials, May 2012. See also United Nations, "Technical Mission to Guinea on Peacebuilding."
21 Author's conversations with director-level staff of civil society organizations in Conakry, Labe, and Pita, May 2012. Generally see Ian D. Quick, "The Peacebuilding Fund in Guinea: Independent Evaluation 2009–12," 2012, www.mdtf.org; Open Society Institute for West Africa, "West Africa's Teetering Tower," 2013, www.osiwa.org; and International Crisis Group, "Putting the Transition Back on Track."
22 Camille Dubruelh, "Guinée: l'opposition annonce une nouvelle vague de manifestations," *Jeune Afrique*, 8 May 2012 (author's translation).
23 Indicatively: Agence France-Presse, "Guinée: 3 morts, plus de 200 blessés en quatre jours de violences à Conakry," 3 March 2013; Christophe Boisbouvier, "Guinée: Conakry sous haute tension," *Jeune Afrique*, 18 March 2013; Agence France-Presse, "Guinée: douze morts et 89 blessés dans les violences a Conakry (bilan official)," 27 May 2013; and Pierre-François Naudé, "Guinée: au moins 12 morts lors de manifestations de l'opposition à Conakry," *Jeune Afrique*, 28 May 2013.

UN peacebuilding in the Republic of Guinea 211

24 Peacebuilding Commission, "Conclusions and Recommendations of the First Review of the Statement of Mutual Commitments between the Government of Guinea and the Peacebuilding Commission," UN doc. PBC/6/GUI/2, 8 June 2012; and Peacebuilding Commission, "Statement by the Guinea Configuration of the Peacebuilding Commission," 6 March 2013 (author's translation). Both accessible via www.un.org/en/peacebuilding.

25 Indicatively: Alexis Arieff, "Guinea: Background and Relations with the United States," US Congressional Research Service, 2012; Manuel M. Gil, "Policy Briefing: The Democratic Transition in Guinea Reaches a Critical Point," Directorate-General for External Policies of the Union, European Parliament, June 2013; Cristina Barrios, "Addressing State Fragility in Guinea-Conakry: A European Success Story?" FRIDE Policy Brief No. 124, 2012; International Crisis Group, "Putting the Transition Back on Track," 2011.

26 UN Development Group, "How to Prepare a UNDAF Part (I): Guidelines for UN Country Teams," January 2010, www.undg.org. See United Nations/Republic of Guinea, "Plan-Cadre des Nations Unies pour l'aide au développement (PNUAD): République de Guinée, 2013–17," 2012.

27 Quick, "The Peacebuilding Fund in Guinea: Independent Evaluation 2009–12."

28 United Nations, "Le bulletin de la paix," Conakry, January 2012.

29 Quick, "The Peacebuilding Fund in Guinea: Independent Evaluation 2009–12," 22–23.

30 *Jeune Afrique*, "Législatives guinéennes: Sidya Touré annonce que l'opposition se retire du comptage des voix," 3 October 2013.

31 UN Peacebuilding Commission/Working Group on Lessons Learned, "Resource Mobilization and Mapping of Relevant Actors: Background Paper for the Meeting on 3 July 2012," 2012. Updated figures after this date compiled by author through private correspondence.

32 EuropeAid, "Vis de marché de services: Assistance Technique au Programme d'Appui à la Réforme du Secteur de la Sécurité République de Guinée," Reference N° EuropeAid/135235/ IH/SER/GN, 2014, eeas.europa.eu.

33 Quick, "The Peacebuilding Fund in Guinea: Independent Evaluation 2009–12," 35–40; and author discussions with bilateral development partners, May–August 2012. See also Erwin van Veen, "The Security Peril of Guinea's Transition: From Military Rule to Weak Policing," *OECD Insights*, 3 March 2014.

34 UN Secretariat, "UN Technical Mission to Guinea on Peacebuilding: 2–10 May 2011," internal report dated 13 June 2011, 13–14; and World Bank/United Nations, "Military Retirement Project Assessment Mission to Guinea: March 12–16," undated internal report, 2012.

35 Author's conversations with bilateral donors in Conakry, May–June 2012.

36 Broadly, see World Bank, "Country Partnership Strategy for Guinea for the Period FY14–17," 4 September 2013, 4–5, www.worldbank.org; Olivier Manlan, "Country Note: Guinea," *African Economic Outlook*, 2013.

37 Republic of Guinea, "Guinea is Back and Ready for Business," Guinea Development Partners and Investors' Conference, October 2013, www.guineemergente.com. See also *notes sectorielles* at same conference, www.guineemergente.com.

212 *Ian D. Quick*

38 UN Peacebuilding Commission/Working Group on Lessons Learned, "Resource Mobilization and Mapping of Relevant Actors," 2012; and author's conversations with members of Peacebuilding Commission in July 2012.
39 United Nations Industrial Development Organization/UNICEF, "Rapport descriptif final: Projet Conjoint d'appui au mouvement de la jeunesse et à certains groupes de jeunes les plus déshérité," 2013, www.mdtf.org.
40 World Bank, "Project Information Document: Guinea Safety Net Project," Report No. PIDC81, 6 January 2012, 2, www.worldbank.org.
41 Author's conversations with World Bank staff and members of PBC, June 2012 and May 2014. The Project Appraisal Document, the linchpin of the bank's project cycle, does not mention either the PBC or the PBF.
42 Guinea was discussed several times but under the agenda item of broader peacebuilding in West Africa. This is well summarized in Security Council Report, "The Security Council and the UN Peacebuilding Commission," 18 April 2013, 31–2, www.securitycouncilreport.org.
43 United Nations, "Report of the Secretary-General; In Larger Freedom: Towards Development, Security and Human Rights for All," UN doc. A/59/2005, 21 March 2005, para. 115. The phrase was also included in the commission's Terms of Reference: General Assembly resolution 60/180, 2005, para. 2.
44 General Assembly, "The Peacebuilding Commission," UN doc. A/RES/60/180, 30 December 2005, para. 2.
45 See Security Council, "Security Council Press Statement on Guinea," UN doc. SC/10992, 29 April 2013, and "Security Council Press Statement on Guinea," UN doc. SC/11159, 24 October 2013.
46 United Nations, "Report of the Secretary-General on Peacebuilding in the Immediate Aftermath of Conflict," UN doc. A/63/881-S/2009/304, 2009, para. 11.
47 International Dialogue on Peacebuilding and Statebuilding, "A New Deal for Engagement in Fragile States," 2011, www.newdeal4peace.org.
48 7143rd meeting of the Security Council, UN doc. S/PV.7143, 19 March 2014.
49 United Nations, "Review of the United Nations Peacebuilding Architecture," UN doc. A/64/868-S/2010/393, 2010, 20.
50 7143rd meeting of the Security Council.
51 Sarah Hearn, Alejandra Kubitschek Bujones, and Alischa Kugel, *The United Nations "Peacebuilding Architecture": Past, Present and Future* (Center on International Cooperation, May 2014), 8.
52 Hearn et al., *The United Nations "Peacebuilding Architecture"*; Security Council Report, "The Security Council and the UN Peacebuilding Commission."
53 UN Development Group, "UN Resident Coordinator Generic Job Description," 2009, www.undg.org.
54 General Assembly resolution 67/226, 21 December 2012, paras. 12, 114, 122.
55 United Nations, "Report of the Secretary-General on Peacebuilding in the Immediate Aftermath of Conflict," para. 33.
56 Nicole Ball and Mariska van Beijnum, "Review of the Peacebuilding Fund," Joint evaluation for Canada, the Netherlands, Norway, Sweden and the United Kingdom, 2009, www.clingendael.nl. At country level see, for

UN peacebuilding in the Republic of Guinea   213

example, Susanna Campbell, Tracy Dexter, Michael Findley, Stephanie Hofmann, Josiah Marineau, and Daniel Walker, "Independent External Evaluation: UN Peacebuilding Fund Project Portfolio in Burundi, 2007–13," 1 February 2014, www.un.org/en/peacebuilding, 49–50.

57 UN Development Program, "Evaluation of UNDP Support to Conflict-Affected Countries in the Context of UN Peace Operations," Evaluation Office, 2013, xv–xvi, www.undp.org.

58 General Assembly, "The Peacebuilding Commission."

59 United Nations, "Note from the Secretary-General: Guidance on Integrated Missions," internal document dated 9 February 2006. For an overview see Ian D. Quick, "Aligning Objectives: Integration of UN Strategy in Haiti, Liberia, Sudan and Timor-Leste," *Peacekeeping Whiteboard*, March 2009; and Arthur Boutellis, "Driving the System Apart? A Study of United Nations Integration and Integrated Strategic Planning," International Peace Institute, August 2013.

60 United Nations, "Report of the Secretary-General on Peacebuilding in the Immediate Aftermath of Conflict," para. 24.

61 United Nations, "Civilian Capacity in the Aftermath of Conflict: Independent Report of the Senior Advisory Group," 2011, para. 14, www.civcapreview.org.

62 United Nations, "Charter of the United Nations and Statute of the International Court of Justice," 1945, ch. 1, art. 2, www.un.org.

Part V

Findings and conclusion

12 The future of the UN Peacebuilding Architecture

Cedric de Coning and Eli Stamnes

- Assessing the impact of the Peacebuilding Architecture
- Establishing peacebuilding as an overarching framework
- Strengthening coordination across the UN system
- A misguided emphasis on resource mobilization
- Recommendations for strengthening the Peacebuilding Architecture
- Shifting the emphasis: From preventing imminent relapse, to sustained international engagement, to addressing root causes of conflict and fragility
- External factors
- Regional approaches to peacebuilding
- National and local ownership
- Conclusion

This chapter aims to assess the overall impact of the United Nations (UN) Peacebuilding Architecture (PBA) on the UN system and wider peacebuilding and development community over its first decade in existence. Based on this assessment, the chapter will generate recommendations for how the PBA can be modified and adjusted to create more synergy and fusion between the UN's peace and development work.

The focus of this chapter is on the whole-of-system impact of the PBA. Some of the other chapters in this volume have looked at the specific institutions that make up the PBA, such as the Peacebuilding Commission (PBC) and Peacebuilding Fund (PBF), their origins and early history, and others have looked at the impact these institutions have had in the specific countries that are on the PBC's agenda. Here the focus moves to the overall effect the PBA has had on the peacebuilding and development community, including the countries where it has been active, with a special interest in its effect within the UN system.

218 *Cedric de Coning and Eli Stamnes*

In essence, the question we seek to answer is: What impact has the establishment of the PBA had on the way peacebuilding is thought about and conducted today? In other words, if we analyze the way the international community approached peacebuilding in 2005 and the way it approaches peacebuilding today, can we attribute any of the changes and developments to the coming into existence and work of the PBA?

In the first section the chapter will base its assessment of the PBA on three dimensions, namely how its establishment contributed to peacebuilding developing into an overarching framework for peace consolidation; how the PBA contributed to strengthening coordination across the UN system, especially at country level; and how it helped the UN system to understand that its emphasis on resource mobilization was misguided.

In the second section the chapter offers a number of recommendations for strengthening and adapting the PBA. The core recommendation offered relates to a shift in emphasis from one on the prevention of imminent relapse into violent conflict to one on sustained medium- to longer-term international engagement aimed at addressing the root causes of conflict and fragility. Other recommendations address external factors, regional approaches, and national and local ownership.

Assessing the impact of the Peacebuilding Architecture

The core question that should form the basis of an assessment of the impact of the PBA is whether it has been able to address the systemic gap that it was meant to fill.[1] Has the PBA made a meaningful contribution to maintaining international attention on countries emerging from conflict and "to focus attention on the reconstruction and institution-building efforts necessary for recovery"?[2] Has it contributed to increased coherence within the UN system and "to improve the coordination of all relevant actors within and outside the United Nations"?[3]

Establishing peacebuilding as an overarching framework

It is important to start our assessment by acknowledging that the UN system's peacebuilding work is much more comprehensive than the PBA. Many, if not all the UN's funds, agencies, and programs work in post-conflict settings and at a minimum their work in these countries needs to be conflict sensitive. However, in many cases they also engage in peacebuilding work. In addition, the UN's special political missions and many of its peacekeeping missions also have peacebuilding mandates. The PBA thus represents just a small part of the larger UN system's peacebuilding effort.

The future of the UN Peacebuilding Architecture 219

The PBA does, however, occupy a strategic position within the system. The PBC is the only member state body with an exclusive focus on peacebuilding. None of the related thematic approaches, such as conflict prevention, peacemaking, peacekeeping, or development, has a dedicated member state body associated with it. The UN Security Council is responsible for all matters pertaining to international peace and security, including peacebuilding. The council authorizes peacekeeping missions, follows countries in crisis, and has debates on key themes such as peacebuilding and security sector reform. It is the most powerful UN body and its decisions have a much larger impact on any specific country or topic than the PBC, but it is not dedicated to any specific theme in the way the PBC has an exclusive focus on peacebuilding. The PBF aims to be catalytic and to influence the rest of the UN system's attention to peacebuilding needs in the countries where it is active. The Peacebuilding Support Office (PBSO) has a number of strategic opportunities to shape the UN's approach to peacebuilding—for instance, it holds the pen on the annual Secretary-General's reports on peacebuilding and the assistant Secretary-General for peacebuilding chairs the Senior Peacebuilding Group.

Our assessment is that the establishment of the PBA and its subsequent work has contributed to a greater awareness in the UN system of peacebuilding as an overarching framework and a specific programmatic approach. Before the establishment of the PBA, peacebuilding was understood as one of the four pillars of the UN's peace work, alongside prevention, peacemaking, and peacekeeping. Peacebuilding was seen as something that comes either after a peacekeeping operation withdraws (post-conflict peacebuilding), or something that contributes to prevention (preventive peacebuilding). Today peacebuilding is understood, both within the UN system and beyond, as an overarching concept that incorporates prevention, peacemaking, and peacekeeping, as well as human rights and aspects of development. It is used as a concept that captures all of the UN's work that has a peacebuilding theory of change as its basis, i.e. that is aimed at contributing to preventing a (re)lapse into conflict.

The work of the PBC in Burundi, Sierra Leone, and elsewhere helped foster the idea of a strategic peacebuilding framework, as the overarching and integrating strategic framework for all the peace consolidation work of the government and the international community. To manage and monitor the framework, and especially the priority plan and related aspects of the PBF, the countries on the PBC agenda created peacebuilding offices or secretariats. For instance, the government of Liberia created a peacebuilding unit in the Ministry of the

220 *Cedric de Coning and Eli Stamnes*

Interior that was not only responsible for managing the government's responsibilities towards the PBF, but also other aspects that were deemed to fall under the peacebuilding framework, such as the country's reconciliation roadmap. The PBA thus helped to establish peacebuilding as an operational concept in those countries on the PBC agenda, and those countries that were recipients of PBF funding.

In those countries that became eligible for the PBF, UN agencies, funds, and offices that have traditionally been seen as development or humanitarian focused, have had to come to grips with the peacebuilding concept and peacebuilding theories of change, so that they could apply for PBF funding. The PBF has contributed to building an understanding of what peacebuilding is and how it differs from development in these agencies, funds, and offices, at the very least at the country level. The requirements of the PBF have also contributed to the agencies, funds and offices, and UN peacekeeping or special political missions, having to coordinate with each other to avoid submitting proposals that overlap or otherwise reflect a lack of coherence with the peacebuilding framework and priority plan, and have thus contributed to ensuring UN system coherence.

Our assessment is that the establishment of the PBA has contributed to how the UN system, and the international community in general, including especially those countries where the PBC and PBF has been active, understand and view peacebuilding today. The work that the PBA has undertaken since its establishment a decade ago has contributed to the peacebuilding concept developing from an idea used by relatively few experts in conflict resolution, to a concept that is now widely used, broadly understood and generally accepted and welcomed, not only in New York and Geneva, but also in Bujumbura, Kinshasa, Monrovia, Free Town, Bangui, Khartoum, and Juba.[4]

Not only is the concept more accepted and in wider use, but there is now also more of a shared understanding that peacebuilding essentially implies a focus on peace consolidation, i.e. a focus on taking steps to prevent a relapse into violent conflict in those contexts where a peace process has been established, or preventing an outbreak of violent conflict in those transitional contexts where peacebuilding is applied as a preventative measure. The PBF in particular has helped to expand the concept of peacebuilding beyond the traditional post-conflict view to now include support to political transitions in order to prevent a lapse into violent conflict.[5]

Despite the fact that a preventive role for the PBA was too controversial to be included when it was established,[6] the PBA has contributed to making the need for early and sustained engagement in

The future of the UN Peacebuilding Architecture   221

prevention, with a focus on ultimately preventing violent conflict, more of a mainstream and widely accepted principle. Much more needs to be done to further operationalize this concept, and the PBC, supported by the PBSO and others, could play a much more central role in assessing and consolidating the knowledge generated by peacebuilding practitioners, evaluators, and researchers, and to provide intergovernmental sanction for the strategic principles and operational guidelines that should direct the UN system and the international peacebuilding community. We will return to what more can be done in this regard in the next section.

Strengthening coordination across the UN system

The operationalization of the PBA has also highlighted the need to strengthen peacebuilding coordination across the UN system. The work of the PBC Country-Specific Configurations (CSCs) and the evaluations of the PBF have confirmed the degree to which the UN—and the international system more generally—lacks coherence and often works at cross-purposes with itself. Much more needs to be done to improve coherence among the international actors involved in peacebuilding, and the PBA should be able to play a much more meaningful role in this regard.

There has been a marked increase in the attention the UN system has devoted to internal coherence as well as to coordination with national counterparts and other international actors. This is at least partly due to the establishment of the PBA and the subsequent performance of the PBC, especially the early work it did to encourage the development of country-level strategic peacebuilding frameworks. Even if some of these experiences initially resulted in high transaction costs for those involved, it laid the foundation for what is now widely accepted as best practice, namely that the relationship between national authorities, local civil society, and international partners needs to be anchored in country-level compacts or strategic frameworks.[7]

The PBF has also contributed to strengthening UN system coherence, as well as coherence between the UN system, other partners, and the host government and civil society. The PBF model has required that the UN system partners agree on a priority plan for PBF allocations, and that this be done through a Joint Steering Committee (JSC), co-chaired by the host government, and including in most cases representatives of civil society and other international partners.[8] The JSC has thus ensured that the key parties engaged in funding and undertaking peacebuilding programs in a specific country take responsibility for adopting a priority plan, based on a conflict analysis, and then consider the applications received as well as the overall results achieved.

This process has resulted in all the participants of the JSC developing an understanding of what peacebuilding is, and is not based on the specific analysis of the conflict and the priority plan adopted, and this knowledge has then also been applied to the work of those involved outside the JSC. The JSC is typically co-chaired by a relevant minister, for instance the minister of internal affairs or development, and the resident coordinator, and is made up of heads of agencies, donor country representatives, and civil society. These kinds of actors also meet in other forums, such as those responsible for development coordination, and the fact that many of them also meet to discuss peacebuilding issues is likely to have helped to bring peacebuilding coordination into the development discourse in these countries.

However, much more remains to be done and particular attention needs to be devoted to how the PBA in general, and the PBC in particular, can further refine and enhance its role in helping to stimulate and support coherence and coordination within the UN system, between the UN and other international partners and at the country level between international, national, and local partners.[9]

A misguided emphasis on resource mobilization

In the early years there was an assumption that one of the benefits of being on the PBC agenda was that more development resources would flow to those countries on the agenda.[10] However, around the first review of the PBA in 2010 it became clear that being on the PBC agenda did not automatically result in increases in aid flows. This assumption proved thus to be flawed. Decisions on aid are not made by permanent representatives in New York. Nor do they have much direct influence on decisions related to aid flows in their capitals. However, the political attention that they are able to generate for the countries on the PBC agenda are likely also to result in their development counterparts taking note, and this has helped these countries to remain on the international agenda. This has not, however, translated into significant increases in aid flows, but it has prevented these countries from becoming aid orphans.

This resource mobilization assumption has generated a number of negative consequences for the PBA. The emphasis on resource mobilization has given the traditional donors undue prominence in the PBA. For example, initially it was assumed that resources would only be mobilized if a CSC was chaired by a prominent donor. This resulted in a PBC narrative that reflected donor nomenclature, and it reduced peacebuilding to something technical and programmatic. Donors dominated the discourse and it was unlikely that non-donor countries

The future of the UN Peacebuilding Architecture 223

could be elected to leading positions, such as chairs of the CSCs. The result was that the PBC became less relevant for non-Western countries. Attempts were made to redress this precedent, for instance by asking Bangladesh to chair the Organizational Committee in January 2012, but by then the damage was done.

This was an unfortunate start because the PBC had the potential as a broadly representative member state body to build understanding across the North–South and East–West divides. It is now necessary to consider what can be done to reverse the damage caused by the donor bias in the PBA design, and how the potential of the PBC to generate strategic coherence among member states can be stimulated and encouraged.

The strong emphasis on resource mobilization also resulted in peacebuilding being understood—in the 2005–10 period—as essentially technical and programmatic. Peacebuilding was presented as development with a peacebuilding theory of change. However, over the 2010–14 period, this understanding of peacebuilding gradually changed, and by 2015 the view that peacebuilding is essentially political and local had gained ground. Over this period, what was understood as the essential added value of the PBC had also shifted from resource mobilization to political accompaniment. This new understanding was partially informed by the failures of the largely top-down "technical-programmatic" approach to peacebuilding and statebuilding, and the relapses in the Central African Republic (CAR), Guinea-Bissau, Timor-Leste, and South Sudan.[11]

The PBA experience has thus contributed to our understanding of peacebuilding as a concept, as well as the relative value of its programmatic and political dimensions in the way it was operationalized in the specific countries on the PBC agenda. The work of the PBC and PBF, including the assessments and evaluations of their work, has thus helped the UN system to realize that too much focus on resource mobilization generates unintended consequences, including reducing peacebuilding to a programmatic and technical undertaking, thus undermining attention to its political dimension.

Recommendations for strengthening the Peacebuilding Architecture

On the basis of our assessment of the overall impact of the PBA on the UN system, other international partners and host governments, this chapter will now offer a number of recommendations for how the PBA can be strengthened in future. However, before we embark on recommendations, we think it is appropriate to address the context within which these recommendations are made and will have to be implemented.

224 *Cedric de Coning and Eli Stamnes*

Our assessment is that the space for the PBA, and thus also for its further development and evolution, is constrained by both internal UN structural tensions and the current turbulent state of global governance. It is not possible to assess the potential for reform of the PBA without taking some of the structural limitations into account.

The PBC is a subsidiary advisory body to the Security Council and the General Assembly. The council has jealously limited the space available to the PBC.[12] Likewise, the Department of Political Affairs (DPA) and Department of Peacekeeping Operations (DPKO), and the large development agencies, funds, and programs have also carefully guarded their respective bureaucratic fiefdoms. The seniority of the head of the PBSO is symbolic of this constrained role, as comparable offices and departments are all headed at the under-Secretary-General level. Future reforms must thus be based on an assessment of the PBA not just in terms of its original design but also in the context of the limited political and bureaucratic space in which it is allowed to operate.

We are currently experiencing a period of global political instability that is unprecedented in modern history. The United States and its Western allies cannot maintain its monopoly on the international system of global governance. The emergence of China and its BRICS (Brazil, Russia, India, China, South Africa) partners has introduced a degree of turbulence in the international system that makes major reforms highly unlikely, as the system lacks the degree of consensus necessary to bring about significant reforms.[13] The Security Council and General Assembly are thus unlikely to entertain radical changes in the role and structure of the PBA, and especially the PBC. However, for the same reason, the international community is likely to rely more on the UN than before, as it is the most credible international body where issues of collective global concern have to be decided.

We thus conclude that major reforms in terms of the role and position of the PBC in the UN peace and security architecture are unlikely. However, there are still many ways in which the effectiveness of the PBA can be enhanced, even given the structural constraints within which it has to operate.[14]

Shifting the emphasis: From preventing imminent relapse, to sustained international engagement, to addressing root causes of conflict and fragility

The founding assumption of the PBA was that the international community and the UN system leave post-conflict engagements too soon, without addressing the root causes. The research by Paul Collier and

The future of the UN Peacebuilding Architecture   225

others which suggested that 25 percent to 50 percent of all peace processes relapse within five to 10 years has been very influential in this regard.[15] It created an evidenced-based rationale for the lesson identified by the UN peace and development community, i.e. that the UN needed to accompany peace processes for longer than the two to four years that was the norm at the time. Following a number of cases in the 1990s, where countries like Liberia, Sierra Leone, and Haiti relapsed into violent conflict after the withdrawal of UN peacekeeping missions, it was realized that the UN needed to remain engaged for longer if it was to support these countries through a period of heightened risk and fragility, until their peace processes were consolidated. As the Security Council had to focus its attention on managing the most critical crises of the day, it was decided to establish the PBA to accompany states in the aftermath of conflict. The assumption was that such a structure would enable the international system to remain engaged longer in countries emerging out of conflict. In this way the root causes of these conflicts could be addressed, thus permanently resolving the conflicts and ultimately reducing the case load for the Security Council.[16]

In our assessment, the establishment of the PBA did help the international community to remain engaged longer than would have been the case in most of the countries on the PBC agenda—perhaps with the exception of CAR.[17] However, the founding assumption that the establishment of the PBA would result in the international system giving more attention to addressing the root causes of conflict never materialized. Instead the opposite seems to have happened. Over the last decade the international response to conflict has steadily shifted from conflict resolution to conflict management. In 2015, 75 percent of UN peacekeepers are deployed in missions where there is no peace agreement in place, and most of the UN's special political missions are managing fragile political transitions, rather than implementing comprehensive peace agreements.

This is, of course, partly due to changes in the nature of conflict and can be linked to shifts in the global order. However, in the context of the PBA, this can also be linked to pressure on the PBC and PBF to demonstrate the PBA's immediate relevance. In other words, the focus has predominantly been on what it can do to avoid imminent relapse in the countries on the PBC agenda. This pressure has resulted in a focus on immediate "problem solving" at the cost of addressing the enduring root causes. As a result, when it comes to the countries on the PBC agenda, the focus of the PBC and the Security Council has been essentially the same—i.e. working to avoid relapse into violent conflict by focusing on the immediate crisis and conflict drivers.

We would recommend that the PBA revert back to its original intended role of addressing the root causes of conflict. It should leave the focus on avoiding immediate relapse to the Security Council, DPA, and DPKO, and it should take the long view. There are many ways in which the PBA can perform this role. For instance, the PBC can follow countries emerging out of crisis or conflict, which are considered fragile, with the goal of supporting and accompanying their medium- to long-term efforts to put in place the capacities needed to sustain their peace processes. The PBC can support their efforts to develop medium- to long-term goals and plans, for instance by supporting the New Deal in countries where this is relevant. They can follow and accompany the "compacts" such countries enter into with international partners, and importantly, the PBC can commission periodic reports that track progress made on these medium- to long-term peacebuilding commitments. In this way the PBA in general, and the PBC in particular, can play an important role of helping to keep the international system, and the host nation and its civil society, focused on those things that need to be done to ensure that the root causes of the conflict are addressed, and on the steps required to put in place capacities needed in the medium to long term.

External factors

Another important contribution the PBA can make is to remind the international system that we cannot deal with conflict and fragility as if they are only due to unique causes that are contained within the borders of a specific nation-state. We have to take into account, for instance, that capital flight is solicited and facilitated by the international banking system that is at the core of the global economy. Fragility is also linked to other external factors such as corruption, transnational organized crime, and extractive industries. If the international community is genuinely interested in making a difference to global poverty, inequality, and fragility, then a significant portion of their effort should be re-focused on controlling the negative side effects of their own economies and citizens. They should ensure that their own laws and markets do not encourage and facilitate exploitation, crime, corruption, and capital flight. These are thus not problems that can be located only on the periphery of the world system, to be tackled through foreign, security, and aid policies. They are also caused by the perversities of their own internal systems, as well as by the international financial, banking, and natural resource management systems. Domestic solutions are needed to deal with criminals and legitimate,

The future of the UN Peacebuilding Architecture 227

but immoral, companies and individuals based or at least banking and spending their illicit gains in the jurisdictions over which these countries have control. The PBC can play a unique role in rallying together states to address these external factors that contribute to fragility and conflict, since it is a member state body made up of countries that are harboring both victims and perpetrators of such illegal activities.

Regional approaches to peacebuilding

The importance of regional approaches to peacebuilding is often recognized in policy documents and public statements, but rarely acted on.[18] Three considerations explain the relevance of regional approaches to peacebuilding, namely: 1 conflicts are rarely isolated within state borders; 2 those who are closer to the problem are often in a better position to understand and influence it; and 3 their proximity ensures that they have a long-term interest in its outcomes. However, this does not mean that regional approaches are automatically benevolent. In some cases those with an interest at stake try to influence the outcome in their favor, often through a local proxy, and in so doing become part of the problem.

The international system, and the international legal framework on which it is based, relies on sovereign states as the building blocks of global governance. The dynamics that drive conflict are, however, rarely limited by the officially recognized boundaries of sovereign states. Often there are regional dynamics that feed on and further modulate these tensions, such as the current spate of narcotics-based transnational organized crime syndicates in West Africa, which use these shared identity networks to smuggle goods and people across national borders.[19]

In these contexts regional approaches to peacebuilding make sense because these conflicts are interlinked and interrelated. Many of the effects of these conflicts, such as refugees, international migration, and the smuggling of weapons and other illicit goods, are also regional in their manifestation, and neighbors are often most affected. Thus they have also the most direct interest to see them resolved. Sovereign state-based approaches to analyzing, preventing, managing, or resolving these conflicts cannot succeed on their own as it is the interlinkages between the various regional actors and the dynamics in the regional conflict system that drive these conflicts. International and regional responses need to be informed by analyses that take these regional dynamics into account, and political and programmatic responses need to be designed to influence and leverage these complex conflict systems.

228   *Cedric de Coning and Eli Stamnes*

In Africa, the UN has started to try to address the regional dynamics of conflicts by deploying regional envoys to West Africa, the Horn of Africa, and to the Great Lakes. This innovation has already generated good results, but unfortunately the rest of the UN system is locked into dealing with conflicts and peacebuilding through programs and missions that are legally and otherwise constrained to specific states. One of the ways to overcome some of these shortcomings is for the UN to work closer with regional organizations and regional and local civil society. In this context, the most important relationship for the PBC is its relationship with the African Union (AU).

All the countries on the PBC's agenda over the last decade have been from Africa, and African countries received approximately 80 percent of the UN PBF's allocations over the 2007–14 period. Approximately 70 percent of the UN's special political missions and peacekeeping operations are also deployed in Africa. The continent has thus been the major regional focus for the PBC and the PBF, and this is likely to continue, although recent trends suggest that in addition to sub-Saharan Africa, the Sahel and the Middle East will be of growing relevance to the UN's PBA.

African capacities to prevent and manage conflict have grown considerably over the past decade and the AU, the Regional Economic Communities (RECs) and Regional Mechanisms (RMs), and African civil society are now more actively engaged in peacebuilding than ever before. In Africa, the UN, the AU, and the RECs/RMs will always operate alongside each other, and close cooperation between the UN and the AU is thus a strategic necessity. The effectiveness of the UN's PBA and these African institutions is mutually interdependent on several levels.

Future reforms should address not only what needs to be done to ensure that the UN's PBA is well connected and complementary to the UN's peace operations, including its regional envoys, but also how the PBC and PBF can enhance their complementarity and support to the AU, RECs/RMs, and African civil society. The first engagement between the PBC and the AU's Peace and Security Council in 2014 could be followed up and become institutionalized in an annual meeting on peacebuilding in Africa to seek greater coherence on strategic priorities between the PBC and the Peace and Security Council. These high-level exchanges need to be underpinned by a desk-to-desk exchange between the UN's PBSO, the AU's Peace and Security Division, and relevant parts of the RECs/RMs.

The UN, AU, and RECs/RMs can also actively cooperate in those countries where they have a shared interest, for instance where both/all have a special political mission or peace operation deployed, and/or

The future of the UN Peacebuilding Architecture   229

where the PBC and PBF have a special interest. The AU, through its Post-Conflict Reconstruction and Development Framework and its African Solidarity Initiative—which encourages South-South cooperation—and the UN, through its PBA and special political missions, have much to learn from each other's approaches, and from seeking greater cooperation, collaboration, and complementarity.

The PBC can play a meaningful role in helping to ensure that international strategic effort is aligned to a coherent framework that encompasses international, regional, and local initiatives.

National and local ownership

The work of the PBA has also helped to highlight various enduring challenges embedded in the peacebuilding concept. Of these, the one that is perhaps the most challenging for a UN architecture that is essentially New York based, anchored in member states and forced to work through the UN system, is national and local ownership, including especially the role of local civil society.[20] The core of the problem with national and local ownership is not that the principle has not been accepted—almost every policy document recognizes that peacebuilding cannot be sustainable without national and local ownership—but that we have failed to internalize the rather radical implications of this principle, namely that peacebuilding is essentially local.[21] The international actors, including the PBA, still dominate the peacebuilding space, with the perverse result that international peacebuilding assistance more often than not generates the opposite effect to what it aims to achieve: it removes much-needed feedback, it prevents local institutions from learning, it generates dependence, it contributes to fragility, and it undermines self-sustainability.

The PBC and PBF can help to empower national and local ownership by giving a greater role to the governments and civil society of the countries on its agenda to undertake self-assessments, to brief the PBC on its vision, plans, and progress, as well as its perception of peacebuilding challenges, including those posed by its regional and international partners, and by playing a leading role in monitoring its own progress towards sustainable peace.

The PBC and PBF can both play an important role in creating space for civil society to participate in shaping the peacebuilding work of the UN and other partners, by participating in, or commenting on, assessments, analysis, coordination, monitoring, and evaluation of peacebuilding plans and programs. In this way the PBA can contribute to facilitating state-society relations and stimulate feedback from civil

230   *Cedric de Coning and Eli Stamnes*

society on the work of the PBA, the UN system, other partners, and the national government. The PBC can also host an annual global consultation with civil society as well as consider regional civil society consultations, for instance in Africa.

Conclusion

This chapter has aimed to assess the overall impact of the UN's Peacebuilding Architecture on the UN system and the wider peace-building and development community over its first decade in existence. We have found that the PBA has contributed to peacebuilding being adopted as an overarching framework for peace consolidation; that it has contributed to improved coordination across the UN system, especially at country level; and that it has helped the UN system to realize that too much focus on resource mobilization generates unin-tended consequences, including reducing peacebuilding to a program-matic and technical undertaking, thus undermining attention to its political dimension. Much more needs to be done to develop an overarching and strategically coherent UN and international response to countries in transition, but over the last decade the PBA has contributed to moderate advances in this direction.

Our assessment is that the space for the PBA, and thus also for its further development and evolution, is constrained by internal UN structural boundaries as well as the current turbulent state of global governance. The Security Council and General Assembly are thus unlikely to entertain radical changes in the role and structure of the PBA, and especially the PBC. However, for the same reason, the inter-national community is likely to rely more on the UN than before, as it is the most credible international body where issues of collective global concern have to be decided.

Despite these constraints, and because of the prominence of the UN in the international system, there are a number of actions the PBA can undertake to enhance its effectiveness. Our recommendations include:

- that the PBA revert to its original intended role of addressing the root causes of conflict. For instance, the PBC can support the efforts of the countries on its agenda to develop medium- to long-term goals and plans, by supporting the New Deal where relevant. The PBC can follow and accompany the compacts such countries enter into with international partners, and the PBC can commission periodic reports that track progress made on these medium- to long-term peacebuilding commitments;

The future of the UN Peacebuilding Architecture 231

- that the PBA, and especially the PBC, use its broad representative base to foster agreement among its members on ways to address external factors such as corruption, transnational organized crime, and extractive industries both globally and specifically in the countries on the PBC agenda;
- that the PBA give serious attention to incorporating regional approaches into its work, including developing a much more cooperative relationship with the AU, sub-regional bodies and African civil society; and
- that the PBA help to empower national and local ownership by giving a greater role to the governments and civil society of the countries on the PBC agenda to undertake self-assessments, to brief the PBC on its vision, plans, and progress, as well as its perception of peacebuilding challenges, including those posed by its regional and international partners, and by playing a leading role in monitoring its own progress towards sustainable peace.

Our conclusion is that although the UN Peacebuilding Architecture faces many challenges, including some that are structural and thus slow or unlikely to change, it has already had an impact on the way the UN system and the global peacebuilding community, including those countries that have engaged directly with the PBA, understand and approach peacebuilding. There are many actors in the international system that have greater leverage than the PBA on avoiding imminent relapse in any given context, but few that have the potential of the PBA to focus international attention on addressing the root causes of conflict and maintaining the long view, so that these countries can avoid relapse and consolidate their peace processes.

Notes

1 See, United Nations, "In Larger Freedom: Towards Development, Security and Human Rights for All," Report of the Secretary-General, UN doc. A/59/2005, 2005, para. 114; and Chapter 1 in this volume.
2 General Assembly, UN doc. A/Res/60/180, 30 December 2005, para. 2b.
3 General Assembly, UN doc. A/Res/60/180, para. 2c.
4 Cedric de Coning, "Clarity, Coherence & Context: Three Priorities for Sustainable Peacebuilding," NUPI and CIPS Working Paper, The Future of the Peacebuilding Architecture Project, University of Ottawa CIPS and NUPI (Oslo: Norwegian Institute of International Affairs, 2010).
5 See, for example, this volume, Chapters 7 and 8, and also Chapter 3.
6 See, for example, Chapter 1 and the volume's Epilogue.
7 Richard J. Ponzio, "Strategic Policy Frameworks as Peacebuilding Tools: A Comparative Study," *Journal of Peacebuilding and Development* 5, no. 2 (2010).

232 *Cedric de Coning and Eli Stamnes*

8 See Chapters 3 and 9.
9 Michael von der Schulemburg, *Rethinking Peacebuilding: Transforming the UN Approach* (New York: International Peace Institute, 2013), 13.
10 Rob Jenkins, *Peacebuilding: From Concept to Commission* (London: Routledge, 2013), 62.
11 For more on the implications of such a technical-programmatic approach, see Eli Stamnes, "Values, Context and Hybridity: How Can the Insights from the Liberal Peace Critique Literature be Brought to Bear on the Practices of the UN Peacebuilding Commission?" NUPI and CIPS Working Paper, Future of the Peacebuilding Architecture Project, University of Ottawa CIPS & NUPI (Oslo: Norwegian Institute of International Affairs, 2010).
12 See the Foreword and Epilogue to this volume.
13 Cedric de Coning, Thomas Mandrup, and Liselotte Odgaard, eds, *The BRICS and Coexistence: An Alternative Vision of World Order* (London: Routledge, 2015).
14 Necla Tschirgi and Cedric de Coning, "Ensuring Sustainable Peace: Strengthening Global Security and Justice through the UN Peacebuilding Architecture," background paper for the Commission on Global Security, Justice, and Governance, The Hague Institute, 2015.
15 Paul Collier et al. estimate a relapse figure of 50 percent, but this has been questioned by Astri Suhrke and Ingrid Samset, who argue for a figure closer to 25 percent. See Paul Collier et al., *Breaking the Conflict Trap: Civil War and Development Policy* (Washington, DC: The World Bank, 2003); and Astri Suhrke and Ingrid Samset, "What's in a Figure? Estimating Recurrence of Civil War," *International Peacekeeping* 14, no. 2 (2007): 195–203.
16 See Chapter 1 and the Epilogue in this volume.
17 Genta Akasaki, Emilie Ballestraz, and Matel Sow, "What Went Wrong in the Central African Republic?" Report 12 (Geneva: Geneva Peacebuilding Platform, 2015).
18 Cedric de Coning, "Regional Approaches to Peacebuilding," United Nations University, Centre for Policy Research, Tokyo, February 2015, cpr. unu.edu/its-broke-so-fix-it-part-ii-peacebuilding.html.
19 Morten Bøås and Liv Elin Torheim, "The Trouble in Mali—Corruption, Collusion, Resistance," *Third World Quarterly* 34, no. 7 (2013): 1280.
20 Eli Stamnes, "Values, Context and Hybridity: How Can the Insights from the Liberal Peace Critique Literature be Brought to Bear on the Practices of the UN Peacebuilding Commission?" NUPI and CIPS Working Paper, The Future of the Peacebuilding Architecture Project, University of Ottawa CIPS and NUPI (Oslo: Norwegian Institute of International Affairs, 2010).
21 Cedric de Coning, "Understanding Peacebuilding as Essentially Local," *Stability: International Journal of Security & Development* 2, no. 1 (2013).

13 Epilogue
The UN Peacebuilding Architecture— good intentions, confused expectations, faulty assumptions

Judy Cheng-Hopkins

- **The purpose of this epilogue**
- **Understanding the different yet interrelated roles of the PBC and PBSO**
- **The PBC and PBSO from an organizational development point of view**
- **The delicate act of defining division of labor**
- **Last words**

The creation of the United Nations (UN) Peacebuilding Architecture (PBA) in 2005 at the UN was heralded as a historic event, finally putting peacebuilding—surely the ultimate *raison d'être* of the UN itself—on the same footing as peacekeeping with its famous and iconic blue helmets. As *The Economist* wrote in 2009, "No wonder that 'post-conflict peacebuilding' … in places such as Sierra Leone and Guinea-Bissau—has come to be seen as the vital second act to peace-keeping."[1]

The general enthusiasm for the UN to prioritize peacebuilding was understandable as the post-Cold War era saw a preponderance and growing number of intrastate (rather than interstate) conflicts that never seemed to end. There was a worrying pattern of relapse, as countries emerging from conflict were very likely to fall back into conflict:

> During the 1990s, an increase in intra-state conflicts generated a growth in focus by the international community on peacebuilding. A sequential approach to the transition from war to peace that had characterized inter-state conflicts did not hold in the complex civil conflicts after the Cold War. Such conflicts did not tend to end in a decisive military victory and post-conflict reconstruction phase, but rather countries were fragile, trapped in cyclical cycles of conflict, with complex causes.[2]

234 *Judy Cheng-Hopkins*

Thus peacebuilding gained prominence as a strategic concept and as a programmatic area of intervention by the international/donor community. Instead of leaving countries to fend for themselves after protracted civil conflicts, the international community started funding national dialogues and reconciliation programs to help heal the wounds of hatred and distrust and prevent revenge and reprisals, especially between different ethnic groups. Investments in security sector reform (SSR, intended to professionalize the all-too-powerful military in these countries) as well as programs to disarm and reintegrate ex-combatants back into society were considered essential. Lastly, it was felt that more systematic efforts to use diplomacy to bring the various parties together as well as to "politically accompany" weak and nascent governments were needed: important as peacekeeping operations were in stabilizing and maintaining the peace, perhaps they were ill suited to go that extra mile to build the peace.

What is different about peacebuilding (as compared to humanitarian or development interventions) is that it is essentially a political activity that shakes up old political/power relationships and the pre-war status quo described above—through SSR, which invariably diminishes the monopoly of power of the military; and rule of law reforms, which provide access to justice for all, not just the few; national dialogues with civil society—involving more than the elites and anti-corruption; and human rights measures, etc. The new peacebuilding architecture with its linchpin Peacebuilding Commission (PBC) could step in, it was felt, and play this role:

> In creating the PBC, there was an explicit recognition that many of the problems plaguing peacebuilding are political ones—challenges of political will, commitment, setting priorities and holding various actors accountable for their commitments—and they require a political body to address them. Hence the decision was made to create the PBC as an intergovernmental body, with membership drawn from across the UN system (seven countries from the Security Council, including the P5 (permanent five members), seven from the General Assembly, seven from the Economic and Social Council, five of the top ten troop contributors to UN peacekeeping, and five of the top ten financial donors to the UN).[3]

The purpose of this epilogue

Much has been written about the genesis of this architecture and whether it was a good or bad idea. For example, Dirk Salomons called the PBC "an optical illusion"[4] that was bound to fail. The epilogue will

Epilogue 235

not repeat, build on or repudiate these publications; it will bring a different and new perspective, which nobody seems to have covered. To be fair, maybe such a perspective is possible only from someone on the inside looking out and not from someone (like a consultant or researcher) on the outside looking in. From the inside, one can see the nuts and bolts and even inherent contradictions that outsiders may fail to notice.

I should also make clear that this epilogue is an essay, an insider's reflection of the missteps and gaps in the creation of this new architecture in 2005. It is not a comprehensive exploration of the concept and practice of peacebuilding, nor an examination of its institutional history in the UN. Much has been achieved and much has been written, over many years now.

This epilogue seeks to shed light on why (because of and) despite the original good intentions, confused expectations and faulty assumptions on the part of the stakeholders—founding member states, post-conflict countries, members of the PBC, the Security Council and General Assembly, and the UN Secretariat—the PBC and the PBA are still viewed with ambivalence today. Will their potential ever be met?

The first section is short, and breaks the three so-called pillars (actually two) of the architecture into their different components, and thus provides clarity regarding their set-up, resources, and limitations. In so doing, I explain the convoluted structure which has contributed to why the PBA is still so misunderstood and, at times, disparaged today. It is only by understanding the roles and limitations of each component part and the possible synergies between them that we can understand how realistic the ambitions and aspirations of its founders were.

The second section presents my inside view. Here I analyze the PBC and Peacebuilding Support Office (PBSO) from an organizational development perspective. Were all the planning steps taken as they would be in any institution-building project? Were the expectations clear? Were the assumptions well thought through, or faulty? Was there someone, some entity, guiding an implementation strategy? Who was in charge?

Understanding the different yet interrelated roles of the PBC and PBSO

The PBC

There is still such a confused understanding among member states today that the PBC and the PBSO are often used interchangeably. I have often been introduced as the head of the PBC, and the PBC has also been assumed to be synonymous with the Peacebuilding Fund (PBF), raising funds, and managing and funding projects.

236   *Judy Cheng-Hopkins*

Here are the facts: the PBC is an intergovernmental body made up of member states (permanent representatives as per the formula described above). What is innovative here is that in addition to the Organizational Committee (the OC, plenary body), there are also Country-Specific Configurations (CSCs), each headed by a chair to advise and advocate for post-conflict countries that have asked to be on the PBC's agenda:

> In an attempt to operationalize the maxim that there is no "one size fits all" approach to peacebuilding, and that every country requires a differentiated response addressing its unique political context, each country on the PBC's agenda would have a unique format, drawing not only upon the 31 PBC members, but also the country itself, the IFIs [international financial institutions], regional organizations, neighboring states, and key bilateral partners.[5]

Today there are six such CSCs—for Burundi, Sierra Leone, the Central African Republic, Guinea-Bissau, Liberia, and Guinea—each headed by a chair: respectively, Switzerland, Canada, Morocco, Brazil, Sweden, and Luxembourg. These are not to be confused with the chair of the OC.

The chairs as well as members are all sitting ambassadors in New York with regular day jobs: obviously, they are neither field based nor operational in the post-conflict countries. They have no operating budgets other than travel budgets (basically two visits per year to the country of the configuration). Thus the role of the PBC must, by necessity, be limited, largely New York based, niche oriented and strategic, leveraging the comparative advantages that an ambassador in New York would have over Secretariat staff at any level: diplomatic skills and good networks within the European Union (EU), the Security Council, the African Union, the G-77, Nordic donor group, regional powers, etc.

In fact, the role to be played by the PBC is so subtle, so nuanced and behind the curtain that it is invisible outside UN Headquarters, which is something many are not used to. One chair tells of a Security Council visit to a West African country on the PBC agenda, lamenting upon their return to New York that they could see no evidence of the PBC's work in that country—as if political accompaniment and advice were immediately tangible.

Then, at the other extreme, an enthusiastic ambassador revealed his ignorance of the very part-time roles and set-up of the PBC by stating that SSR should be taken out of the UN Department for Peacekeeping Operations' (DPKO) area of responsibility and given to the PBC—as if it had a permanent structure and resources comparable to those of the DPKO!

The PBSO

As for the PBSO, it is a Secretariat body in New York headed by an assistant Secretary-General (ASG) with 26 staff in all, only 14 of whom are funded by the regular budget. The rest are secondees whose secondment may or may not be renewed by the contributing organization—the Office of the UN High Commissioner for Refugees (UNHCR), the UN Population Fund (UNFPA), etc. The problem is not the size of the office per se, but the unpredictability from year to year of what staff resources will be available the following year—hardly ideal for planning purposes. The ASG reports to the Secretary-General and is a part of his senior management group.

The PBSO (see Figure 13.1 and Figure 13.2):

- provides logistical and substantive support to the PBC (helping draft speeches, researching relevant publications and news reports related to the post-conflict country, liaising with the field and relevant departments, and funds and programs);
- manages the PBF (which has US$80–100 million a year, 3 percent of which is put aside to fund all the staff of the PBF section); and
- has an embryonic Policy Branch to develop and coordinate peacebuilding policy within the UN system as a knowledge center, disseminating best practices, lessons learnt, etc.

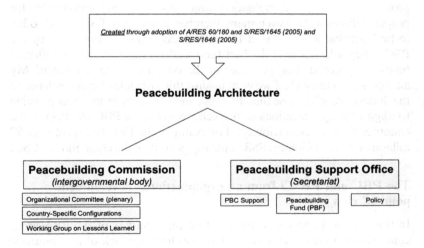

Figure 13.1 The UN Peacebuilding Architecture
Source: Peacebuilding Support Office, 2015.

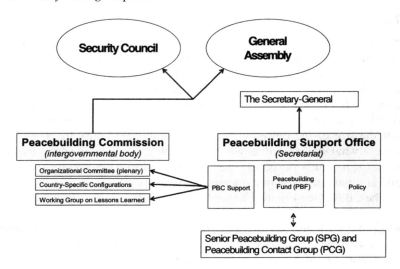

Figure 13.2 Relationships and reporting lines
Source: Peacebuilding Support Office, 2015.

The largest donors to the PBF have stated quite emphatically that they would like the fund to be managed independently and rigorously, with proper monitoring and evaluation, and with the PBSO accountable for proper utilization. However, many member states are still surprised today to find out that allocations of the PBF to countries are not made by the PBC. They ask, where is the beef (and teeth) if the PBC cannot allocate funds for peacebuilding priorities in the countries under its watch? My answer is as follows: (1) if we went against this principle of independence of the donors, we might lose their funding; and (2) we try as much as possible to align funding allocations with specific priorities of PBC chairs (and the countries themselves, obviously). For example, the PBF has spent over $7 million on SSR in Guinea; SSR is the top priority of the chair and the CSC.

The PBC and PBSO from an organizational development point of view

In this section I show how inconsistent the founders of the PBA were, contributing to a difficult birth, and also how the lack of an organizational development strategy—no thanks to diffuse leadership—led to continued confusion, faulty assumptions, and turf wars.

Epilogue 239

Bold vision, modest prescription

According to Dirk Salomons:

> [The then] Secretary-General, Kofi Annan, saw the forthcoming sixtieth anniversary of the United Nations as an opportunity to set a new course for the Organization, and he commissioned a High Level Panel on Threats, Challenges and Change to map out how the UN system could best channel its energies. In its report, the Panel paid considerable attention to the need to preserve or restore peace through non-military means. It noted the void created by an institutional gap, as no agency had a primary mandate in the field of early recovery, and it stressed that the United Nations system could play a unique role.[6]

The concept of a "gaping hole" was echoed in Kofi Annan's report *In Larger Freedom*: "There is a gaping hole in the United Nations institutional machinery: no part of the United Nations system effectively addresses the challenge of helping countries with the transition from war to lasting peace."[7]

With hindsight, we must ask: Was there a gaping hole? The UN Department of Political Affairs (DPA) had set up its first peacebuilding missions in 2005, mandated by the Security Council. The first such missions with explicit peacebuilding objectives were set up in East Timor (2005 to 2006, when renewed conflict cut the mission short) and Sierra Leone (2005; it changed from a peacekeeping mission to a peacebuilding office), each headed by a special or executive representative of the Secretary-General (SRSG/ERSG), very senior staff at under- or assistant Secretary-General levels. Their terms of reference invariably included being head of and coordinator of the entire UN system in-country and representing the Secretary-General in contacts with government, all political actors, member state representatives, regional organizations, etc. I return to this delicate relationship and division of labor between PBC chairs and SRSG/ERSGs below.

Similarly in DPKO, awareness had set in since 2000, the year of the seminal *Brahimi Report*, which pointed to the need to focus on peacebuilding as well if all investments in "boots on the ground" were not to be lost by recurring relapses into violent conflict. The *Brahimi Report* had emphasized the need for integrated, multidimensional peacekeeping missions so that the important business of consciously and painstakingly building the peace is not overlooked. This has evolved, especially in 2011, when a strategy was developed for peacekeepers as "early

240   *Judy Cheng-Hopkins*

peacebuilders" and with the adoption of a Security Council resolution on this role in early 2013.

Lastly, the UN Development Programme (UNDP), quick to see gaps and niches, had set up a Bureau for Conflict Prevention and Early Recovery (BCPR) in 2001, when the void in peacebuilding at the UN had become evident.

In other words, it was not exactly virgin territory for the new peace-building architecture to flourish in. Why had member states not given these existing mechanisms a chance to succeed? Or could it be that other structures did exist, but were not living up to the task at hand? In that case, could we not have been more analytical in terms of identifying weaknesses and gaps and then coming up with a reform process that might have led to the new peacebuilding architecture?

I am not in a position to provide answers here, but I have certainly experienced the consequences of inevitable turf wars between these elephants (in terms of size of budget and staff) and the mouse that PBSO was, and still is. Mind you, Secretariat entities do not generally pick fights with member state entities (the PBC, in this case). They pick on their own kind—which here would be the PBSO.

The second question is: If there was indeed a "gaping hole," why was the response so modest and self-limiting? First let's tackle the question of the wisdom of separating conflict prevention from peacebuilding, knowing what we knew by then:

> For the (then) Secretary-General, however, these recommendations were too bold, and in his own report to the sixtieth session of the General Assembly, entitled "In larger freedom," he presented a diminished version. To fend off all controversy, the Secretary-General introduced his proposal with the statement that "I do not believe that such a body should have an early warning or mon-itoring function." Instead of a robust, preventive and proactive mandate as envisaged by the High-Level Panel, the Peacebuilding Commission's tasks would now be limited to a few activities to be undertaken only after war: improve planning, help ensure finan-cing, provide a forum, improve coordination, review progress, and make sure that international attention would remain focused on countries coming out of crisis.[8]

So "conflict prevention" was a no-go zone for both the PBC and the PBSO. What was incomprehensible was this: If Paul Collier, among many others, had established that countries seldom emerge perma-nently from conflict—there is a very high likelihood that they (for lack

Epilogue 241

of trust, reconciliation not complete, weak institutions, etc.) will relapse into conflict—why and how would one forbid peacebuilders from engaging in prevention as well?

Second, what has always intrigued me was why "support" was part and parcel of the name of my outfit, the PBSO, when only one branch of three has a support function (supporting the PBC). Is not everything that international actors do in relation to developing countries (whether it is in development or in peacebuilding) strictly "support"? We *support* capacity and institution building, we never "do" it on their behalf—in theory. So why are other programs not called "support" programs? I would venture to say that it was to appease the giants—a support office is no threat.

The 2009 report "Peacebuilding in the Immediate Aftermath of Conflict," the guiding note to operationalizing the new peacebuilding architecture, is yet more evidence that in those early days, everybody was bending over backwards to soothe and assure the giants that this new mechanism was not going to infringe on their territory; it was just going to show itself in the "immediate aftermath"—not before, not after. How wrong that has turned out to be—yet nobody seems to be complaining.

As stated in the PBC's 2005 founding resolutions by the General Assembly (resolution 180) and Security Council (resolution 1645), both bodies:

> Reaffirm [...] [their] request to the Secretary-General to establish, within the Secretariat, from within existing resources, a small peacebuilding support office staffed by qualified experts to assist and support the Commission, and recognize [...] in that regard that such support could include gathering and analysing information relating to the availability of financial resources, relevant United Nations in-country planning activities, progress towards meeting short and medium-term recovery goals and best practices with respect to cross-cutting peacebuilding issues.[9]

Note that it would be created from within "existing resources." "Small," I have no problem with—but "within existing resources" has proven a challenge, given that no bureaucracy in the world would ever give up resources willingly. As noted, out of the 26 total posts in my office, 12 were extra-budgetary, usually depending on the goodwill of friends like the UNHCR and UNFPA. However, as we have learnt, such staff can be withdrawn at short notice, making even medium-term planning impossible.

242 *Judy Cheng-Hopkins*

This is where the schizophrenia and contradictions come in: if the institutional hole was gaping and the need so urgent, why were the prescriptions so modest and limiting, as if a restraining circle had to be drawn around the new kids on the block? As Sarah Hearn points out, "Initially, PBSO was to provide strategic input alongside the national governments seeking assistance, but this mandate quickly unravelled as some countries and UN departments pushed back on a leadership role for the new office, a point from which PBSO has not recovered."[10]

Upon further reflection, I find this statement dated. The PBSO did recover, albeit through another route. It focused on its greatest asset and leverage, its most sought-after tool (within the UN agencies and missions at least): the PBF. The PBSO was able to find its way into playing a strategic role, especially alongside national governments, in defining and shaping their peacebuilding priorities and frameworks through the PBF. In the aid business, talk is cheap. It is both more realistic and more credible to discuss meaningful reforms with governments when some funding is available at the end, at least to kick-start its implementation. Hearn seems to have forgotten that there are usually many paths to the same objective—and that coordination of national programs matters in the field, not at headquarters.

A difficult birth

The PBC is listed on the Security Council website as the *only* advisory body to the council. Yet, the relationship to this parent body has been problematic, as pointed out by the 2010 review of the PBA:

> The interaction between the Security Council and the Commission has been limited. The problem appears to be twofold: the Security Council perceives that the advice of the Commission does not provide much added value and the Commission does not provide more focused advice in part because the Security Council does not make more specific requests. The situation is one of missed opportunities, and falls short of the hopes and expectations of 2005.[11]

One view was that the PBC was the ultimate compromise in a period of failed Security Council reform. Many non-P5 countries, which included the largest official development assistance donors, the G-77 and those who aspired to be in an expanded and more diversified permanent member group in the Security Council, accepted as a second-best option the establishment of the PBC as an alternative platform for

Epilogue 243

discussion of peace and security issues. The P5, on the other hand, were either indifferent or accepted the PBC grudgingly.

Needless to say, the debates leading up to the adoption of the resolutions in 2005 were long and painful, for reasons stated above. Maybe it is human nature, but once bitter compromises are arrived at, most people are exhausted and never want to hear of the subject matter again. After a difficult birth, the poor PBA became not the darling but the stepchild. This may have had repercussions on relations with its reluctant parents, as described in the 2010 review cited above.

As if that were not bad enough, it took the PBC so long to get its act together (formula for membership, etc.) and to communicate what this new entity in New York was about, that skepticism and cynicism had already begun. This was true especially among actors in the field, who suspected yet another headquarters-inspired concoction to duplicate and coordinate their work:

> In the PBA's first year in 2006, we found that the PBC's immediate procedural and negotiation obstacles had resulted in long delays, frustration, and confusion in the field and at headquarters about what the PBC was for. Cumbersome negotiations had already resulted in the development of an institution that was considerably larger than first envisioned, but with no institutional weight, resources or other tools to assert it. By the end of its first year, a degree of self-fulfilling scepticism about whether the PBC could fulfil its mandate effectively or efficiently had already started to set in.[12]

Hardly any attention was paid to details on how the PBC would function. How would it relate to SRSG/ERSGs, who have Security Council mandates after all? Only mechanical issues like membership numbers, from what groupings, etc., were discussed and agreed upon. Many thus considered it a "hollow mandate." This was their first faulty assumption: just because a resolution was passed, it was assumed that everybody would understand and jump into their respective roles and onto a crowded field. The PBA, for all intents and purposes, was dropped into this crowded field.

Who is in charge?

From my insider perspective, I have always felt uneasy about this question. The PBA is a hybrid entity that combines a member state organization with a Secretariat organization—the two are intrinsically linked, yet neither reports to the other. The work and credibility of one

244 *Judy Cheng-Hopkins*

depends on the other. The PBSO does not report to the PBC but to the Secretary-General, and the PBC is somehow accountable to the Security Council and General Assembly. Discussions about lines of authority are just left unaddressed. This is unlike any other UN system entity, where such basic matters are articulated and understood (see Figure 13.2 on relationships and reporting lines between the PBC and PBSO).

The PBC is an intergovernmental entity made up of ambassadors, and my office supports them. So how could we possibly be in charge of defining their role, of how they prioritize, their relationships with governments and UN entities? On the other hand, they rotate (the chair of the OC rotates annually and chairs of CSCs may eventually be reassigned as permanent representatives). The institutional memory rests with my office, yet we have to tread lightly, stealthily. For the most part, our relations have been smooth and mutually reinforcing, but there have been occasional hiccups in the years of the PBC's existence, especially when we feel that chairs ought to be more engaged and proactive in one peacebuilding area or another. Yet we have to defer to their expertise and hierarchy in matters of diplomacy. Occasionally, UN departments complain that Security Council members do not understand what the role of the PBC is in a particular country: Where is the "value-added"? they ask. However, did anyone really understand what the value-added was meant to be when nothing was defined in those early days? Certainly not what "political accompaniment" meant, as I describe later.

Of course, my office, like any other Secretariat office, has strong and sometimes not so strong staff, especially when it comes to grasping the subtle and nuanced role of the PBC in political accompaniment. In July 2009, *The Economist* stated: "Beneath the thickets of UN-speak lie three priorities. The first is the need for a strong leader to stop international agencies' turf wars. Somebody needs to bang bureaucratic heads together and set an agenda."[13]

Who is the strong leader they are talking about? It would be terribly presumptuous and arrogant to think that it would be me—but who then? Has the chair of the OC, who is a full-time ambassador and rotates every year, the time and inclination to understand the inner workings of UN agencies and departments and "bang bureaucratic heads together"? Or the chairs of CSCs? How about the SRSG/ERSGs?

The delicate act of defining division of labor

I have heard that in the early days, because of lack of communication on the role of the CSC chairs, fireworks exploded when they visited countries on the agenda. SRSG/ERSGs could not fathom what the

Epilogue 245

chairs would do in the country; when chairs assumed a superior air, the SRSG/ERSGs went into passive-aggressive mode. Some even refused to clear mission dates of chairs to the country, making excuses that the timing was inconvenient. On the other hand, some chairs stepped right into the minefield that UN Country Team coordination is, castigating this or that agency for moving too slowly.

Let us recall that the CSC chairs had generally phrased terms of reference. The mandate of a chair according to the founding resolutions was advocating for and keeping international attention on the country, mobilizing resources and bringing about policy coherence among all international actors in the country concerned. In an overarching sense, it would politically accompany nascent governments out of conflict, and into sustainable peace.

Undoubtedly, the Terms of Reference of the chairs and SRSG/ERSGs could be seen as duplicative—advocating for the country, mobilizing resources, and bringing coherence amongst aid programs. The most successful chairs, in my observation, are those most conscious of their own comparative advantage—the ability to convene and speak frankly with other ambassadors in-country and thus gather valuable information; the ability to have a tête-à-tête with heads of state as government to government, or (crudely put) as a donor government to a recipient government. I always say that chairs cannot be made *persona non grata* the way SRSGs can. Ambassadors may also convene the highest-level of IFI to strategize and work together the way no Secretariat personnel can because they represent member states and most are board members at IFIs as well. Lastly, chairs have their configuration comrades to call on when a difficult position is necessary—vis-à-vis a recalcitrant government engaging in human rights abuses against the opposition, for instance. These could be countries in the same language groupings, in regional groupings or just good personal friends and colleagues in New York with whom they socialize.

The most successful relationships between CSC chairs and SRSG/ERSGs have come about when the former actually exploit their comparative advantages and the latter are able to conceptually understand the former's advantages and use them to their own benefit—call it what you will: division of labor, good cop/bad cop, etc.

The second faulty assumption was to assume that everybody, including the chairs, knew their roles, knew the SRSG's role and what political accompaniment meant. As CSCs were long term, up to 8–10 years, trust had to be built up with governments, civil society, etc. It was not fly-by-night. This meant that chairs had to be empathetic and work behind the scenes, behind the curtain—no headline news.

246 *Judy Cheng-Hopkins*

Obviously, then, the PBC could not be "visible" on the ground. It is a New York-based body that facilitates political consensus based on broad political support for a country emerging from conflict and the relevant transitional processes.

The conundrum is how a body that is meant to act behind the scenes in a manner so non-reminiscent of past "advisors" from ex-colonial masters, is supposed to be more "visible" and show more impact. How could it ever prove it has impact?

Making the best out of a bad situation

Let me share my strategy in 2009, my first year as head of the PBSO. I was aware that my predecessors had not lasted very long on the job— they had obviously been trying to get a new institution off the ground, but little did I know the extent of the acrimony over turf. At one point, a very senior colleague in one of the departments even suggested that, since the PBSO and especially the PBC (and the PBC support branch) was doing so poorly, I should just call it a day and hand over all substantive backstopping responsibilities to his department, leaving logistics support only to the PBSO. (I have kept that email as a souvenir.)

It was too complex to try to get this entity called the PBC right—it was too multi-faceted, with too many different perspectives. All that I managed to achieve in the early years was, mindlessly and desperately, to get two new countries on the PBC agenda, Liberia and Guinea, in addition to the four already on since 2006–07. I felt I had to overcome the criticism of why only the same four countries were on the agenda. My deputy worked on one while I worked on the other.

So I turned all my efforts and attention to the PBF. Thanks to the enthusiasm over the establishment of the PBA and the PBF, by 2008, contributions to the latter had far exceeded the target set in the founding resolution of $250 million, with over 50 countries contributing. However, this remained untapped, unutilized. It was as if everyone had forgotten that $250 million was sitting in the bank waiting to be programmed. Internal wrangling over PBC membership and perennial external tensions consumed everybody's attention. My first meeting with some of the largest donors was the strangest encounter I have ever had with a donor. They told me not even to mention new contributions until we started spending what we had. The message was crystal clear—so spend we will, I assured them. Not only did disbursements jump up in 2009 and 2010 but we corrected the then totally lopsided situation where 80 percent of all disbursements went to one organization alone, breeding suspicion and disinterest on the part of other funds and programs.

Epilogue   247

We went about reinventing the PBF. First we had to brand it as "fast, catalytic and risk taking." As I always tell my team, in the aid world, if you are fast (without compromising quality, of course), you get noticed. If you are relatively small, you must be able to catalyze more resources, either by piloting risky activities or via rapid bridging funding. That way we have a chance of having, one day, some impact when others scale up what we started. The needs in post-conflict settings are simply too big for a small peacebuilding fund to meet. Next, we introduced more systematic programming steps such as appraisal committees, beefed-up monitoring and evaluation, etc. However, perhaps the most important thing I did was hire a savvy fund manager with extensive field experience and a personable, honest manner with the donors at the working level—who, after all, greatly influence their bosses regarding which funds to support among many options.

In spite of a general shrinking of aid, the PBF is still going strong today, able to reach its fundraising as well as its allocation targets of between $80 million and $100 million a year. It helped that the PBF received positive ratings (in fact, "A" the second time around) from one of its top donors known for tough, discriminating standards.

With hindsight, that was the smartest thing we did. It is known to those working with aid that humanitarian aid and development aid have clear provisions in aid budgets in donor capitals built up over the years. However, anything to do with transitional settings (that which is neither emergency/humanitarian nor development) has a hard time getting a budget provision. I remember from my time at the UNHCR that while funds were usually available when refugees crossed borders (the "CNN effect"), when that happy day arrived when they were to return home, funds were seldom available. My ex-colleague Jeff Crisp used to write that sadly all we could offer a returnee was a "cooking pot and a handshake!"

Thus one can imagine how ecstatic the SRSGs, deputy SRSGs, resident coordinators (RCs) and others were when the PBF showed up. The Immediate Response Facility (IRF) of the PBF has a ceiling of $10 million. What a dream it was for the SRSG of the Central African Republic, for instance, to be able to draw on this amount from the PBF/IRF within six months of the onset of conflict. To cut a long story short, when I shared pie charts with heads of departments, showing where the funds had gone, including to their departments and agencies, the turf wars stopped, or at least subsided.

It was only after the PBF was on a sound footing with a solid team and, I might add, with a star-studded cast of peacebuilding experts on its advisory group, that I could turn my full attention to the PBC. I attended every OC and CSC meeting and made it a point always to

248 *Judy Cheng-Hopkins*

make brief remarks supporting the chair, for example in announcing new PBF projects in line with priorities that they had expressed. I also felt that the Peacebuilding "Support" Office should play a more proactive role, for instance in helping to orient new chairs to the job by talking through their experiences and exchanging ideas. In fact, this was a "faulty assumption" on my part—thinking that ambassadors would find it insulting to be trained. Most of them appreciated the opportunity to demystify the concept of "political accompaniment." We used the "fishbowl" technique where a moderator would facilitate this conversation between themselves only. The rest of us, including those supporting the chairs, sat around the fishbowl, observing and listening.

Is there any hope?

The 2010 review stated:

> Five years later, despite committed and dedicated efforts, the hopes that accompanied the founding resolutions have yet to be realized. We are now at a crossroads: Either there is a conscious recommitment to peacebuilding at the very heart of the work of the United Nations, or the Peacebuilding Commission settles into the limited role that has developed so far. Our consultations suggest that the membership strongly favours the former path.[14]

In my opinion, the PBC as an institution will never win the Nobel Peace Prize, but between winning the peace prize and doing away with the PBC altogether are invaluable opportunities that will be lost for peacebuilding if we opted for the latter, because of the important niche that the PBC occupies or could occupy. My view is that there was no gaping hole: on the contrary, it was a crowded field. However, the PBC does have invaluable comparative advantages, and there is a clear niche within which these advantages can be strategically utilized. The key is to tease them out, to talk them through, and to internalize them—and not live with the faulty assumption that something so complex and nuanced is easily understood by all.

Last words

I will not list here recommendations for improving the PBC or PBSO. That was not the intent of this chapter, which was instead to provide an inside view, insights into the machinery which seemed painfully

Epilogue 249

foggy to so many. It is for the 10-year review of the PBA to come up with recommendations—rigorously and comprehensively.

Adjustments to the original concept are obviously necessary because:

- in reality the PBC is intervening not in the "immediate aftermath" of conflict but sometimes several years later;
- in the case of the Central African Republic today, the PBC and PBF are engaged in the midst of conflict;
- up to now there has been a reluctance to discuss exit strategies, so when is the PBC's work finished?
- The founding resolutions were clear that the PBA should intervene to prevent "a lapse or relapse into conflict." Is it timely now to look into the "lapse" side of the equation, i.e. prevention?

On the question of diffuse leadership and who is in charge, should the question of having the PBC chair (of the OC) stay for a minimum of two years or three be contemplated? I know the argument is that the presidents of the Security Council and the General Assembly rotate as well but these are not startup organizations—they have been around for decades. Later on, once the PBC is fully established then annual rotations may make sense. Again, this is from an organizational development perspective.

The three keywords or phrases that summarize this chapter's contents are: "insider's view," "organizational development perspective," and "confused expectations and faulty assumptions." I hope I have shed light and contributed to continuous learning in this respect.

Notes

1 *The Economist*, "After the Peacekeepers Come the Peacebuilders," 1 July 2009.
2 Sarah Hearn, Alejandra Kubitschek Bujones, and Alischa Kugel, *The United Nations "Peacebuilding Architecture": Past, Present and Future* (Center for International Cooperation (CIC), New York University, May 2014), 2.
3 Vanessa Wyeth, "Peacebuilding at the UN over the Last 10 Years," International Peace Institute, essay series no. 06/2011, 2011, 6.
4 Dirk Salomons, "On the Far Side of Conflict: The UN Peacebuilding Commission as an Optical Illusion," in *United Nations Reform and Collective Security*, ed. Peter Danchin and Horst Fischer (Cambridge: Cambridge University Press, 2010).
5 Wyeth, "Peacebuilding at the UN over the Last 10 Years," 6.
6 Salomons, "On the Far Side of Conflict," 197.

250 *Judy Cheng-Hopkins*

7 United Nations, "In Larger Freedom," Report of the Secretary-General of the United Nations for decision by heads of state and government in September 2005, UN doc. A/59/2005, 21 March 2005, 31.
8 Salomons, "On the Far Side of Conflict," 199.
9 Security Council resolution 1645, 2005, para. 23.
10 Hearn et al., *The United Nations "Peacebuilding Architecture,"* 4.
11 United Nations, "Review of the United Nations Peacebuilding Architecture," UN doc. A/64/868–S/2010/393, 21 July 2010, 27, para. 106.
12 Hearn et al., *The United Nations "Peacebuilding Architecture,"* 4.
13 *The Economist*, "After the Peacekeepers Come the Peacebuilders."
14 United Nations, "Review of the United Nations Peacebuilding Architecture."

Index

2010 Review of the United Nations Peacebuilding Architecture 1–2, 182, 185–6, 207, 248; Guinea-Bissau 185–6, 187, 189; PBC 2, 77–8, 183, 191

2015 Review of the United Nations Peacebuilding Architecture xxx, 2, 102–103, 105

Abdenur, Adriana Erthal 16, 181–95
Advisory Group of Experts 2, 3–5, 19, 228; 'sustaining peace' 3
Africa 228
African Development Bank 119, 195
An Agenda for Peace xx, 121, 182; Boutros-Ghali, Boutros 26, 121, 148, 182; conflict prevention 26, 38; *Supplement to an Agenda for Peace* 38
AIAF (Afghan Interim Authority Fund) 34
Annan, Kofi xxvi, 6, 24, 44; PBA, beginnings 25, 27, 29, 30, 36, 181, 239; *see also In Larger Freedom*
ASG (assistant secretary-general) xxiv, 61, 63, 69, 237; ASG Peacebuilding group xxviii; coordination on peacebuilding among UN departments and programs xxiii
Asia Infrastructure Investment Bank 5
AU (African Union) 5, 106, 117, 119, 228–9; African Solidarity Initiative 229; Post-Conflict Reconstruction and Development Framework 229

Bailey, Mark 7, 23–39
Ball, Nicole 190
Ban Ki-moon 44, 185; 2009 *Peacebuilding in the Immediate Aftermath of Conflict* 12, 53, 101–102, 103, 109, 110, 111, 117, 206–207, 208, 241; 2010 *Women's Participation in Peacebuilding* 99, 101–102, 103; 2014 *Civilian Capacities in the Aftermath of Conflict* 112, 116–19
Berdal, Mats 41
Bernardino, Luís 184
Bolton, John 31
Brahimi Report xxv, 26, 28, 239
BRICS (Brazil, Russia, India, China, South Africa) 87, 91, 224; New Development Bank 5
Burundi xxii–xxiii, 13–14, 127–44; Arusha Peace and Reconciliation Agreement 127; BINUB 128, 129, 134, 142; BNUB 129, 134; Burundian police 130; civil war 127; CNDD-FDD 129, 131, 132; CNIDH 132; *colline* 129, 131, 133, 143; CSC xxiv, 45–6, 135 (chair 13, 135, 136, 143); elections 127, 131–2; FDN 130, 143; gender-related issues 100, 101, 132; JSC 137, 138, 144; Norway xxiv; PBA 127–8 (key areas covered 132, 142); PBC 134–6, 143; PBSO 128, 135, 136–8, 149; Peacebuilding Priority Plan 144; PNG 135; research and methodology 129; RUNO 128, 134, 136–7, 139;

252   *Index*

shortcomings 137–8; SNR 130; TFC 134, 138, 139, 144; UNDP 136, 142; *see also* Burundi and PBF support; ONUB
Burundi and PBF support 13, 127, 142, 187–8; context 129; oversight, guidance, support, implementation mechanisms and instruments 133–4; PBF I 13, 128, 132, 134, 138–9, 142; PBF II 13, 128, 132–3, 134, 138–9, 142, 144; Period I: deadlock in parliament 129–30; Period II: deadlock in negotiations with the FNL 130–1; Period III: 2010 election period 131–2; Period IV: consolidation of political power in the post-2010 phase 132–3; recommendations for improvement 140–2; shortcomings 13, 54, 128, 131–2, 133, 134, 138, 139 (negative impact/harm 128, 131, 133, 140; poor project design, implementation, monitoring 13–14, 128); success 13, 14, 129–31, 133, 140; *see also* Burundi

C34 (Special Committee on Peace-keeping Operations) 88, 92, 94
Campbell, Susanna 13–14, 127–44
Caparini, Marina 15–16, 159–80
Caplan, Richard 52–3
CAR (Central African Republic) 47, 78, 143, 185, 198, 223, 225, 236, 249; CSC chair 191
Cavalcante, Fernando 14–15, 145–58
CCC (Civilian-Contributing Country) 110, 111, 121
Cheng-Hopkins, Judy 5, 6–7, 44, 52, 165, 233–50
CIVCAP (Civilian Capacity initiative) 12–13, 109–23; CAPMATCH 114–16, 118; CIVCAP reform 12, 110–11, 114, 117, 121; CIVCAP Steering Committee 112, 122; *Civilian Capacity in the Aftermath of Conflict* 112, 116–19; civilians: crucial role in peacebuilding 12, 109–110, 117, 121; end of 116; future directions 120; Global South 112–13, 115, 118; historical

background of 109–113; lessons learned 117–19; national owner-ship 12, 112, 117, 120; PBA, implications for 119; *Peacebuilding in the Immediate Aftermath of Conflict* 12, 109, 110, 111, 117; recommendations to the UN system 120, 121; results 116–17; Senior Advisory Group's report 12, 110, 111–12; South-South cooperation 12, 110, 111, 118–19, 120, 121; South Sudan 113–14; triangular cooperation 12, 110, 111, 114, 118–19, 120, 121
civil society 234; crucial role in peacebuilding 12, 109–110, 117, 121; implementer in peacekeeping field xxv; local ownership 229; PBA, beginnings 31; PBA, recommendations for improvement 18, 228, 229–30, 231; PBC xxii, 4, 7, 31–2, 229–30; PBF 4, 34, 229; Sierra Leone 147, 153; *see also* INGO; NGO
civil war: Burundi 127; cost of 25; Guinea-Bissau 183, 185, 192; Liberia 160; *see also* conflict
Cliffe, Sarah 112
Collier, Paul xxix, 25, 224–5, 232, 240
Condé, Alpha 201, 202–205, 206, 207; *see also* Guinea
conflict: conflict/development link xx; external factors that contribute to 226–7, 231 (corruption, organized crime, extractive industries 18, 226–7, 231); intrastate conflict 233; regional dynamics that drive conflict 227; root causes of conflict 18, 224–6, 230; *see also* civil war; conflict prevention; conflict, relapse into; post-conflict country
conflict prevention xxvi, xxx, 6; *An Agenda for Peace* 26, 38; conflict-prevention/post-conflict peacebuilding relationship 26; Guinea 55; PBA 26–7, 181, 220–1; PBC, conflict prevention role 7, 24–5, 29–30, 78, 191, 240, 249 (sovereignty 7, 36, 43, 79, 182,

Index 253

191); PBF 55; peacebuilding 26–7, 36, 63, 148; separating conflict prevention from peacebuilding 8, 55, 240–1; *see also* conflict; conflict, relapse into

conflict, relapse into xxi, 25, 135, 223, 224–6, 232, 231; pattern of 233; peacebuilding 6, 220, 225, 240–1; *see also* conflict; conflict prevention

Coning, Cedric de 1–20, 217–32

CSC (Country-Specific Configuration) xxiv–xxv, 44, 45–7, 221, 236; Burundi xxiv, 45–6, 135; functions 47; Guinea 198 (peer advice 17, 206, 207); Liberia 161; PBC's main instrument for peacebuilding 45; shortcomings 10 (marshalling resources xxvii; path dependency 47); Sierra Leone xxiv–xxv, 45–6, 146, 147, 153; success 80, 91, 183; *see also* CSC chair; IPBS; PBC

CSC chair 80, 81, 91, 135, 183, 236, 244–6; Burundi 13, 135, 136, 143; chair/SRSG/ERSGs relationship 245–6; donor xxiv, 83, 222–3; Guinea 201, 202; Guinea-Bissau, Brazilian CSC chair 16, 189–90, 191–2; *persona non grata* 135, 245; Sierra Leone 153; training 248; *see also* CSC

CSSO (civil service support officer) 114

DDR (disarmament, demobilization, and reintegration) 234; Sierra Leone 14, 145

development: conflict/development link xx; development assistance, history of xxix; Guinea, underdevelopment 199–200; Guinea-Bissau, underdevelopment 16, 188, 192; peace/security/development/ human rights link xxvi, xxvii, xxix, 23–4; peacebuilding/development distinction 234; peacebuilding/ development link 148–50; security/ development link 16, 182

Dexter, Tracy 13–14, 127–44

DOCO (UN Development Operations Coordination Office) 53

Doyle, Michael 26

DPA (UN Department of Political Affairs) 6, 28, 51, 68, 224; closing the UN's institutional peacebuilding gap 80, 93; peacebuilding missions 239

DPKO (UN Department of Peacekeeping Operations) 6, 32, 51, 68, 142, 224; closing the UN's institutional peacebuilding gap 80, 93; *see also* peacekeeping operation

ECOSOC (UN Economic and Social Council): Guinea-Bissau 184, 185, 186, 192, 195; PBC xxiv, 29, 44, 234 (reporting to ECOSOC 7, 30–1)

ECOWAS (Economic Community of West African States): Guinea 17, 197, 199, 201, 203, 207; Guinea-Bissau 184, 185, 186, 192, 195

ECPS (Executive Committee on Peace and Security) 28

EISAS (ECPS Information and Strategic Analysis Section) 28

Embaló, Birgit 184, 193

EOSG (Executive Office of the Secretary-General) 28, 33, 34

ERSG (executive representative of the secretary-general) 128, 239; chair/SRSG/ERSGs relationship 245–6

EU (European Union) 106, 119; Guinea-Bissau 186–7; PBF 9, 67

FAO (Food and Agriculture Organization) 142

Fearon, James 28

Felix da Costa, Diana 114

Fernández-Taranco, Oscar 20

Findley, Michael 13–14, 127–44

Forman, Shepard 28

Forrest, Joshua 192

fragile state xxix, 118, 233; external factors that contribute to fragility 226–7; Guinea 198; Guinea-Bissau 183, 184, 185; Liberia 160; sustainable development xxix

254 *Index*

g7+ group 81, 90–1, 113, 118
G-77: PBC 30, 79, 100, 242 (preventive mandate 7, 24, 29, 43)
gender-related issues 31; 2015 PBA review 102–103, 105; Burundi 100, 101, 132; Guinea 17, 200, 205; Guinea-Bissau 187, 188; McAskie, Carolyn 100–101; PBA and gender 99, 100–101, 102, 103–104 (failure to deliver on 'gender-sensitive peacebuilding' 97, 99, 103, 105); PBC 100, 101, 103, 105; PBF 100–101, 103, 104 (GPI 71–2, 74, 75); PBSO 100–101, 102, 103, 105; Seven-Point Action Plan 71, 103; WGLL 101, 102; women's inclusion in peacebuilding 103–104; *Women's Participation in Peacebuilding* 99, 101–102, 103; *see also* WPS
Ghani, Ashraf 32
global governance 19, 227; turbulent state of 18, 224, 230
Global Review 64, 65, 67, 68, 69, 70, 71, 72; *see also* PBF
Global South 54, 87, 91; CIVCAP 112–13, 115, 118 (South-South cooperation 12, 110, 111, 118–19, 120, 121); *New Deal*, South-South dialogue 10–11, 81, 90; South-South cooperation 229
GPP (government-provided personnel) 110, 111, 113, 117, 121
Guéhenno, Jean-Marie 111
Guinea 16–18, 196–213; CMRN 197, 199; CNDD 196, 197–8, 204; conflict prevention 55; country context 197–8; crisis diplomacy 17, 203; economic sector 199–200, 205, 206; ECOWAS 17, 197, 199, 201, 203, 207; elections 17, 198, 200–201; FOSSEPEL/FOSSEL 203, 204; fragile state 198; instability 17, 206; International Contact Group 197, 201, 206, 207; National Assembly 198, 201, 203; national reconciliation 198; Ouagadougou agreement 196, 197–8, 204; SSR 17, 199, 204–205, 206, 238; transition from military to

elected civilian regime 17, 196, 198–200, 206; UN Office for West Africa 17, 201, 203, 207–208; underdevelopment 199–200; violent street politics 17, 198, 199–200, 202, 203–204, 205; World Bank 200, 205–206; youth/women dimension 17, 200, 205; *see also* Condé, Alpha; Guinea and PBA; Touré, Sidya
Guinea and PBA 200–206; between UNSC peacekeeping/political mission and development 'business as usual' 17–18, 207–209; CSC 198 (chair 201, 202; peer advice 17, 206, 207); PBC 198, 199, 201, 202; PBF 198, 199, 202–203, 204, 206; PBSO 203; shortcomings 203, 204–205, 206–208 (lack of a country-level counterpart 202; lack of inclusive approach to peacebuilding 206–208); a test case 196; *see also* Guinea
Guinea-Bissau 16, 181–95; 2012 *coup d'état* 16, 182, 186, 187, 191, 192; civil war 183, 185, 192; CPLP 184, 186, 192–3, 195; drug and human trafficking 16, 184, 185, 188, 192; ECOWAS 184, 185, 186, 192, 195; elections 85, 186, 187–8, 194; fragile/failed state 183, 184, 185; gender-related issues 187, 188; ICG-GB 184, 189, 194; instability 183, 184, 186, 193 (causes of 16, 181, 183, 190–1; recurring political instability 16, 182, 183, 185, 188, 192); low attention by the international community 16, 181–2, 184, 186–7, 192; poverty 182, 183, 188; security/development link 16, 182; UN Security Council 184, 192; underdevelopment 16, 188, 192; World Bank 183, 194, 195; *see also* Guinea-Bissau and PBA; UNIOGBIS
Guinea-Bissau and PBA: 2010 review 185–6, 187, 189; an 'awkward fit' 181, 185–6, 192; Brazilian CSC chair/PBC presidency 16, 189–90, 191–2, 193; challenges 16, 78, 183;

Index 255

Guinea-Bissau and debates on UN peacebuilding 188–92; PBC 185, 186–8 (inclusion on the PBC agenda 184–5, 186, 195); PBF 185, 186, 187–8, 196; recommendations for improvement 16, 187–8, 189–91 (need for more preventive action by the PBA 186, 191; PBA/UN agencies/stakeholders coordination 16, 188–9; PBC, reacting effectively to changing situations on the ground 16, 190); shortcomings 185–6, 187, 189–91, 192; success 186–7; suspension of PBA activities 16, 182, 186, 189, 192; *see also* Guinea-Bissau

Hearn, Sarah 48, 78, 80–1, 87–8, 242
High-Level Panel on Threats, Challenges and Change 182; PBA, beginnings xxi, xxv, 24, 27, 29, 33, 239; PBC 42, 107
Hofmann, Stephanie 13–14, 127–44
human rights: CNIDH 132; peace/security/development/human rights link xxvi, xxvii, xxix, 23–4

IDPS (International Dialogue on Peacebuilding and Statebuilding) 207; g7+ group 81; *New Deal for Engagement in Fragile States* 10, 54, 70, 170, 207 (donor dominated 90; inclusive processes of political dialogue 207; South-South dialogue 10–11, 81, 90; supporting political dialogue and leadership 90, 94); PBA 8, 10, 53, 55; PBC 10–11, 81, 90, 226, 230; PBSO 53, 55
IFI (international financial institution) 5, 28, 86, 87, 119, 236; 'liberal peace' approach 15; *see also* IMF; World Bank
IGAD (Intergovernmental Authority on Development) 114, 122
ILO (International Labour Organization) 142
IMF (International Monetary Fund) 183, 194

INGO (international nongovernmental organization) 9, 28, 70–1, 75; *see also* civil society; NGO
International Crisis Group 195
International Peace Academy/Institute xxi
IOM (International Organization for Migration) 62, 68
IPBS (Integrated Peacebuilding Strategy) 8, 14, 46–7, 52, 155; *see also* CSC
IRF (Immediate Response Facility) 8, 35, 61, 65–6, 247; a project-based financing facility 9, 65; rapid funding for immediate peacebuilding needs 9, 64, 66, 73; underutilized 9; *see also* PBF

Jenkins, Rob 43, 56, 184, 185
JSC (Joint Steering Committee) 9, 136, 138, 141, 144, 222; Burundi 137, 138, 144; PBF 62, 65, 134, 136, 221–2

Karlsrud, John 12–13, 109–23
Kluyskens, Jups 8–9, 61–76
Kubitschek Bujones, Alejandra 48, 78, 80–1, 87–8, 242
Kugel, Alischa 48, 78, 80–1, 87–8, 242

Laitin, David 28
In Larger Freedom xxi, xxv, xxvi, 29, 30, 56, 107, 182, 239, 240; *see also* Annan, Kofi
League of Arab States 117, 119
Liberia 15–16, 159–80, 219–20; 2003 Comprehensive Peace Agreement 160, 168; 2014 Ebola crisis 171, 174, 175; civil war 160; CSC 161 (chair 161); fragile state 160; government 16, 175, 176 (corruption, lack of accountability, impunity 15, 175); Liberian experience for the peacebuilding debate 175–6 (bottom-up approach 15, 175; 'liberal peace' approach 15, 175; 'problem-solving' approach 15, 175); LPP 163, 169–70; national/local ownership

256 *Index*

15, 172, 175; PBA 160–3, 172, 175; PBC 160, 161; PBF 161, 164–5, 187; PBSO 165, 170; recommendations 15–16, 173, 176; shortcomings 165–6, 168, 169, 171–2, 174; SMC 161–2, 163, 168, 171; success 165, 167, 172–3, 174, 175; *see also the entries below for* Liberia; UNMIL
Liberia, national reconciliation 15, 16, 160, 161, 163, 167–72, 174, 175, 176; addressing impunity/retributive justice 167–8, 171, 178; Palava hut 163, 169, 170, 171; restorative justice 171, 174; specific outputs 169; Strategic Roadmap for National Healing, Peacebuilding and Reconciliation 169–71, 172; TRC 163, 168, 169, 171, 178; *see also* Liberia
Liberia, rule of law 15, 160, 161–2, 163, 172–3, 175; customary law 161–2, 164, 174, 175–6; decentralization 16, 164, 166; regional justice hubs 160, 164–7, 172, 174; *see also* Liberia
Liberia, SSR 15, 160, 161, 163, 172–3, 175; AFL 162; BIN 162; decentralization 16, 164, 166; LNP 162; regional security hubs 160, 164–7, 172, 174; *see also* Liberia
local ownership 4–5, 18, 53, 120, 172, 175, 229–30, 231
Lute, Jane Holl 20, 44, 51

Malcorra, Susana 112, 122
Marineau, Josiah 13–14, 127–44
McAskie, Carolyn xx–xxxi, 5–6, 43, 44, 51
MDTF (multi-donor trust fund) 33, 34
M&E (monitoring and evaluation) 72, 75
Millennium Development Goals xxix, 2, 97
MINUSTAH (UN Stabilization Mission in Haiti) 32
MPTF-O (Multi-Partner Trust Fund Office) 63, 136, 137, 144

NAM (Non-Aligned Movement) 43, 79
national/local ownership 53, 120, 229; CIVCAP 12, 112, 117, 120; IGAD initiative 114; Liberia 15, 172, 175; local civil society 229; PBC 36, 143, 229; PBF 229; recommendations 4–5, 18, 229–30, 231; Sierra Leone 15, 147, 155
national reconciliation 234; Guinea 198; *see also* Liberia, national reconciliation
NATO (North Atlantic Treaty Organization) 106
NGO (nongovernmental organization): advocacy group 31; WPS 98, 99, 101 (NGO Working Group on WPS 101); *see also* civil society; INGO
Nilaus Tarp, Kristoffer 114
North–South divide 30, 43, 79, 90, 223
Norway xxiv, 101, 122

OC (Organizational Committee) xxi, 8, 42, 44–5, 236; chair 44–5, 52, 92, 236, 244, 249; functions xxviii, 48; membership 35, 44; recommendations for improvement 91–2; shortcomings 78, 91 (civil society, lack of representation 32, 45; inefficiency 10, 80); *see also* PBC
OCHA (UN Office for the Coordination of Humanitarian Affairs) 32, 51; CERF 34
OECD (Organisation for Economic Co-operation and Development) xxix, 49, 79
O'Gorman, Eleanor 103, 104
OHCHR (Office of the High Commissioner for Human Rights) 142
OIOS (UN Office for Internal Oversight Services) 50
ONUB (UN Operation in Burundi) 32, 129

P5 (Permanent five members of the Security Council) 43, 47, 79, 234, 242–3
Patrick, Stewart 28

Index 257

PBA (UN Peacebuilding Architecture) 99, 218–19, 237; aim 1, 40–1, 55–6, 134; a catalytic mechanism 7, 41; challenges 3–5, 231; conflict prevention 220–1; funding xxvii; gender-related issues 99, 100–101, 102, 103–104 (failure to deliver on 'gender-sensitive peacebuilding' 97, 99, 103, 105); a hybrid entity 243; lessons learned xxvi, 36; relationships and reporting lines 238, 243–4; *see also the entries below for* PBA; PBC; PBF; PBSO

PBA, beginnings 1, 5–6, 23–39, 182, 237, 238; 2005 World Summit xxv, 40 (Outcome Document xxi, 6, 23–4, 32, 33, 35–6, 39); Annan, Kofi 25, 27, 29, 30, 36, 181, 239; civil society 31; conflict prevention 26–7, 181; democratic legitimacy 27; a difficult birth 242–3; establishment of 35–6; G-77: 7, 24, 29, 43; a 'gaping hole' 6, 29, 239–40, 248; High-Level Panel on Threats, Challenges and Change xxi, xxv, 24, 27, 29, 33, 239; negotiation process 24–5, 27, 29–31, 36; origins xx–xxi, xxv; peacebuilders 27–8; peacebuilding 26–8, 30; private sector 31; reform proposals/achieved results gap 24, 36; UN General Assembly 7, 30, 31, 32; UN:A/RES/60/180—S/RES/1645: 35, 42, 55, 61, 182, 237, 241, 243, 249; UN reform 24, 27, 28; UN Secretariat 24; UN Security Council 26; US 24; *see also* PBC, mandate; peacebuilding

PBA, impact of 2–3, 18, 53–4, 218–23, 231; Burundi 13, 14, 129–31, 133, 140; CSC 80, 91, 183; establishing the foundations for peacebuilding knowledge 8, 54; establishing peacebuilding as an overarching framework 18, 218–21, 230; establishing the political dimension of peacebuilding 18, 223, 234; greater coherence to/a common appreciation of peacebuilding 8,

53–4; Guinea-Bissau 186–7; helping to understand the misguided emphasis on resource mobilization 18, 222–3, 230; Liberia 165, 167, 172–3, 174, 175; PBF xxv, xxvii, 19, 51, 72–3, 220, 221, 247 (proof of concept' 8, 54); PBSO 54, 242; Sierra Leone 14–15, 146, 148, 153, 154, 155; strengthening coordination across the UN system 18, 221–2, 230 (PBC 83, 84–5); *see also* PBC, achievements; PBC and client country; PBF allocations; PBF, country-specific impact; PBSO, country-specific impact

PBA, recommendations for improvement xxvii–xxix, 3–4, 18, 223–30; addressing external factors that contribute to conflict 226–7, 231 (corruption, organized crime, extractive industries 18, 226–7, 231); addressing the root causes of conflict 18, 224–6, 230; Burundi 140–2; civil society 18, 228, 229–30, 231; improving the coherence/interconnectedness of the UN system 19, 36, 222, 230; incorporating regional approaches 18, 227–9, 231; Guinea-Bissau 16, 186, 187–8, 189–91; Liberia 15–16, 173, 176; national/local ownership 4–5, 18, 229–30, 231; OC 91–2; partnership 5; PBF 4, 9, 65, 73–5, 140–2, 156; PBSO 11, 140–2, 155–6; political will xx, xxviii, 6; (re) commitment of member states xx, xxix, xxx, 6; (re) commitment of UN senior management xx, xxix, xxx, 6; Sierra Leone 155–6; WGLL 11, 92; *see also* PBC, recommendations for improvement

PBA, shortcomings 8, 36, 54–5; ambitious/confused expectations and faulty assumptions 6, 7, 235, 238–48, 249; Burundi 13–14, 54, 128, 131–2, 133, 134, 137–8, 139, 140; criticism 18–19; failing to co-lead the IDPS 8, 10, 53, 55; failure to deliver on 'gender-

258   *Index*

sensitive peacebuilding' 97, 99, 103, 105; fragmented nature 42, 56; Guinea 202, 203, 204–205, 206–208; Guinea-Bissau 185–6, 187, 189–91, 192; Liberia 165–6, 168, 169, 171–2, 174; limited progress in addressing effectively critical conflict drivers 8, 54; marshalling resources xxvii, xxx; PBF 36, 48, 50; PBSO 36, 53, 88, 136, 224; separating conflict prevention from peacebuilding 8, 55, 240–1; Sierra Leone 15, 54, 147, 155; UN system constraints 18, 19, 41, 224, 230, 242 (structural limitations 224); WGLL 10, 47, 88, 91, 92; *see also* PBC, shortcomings

PBC (UN Peacebuilding Commission) 42–8, 236; 2006–08: 'survival' phase 40; 2010 review 2, 77–8, 183, 191; added value of 86–8, 92; challenges 77, 78–82, 92; civil society xxii, 4, 7, 31–2, 229–30; gender-related issues 100, 101, 103, 105; 'graduation' from 14, 52–3, 84, 249; national/local ownership 36, 143, 229; North–South divide 30, 43, 79, 223; origins xxi–xxii, xxv, xxviii, 23, 30, 31, 35, 42–3, 99, 107 (political context 43–4, 100); staff xxvii; uniqueness xxviii, 86, 219; *see also the entries below for* PBC; CSC; OC; WGLL

PBC, achievements 10–11, 36, 82–6, 219; advocacy and providing strategic momentum 83, 85–6; coordination and coherence 83, 84–5; resource mobilization 83–4; *see also* PBC, mandate

PBC and client country xxii–xxiii, 6, 30, 36, 44, 55, 83, 87, 182; Burundi 134–6, 143; countries in PBC agenda 47, 76, 83, 143, 228, 236, 246; Guinea 198, 199, 201, 202; Guinea-Bissau 185, 186–8 (inclusion on the PBC agenda 184–5, 186, 195); peacebuilding, 'internally led'/'externally

supported' xxiv; Liberia 160, 161; *see also* Sierra Leone and PBC

PBC, mandate 7, 10, 55–6, 77, 79, 99–100, 182–3, 208, 219, 234; adjustments to 249; advisory body xxiii–xiv, 32, 42, 46, 79, 81, 85, 89–90, 236, 242; civil society 7; conflict prevention role 7, 24–5, 29–30, 78, 191, 240, 249 (sovereignty 7, 36, 43, 79, 182, 191); a diplomatic body 10, 85, 86–7, 88, 89–90, 135–6, 245; gender-related issues 100; a 'hollow mandate' 243; objectives and functions xxi, 29, 35, 42, 82–6, 88, 92–3, 143, 160–1, 172, 236; political accompaniment 10, 87–8, 223, 236, 244, 245, 248; private sector 7; subsidiary role xxiii–xiv; sustainable development xxi, 35, 42; *see also* PBC

PBC membership xxii, 29, 44, 80, 89, 99, 106, 234; civil society xxii, 4, 31–2; donor xxv, xxvii, xxix–xxx, 29; fixed and formulaic membership 48, 80; mistrust among member states xxi, 6, 89, 100; observer status xxii; *see also* PBC and UN system

PBC, recommendations for improvement 10–11, 87, 88–92, 229, 248; adjusting organizational set-up of PBC entities 91–2; discussions of crises in non-PBC countries 11; identifying PBC complementarities 90–1; IDPS/*New Deal* 10–11, 81, 90, 226, 230; 'internal track' of advice 10; reducing meeting activity 11, 91–2; revisiting the advisory objective 89–90; Trusteeship Council Chamber, turning over to PBC xxx; *see also* PBC

PBC, shortcomings 2, 9–10, 19, 36, 77, 78–82, 246; attaching a stigma to serving on the PBC's agenda 8, 55, 154; attempts to serve as a knowledge hub 88; criticism 77, 78, 79, 85–6, 88, 92, 246; CSC xxvii, 10, 47; failing to co-lead the

IDPS 10, 81; failing to mobilize resources 70, 81, 83, 183; inability to inform the Security Council on major conflicts 10, 78; inability to prevent conflict escalation in PBC countries 9–10, 78; lack of cross-fertilization between its three configurations 8, 47–8, 91; minimal contributions to facilitate peacebuilding strategies 8, 88; OC 10, 32, 45, 78, 80, 91; skepticism about PBC 9, 77, 78, 88, 149, 243; *see also* PBA, shortcomings; PBC and UN system

PBC and UN system xxii, 106; dual reporting 31, 42; ECOSOC xxiv, 29, 44, 234 (reporting to ECOSOC 7, 30–1); PBC, insufficiently connected to UN lead departments 80; PBF/PBC relationship 9, 48, 67, 69–70, 73, 75, 83, 246–7; structural limitations 224; UN General Assembly xxi, xxiv, 35, 44, 89, 224, 234 (reporting to General Assembly 7, 31, 42, 238); UN Secretariat 6; UN Security Council xxi, xxiii, xxiv, xxvii, 29, 30–1, 44, 89, 224, 234 (P5: 43, 47, 79, 234, 242–3; PBC as advisory body to the Council 6, 89, 224, 242; PBC/Security Council working relations 10, 78, 79, 81, 89, 242); *see also* PBC

PBF (UN Peacebuilding Fund) 8–9, 48–51, 61–76; 2005 World Summit, Outcome Document 34; 2006–08: 'survival' phase 40; budget xxv, 49, 62; catalytic effect of 9, 35, 49, 50, 64–5, 67, 74, 219, 247; civil society 4, 34, 229; conflict prevention 55; donors 49, 62, 64, 65, 74, 238; gender-related issues 100–101, 103, 104 (GPI 71–2, 74, 75); 'high-risk' projects 8, 13–14; *In Larger Freedom* 33; management xxv, xxvii, 6, 49, 61; MPTF-O 136, 137, 144; national/local ownership 229; niche in peacebuilding 8, 34, 48–51, 64–5, 73, 74; objectives and functions

8–9, 34, 48–9, 61, 62, 64, 100; OIOS evaluation 50; origins xxi, 31, 33–5, 48, 61, 99; PBF/PBC relationship 9, 48, 67, 69–70, 73, 75, 83, 246–7; PBSO 49, 61, 63, 73, 75, 100, 136, 140, 237, 242; recommendations for improvement 4, 9, 65, 73–5, 140–2 (Sierra Leone 156); shortcomings 36, 48, 50; staff xxv, 6, 50, 63, 140, 208; success xxv, xxvii, 19, 51, 72–3, 220, 221, 247 (proof of concept' 8, 54); ToR 48–50, 71, 104 (2009 revision 8, 48, 49, 50, 51); UN Secretariat xxv, 34, 49, 50; value for money 72; *see also the entries below for* PBF; IRF; Global Review; PRF

PBF Advisory Group 63

PBF allocations 8–9, 50, 61–2, 65, 220, 221, 238, 247; African countries 228; criteria for 34–5, 64, 70, 73, 74; exit strategy for PBF funding 70, 73, 75, 141–2; financing peacebuilding 48, 49, 83; JSC 62, 65, 134, 136, 221–2; priority areas 34, 62, 71–2; Windows 49–50; *see also* PBF

PBF, country-specific impact: Guinea 198, 199, 202–203, 204, 206; Guinea-Bissau 185, 186, 187–8, 196; Liberia 161, 164–5, 187; Sierra Leone 14–15, 68–9, 145–6, 150–3, 155, 187–8 (thematic areas 150–1, 152; uneven distribution of PBF support 151–2); *see also* Burundi and PBF support

PBF, partnerships 9, 67–9, 73, 74, 75; INGOs and government 9, 70–1, 75; regional banks, EU, World Bank 9, 67–8; UN agencies 9, 62, 68, 73, 74 (UNDP xxv, 62, 68); *see also* PBF

PBSO (UN Peacebuilding Support Office) 33, 51–3, 237; 2005 World Summit, Outcome Document 33, 39; 2006–08: 'survival' phase 40; budget xxviii ('within existing resources' xxii, 6, 39, 241); design flaw 80; DSG xxviii; gender-related issues 100–101, 102, 103,

260 *Index*

105; IDPS 53, 55; minimalist version 33; origins xxi–xxii, 30, 31, 33, 35, 39, 99; PBF 49, 61, 63, 73, 75, 100, 136, 140, 237, 242; *Peacebuilding in the Immediate Aftermath of Conflict* 53; recommendations 11 (Burundi 140–2; Sierra Leone 155–6); shortcomings 36, 53, 88, 136, 224; staff xxiii, xxviii, 33, 39, 51, 54, 105, 237, 241; structure and accountability mechanisms 136; success 54, 242; UN Secretariat 33; UNDP 51, 136; Units 51–2; 'virtual' pillar of the PBA 52; *see also the entries below for* PBSO

PBSO, country-specific impact: Burundi 128, 135, 136–8, 149; Guinea 203; Liberia 165, 170; Sierra Leone 149, 153; *see also* PBSO

PBSO mandate xxviii, 51, 219, 241–2; not operational nature xxiii; objectives and functions xxiii, xxviii, 39, 52, 57, 100; PBC secretariat 8, 51, 52, 88, 100, 237; peacebuilding knowledge base 8, 51, 52, 53, 237; supporting role 5, 10, 39, 45, 135, 241, 244, 248; *see also* PBSO

peace: peace/security/development/ human rights link xxvi, xxvii, xxix, 23–4; 'sustaining peace' xx, 2, 3, 4, 23–4, 63, 111, 148

peacebuilding xx, 26–8, 234; Annan, Kofi 44; bottom-up approach 15, 175; concept 26–7, 63; conflict prevention 26–7, 36, 63, 148; conflict-prevention/post-conflict peacebuilding relationship 26; context specificity 47, 140, 159, 236; criticism 159, 175; 'internally led'/'externally supported' xxiv; 'liberal peace' approach 15, 27, 159, 175; national reconciliation 167, 172, 175; peacebuilding/ development distinction 234; peacebuilding/development link 148–50; a 'post-conflict' activity 26; 'problem-solving' approach 15,

175, 225; regional approaches 18, 227–9, 231; relapse into conflict 6, 220, 225, 240–1; scope 26, 30, 148, 219; sequencing of 27, 30, 185, 190; UN Security Council 26; UN system 3, 15, 24, 75, 218, 233 (fragmentation and compartmentalization 3–4, 28; one of four pillars of the UN's peace work 219)

Peacebuilding Contact Group 63, 68

peacekeeping operation 153, 156, 190, 228, 234, 239–40; *see also* DPKO

Ping, Jean 30

Ponzio, Richard 7–8, 40–57

post-conflict country 109, 159, 236; 2009 *Peacebuilding in the Immediate Aftermath of Conflict* 12, 101–102, 103, 109, 110, 111, 117, 206–207, 208, 241; conflict-prevention/post-conflict peacebuilding relationship 26; PBC 99–100, 136, 174; PBF 49, 62, 173; PRF 9, 63, 66; sustainability of peace in xx, 24; transition from war to peace 25, 174; UN 24

prevention xx, 2, 3, 4, 23–24, 63, 111, 148

PRF (Peacebuilding and Recovery Facility) 8, 34, 61, 66–7, 73; longer-term support to post-conflict countries 9, 63, 66; the most used instrument to support peacebuilding 63; the primary vehicle for PBF funding 9, 66; recommendations for improvement 9; *see also* PBF

private sector 7, 31, 32

Quick, Ian D. 16–18, 196–213

R2P (Responsibility to Protect) 24, 27, 105–106

Rosén, Frederik 114

Rosenthal, Gert 2

RUNO (Recipient UN Organization) 128, 138, 140–2, 144; Burundi 128, 134, 136–7, 139

Index 261

Salomons, Dirk 28, 234, 239
Sambanis, Nicholas 26
Samset, Ingrid 232
security: peace/security/
development/human rights link
xxvi, xxvii, xxix, 23–4; security/
development link 16, 182; *see also*
SSR
Senior Advisory Group 12, 110,
111–12, 113; 2011 *Civilian
Capacity in the Aftermath of
Conflict* 113, 209
Senior Peacebuilding Group 63, 68,
219
Sierra Leone xxii, xxiii, 14–15, 145–58;
Agenda for Change 148, 153; civil
society 147, 153; CSC xxiv–xxv,
45–6, 146, 147, 153; DDR 14, 145;
elections 14, 145, 150, 153; energy
sector development 147, 149–50,
155; Freetown, centralization of
power in 14, 145, 147, 155;
Human Development Index xxx,
145; national/local ownership 15,
147, 155; PBA 145, 155; PBA,
future involvement in 153–4; PBF
14–15, 68–9, 145–6, 150–3, 155,
187–8 (thematic areas 150–1, 152;
uneven distribution of PBF
support 151–2); PBSO 149, 153;
PCF 14, 146, 147–8, 149, 151, 155;
peacebuilding priorities 146–7;
poverty 14, 145; recommendations
155–6; shortcomings 15, 54,
147, 155; success 14–15, 146, 148,
153, 154, 155; youth exclusion
14, 145, 155; *see also* Sierra
Leone and PBC;
UNIPSIL
Sierra Leone and PBC 146–50, 155,
155–6; contributions to peacebuilding 14, 145; 'graduation' from
PBC 14, 84, 146, 153–4; inclusion
on the PBC agenda 149;
'test case' 14, 145; *see also*
Sierra Leone
Smith, Dan 78, 82, 85, 88
South Sudan 113–14
Souza Neto, Danilo Marcondes de
16, 181–95

sovereignty 25, 81, 90, 241; international system 227; PBC, preventive
mandate 7, 36, 43, 79, 182, 191
SPU (Strategic Planning Unit) 33, 34
SRSG (special representative of the
secretary-general) 32; chair/SRSG/
ERSGs relationship 245–6; WPS
98, 106
SSR (security sector reform) 234;
Guinea 17, 199, 204–205, 206,
238; *see also* Liberia, SSR
Stamnes, Eli 1–20, 217–32
Suhrke, Astri 232
sustainable development 2, 24, 100;
fragile state xxix; PBA 2; PBC xxi,
35, 42
Sustainable Development Goals 2
'sustaining peace' xx, 2, 3, 4, 23–4,
63, 111, 148

Tavares, Rodrigo 184
theory of change 133, 143, 219, 220,
223
Touré, Sidya 200, 202; *see also*
Guinea
Tryggestad, Torunn L. 11–12, 97–108
Tschirgi, Necla 7–8, 40–57

UN (United Nations) 224, 230; 2005
World Summit xxv, 40 (Outcome
Document xxi, 6, 23–4, 32, 33, 34,
35–6, 39); 2015 reviews 97;
CIVCAP, recommendations from
120, 121; leadership 7, 24, 36, 244;
reform 24, 27, 28, 36, 110–11; UN
system constraints and limitations
13, 18, 19, 41, 224, 230, 242; *see
also* peacebuilding
UN General Assembly 208, 230;
PBA, beginnings 7, 30, 31, 32;
PBC xxi, xxiv, 35, 44, 89, 224, 234
(reporting to General Assembly 7,
31, 42, 238); Resolution 60/180:
35, 42, 55, 61, 182, 237, 241, 249
UN High-level Independent Panel on
Peace Operations 2, 4–5
UN Office for West Africa 17, 191,
201, 203, 207–208
UN Secretariat 3, 4; PBA, beginnings
24; PBC, duplication of roles in

262 *Index*

the field 6; PBF xxv, 34, 49, 50; PBSO 33; *see also* ASG; ERSG; SRSG

UN Security Council 219, 225, 230; Guinea-Bissau 184, 192; inclusive approach to peacebuilding 207; PBA, beginnings 26; PBC xxi, xxiii, xxiv, xxvii, 6, 29, 30–1, 44, 89, 224, 234 (P5: 43, 47, 79, 234, 242–3; PBC as advisory body to the Council 6, 89, 224, 242; PBC/Security Council working relations 10, 78, 79, 81, 89, 242); reform xxvii, 79, 89, 242–3; Resolution 1325: 2, 11, 71, 98, 100 (follow-up resolutions 98–9, 106; implementation 98, 106); Resolution 1645: 35, 42, 55, 61, 182, 237, 241, 249; Resolution 1889: 101, 106

UN Security Council Resolution 1325: 2, 11, 71, 98, 100 (follow-up resolutions 98–9, 106

UN Women 99, 103, 105, 142, 170; PBF 68, 72; *see also* UNIFEM

UNCT (UN Country Team) 68, 72, 128, 142

UNDP (UN Development Programme): BCPR 34, 93, 110, 111, 121, 240; Burundi 136, 142; closing the UN's institutional peacebuilding gap 80, 93; Human Development Index xxvi, xxx, 145, 183, 199; PBF xxv, 62, 68; PBSO 51, 136; peacebuilding and prevention of conflict recurrence 6

UNFPA (UN Population Fund) 62, 142, 237, 241

UNHCR (Office of the UN High Commissioner for Refugees) 142, 237, 241, 247

UNICEF (UN Children's Fund) 62, 68, 170

UNIFEM (UN Development Fund for Women) 99, 100, 101, 142; *see also* UN Women

UNIOGBIS (UN Integrated Peacebuilding Office in Guinea-Bissau) 184, 186, 188, 189, 191

UNIPSIL (UN Integrated Peacebuilding Office in Sierra Leone) 146, 150, 153, 154, 155

UNMIL (UN Mission in Liberia) 32, 160, 161, 162, 163, 164, 166, 170, 175

UNMISS (UN Mission in South Sudan) 113

UNOPS (UN Office for Project Services) 62

US (United States) 24; 2003 invasion of Iraq 36, 43

Van Beijnum, Mariska 9–11, 77–94

Vermeij, Lotte 12–13, 109–23

Vester Haldrup, Søren 114

Walker, Daniel 13–14, 127–44

WGLL (Working Group on Lessons Learned) 8, 44, 47–8, 52, 54, 80; functions 47–8; gender-related issues 101, 102; PBF 75; recommendations for improvement 11, 92 (integrating the lessons learned into the OC functions 11); shortcomings 10, 47, 88, 91, 92; *see also* PBC

Williams, Abiodun 7, 23–39

World Bank 5, 32, 50; *Conflict, Security and Development* 113; Guinea 200, 205–206; Guinea-Bissau 183, 194, 195; PBF 9, 67

WPS (Women, Peace and Security Agenda) 11–12, 97–108; an 'add-on' component 11, 103; agenda 98–9, 105–106 (acknowledgment in academic circles and think-tanks 104–105); challenges and concerns 11, 103, 104–105; NGO 98, 99, 101 (NGO Working Group on WPS 101); Norway 101; recommendations for improvement 11–12, 104, 105; SRSG 98, 106; UN Security Council Resolution 1325: 2, 11, 71, 98, 100 (follow-up resolutions 98–9, 106; implementation 98, 106; Resolution 1889: 101, 106); *see also* gender-related issues

Routledge Global Institutions Series

121 UN Peacebuilding Architecture (2016)
The first 10 years
edited by Cedric de Coning (Norwegian Institute of International Affairs) and Eli Stamnes (Norwegian Institute of International Affairs)

120 Displacement, Development, and Climate Change (2016)
International organizations moving beyond their mandates
by Nina Hall (Hertie School of Governance)

119 UN Security Council Reform (2016)
by Peter Nadin

118 International Organizations and Military Affairs (2016)
by Hylke Dijkstra (Maastricht University)

117 The International Committee of the Red Cross (2nd edition, 2016)
A neutral humanitarian actor
by David P. Forsythe (University of Nebraska–Lincoln) and Barbara Ann J. Rieffer-Flanagan (Central Washington University)

116 The Arctic Council (2016)
Governance within the Far North
by Douglas C. Nord (University of Umeå)

115 Human Development and Global Institutions (2016)
Evolution, impact, reform
by Richard Ponzio (The Hague Institute for Global Justice) and Arunabha Ghosh (Council on Energy, Environment and Water)

114 NGOs and Global Trade (2016)
Non-state voices in EU trade policymaking
By Erin Hannah (University of Western Ontario)

113 Brazil as a Rising Power (2016)
Intervention norms and the contestation of global order
edited by Kai Michael Kenkel (IRI/PUC-Rio) and
Philip Cunliffe (University of Kent)

112 The United Nations as a Knowledge System (2016)
by Nanette Svenson (Tulane University)

111 Summits and Regional Governance (2016)
The Americas in comparative perspective
edited by Gordon Mace (Université Laval), Jean-Philippe Thérien
(Université de Montréal), Diana Tussie (Facultad Latinoamericana de
Ciencias Sociales), and Olivier Dabène (Sciences Po)

110 Global Consumer Organizations (2015)
by Karsten Ronit (University of Copenhagen)

109 Expert Knowledge in Global Trade (2015)
edited by Erin Hannah (University of Western Ontario), James Scott
(King's College London), and Silke Trommer (University of Helsinki)

108 World Trade Organization (2nd edition, 2015)
Law, economics, and politics
by Bernard M. Hoekman (European University Institute) and
Petros C. Mavroidis (European University Institute)

107 Women and Girls Rising (2015)
Progress and resistance around the world
by Ellen Chesler (Roosevelt Institute) and
Theresa McGovern (Columbia University)

106 The North Atlantic Treaty Organization (2nd edition, 2015)
by Julian Lindley-French (National Defense University)

105 The African Union (2nd edition, 2015)
by Samuel M. Makinda (Murdoch University),
F. Wafula Okumu (The Borders Institute),
David Mickler (University of Western Australia)

104 Governing Climate Change (2nd edition, 2015)
by Harriet Bulkeley (Durham University) and
Peter Newell (University of Sussex)

103 The Organization of Islamic Cooperation (2015)
Politics, problems, and potential
by Turan Kayaoglu (University of Washington, Tacoma)

102 Contemporary Human Rights Ideas (2nd edition, 2015)
by Bertrand G. Ramcharan

101 The Politics of International Organizations (2015)
Views from insiders
edited by Patrick Weller (Griffith University) and
Xu Yi-chong (Griffith University)

100 Global Poverty (2nd edition, 2015)
Global governance and poor people in the post-2015 era
by David Hulme (University of Manchester)

99 Global Corporations in Global Governance (2015)
by Christopher May (Lancaster University)

98 The United Nations Centre on Transnational Corporations (2015)
Corporate conduct and the public interest
by Khalil Hamdani and Lorraine Ruffing

97 The Challenges of Constructing Legitimacy in Peacebuilding (2015)
Afghanistan, Iraq, Sierra Leone, and East Timor
by Daisaku Higashi (University of Tokyo)

96 The European Union and Environmental Governance (2015)
by Henrik Selin (Boston University) and
Stacy D. VanDeveer (University of New Hampshire)

95 Rising Powers, Global Governance, and Global Ethics (2015)
edited by Jamie Gaskarth (Plymouth University)

94 Wartime Origins and the Future United Nations (2015)
edited by Dan Plesch (SOAS, University of London) and
Thomas G. Weiss (CUNY Graduate Center)

93 International Judicial Institutions (2nd edition, 2015)
The architecture of international justice at home and abroad
by Richard J. Goldstone (Retired Justice of the Constitutional Court of South Africa) and Adam M. Smith (International Lawyer, Washington, DC)

92 The NGO Challenge for International Relations Theory (2014)
edited by William E. DeMars (Wofford College) and Dennis Dijkzeul (Ruhr University Bochum)

91 21st Century Democracy Promotion in the Americas (2014)
Standing up for the Polity
by Jorge Heine (Wilfrid Laurier University) and Brigitte Weiffen (University of Konstanz)

90 BRICS and Coexistence (2014)
An alternative vision of world order
edited by Cedric de Coning (Norwegian Institute of International Affairs), Thomas Mandrup (Royal Danish Defence College), and Liselotte Odgaard (Royal Danish Defence College)

89 IBSA (2014)
The rise of the Global South?
by Oliver Stuenkel (Getulio Vargas Foundation)

88 Making Global Institutions Work (2014)
edited by Kate Brennan

87 Post-2015 UN Development (2014))
Making change happen
edited by Stephen Browne (FUNDS Project) and Thomas G. Weiss (CUNY Graduate Center)

86 Who Participates in Global Governance? (2014)
States, bureaucracies, and NGOs in the United Nations
by Molly Ruhlman (Towson University)

85 The Security Council as Global Legislator (2014)
edited by Vesselin Popovski (United Nations University) and Trudy Fraser (United Nations University)

84 UNICEF (2014)
Global governance that works
by Richard Jolly (University of Sussex)

83 The Society for Worldwide Interbank Financial Telecommunication (SWIFT) (2014)
Cooperative governance for network innovation, standards, and community
by Susan V. Scott (London School of Economics and Political Science) and Markos Zachariadis (University of Cambridge)

82 The International Politics of Human Rights (2014)
Rallying to the R2P cause?
edited by Monica Serrano (Colegio de Mexico) and Thomas G. Weiss (The CUNY Graduate Center)

81 Private Foundations and Development Partnerships (2014)
American philanthropy and global development agendas
by Michael Moran (Swinburne University of Technology)

80 Nongovernmental Development Organizations and the Poverty Reduction Agenda (2014)
The moral crusaders
by Jonathan J. Makuwira (Royal Melbourne Institute of Technology University)

79 Corporate Social Responsibility (2014)
The role of business in sustainable development
by Oliver F. Williams (University of Notre Dame)

78 Reducing Armed Violence with NGO Governance (2014)
edited by Rodney Bruce Hall (Oxford University)

77 Transformations in Trade Politics (2014)
Participatory trade politics in West Africa
by Silke Trommer (Murdoch University)

76 Rules, Politics, and the International Criminal Court (2013)
by Yvonne M. Dutton (Indiana University)

75 Global Institutions of Religion (2013)
Ancient movers, modern shakers
by Katherine Marshall (Georgetown University)

74 Crisis of Global Sustainability (2013)
by Tapio Kanninen

73 The Group of Twenty (G20) (2013)
*by Andrew F. Cooper (University of Waterloo) and
Ramesh Thakur (Australian National University)*

72 Peacebuilding (2013)
From concept to commission
by Rob Jenkins (Hunter College, CUNY)

71 Human Rights and Humanitarian Norms, Strategic Framing, and Intervention (2013)
Lessons for the Responsibility to Protect
by Melissa Labonte (Fordham University)

70 Feminist Strategies in International Governance (2013)
*edited by Gülay Caglar (Humboldt University, Berlin), Elisabeth Prügl
(the Graduate Institute of International and Development Studies,
Geneva), and Susanne Zwingel (the State University of
New York, Potsdam)*

69 The Migration Industry and the Commercialization of International Migration (2013)
*edited by Thomas Gammeltoft-Hansen (Danish Institute for International
Studies) and Ninna Nyberg Sørensen (Danish Institute for
International Studies)*

68 Integrating Africa (2013)
Decolonization's legacies, sovereignty, and the African Union
by Martin Welz (University of Konstanz)

67 Trade, Poverty, Development (2013)
Getting beyond the WTO's Doha deadlock
*edited by Rorden Wilkinson (University of Manchester) and
James Scott (University of Manchester)*

66 The United Nations Industrial Development Organization (UNIDO) (2012)
Industrial solutions for a sustainable future
by Stephen Browne (FUNDS Project)

65 The Millennium Development Goals and Beyond (2012)
Global development after 2015
edited by Rorden Wilkinson (University of Manchester) and David Hulme (University of Manchester)

64 International Organizations as Self-Directed Actors (2012)
A framework for analysis
edited by Joel E. Oestreich (Drexel University)

63 Maritime Piracy (2012)
by Robert Haywood (One Earth Future Foundation) and Roberta Spivak (One Earth Future Foundation)

62 United Nations High Commissioner for Refugees (UNHCR) (2nd edition, 2012)
by Gil Loescher (University of Oxford), Alexander Betts (University of Oxford), and James Milner (University of Toronto)

61 International Law, International Relations, and Global Governance (2012)
by Charlotte Ku (University of Illinois)

60 Global Health Governance (2012)
by Sophie Harman (City University, London)

59 The Council of Europe (2012)
by Martyn Bond (University of London)

58 The Security Governance of Regional Organizations (2011)
edited by Emil J. Kirchner (University of Essex) and Roberto Domínguez (Suffolk University)

57 The United Nations Development Programme and System (2011)
by Stephen Browne (FUNDS Project)

56 The South Asian Association for Regional Cooperation (2011)
An emerging collaboration architecture
by Lawrence Sáez (University of London)

55 The UN Human Rights Council (2011)
by Bertrand G. Ramcharan (Geneva Graduate Institute of International and Development Studies)

54 Responsibility to Protect (2011)
Cultural perspectives in the Global South
edited by Rama Mani (University of Oxford) and Thomas G. Weiss (The CUNY Graduate Center)

53 The International Trade Centre (2011)
Promoting exports for development
by Stephen Browne (FUNDS Project) and Sam Laird (University of Nottingham)

52 The Idea of World Government (2011)
From ancient times to the twenty-first century
by James A. Yunker (Western Illinois University)

51 Humanitarianism Contested (2011)
Where angels fear to tread
by Michael Barnett (George Washington University) and Thomas G. Weiss (The CUNY Graduate Center)

50 The Organization of American States (2011)
Global governance away from the media
by Monica Herz (Catholic University, Rio de Janeiro)

49 Non-Governmental Organizations in World Politics (2011)
The construction of global governance
by Peter Willetts (City University, London)

48 The Forum on China-Africa Cooperation (FOCAC) (2011)
by Ian Taylor (University of St. Andrews)

47 Global Think Tanks (2011)
Policy networks and governance
by James G. McGann (University of Pennsylvania) with Richard Sabatini

46 United Nations Educational, Scientific and Cultural Organization (UNESCO) (2011)
Creating norms for a complex world
by J.P. Singh (Georgetown University)

45 The International Labour Organization (2011)
Coming in from the cold
by Steve Hughes (Newcastle University) and
Nigel Haworth (University of Auckland)

44 Global Poverty (2010)
How global governance is failing the poor
by David Hulme (University of Manchester)

43 Global Governance, Poverty, and Inequality (2010)
edited by Jennifer Clapp (University of Waterloo) and
Rorden Wilkinson (University of Manchester)

42 Multilateral Counter-Terrorism (2010)
The global politics of cooperation and contestation
by Peter Romaniuk (John Jay College of Criminal Justice, CUNY)

41 Governing Climate Change (2010)
by Peter Newell (University of East Anglia) and
Harriet A. Bulkeley (Durham University)

40 The UN Secretary-General and Secretariat (2nd edition, 2010)
by Leon Gordenker (Princeton University)

39 Preventive Human Rights Strategies (2010)
by Bertrand G. Ramcharan (Geneva Graduate Institute of International
and Development Studies)

38 African Economic Institutions (2010)
by Kwame Akonor (Seton Hall University)

37 Global Institutions and the HIV/AIDS Epidemic (2010)
Responding to an international crisis
by Franklyn Lisk (University of Warwick)

36 Regional Security (2010)
The capacity of international organizations
by Rodrigo Tavares (United Nations University)

35 The Organisation for Economic Co-operation and Development (2009)
by Richard Woodward (University of Hull)

34 Transnational Organized Crime (2009)
by Frank Madsen (University of Cambridge)

33 The United Nations and Human Rights (2nd edition, 2009)
A guide for a new era
by Julie A. Mertus (American University)

32 The International Organization for Standardization (2009)
Global governance through voluntary consensus
*by Craig N. Murphy (Wellesley College) and
JoAnne Yates (Massachusetts Institute of Technology)*

31 Shaping the Humanitarian World (2009)
*by Peter Walker (Tufts University) and
Daniel G. Maxwell (Tufts University)*

30 Global Food and Agricultural Institutions (2009)
by John Shaw

29 Institutions of the Global South (2009)
*by Jacqueline Anne Braveboy-Wagner (City College of
New York, CUNY)*

28 International Judicial Institutions (2009)
The architecture of international justice at home and abroad
*by Richard J. Goldstone (Retired Justice of the Constitutional Court of
South Africa) and Adam M. Smith (Harvard University)*

27 The International Olympic Committee (2009)
The governance of the Olympic system
*by Jean-Loup Chappelet (IDHEAP Swiss Graduate School of Public
Administration) and Brenda Kübler-Mabbott*

26 The World Health Organization (2009)
by Kelley Lee (London School of Hygiene and Tropical Medicine)

25 Internet Governance (2009)
The new frontier of global institutions
by John Mathiason (Syracuse University)

24 Institutions of the Asia-Pacific (2009)
ASEAN, APEC, and beyond
by Mark Beeson (University of Birmingham)

23 United Nations High Commissioner for Refugees (UNHCR) (2008)
The politics and practice of refugee protection into the
twenty-first century
by Gil Loescher (University of Oxford), Alexander Betts (University of Oxford), and James Milner (University of Toronto)

22 Contemporary Human Rights Ideas (2008)
by Bertrand G. Ramcharan (Geneva Graduate Institute of International and Development Studies)

21 The World Bank (2008)
From reconstruction to development to equity
by Katherine Marshall (Georgetown University)

20 The European Union (2008)
by Clive Archer (Manchester Metropolitan University)

19 The African Union (2008)
Challenges of globalization, security, and governance
by Samuel M. Makinda (Murdoch University) and F. Wafula Okumu (McMaster University)

18 Commonwealth (2008)
Inter- and non-state contributions to global governance
by Timothy M. Shaw (Royal Roads University)

17 The World Trade Organization (2007)
Law, economics, and politics
by Bernard M. Hoekman (World Bank) and Petros C. Mavroidis (Columbia University)

16 A Crisis of Global Institutions? (2007)
Multilateralism and international security
by Edward Newman (University of Birmingham)

15 UN Conference on Trade and Development (2007)
by Ian Taylor (University of St. Andrews) and
Karen Smith (University of Stellenbosch)

14 The Organization for Security and
Co-operation in Europe (2007)
by David J. Galbreath (University of Aberdeen)

13 The International Committee of the Red Cross (2007)
A neutral humanitarian actor
by David P. Forsythe (University of Nebraska) and
Barbara Ann Rieffer-Flanagan (Central Washington University)

12 The World Economic Forum (2007)
A multi-stakeholder approach to global governance
by Geoffrey Allen Pigman (Bennington College)

11 The Group of 7/8 (2007)
by Hugo Dobson (University of Sheffield)

10 The International Monetary Fund (2007)
Politics of conditional lending
by James Raymond Vreeland (Georgetown University)

9 The North Atlantic Treaty Organization (2007)
The enduring alliance
by Julian Lindley-French (Center for Applied Policy,
University of Munich)

8 The World Intellectual Property Organization (2006)
Resurgence and the development agenda
by Chris May (University of the West of England)

7 The UN Security Council (2006)
Practice and promise
by Edward C. Luck (Columbia University)

6 Global Environmental Institutions (2006)
by Elizabeth R. DeSombre (Wellesley College)

5 Internal Displacement (2006)
Conceptualization and its consequences
*by Thomas G. Weiss (The CUNY Graduate Center) and
David A. Korn*

4 The UN General Assembly (2005)
by M. J. Peterson (University of Massachusetts, Amherst)

3 United Nations Global Conferences (2005)
by Michael G. Schechter (Michigan State University)

2 The UN Secretary-General and Secretariat (2005)
by Leon Gordenker (Princeton University)

1 The United Nations and Human Rights (2005)
A guide for a new era
by Julie A. Mertus (American University)

Books currently under contract include:

The Regional Development Banks
Lending with a regional flavor
by Jonathan R. Strand (University of Nevada)

Millennium Development Goals (MDGs)
For a people-centered development agenda?
by Sakiko Fukada-Parr (The New School)

The Bank for International Settlements
The politics of global financial supervision in the age of high finance
by Kevin Ozgercin (SUNY College at Old Westbury)

International Migration
by Khalid Koser (Geneva Centre for Security Policy)

The International Monetary Fund (2nd edition)
Politics of conditional lending
by James Raymond Vreeland (Georgetown University)

The UN Global Compact
by Catia Gregoratti (Lund University)

Institutions for Women's Rights
by Charlotte Patton (York College, CUNY) and Carolyn Stephenson (University of Hawaii)

International Aid
by Paul Mosley (University of Sheffield)

Coping with Nuclear Weapons
by W. Pal Sidhu

Global Governance and China
The dragon's learning curve
edited by Scott Kennedy (Indiana University)

The Politics of Global Economic Surveillance
by Martin S. Edwards (Seton Hall University)

Mercy and Mercenaries
Humanitarian agencies and private security companies
by Peter Hoffman

Regional Organizations in the Middle East
by James Worrall (University of Leeds)

Reforming the UN Development System
The politics of incrementalism
by Silke Weinlich (Duisburg-Essen University)

The International Criminal Court
The politics and practice of prosecuting atrocity crimes
by Martin Mennecke (University of Copenhagen)

BRICS
by João Pontes Nogueira (Catholic University, Rio de Janeiro) and Monica Herz (Catholic University, Rio de Janeiro)

The European Union (2nd edition)
Clive Archer (Manchester Metropolitan University)

Protecting the Internally Displaced
Rhetoric and reality
Phil Orchard (University of Queensland)

For further information regarding the series, please contact:

Nicola Parkin, Editor, Politics & International Studies
Taylor & Francis
2 Park Square, Milton Park, Abingdon
Oxford OX14 4RN, UK
Nicola.parkin@tandf.co.uk
www.routledge.com

eBooks
from Taylor & Francis

Helping you to choose the right eBooks for your Library

Add to your library's digital collection today with Taylor & Francis eBooks. We have over 50,000 eBooks in the Humanities, Social Sciences, Behavioural Sciences, Built Environment and Law, from leading imprints, including Routledge, Focal Press and Psychology Press.

Choose from a range of subject packages or create your own!

Benefits for you
- Free MARC records
- COUNTER-compliant usage statistics
- Flexible purchase and pricing options
- 70% approx of our eBooks are now DRM-free.

Benefits for your user
- Off-site, anytime access via Athens or referring URL
- Print or copy pages or chapters
- Full content search
- Bookmark, highlight and annotate text
- Access to thousands of pages of quality research at the click of a button.

Free Trials Available

We offer free trials to qualifying academic, corporate and government customers.

eCollections

Choose from 20 different subject eCollections, including:

- Asian Studies
- Economics
- Health Studies
- Law
- Middle East Studies

eFocus

We have 16 cutting-edge interdisciplinary collections, including:

- Development Studies
- The Environment
- Islam
- Korea
- Urban Studies

For more information, pricing enquiries or to order a free trial, please contact your local sales team:

UK/Rest of World: **online.sales@tandf.co.uk**
USA/Canada/Latin America: **e-reference@taylorandfrancis.com**
East/Southeast Asia: **martin.jack@tandf.com.sg**
India: **journalsales@tandfindia.com**

www.tandfebooks.com